THE MURDER OF WILLIAM OF NORWICH

THE MURDER OF WILLIAM OF NORWICH

The Origins of the Blood Libel in Medieval Europe

E. M. ROSE

OXFORD
UNIVERSITY PRESS

OXFORD
UNIVERSITY PRESS

Oxford University Press is a department of the University of
Oxford. It furthers the University's objective of excellence in research,
scholarship, and education by publishing worldwide.

Oxford   New York
Auckland   Cape Town   Dar es Salaam   Hong Kong   Karachi
Kuala Lumpur   Madrid   Melbourne   Mexico City   Nairobi
New Delhi   Shanghai   Taipei   Toronto

With offices in
Argentina   Austria   Brazil   Chile   Czech Republic   France   Greece
Guatemala   Hungary   Italy   Japan   Poland   Portugal   Singapore
South Korea   Switzerland   Thailand   Turkey   Ukraine   Vietnam

Oxford is a registered trademark of Oxford University Press
in the UK and certain other countries.

Published in the United States of America by
Oxford University Press
198 Madison Avenue, New York, NY 10016

Library of Congress Cataloging-in-Publication Data
Rose, E. M., author
The murder of William of Norwich: the origins of the blood libel in medieval Europe /
E. M. Rose.
pages cm
Includes bibliographical references and index.
ISBN 978–0–19–021962–8 — ISBN 978–0–19–021963–5 — ISBN 978–0–19–021964–2—
ISBN 978–0–19–021965–9   1. Antisemitism—Europe—History.   2. Blood
accusation.   3. Jews—Persecutions—Europe—History.   4. Christianity and
antisemitism.   5. Europe—Ethnic relations—History.   I. Title.
DS145.R67 2015
305.892′4040902—dc23
2014043379

9 8 7 6 5 4 3
Printed in the United States of America
on acid-free paper

To My Family

Contents

List of Illustrations

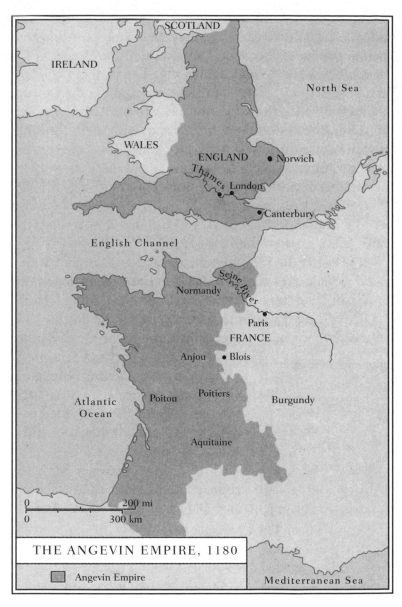

THE ANGEVIN EMPIRE, 1180

Angevin Empire

Map of Europe in 1180 with Norwich.

Timeline

1066	Norman Conquest of England
1096	Foundation of Norwich Cathedral
1119	Death of Bishop Herbert Losinga
1135	Death of Henry I; nephew Stephen of Blois becomes king
	Civil war
1144	(March) Death of apprentice William
1145	Bishop Eborard of Norwich retires to Fontenay in Burgundy
1145	(December) Pope Eugenius III issues papal bull *Quantum praedecessores*
	King Louis VII of France promotes crusade at Christmas court
1146	(March) Bernard of Clairvaux preaches crusade at Vezelay, Burgundy
1146	(summer and autumn) Ralph "the barker" preaches the crusade
1146/1147	William Turbe elected bishop of Norwich; Sheriff John de Chesney dies
1147–1149	**Second Crusade**
1147	(June) Anglo-Normans join French crusaders on the Continent
1148	(January) French and remnants of German army ambushed; William de Warenne, earl of Surrey, among the dead
1149	Crusaders straggle back to western Europe

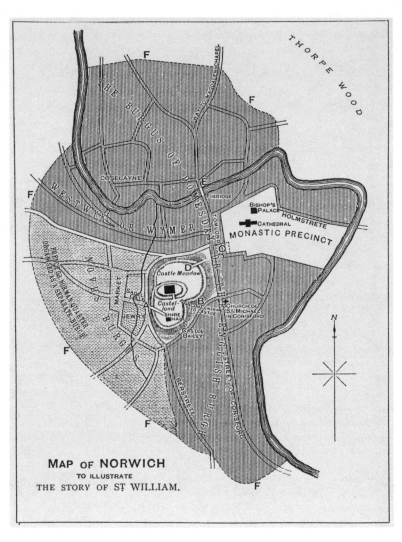

Map of Norwich in the 1140s.

THE MURDER OF WILLIAM OF NORWICH

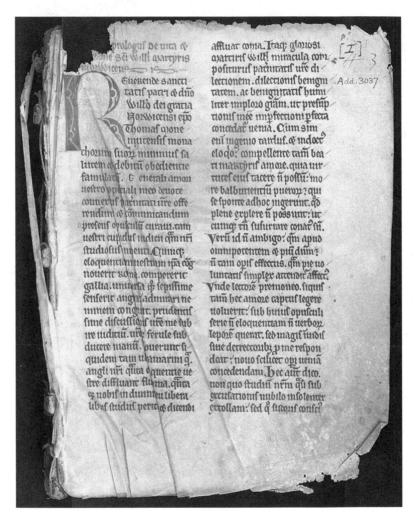

FIGURE I.1 The sole surviving text of *The Life and Passion of St William of Norwich* by Thomas of Monmouth, appears in a manuscript of the late twelfth century, Cambridge University Library Add MS. 3037, f. 1–77r.

PART I   *The Monk, the Knight, the Bishop, and the Banker*

The origin of the blood libel, or the ritual murder charge—the accusation that Jews killed Christian children in order to use their blood for medicinal or ritual purposes and in mockery or hatred of Christ—has never been determined.[1] Such accusations appear in accounts from medieval, Reformation, and modern Europe, and in England, France, Spain, Italy, Germany, Poland, Hungary, Greece, and Russia. It has cropped up in some communities in the United States, and, since the nineteenth century, in Islamic countries as well. Nonetheless, ritual murder has become a quintessential "medieval" accusation, one that for many people seems to sum up all that is darkest about the Middle Ages.

Most charges were never formally investigated, and only in a few cases was official evidence submitted to a legal tribunal (usually after torture had been employed). The Church repeatedly denounced such allegations, as did Christian emperors, kings, and a Turkish sultan, not to mention Jews themselves and many Jewish converts to Christianity.[2] It was well known that Jewish law prohibits the consumption of blood.

No charge has withstood historical scrutiny. No alleged victim remains in the Roman Catholic calendar of saints.[3] Yet some notion of the blood libel accusation has endured to the present. The earliest-known story comes from England in the mid-twelfth century. In 1150 Thomas of Monmouth, a Benedictine monk living in the cathedral priory in Norwich, East Anglia, began collecting notes for a narrative that he completed more than twenty years later, called *The Life and Passion of Saint William of Norwich*. Thomas's text exists in a single contemporary manuscript now in the Cambridge University Library.[4] Brother Thomas, as we will call him, reported that a few years earlier, before he had arrived in Norwich, a young apprentice leatherworker in the city, named William, had been persuaded to leave home with the promise of a job in an archdeacon's household. He was taken instead to the house of an eminent Jew, where he remained for a few days. Thereafter, at the direction of the homeowner, one of Norwich's leading bankers, William was secretly held, subjected to "all the tortures of Christ," and finally murdered. According to Thomas, after the Jews had crowned William with thorns, tightened a knotted rope around his head and placed a gag in his mouth, they took the young man's mutilated body out to the woods and hung it up.[5] The body was eventually found under a tree outside the city walls.

Brother Thomas claimed that Jews performed this alleged ritual in imitation of the Crucifixion and in mockery of the Christian religion, and that William, therefore, should be regarded as a saint. His account comprises two books, in which he details William's life and sufferings, and five further books, in which he recounts the miracles the saint was said to have performed after death. Brother Thomas maintained that William was worthy of veneration and claimed him as an important patron for Norwich Cathedral. Although William's contemporary fame proved ephemeral and quickly died out, even in Norwich (albeit with a short-lived revival of interest in the late Middle Ages), the outline of his tale spread beyond that city, and the idea that Jews engaged in ritual murder became firmly rooted in the European imagination.[6]

This book reconsiders the circumstances surrounding William of Norwich's death and Brother Thomas's interpretation of it, by focusing on the author and the major protagonists of his story.

The purpose is to place the original accusation in its immediate and pertinent contexts, viewing it not merely against a generalized backdrop of Christian-Jewish encounters over the centuries but in the specific and localized contours of a provincial Anglo-Norman city during the High Middle Ages. It centers on another event recounted in Thomas of Monmouth's *Life and Passion of Saint William of Norwich*, a homicide trial following a different murder, one that took place in 1150, in which William's death was invoked. The victim of the second murder was a Jewish banker and the accused was a knight, Simon de Novers, who could not pay his debts. The knight's bishop, William Turbe, defended him before the royal court in London by insisting that the slain banker and the entire Jewish community should be charged with killing young William. It was in the aftermath of that trial that Brother Thomas composed his story.

It is said, correctly, that Brother Thomas's *Life and Passion* is a treatise on martyrdom rather than a legal document—an imaginative, emotional appeal rather than a presentation of forensic evidence.[7] The monk acknowledges that his account of the knight's trial is imagined, and indeed there is no question that his text poses challenges to our concepts of historical evidence.[8] Brother Thomas's account of the trial, however, while a rhetorical tour de force, should not be viewed as mere fiction. No matter how much he may have shaped it, Brother Thomas could hardly have imagined the presence of King Stephen; many of the protagonists of the trial, moreover, were still alive years later when he completed his work.[9] Brother Thomas's text was rhetorically and imaginatively crafted to fit within the existing literary genres of saints' lives and, especially for the trial he describes, of Jewish-Christian disputations.[10] But it intersects history in at least two important ways: first, in the manner in which he writes of historical figures and events, local sites, and chronology with such detail that he could have consulted an almanac;[11] and second, in the expectation that once copied and circulated, his text would be understood by later readers as an authoritative account of what happened.[12] Whatever its nature as a literary document,

Brother Thomas's text provides us with an account of the earliest-known case of ritual murder, and it therefore constitutes the de facto origin. Analyzing key elements and features of his account against other kinds of historical evidence provides us with new insights into the events he treats, as well as into the manner in which the child murder accusation was fashioned and given form.

These events took place during the High Middle Ages, a period of rapid social, political, and economic change. The so-called "renaissance" of the twelfth century witnessed significant population growth, expanded trade, promotion of the crusades, the revival of Greek science and Roman law, and the bureaucratic development of the European nation-state.[13] The establishment of schools and universities, rapid urbanization, and improvements in agriculture led to an intellectual flowering that witnessed advances in architecture (the culmination of Romanesque and the beginnings of Gothic), poetry, romance, and historical writing, philosophical debates, and the development of chivalric ideals. A religious emphasis on pilgrimage and the veneration of relics of the saints anticipated a lively interest in devotion to the Virgin Mary and a focus on Eucharistic piety that would reach maturity in the following century. There was also an increasing emphasis on affective piety and emotional engagement in religious devotion. There is little hint of the demographic crises to come during the "disastrous" fourteenth century and the Black Death (1348–1350). But at the same time, this twelfth-century cultural flowering was accompanied by a crisis of lordship, new attempts to channel violence into acceptable paths, and an increasing effort to identify, marginalize, and punish those on the edges of Christian society.[14]

The murder of William of Norwich occurred almost a century after the Norman Conquest (1066), after which England was ruled by Norman kings who also had significant interests across the Channel. The Conquest had had a dramatic effect on Norwich; many houses in the center of the old town were destroyed, and a new French borough was established. By the twelfth century the French-speaking

Anglo-Norman elite still ruled, but by now had intermarried, had adapted to the English-speaking Anglo-Saxon majority, and had created a vibrant new social and political culture.[15]

Although there is a strong English (i.e., Anglo-Saxon) element in the story of William's death, there is little indication of ongoing conflict between descendants of the Norman conquerors and the Anglo-Saxon natives. In mid-twelfth-century Norwich, far more important than the distant Conquest were the immediate concerns of the civil war and the Second Crusade. After William the Conqueror's youngest son Henry I died in 1135, his daughter Matilda, wife of the Count of Anjou, and his nephew Stephen of Blois, count of Boulogne, vied for control, resulting in a long civil war between the cousins and the "Anarchy"; the political situation was not fully resolved until Matilda's son Henry, the first Plantagenet king of England, succeeded King Stephen in 1154. It was during this violent period that young William was killed. The Second Crusade (1147–1149) added to the turmoil by raising expectations, draining money, and increasing the uncertainty about political authority. It was difficult to rebuild infrastructure and reconstitute civil society in East Anglia after the war when so much attention, enthusiasm, and resources were focused on the Holy Land and the anticipated victories, both spiritual and practical.

Norwich, where the murder occurred, was the second-largest city in medieval England. A few days' ride northeast of London, the booming Norman city, rebuilt on ancient foundations, was the governmental, ecclesiastical, and economic center of eastern England (East Anglia), reflected in its thriving market, its massive fortified castle, and its elaborate cathedral complex, among the greatest works of Romanesque architecture of the time. The river Wensum, which runs through the city, and the river Yare, which flows to the port of Great Yarmouth, gave Norwich convenient access to the hinterland for wool and cattle and to the sea for international trade. The growing city was well supplied with peat for energy and fish for food.[16]

The Jews had first come to England with the Normans in the wake of the Conquest but had spread out only recently from London. Brother Thomas's mention of them in Norwich is the first indication that they were settled there. Little is known about Jewish communities in the early twelfth century: most of what is surmised about them has been inferred from a tax list (*donum*) of 1159, which has allowed an estimate of the relative size and prosperity of the different communities that existed at that date. Jews in Norwich constituted a community of about two hundred people in a city of perhaps five thousand residents by the beginning of the thirteenth century.[17] Rapid growth suggests that Norwich was one of the places in which Jews chose to settle from abroad. It was a flourishing city with a strong Norman presence, a port outlet, with close cultural ties to the Continent, and one of Stephen's strongholds during the civil war. Demographic and financial evidence confirm the city's appeal. By 1159 Norwich was second only to London in the taxes its Jews could pay the king, despite the fact that Jews had been there for less than a generation.[18] For the Jews it was also a bastion of learning, intellectual patronage, and international trade.[19] Norwich became a place of refuge for Jews later in the century, when other English locales such as Thetford, Norfolk and Bungay, Suffolk, became inhospitable.

Jews in twelfth-century England had diverse occupations, chief among them moneylending, but not exclusively so. They were also involved in a variety of trades and commerce, were especially well regarded as doctors, and in Europe in this period (so likely in England as well) were known for work with precious metals, as artisans, mintmasters, and moneyers. In the 1140s, they seem to have been closely connected to the exchange of foreign coinage. Although there are repeated hints in Brother Thomas's *Life and Passion* of the difficulties Jews faced integrating into Christian England, in fact the twelfth century was a fairly peaceful time for them—lasting until the riots that surrounded Richard I's accession in 1189 and their expulsion from the kingdom a century later (1290). England had no outbreak of violence as early as the Rhineland massacres of Jews during the First Crusade (1096). Brother Thomas's creation of the ritual murder accusation is therefore taken as a turning point in the history of the Jews in medieval England.

THIS BOOK IS ABOUT people at the heart of medieval urban life, rather than great men or powerful people, such as kings and earls, popes and archbishops, scholars and chancellors, queens and courtesans. Nor does it concern the rural masses, deluded peasants, abandoned wives, ignorant plowmen, or mute rustics possessing heretical views. The principal actors are people of some substance, some education, and conventional piety. They were sufficiently important to have had their names recorded, to have held land, made donations, joined battles, taken public vows, administered property, witnessed documents, appeared in court, paid for medical care, read books, traveled abroad, educated and provided for their children, and to have been remembered by their families, friends, and colleagues. They seem to have been fairly typical members of the communities in which they lived.

None of these men and women appear to have been uncommonly foolish, easily duped, or especially sinister. Yet the trial of the knight, the event that drew them together, produced one of the most malevolent tales of medieval and early modern history. The claim that Jews killed children and obtained their blood was to have a pernicious and long-lasting history, and left its mark in the realms of both popular imagination and elite opinion.

In the centuries since its appearance—beginning with Brother Thomas's account—the accusation of ritual murder led to instances of the torture, the death, and the expulsion of thousands of individual Jews throughout Europe and to the extermination of hundreds of communities. In the wake of the accusation, a large number of Jews were exiled, executed, burned at the stake, or died in prison. Accusations of ritual murder—at times mere rumors of it—provoked riots in every century well into the twentieth, some eight centuries after the death of William of Norwich. Even in instances where Jews were placed on trial for the death of a child and were found not guilty, attempts to blame them laid the groundwork for their communal condemnation and expulsion.

Now that Jewish ritual murder is no longer accepted as historical truth, there are understandable reasons to diminish or deny the past importance of the accusation. Christians and Jews alike, unable to agree on the origins of the accusation or to account for its force, are eager not to dwell on the tragic effects and the lasting enmity it engendered. Most prefer to focus on positive examples of interfaith dialogue, cultural borrowings, and peaceful coexistence (*convivencia*), rather than on examples of extreme and incomprehensible antipathy. That is why ritual murder and blood libel tend to be treated as a characteristic of a distant medieval past. Yet the concept of the blood libel remains so emotionally charged and so deeply rooted in cultural memory that even today, whether visually or verbally, it endures as a touchstone of historical malevolence.[20]

The blood libel had a profound impact, but its importance is not easily quantified and cannot be measured by a simple tally of the cases that appear in history books and encyclopedias. Some individual accusations resulted in lengthy imprisonments, mass deaths, and communal expulsions and were remembered for centuries. Others were mentioned only in passing, recorded in documents long forgotten and quickly dismissed by officials. Most of the twelfth- and thirteenth-century charges were treated as felony crimes and were taken seriously, initiated by or brought to the attention of the highest governmental authorities. Others appear to have been crafted as literary or rhetorical constructions, or satirical allusions not intended to be regarded as "fact." The best-known literary example is the Prioress's Tale of the late fourteenth century, from Chaucer's *Canterbury Tales*. The tale ends with an allusion to the case of Hugh of Lincoln in the previous century. Many more are fabrications or misunderstandings by later authors intent on highlighting Jewish perfidy or, alternatively, Jewish victimization. In either instance they rely on inaccurate lists, passed down the centuries and garbled in the process.

One needs to take care neither to discount the historical, social, and cultural importance of the ritual murder accusation nor to exaggerate its influence. It has been suggested, for example, that in a late medieval society permeated by violence, the ritual murder accusation was unremarkable.[21] But the frequency of such accusations does not provide a reliable or adequate measure of their cultural, economic, or legislative impact. Some cases were ephemeral. Others, however, such as those of Hugh of Lincoln (England) in the thirteenth century, and Simon of Trent (Italy) in the fifteenth, had profound repercussions, both in their own time and centuries later. The accusations in the cases in Damascus in the nineteenth century and in Kiev in the twentieth (the trial in 1913 of Mendel Beilis) were likewise the focus of great public interest. They were covered extensively at the time in the popular press, were analyzed subsequently in serious books addressed to general readers, and are the topics of exhaustive scholarship even today.[22]

The ritual murder accusation was widespread geographically and chronologically, extending across northern and southern Europe, from the Mideast to America, from the twelfth century to the twentieth. It also had immensely powerful political, economic, and legal effects. The blood libel was much more than a simple or commonplace motif of religious folklore, as it is now often described.

An enumeration of specific charges of ritual murder in the Middle Ages does not take into account the immediate cultural contexts in which the accusation was disseminated. Variously enshrined in cathedrals, celebrated in ballads and songs, or depicted with the Virgin Mary in panel paintings and altarpieces, the purported victims of ritual murder were honored, and their stories became foundational legends of churches the length and breadth of Europe. Jews murdering such victims were portrayed in manuscripts, sculpture, paintings, and stained glass. In the modern era, such depictions appeared in prints, posters, and postcards and even on magazine covers prominently displayed at bus stops, company cafeterias, and public parks.[23] Long after its legal, financial, and theological roots had withered, the ritual murder accusation remained a powerful cultural concept.[24]

Explanations that seek to account for the appearance of the ritual murder accusation in so many periods and places and under markedly different social, religious, and political circumstances necessarily rely on wide-ranging theories derived from the disciplines of anthropology, folklore, psychology, and the social sciences, rather than from history. For a long time, scholars believed that the accusation was a holdover from Antiquity, a continuation of Roman attacks on Christians, who were once looked upon as a Jewish sect.[25] Some have sought its origins in such varied areas as the Jewish customs of circumcision, kosher butchering practices, Purim festivities, Jewish holiday food such as *matzah, haroset*, and *hamentaschen*, the martyrdoms of the First Crusade, or guilt over child neglect and abandonment.[26] Many modern writers see the blood libel accusation either as perverse or as an excuse to demonize Jews, particularly Jews to whom money was owed.[27] Others view it as an example of psychological projection.[28] Christians' doubts about their own beliefs, it has been argued, fostered "irrational fantasies," such as those of the ritual crucifixion imagined by Brother Thomas to reinforce his own sense of religious security. Indeed, writing about the early history of the blood libel now has its own extensive history.[29] William of Norwich, in particular, has received a considerable amount of attention, ever since the full text of his story was discovered in a Suffolk parish library at the end of the nineteenth century by the antiquarian M. R. James, who edited and published an influential translation with Augustus Jessopp, an honorary canon of Norwich Cathedral.[30] Brother Thomas's *Life and Passion* has now been re-translated for a modern readership, including passages that the fastidious Victorian translators passed over.[31]

It is widely assumed today that the accusation of ritual murder was a pan-European phenomenon and that its historical "truth" will never be known.[32] The literature on this topic—polemical, religious, scholarly, and apologetic—is extensive and sometimes contradictory.[33] But to label the ritual murder accusation as a "myth," characterize it as "folklore," call it a "legend," refer to it as a "fable" or "literary motif," or dismiss it as mere "fantasy" or "unfounded rumor" is to imply that there is some timeless basis to the original story. Rather than diminishing it, to claim that it is beyond history or historical investigation is to give it unwarranted power and implicitly to place the blame on the victims of the accusation. Indeed, Jewish customs, such as those mentioned above, that supposedly gave rise to the accusation often receive more attention than the accusation itself.

Although the ritual murder accusation is perceived as medieval, it spread most widely during the modern period. Jews were accused of ritual murder more frequently in the Early Modern period than during the Middle Ages, and more in the nineteenth century than in all preceding centuries combined, particularly between 1870 and 1935.[34] The recorded dates of accusations are often misleading because many, if not most, charges were made retrospectively, sometimes years after the supposed events, sometimes decades, or even centuries later.[35] If it did not happen this time, it could be said, it had happened at some previous time. Blood libel, later combined with the accusation that Jews desecrated the Host (the Eucharistic wafer), became a stock accusation with recognizable characters that could be reworked and filled in with local and timely detail in each succeeding generation.

This book, therefore, is primarily about the first tellers of the tale, rather than its subjects. It does not consider what "timeless" anonymous Jews allegedly did, thought, said, and believed, but what certain Christians did, thought, said, and believed at a particular time, in a particular and distinct geographic, political, and religious context. It is less about what these individuals imagined than what actions they took on the basis of those beliefs. My subject is not eternal truths of the Christian-Jewish encounter, but one particular encounter—its creation, elaboration, interpretation, cultural construction, and its dissemination as an enduring narrative.

FIGURE 1.1 Mousehold Heath today (then known as Thorpe Wood) outside Norwich, where the body of William of Norwich was discovered in 1144.

CHAPTER 1   *The Discovery of a Dead Body*

The story of the first ritual murder accusation begins with the discovery of a dead body. In March 1144, William, a young apprentice, was killed and left under a tree on the outskirts of Norwich. Finding a dead body is invariably an awkward experience. It raises troubling questions, draws unwanted attention to the finder, and generally entangles the discoverer in costly officialdom and paperwork, not to mention emotional distress. This was particularly true in medieval England, where detailed rules specified the proper procedures for dealing with corpses.[1] Then, as now, homicide was a serious business involving families, communities, courts, and an entire hierarchy of justice. Many considered it advisable to move a dead body elsewhere, bury it quickly, or hope that it might be devoured by animals or consumed by the elements before it was discovered.

When a peasant stumbled upon a corpse tangled in the underbrush not far from a major thoroughfare outside the city of Norwich, therefore, he knew exactly what to do: at first he ignored it.[2] Earlier that same day, another person who came upon the corpse, a Norman aristocratic nun, Lady Legarda, likewise failed to alert the authorities or to take any responsibility. She said prayers around the corpse with her fellow nuns, and then retreated to her convent, apparently untroubled.[3] The presence of birds circling around the cadaver indicated that it lay unprotected in the open. As was typical in many such cases, the "first finder" of the body was actually the last of several people who encountered it, but the first one who was legally obligated to investigate the death.[4]

On Holy Saturday (March 25), the day before Easter, the forester Henry de Sprowston was shown the corpse while he was riding through the woods in the course of his duties, looking for people who might be making mischief or, more likely, cutting timber without a license.[5] He was patrolling Thorpe Wood on behalf of his ecclesiastical employer, the Norwich bishop and monks. The right to cut lumber was a valuable privilege that was jealously guarded. Wood was used for heating and cooking, for building halls, cathedrals, parish churches, homes, docks, and the boats needed for the hundreds of shiploads of fine limestone brought from Normandy to build Norwich Cathedral and castle. Good English oak was especially highly prized: tree trunks were employed for the construction of heavy beams in houses, halls, and barns, the branches were used to make charcoal or were dried for firewood, the bark was boiled for tannin used in leatherworking, and the fiber beneath the bark could be used to make rope.[6] This was a period of great deforestation throughout Europe as the population expanded and land was cleared for planting, especially around Norwich, one of the fastest-growing boroughs in the country in an already densely populated region. Landlords, therefore, vigorously enforced restrictions on access to woodland.

The forester's role was judicial and economic as well as agricultural. In a complicated plan to divide one of their major assets, the bishop owned Thorpe Wood, but part had been given to the monks of Norwich Cathedral Priory, the monastery attached to the cathedral.[7] The woods were to be managed for the joint benefit of monastery and bishop, and each had to approve the trees that the other marked before they were cut down.[8] They also had to agree to any timber sales to a third party. The discovery of a dead body on their land was of consequence to the church authorities in their capacity as landowners as well as comforters of the dead youth's family.

To deflect attention from his own possibly illicit activities, the peasant led Henry de Sprowston to the dead body. Neither the woodcutter nor the forester recognized the young man, and neither could account for how the body came to be in the woods. Henry de Sprowston launched an inquiry into the death, and while nothing apparently came of his investigation, the body was identified as that of William, a young apprentice leatherworker and son of Wenstan and Elviva.[9] The news spread and people from the city rushed to the woods to see what had happened. After William's uncle, brother, and cousin identified the body, the dead youth was laid to rest with minimal ceremony and no elaborate marker.[10]

Information about William and the resulting homicide inquiry comes from Brother Thomas's account of the *Life and Passion of William of Norwich*, which is one of the only surviving texts from the large library of twelfth-century Norwich Cathedral. Thomas arrived at the monastery a few years after the discovery of William's body and took a passionate interest in the dead boy, for reasons that will become clear. Six years after the murder, Brother Thomas claimed to have pieced together what had happened during the fateful Holy Week of 1144. He set out to prove that William had been killed for his faith and therefore deserved to be hailed as a saint.

The story, as Brother Thomas was later to recount it, offered an intriguing mystery, one in which he features himself prominently as a crusading detective. Relying on information provided by the victim's family, Thomas claimed that young William was induced to accompany a man who offered him a job working for the archdeacon's cook. That, at least, was what the archdeacon's man told William's mother, who acquiesced to his employment despite her misgivings.[11] When the man (the mother was not certain whether he was a Christian or a Jew) checked with the boy's aunt the next day, she was sufficiently suspicious to send her daughter to follow William. The daughter reportedly saw the man and William enter a certain Jew's house.[12] There, after some time, Brother Thomas insisted, William was sacrificed in a bloody mockery of the Crucifixion, after which his abused body was abandoned in the woods outside the town, where it was eventually discovered. William's uncle reported that, as soon as the mother learned of her son's death, she blamed local Jews. According to Thomas's account, Bishop Eborard of Norwich tried to have these Jews brought to court to testify, but the sheriff, a man named John de Chesney, protected them, so that any hopes of prosecuting them soon passed.

Although William's family made a fuss, the case seemed to die down fairly quickly. Bishop Eborard let the boy's uncle speak at an ecclesiastical gathering, the regular synod he convened the following month, but he does not seem to have investigated any further. Once it was identified, the body was eventually buried where it was discovered, on land owned by the bishop and the cathedral priory, and little more thought was given to William.[13] By the time Brother Thomas began his imaginative work, the dead boy's brother had become a fellow monk at the cathedral priory.

Scholars have taken Thomas at his word, believing that he wrote his account relatively close in time to the death and with sufficient knowledge of and access to the protagonists and other interested parties that he could not have manipulated the facts without provoking comment.[14] Although he began writing just six years after William's death, he did not refine and complete his text for another two decades.

We need therefore to separate the various layers of accretions that have enveloped this medieval "whodunit": the immediate events surrounding the death and the initial discovery of the body; the subsequent events when a story was woven about the dead boy and his alleged murderers; the completion of that story a generation later, when a cult was created around the remains; and the dissemination of the outlines of the story far beyond Norwich. Although Brother Thomas strains to appear forthright with his readers, he is quite selective in the information he provides. He does not mention, for example, that it was standard procedure for bodies to remain exposed for three days.[15] He ignores other events that are important to consider if we are to understand his claims for William's sanctity, and which played a significant role in his interpretation of what took place. One of the most important was the violent civil war that beset the area, which may explain the boy's death and the lack of attention it received at the time. Other important factors are the close connections and relationships between the family, the members of the priory, and the bishop's household, and the legal proceedings related to the alleged murder (which Thomas misrepresents). All these circumstances were underplayed. What was overemphasized was the demand for the boy's relics.

Until 1150, when Thomas began his work, no one apparently gave the young apprentice a second thought.[16] Local disinterest concerning William at the time of his death stands in marked contrast to the popular attention garnered by some of his holy contemporaries, such as St. Wulfric of Haselbury, St. Godric of Finchale (whose *Lives* appear in the same manuscript with that of William), and St. Thomas Becket, men who were instantly acclaimed as powerful heavenly intercessors when they died.[17] Veneration of Becket was immediate, dynamic, and long lasting. When in 1170 he was murdered in his cathedral in Canterbury, pilgrims dipped their handkerchiefs in the martyr's blood before it had dried. Within two years of his death, admiring monks composed miracle stories about his wonder-working remains. Within three years, Becket of Canterbury was called on to shore up other cults: he was invoked in visions as a supporter of other saints, indicating the quick spread of his fame.

In the case of William of Norwich, it was convenient to recall portents that supposedly presaged his martyrdom: a sweet smell, a mother's dream, an aunt's dream, flowers blooming in winter, an easy labor during pregnancy.[18] However, William's most avid proponent could find information concerning only those five miracles; none was particularly remarkable.[19] A bright light shining over William's corpse indicated his sanctity.[20] There is no mention of dipping handkerchiefs, rending clothes, bringing gifts, or begging for cures. This suggests that the few miracles recorded for the period 1144–1150 were later recollections of natural phenomena.

The lack of attention initially paid to young William was likely due to the fact that his death occurred during a civil war between Stephen and Matilda, the children of Henry I.[21] Scholars debate the extent of the war's devastation, but there is no doubt that around 1144, it raged with particular ferocity in East Anglia and its swampy fenlands.[22] In the oft-quoted phrase of the Peterborough version of the *Anglo-Saxon Chronicle*, one of the main sources of information about the civil war, "They said openly that Christ and his saints were asleep."[23]

It was not only armed combatants and peasants who suffered; townsmen and artisans, such as William and his prosperous family, were targeted for persecution and extortion.[24] The garrisons seized "such of the *vavasours* and country-people as were reputed to be possessed of money, they compelled them, by extreme torture, to promise whatever they thought fit."[25] The Peterborough chronicler reports in explicit detail that soldiers during the war

> perpetrated every enormity . . . both by night and day they took those people that they thought had any goods—men and women—and put them in prison and tortured them with indescribable torture to extort gold and silver—for no martyrs were ever tortured as they were. They were hung by the thumbs or by the head, and corselets were hung on their feet. Knotted ropes were put round their heads and twisted till they penetrated to the brains. . . . In many of the castles was a "noose-and-trap". . . . It was so made that it was fastened to a beam, and they used to put a sharp iron around the man's throat and his neck, so that he could not in any direction either sit or lie or sleep, but had to carry all that iron.[26]

The tortures described by the Anglo-Saxon chronicler correspond to those described by William of Malmesbury in the *Historia Novella* and by the author who continued the work of Simeon of Durham.[27] They also correspond to the tortures apparently suffered before his death by William of Norwich, who was "hung from a tree" and whose "head was bound." The Peterborough chronicler wrote his account not far from Norwich.

Vicious attacks occurred throughout England. In the west, on the highways outside Bristol, innocent bystanders were hacked to pieces and the knights of the castle nailed the noses of their victims to trees.[28] In eastern England, Geoffrey de Mandeville, who organized a kidnapping ring as a way to extort money, was equally ruthless.[29] He used the civil war to wrest charters from both Stephen and Matilda. After brutalizing the abbeys of Ramsey and the Isle of Ely, the infamously vicious earl, still rebellious, died of his wounds in late summer of 1144, not long after William's murder, at Mildenhall in Suffolk. Mandeville's cohorts may have attacked the outskirts of Norwich earlier that spring, for Mildenhall is less than a day's ride away. There is no question that the unrest spread to the heart of Norwich: the bishop's large library was burned during the civil war—not, as generally believed, in town riots of the following century.[30] A number of knights were threatening violence and wreaking havoc on civil society in and around Norwich, extorting lands from leading ecclesiastics with holdings in East Anglia. The foremost lords of the region, including Hugh Bigod and William de Warenne, had no compunction about using intimidation to get what they wanted. The counties of Norfolk and Suffolk, which together were the most lucrative source of royal revenue in 1130 and for most of Henry II's reign, were able to contribute almost nothing to the royal treasury immediately after the civil war.[31]

Under the circumstances, it is therefore not surprising that local authorities did not investigate the death of a young apprentice with more vigor. A thorough investigation of William's death might have exacerbated bitter divisions in the community, and no good was likely to come of it. The inhabitants of Norwich were subject to pressure from all sides: from Stephen's loyalists (many, like the Chesneys, tenants on lands that were King Stephen's personal holdings as Lord of Eye and Boulogne); from supporters of Matilda (such as

Bishop Eborard, a native of Calne in Salisbury, the heartland of Matilda's power); and from Hugh Bigod, Earl of Norfolk, who shifted back and forth in his alliances.

The initial judicial inquiries and proceedings that Brother Thomas describes do not reflect or conform to contemporary practice. The elaborate detail he offers ignores the fact that there was no inquest or jury of presentment, which would have been typical at that time for a homicide case. Uncle Godwin appealed for justice to a diocesan synod, the annual meeting or church council called by the bishop to review pastoral care and mete out discipline. At the synod, according to Brother Thomas, Godwin announced that Jews had been responsible for the death of his nephew and offered to back up his words by resort to a judicial ordeal.[32]

Unlike secular courts, an ecclesiastical court could offer recourse to a judgment by God, that is, through a trial by ordeal (*iudicium dei*). Defendants were dipped in water, subjected to fire, or forced to do battle with a champion—all methods often used in cases where proof was lacking or evidence difficult to obtain.[33] Yet from the time of Charlemagne three centuries earlier, Jews had usually been exempted from such ordeals.[34] If Godwin hoped to achieve something by recourse to a trial by ordeal, he was disappointed. Although the Jews were dreadfully afraid of the trial by ordeal, as Brother Thomas put it, they were adequately protected by the sheriff, the aforementioned John de Chesney.[35] Nonetheless, trial by ordeal later became a consistent theme underlying similar accusations against Jews, so Thomas's report that it was suggested may reflect subsequent literary embellishment.[36] What is clear is that no prosecution succeeded.

Thomas's account of an appeal to a synod was likely included in the later *Life* to emphasize the importance of the ecclesiastical context and to highlight the failings of Sheriff de Chesney, for in Brother Thomas's judgment, it was the sheriff who should have been responsible for taking action against the perpetrators. Instead, the sheriff sided with the Jews (and like Judas, he suffered a violent death).[37]

According to Brother Thomas, Bishop Eborard had attempted in vain to bring Jews to his court, but until tempers cooled the sheriff took them under his protection in Norwich Castle.[38] William may have been a victim of foul play, but there was little effort to find a perpetrator, and evidently no one was ever prosecuted for his killing. Apparently neither the family nor the authorities sought to mobilize the secular legal apparatus, even though homicide on the king's roads was a serious offense and was profitable to prosecute.[39] The accusation against the Jews may have been an early form of extortion, for Jews were widely reputed to have money. If the purpose of the denunciation was primarily to negotiate a financial settlement, then Godwin was well advised to lay his complaint before the diocesan synod.[40]

Godwin's eagerness to point the finger at the Jews may have been intended to draw attention away from William and the possibility that he died by his own hand. Then, as now, adolescent suicide was not uncommon.[41] As a suicide, William would have been deprived of burial in consecrated ground and his family subject to scandal, tainted by association with the most famous suicide of all, that of Judas Iscariot. A peasant who hanged himself was regarded as a coward inspired by the devil. His corpse was subject to abuse, his soul was bound for hell, his property was subject to confiscation, and his family was shamed and humiliated.[42] Godwin would thus have been motivated to assign blame to someone other than the victim.

The Jews of Norwich were not alone in being blamed for William's death, so too was their perceived associate, the sheriff at the time, John de Chesney, who died soon after. The shift of blame to the sheriff may have occurred during a brief interim (roughly 1154–1156) when one of the Chesneys no longer held the office of sheriff. Sheriff John de Chesney had succeeded his father Robert fitzWalter and was succeeded in turn by his brother William de Chesney (d. 1174); together they ruled East Anglia as royal representatives for fifty years, from 1115 into the 1160s, and wielded unprecedented power in the locale. Once the family was back in power in the later 1150s, attention shifted in turn to the Jews they protected.[43] The monks of Norwich were highly motivated to attack the reputation of John de Chesney, because he had seized ecclesiastical land during the civil war, which they were eventually able to reclaim.[44] On his deathbed in 1146, two years after the death of William of Norwich, John de Chesney was so overcome by the sins he had apparently committed during the war that he directed his brother to found Sibton Abbey on his behalf.[45] It was Sibton Abbey that later preserved the surviving copy of Thomas of Monmouth's work.[46]

Bishop Eborard, as well as Uncle Godwin, may have had motives to prosecute William's murder that had nothing whatever to do with efforts to discover the identity of the perpetrators. The bishop could have seized the initiative on the grounds that he had authority over Thorpe Woods, the land on which the body was found, which had originally been a gift from Henry I. He may have sought to buttress his claim over the territory by prosecuting malefactors there, prompted by the knowledge that both Ely and Bury held large tracts of land with royal rights within his diocese. This was no minor matter. A few years later, in the same diocese, on the basis of an ancient gift of royal rights, the abbey of Bury St. Edmunds successfully defended abbey knights from royal prosecution for treason.[47] Perhaps the bishop was trying to set a precedent for prosecuting crimes of this type. If—in what was a familiar medieval strategy—he was testing the waters for increased autonomy and status for his cathedral on the basis of the possession of saintly relics, he did not succeed.

Bishop Eborard's interest in William's sanctity appears to have remained lukewarm. Once the bishop retired from Norwich in 1145 to the abbey of Fontenay in Burgundy, there is no evidence that the case continued through official channels, either religious or secular.[48] Within the year, Eborard was in close contact with the papal legate, but he does not seem to have raised the issue of William's death either with him or in a letter that he wrote to the pope later that year. He apparently never said a word about the homicide that William's uncle explicitly and publicly characterized as "an affront recently committed against all Christians."⁴⁹ Bishop Eborard's successor, William Turbe, who had been prior at the time of William's death in 1144, also failed, apparently, to bring up the case when he met with colleagues and superiors. No further mention was made of William, no miracles are recorded, and relations between Christians and Jews appear to have continued uneventfully for the next few years. In the *Life* Thomas admits as much when he says that the memory of William had all but died out.⁵⁰

Once Brother Thomas was on the case in 1150, everything changed. A year after the removal of William's body from the Norwich churchyard into the chapter house, his remains were moved again and elevated to the high altar; after that, he was moved into a special chapel dedicated to the martyrs. William now had a personal sacrist (Brother Thomas, then working on his *Life*) assigned to care for the relics and take note of the miracles that occurred around his tomb. Artwork was commissioned, and he could boast of his own feast day. The restoration of William's reputation had begun.

By the time Brother Thomas began his work, it was important to present William's credentials for sanctity and to backdate them to the year of his death. Since the appeal of a holy cult centered on a dead apprentice was not immediately obvious to the citizens of Norwich, Brother Thomas took care to explain that while Norwich had been unappreciative of its prized remains, others knew their value. Threats of theft, even if invented, or stories of actual thefts enhanced the allure of relics and guaranteed their authenticity.⁵¹

Brother Thomas reports that the inspiration for moving William's body to the protection of the monastic confines came from an outsider. Aimery, prior of the wealthy abbey of St. Pancras in Sussex, heard Godwin's story while they were attending the synod together, and he offered to take the boy's body. Aimery's interest would seem to suggest that by then William's story—as well as the accusation of ritual murder—was known throughout England.⁵² As the head of the Cluniac mother house in England, the prior of St. Pancras was influential in East Anglian monastic circles. Aimery, however, did not have the stature of his predecessors and died not long after his accession.[53]

The threat of robbery was sufficient to alert the monks and to make William's relics appear to be in high demand. This was a literary commonplace of long standing, found, for example, in the case of St. Wulfric (d. 1154), whose remains were fought over by the monks of Montacute, Osbern the priest of Haselbury, and his parishioners. Prior Aimery's reported eagerness to acquire William's relics may have been invented after the fact, a possibility enhanced by the prior's brief and unmemorable tenure in office.

The monks may have welcomed the transfer of William's body to their cemetery, if only because burials added to their income.[54] In the early twelfth century, the right to bury Roger Bigod, the father of Hugh Bigod, first earl of Norfolk, in Norwich Cathedral was the subject of a bitterly fought body-snatching case argued before the royal court, pitting the first bishop of Norwich, Herbert Losinga, against the monks of Thetford.[55] In the mid-twelfth century, the monks of St. Margaret's, King's Lynn, Norfolk, received permission, confirmed by papal charter, to bury those who died in boating accidents.[56] Disputes over burial rights and fees arose frequently between monks and friars in the thirteenth century and festered for years.[57]

Burial in the monks' cemetery did not necessarily imply a religious distinction, but it certainly registered social distinction. Social divisions were reinforced in medieval burial practices, and the placement close to the church or saints (*ad sanctos*) was a critical indicator. Different social zones were defined in the churchyard, with the church walls reserved for the elite and the periphery of the cemetery for slaves and lepers. At many Anglo-Norman monasteries, wealthy individuals and families could purchase confraternity with the monks. In exchange for a donation, they would be guaranteed burial among the professed brothers and would be included in their prayers. An example of a Norwich confraternity contract survives in the episcopal letters and charters, perhaps referring to William's own family.[58] William's mother was buried with the Norwich monks, possibly under some form of confraternity arrangement, although Brother Thomas says "because of the devotion we had for the son, we buried the mother honourably in our cemetery."[59]

Brother Thomas's account of the day of William's move to the churchyard (which he did not witness) corresponds to arrangements for the funeral of a socially prominent individual.[60] The body was washed, prepared, and laid on a bier in the center of the cathedral while a requiem mass was recited, after which it was to be placed in a simple wooden coffin and interred in the cemetery adjacent to a wall of the chapter house.[61] While the grave was dug, a sarcophagus was found and William was placed in it. Stone sarcophagi recycled from burials in Late Antiquity often enhanced the stature and lent an aura of continuity and legitimacy to the tombs of twelfth-century aristocrats.[62] At most translations of sanctified relics, the official guest list was of critical concern, and the ritual was carefully considered.[63] No distinguished guests are known to have attended William's memorial service.

The violent nature of William's death—whatever the nature of the violence—also played a part in the process of his sanctification. The Anglo-Saxons had a long tradition of associating sudden violence with holy death.[64] In 1147, Englishmen in Portugal on the Second Crusade hailed their companions killed in battle as martyrs (contrary to church teaching) and immediately following their deaths reported miracles around their corpses.[65] At Rochester, Kent, the baker William of Perth was ambushed and killed as he set out on pilgrimage in 1201; his body was graced with all kinds of miracles. Popular tradition suggested that it was the character of one's death, rather than the identity of the perpetrators, that determined a body's holiness.[66] Brother Thomas, however, claimed to accept the theologically correct line articulated by his opponents that "the cause, not the suffering, makes the saint."[67]

The most telling context in which to consider William's sanctification comes from the pen of Abbot Guibert of Nogent, in northern France, who wrote a treatise on saints and relics in addition to his memoirs and works of history and theology. Two decades before William's death, Guibert (d. 1124) ridiculed the prevalent notion that a boy from a good family, killed around Easter, ought reflexively to be regarded as particularly holy:

> I have indeed seen, and blush to relate, how a common boy, nearly related to a certain most renowned abbot, and squire (it was said) to some knight, died in a village hard by Beauvais, on Good Friday, two days before Easter. Then, for the sake of that sacred day whereon he had died, men began to impute a gratuitous sanctity to the dead boy. When this had been rumored among the country-folk, all agape for something new, then forthwith oblations and waxen tapers were brought to his tomb by the villagers of all that country round. What need of more words? A monument was built over him, the pot was hedged in with a stone building, and from the very confines of Brittany there came great companies of country-folk, though without admixture of the higher sort. That most wise abbot with his religious monks, seeing this, and being enticed by the multitude of gifts that were brought, suffered the fabrication of false miracles.[68]

Guibert was describing a situation remarkably similar to that of William of Norwich. Like the boy of Beauvais, William came from a respected family; his mutilated body was divinely pointed out on Good Friday and was discovered in the woods on Easter Saturday; the local monks were to promote his cause. But Norwich residents shared the kind of skepticism that Guibert evinced about the boy in Beauvais. To judge from Brother Thomas's fierce and frequent denunciations of his unnamed opponents in the *Life and Passion*, many doubted the justice of his cause. "They are most eager to detract and unwilling to praise ... they injure [William's] reputation by belittling the enhancement of his praise ... and so persecute him by diminishing him," Brother Thomas complained of his opponents, adding, "What they call presumption—to hold as a saint one who is not—we assert the same without a shadow of a doubt."[69]

The flurry of interest surrounding the violent and sudden death of William—whatever the opinion of what had caused it—indicates fervent belief in the sanctifying effects of innocent death, young death. These attitudes belong to Anglo-Saxon and pagan traditions and continued into the late eleventh and twelfth centuries; the English long maintained a fascination with sexual purity and the innocence of youthful martyrs.[70] Some medieval victims enjoyed a certain repute and were immediately and actively mourned by their families and neighbors, but few of these generated a viable cult when they came under the scrutiny of religious authorities. William of Norwich, like the baker of Perth or the boy of Beauvais, at first appeared to have commanded only local and ephemeral fame; it would take a few years, the endorsement of the bishop, and the backing of the priory to make William into a saint.

One of the most striking elements of William's death involves the status and identity of his extended family, about which Brother Thomas informs us, although only in bits and pieces. Retellings of William's story consistently describe him as a poor, young child. Brother Thomas describes William as innocent, young, and vulnerable, and emphasizes his naiveté; later readers assumed he was born a peasant and ended his short days as an urban ragamuffin eking out a living.[71] But William's supposedly pitiable circumstances are part of the later literary tradition of his cult. On closer scrutiny, he appears to have been an integral and substantial member of Norwich society.

What little circumstantial evidence survives indicates that William was born into a notable family, one that was relatively wealthy and educated and that possessed long-standing ties to the region. Contemporary documents appear to connect the family with the town of Bury, the miracles of St. Edmund, ownership of a church in Norwich, and patronage of the cathedral priory. In short, although Anglo-Saxon rather than part of the Norman ruling class, William's family were members of the East Anglian clerical elite, and William himself appears to have been a youth with a promising future.

In his commentary on Brother Thomas's work published in 1896, M. R. James says of William's father, Wenstan, "we hear nothing save that he lived in the country and was a farmer, comfortably off."[72] James extrapolates Wenstan's occupation as farmer from the description of his family as "rural" (*ruri*). Brother Thomas alludes to ten members of the saint's immediate family, including William's parents and elder brothers, and not one of them is ever identified as a farmer or peasant. The *Life* opens by saying merely, "his father was a certain Wenstan by name. His mother was called Elviva, and they lived a decent life in the countryside, abundantly supplied with all those things needed for living."[73] Indications that the family was above the peasant class suggest that Brother Thomas is revealing his own social snobbery when he adds that the future saint was "from humble parents" (*ab infimis parentibus*).[74] That judgment of an Anglo-Saxon family by a Norman writer appears a matter of perspective and degree rather than an objective measure of the youth's status within his own community.

William's parents came from the countryside, but they were not provincial in the pejorative sense of the word.[75] William was baptized at Haveringland, nine miles from Norwich, and presumably was raised there.[76] The tower of the windswept Norman church where William may have been brought to the font survives. William moved to the center of town as a boy and thereafter was very seldom in the country, but was occupied in the city.[77] William lived in Norwich with a family friend named Wlward, probably a relative, for it was typical in this period for a boy to apprentice with an uncle or cousin.[78] The Anglo-Saxon *Wlward*, the name of his maternal grandfather, may have been passed down the family as the Norman name *William*.

Thus William was a new member of the urban commercial world who had not lived with his parents in the country for some time. His mother remained in the country, and it took time for news to travel to her and for her to come to the city.[79] He was, according to Brother Thomas, "gifted with a teachable disposition and bringing industry to bear upon it, in a short time he far surpassed lads of his own age in the craft aforesaid [leatherworking], and he equaled some who had been his teachers."[80] It was here as well that he would have come into contact with Norwich's Jewish population who were involved in trade. The Jews made a point of seeking him out, either because he charged less, as Brother Thomas would have it, or because some were among the wealthiest members of the urban merchant community and they could afford to pay well for skilled work.[81]

From what Brother Thomas tells his readers, William was ambitious and educated. He knew the traditional prayers by heart and could also read.[82] Despite his success in leatherworking, William was allegedly offered a post with the archdeacon's cook. Such an offer, if authentic, would have been enticing. Cooks were well-regarded in medieval England: so much so that they amassed land, made donations, and joined bishops, knights, and officeholders in attesting documents and confirming grants. The position of cook was both respected and highly profitable, and the household of an archdeacon of Norfolk could be an important steppingstone to prominence. William would have been well placed to take advantage of the opportunities offered.

Literate, well-connected, and well-spoken, with English (his native Anglo-Saxon) and possibly some commercial French (which was spoken by the Anglo-Norman elite) and with a smattering of Latin by the age of twelve, William was no rude rustic; he was a young man embarking on an auspicious professional life. In the same decade that one archdeacon was said to have recruited young William the apprentice, another archdeacon recruited a promising young man whose family hailed from Bec. By 1143 that protégé, Thomas Becket, was in the household of Archbishop Theobald of Canterbury, where he began his meteoric rise. The implications of such a career path would not have been lost on ambitious Norwich households. Brother Thomas perhaps hoped to make William a posthumous success on the scale of St. Thomas Becket. He completed his book on William within a few years of the archbishop's death in 1170.

William's future looked bright, and knowing the advantages an archdeacon's patronage might confer, the readers of Brother Thomas's *Life* would not question too closely the circumstances under which William's mother relinquished her son to an unknown man in the days immediately before Easter. It was only after the alleged martyrdom that she claimed that the man who took her son "claims to be the archdeadon's cook, but she does not trust him at all."[83] Curiously, William remained in the Jews' home, where he was treated kindly, "ignorant of what business was being prepared for him, and he was kept until the morrow."[84] This delay suggests that he had some familiarity with the people who took him. Thomas wanted to emphasize the literary overtones, for he adds that, like Christ, William was "an innocent lamb led to the slaughter"—a motif that became a stock element of later accusations of blood libel. William's mother, moreover, is portrayed as mercenary in accepting money for her son. The three shillings (36 pence) she received for William's apprenticeship may be a rhetorical flourish, or it may actually suggest his considerable value as an employee; this Judas motif, like that of the fatted calf, became a literary commonplace. The literary coloring of the text, however, could not disguise the possibility that readers would accept without surprise William's ongoing and long-standing interaction with Jewish neighbors.[85]

Thomas describes William's background as lowly and characterizes him as "neglected" (*pauperculum atque neglectum*), but he may refer to a fatherless individual in an otherwise successful family. As noted, William's parents do not seem to have been peasant farmers, as were most of the population; he himself was an urban resident, a skinner at a time when leatherworking was a lucrative skill in a growing industry. Leather was the basis for England's second-largest export product after wool; it was the greatest trade of thirteenth-century Norwich.[86] His connections were long remembered: in the fourteenth century the Guild of Leatherworkers adopted William as their patron saint, and they set out to raise his profile through their renewed contributions in his name and by sponsoring annual feasts (all surviving pictures of William date from this later period).[87] William and at least one of his brothers and a cousin had employment options that were not available to most English boys of Norwich: positions as artisan, cook, monk, and deacon were all respectable careers with many advantages, far removed from field work.

William's family of churchmen may have come from Bury St. Edmunds. Although unprovable, if this is so, it suggests one further motivation for the particular interest of the Norwich ecclesiastical establishment in the boy. Bury and Norwich had been at odds for decades. Bury St. Edmunds was one of the wealthiest abbeys in England, and had long treasured its independence and the power of its abbot. Since the establishment of the episcopal seat at Norwich, the bishops had tried vigorously to control or to lay claim to the abbey and the relics of St. Edmund, king and martyr, which the abbey preserved.[88]

William's maternal grandfather was "Wlward the priest, a man famous in his time," in Thomas's description, very likely the *Wlwardus presbiter* who attested (witnessed or authenticated later) three documents in Bury St. Edmunds.[89] The first, a charter of Abbot Albold of Bury (made between 1114 and 1119) was a grant to the widow of Jocelin of Loddon, of land that her husband had held from the abbey of St. Edmunds.[90] Loddon, a small town on the road between Bury and Norwich, was one of the few places that possessed a depiction of St. William during the later Middle Ages.[91] *Wlwardus presbiter* attested two other charters of Abbot Albold; he also attested a charter of Albold's successor, Abbot Anselm of Bury (1121–1148).[92] "Wulward" was also the name of William's landlord and may have been William's original Anglo-Saxon name.[93] Wlward, Wulfward, and Wluuard are alternative spellings of the same name.

It should not be surprising to learn that the priest was also a grandfather, for married priests were still common in East Anglia and continued to be for the next hundred years, even though canon law had recently dictated otherwise. When urged by his superiors to restrict the practice, Bishop Herbert of Norwich had lamented that there would hardly be a church served were he to deprive all the married clergy in his diocese.[94]

There is further documentation of *Wlward presbiter* in and around Bury, and of a daughter as well. The *Miracles of St. Edmund* recount an episode in which passengers on a storm-tossed ship successfully invoked St. Edmund, among whom were Wulward the priest and Robert, both of St. Edmunds.[95] Given the wide circulation of these miracle stories by the twelfth century, such a mention would have been sufficient to guarantee considerable status to those favored by the saint.[96] This storm-tossed devotee of St. Edmund may therefore be William's grandfather, the famous *Wlward presbiter*, referred to in the *Miracles of St. Edmund* as a "man of discernment" and in the *Life and Passion of William of Norwich* as "having great skill in the interpretation of visions."[97]

William's aunt, Wlward's daughter, may also have been documented in the earlier miracle stories. Immediately preceding his account of the storm at sea, Hermann, the author of the *Miracles of St Edmund*, writes of a young girl named Levive, who had her sight restored after spending the night near the relics of St. Edmund, which had just been translated to the elaborate new church at Bury in 1095.[98] According to this document, Levive had come to the new church with her parents.[99] If her family resided near Bury, one might have expected them to visit when the relics of St. Edmund were ceremonially installed in his sumptuous new shrine and to seek a cure from the local patron saint. Wlward the priest might well have reported to the abbey registrar at the same time both his daughter's cure and his safe return home from sea. Thus, decades before William of Norwich became a wonder-working saint, there seems some family connection with the cult of another English martyr.[100] Other people mentioned in Brother Thomas's *Life and Miracles* likewise enjoyed miraculous blessings from various saints: Bishop Eborard, for example, apparently benefited from a miraculous cure by St. Aldhelm while he was an archdeacon of Salisbury in

Wiltshire.[101] The overlap and interpenetration of themes, stories, miracles, and people further indicate that the elements of the story Brother Thomas told had conventional appeal and were typical of the society in which it was created.[102]

William's family continued to appear in official Norwich documents after the boy's death. Sometime after 1155—a full decade after William's death—Bishop Turbe supervised a settlement made between a *Wlward of Timsworth* (a tiny hamlet four miles from Bury St. Edmunds) and *Rainald of Acle* (a village ten miles from Norwich in the Norfolk Broads).[103] The settlement concerned a dispute over St. Michael Coslany in Norwich, a church that still stands near the center of the city and the only church (apart from the cathedral itself) known to have had an altar dedicated to St. William.[104] The agreement between the two men hints that it might have been William's relative who owned, or claimed to own, a church in the city of Norwich.[105] Brother Thomas was apparently happy to take the part of William's family not only by endorsing the posthumous cult and composing its major text, but also by casting aspersions in his text on another priest of St. Michael's. Wlward's adversary, Rainald of Acle, who was the vicar of St. Michael Coslany, must have been a colleague of Ralph, a priest of St. Michael's at Norwich, whom Brother Thomas accuses of surreptitiously taking and then returning the book of psalms that Thomas had copied for his own use.[106]

All the other identifiable members of William's maternal family were connected with the church by work or marriage. His mother's first cousin was married to a priest in Taverham, Norfolk; his grandfather and uncle were priests, his cousin a deacon, and his brother a monk.[107] Taking such extensive ecclesiastical employment into account, it seems less likely that his brother Robert was welcomed into the Norwich priory as the sibling of a saint than that Robert's own clerical contacts, which were considerable, aided his entry. Moreover, Thomas says that William's mother was buried in the monk's graveyard in the Norwich Cathedral Priory, sometime later.[108] In no other case of alleged ritual murder was the mother of a child martyr buried with the same or similar honors as her child.[109] William's family was clerical in death as in life.[110]

It appears that there were close, long-standing connections between Norwich Cathedral and William's uncle Godwin Sturt, the priest who accused the Jews of William's murder, and who became a prime mover in William's cult. It is possible that Godwin was addressed directly in letters sent from the first bishop of Norwich, Herbert Losinga (d. 1119). If such were the case, it suggests that William's family was more closely allied to the cathedral hierarchy than previously considered. Such connections may have played an important role in William's subsequent elevation as a local saint—as important a role, perhaps, as the story of his murder.

Around 1154, Brother Thomas describes Godwin as a priest, but he was probably still a deacon (a lower position in the clerical hierarchy) when he was mentioned in one of the letters that Bishop Herbert of Norwich directed to a certain Godwin and his brother William.[111] Bishop Herbert reassures the brothers about their father's reconciliation with his brother.[112] The same Deacon Godwin is also addressed by the bishop on an earlier occasion, when the bishop reproves him for his fickleness in repudiating his monastic vow: "But as you became a fellow citizen of ours and a monk in our cloister, why do you live in the country?"[113]

A deacon named Godwin and his wife presented a generous gift to the church and monks of the cathedral in a document signed by Bishop Losinga sometime before 1119. The husband donated all the goods, land, and appurtenances of "my church of Cressingham" so that he and his wife would be received by the monks "for my soul and the soul of my wife."[114] He went on to promise that he would return to the monks: "I promise that in the church aforesaid I will assume the sacred habit of religion, and become a monk, when God shall have inspired my soul with such resolution and when my lord Herbert the bishop shall have enjoined me, after the death of my wife Ediva."[115] While we cannot be sure, the chances that there would have been another cleric named Godwin with a wife and sister-in-law named Ediva (sometimes Elviva or Leviva) are small. They were almost surely William's aunt and uncle.

As the grant specified, both husband and wife would have had entrance to the monks' graveyard.[116] In the manuscript copy of Godwin and Ediva's charter kept in the cathedral treasury, the words "soul of my wife" (*anima uxoris*) have been underlined, suggesting that the manuscript was consulted, perhaps when the privilege of monastic burial was utilized.[117] It is possible that William's mother made similar arrangements, and that, like her brother and sister-in-law, she may have been buried in the monk's cemetery because of previous contractual arrangements, separate from the postmortem miracles of her son. William's family may therefore have had more complex and extensive connections to the priory than the extant documentation indicates.

While the identifications suggested above are intriguing, they are admittedly speculative. One is on firmer ground in stating simply that William's family was a family of clerics, as indicated in Brother Thomas's *Life and Passion*. They appear to have benefited from a particularly close relationship with the church. Among relations, one finds three priests, two monks, and a mother buried in the monks' cemetery.[118] At one point William may have himself been intended for a clerical life. "He frequented the church most willlingly," writes Thomas. "He learned letters, psalms and prayers and worshipped with the greatest reverence all that was related to God."[119] In a vision, William appears and particularly requests to rest under the seats of the boys in the chapter house. It was "above all boys and youths" who came to see William's body in Thorpe Wood, says Thomas. Inasmuch as they included William's brother Robert, these may have been students at the priory school, which was said to have been founded by Bishop Herbert.[120]

William's family enjoyed job security, income, and education. The family must have been able to afford a generous contribution when Robert joined the monks. As noted above, he entered when the monastery had not yet greatly profited from the presence of his brother's relics. Families of other monks made significant contributions to be accepted into the cathedral community. Sir Matthew Peverel, for example, gave lands in Great Melton, Norfolk, on the entry of his brother Peter.[121] Hermer de Ferrars likewise made a donation to the monastery when his brother Richard joined, or soon after; Richard's nephew later made a contribution in memory of his uncle the prior.[122] One of those who would later benefit from St. William's intercession, Sibald son of Brunstan, gave land at Conesford in Norwich when his nephew Gregory entered the monastery of St. Benet of Holme.[123] It is likely that William's mother, as well as his brother, gave something of value for the privileges they enjoyed—presumably something more tangible than the potential earning power of a wonder-working relic.

An illustration of the difficulty of entering a monastery *without* having made a significant donation can be seen in the example recorded in the story of the "Holy Rood of Bromholm." The proposed donation of this relic and others was insufficient to admit the owner, a poor Crusader cleric and his two sons, into a number of monasteries in East Anglia, during the early thirteenth century. It was only when the cleric came to the impoverished Norfolk house of Bromholm Priory with his souvenirs of the Holy Land, including a piece of the True Cross, that he was welcomed to stay. Once Bromholm possessed this relic (the Holy Rood), the priory lost no time in publicizing its valuable possession, which is mentioned in *Piers Plowman* and by Chaucer in the *Reeve's Tale*; the monastery was to become an important pilgrimage site of late medieval England. The interest of this account lies in the difficulty a poor local cleric faced in trying to join a monastery—any monastery—lacking funds to make a suitable donation on entry. There is no suggestion that William's family faced any such difficulty.

William's father, with the uncommon name Wenstan (Wynstan), died years before his son William. He also may have been a tenant of the abbey of Bury St. Edmunds. In a record of the later twelfth century, a list of tenants mentions one Aelfwine, the son of Wenstan, who holds four acres and pays four pence in tax. Nearby, the widow Leveva also holds four acres and also pays four pence.[124] One of the few references to a Wenstan in twelfth-century England is to a moneyer who minted coins at Hastings early in Stephen's reign.[125] It was not unusual for clerics to be involved with monetary production, and the occupations of currency exchange and coin manufacture ran in priests' families.[126] Moneyers traveled long distances and worked in different parts of the country, and their office was passed down through the generations.[127] If Wenstan the moneyer was St. William's father, much would be explained. It would suggest a basis for the familiarity between William and the Norwich Jewish population, for he had frequent dealings with the Jews, something for which William was taken to task by his uncle Godwin and his landlord Wulward.[128] Jews in this period were often involved in the manufacture and exchange of money, as well as in making loans. The possibility that Wenstan the moneyer was William's late father might also explain the family's wealth and status: moneyers, most of whom were native English, ranked second only to royal officials in power, and were established in the highest group of urban society—but after the purges of moneyers in 1124 and in 1158 (in the first of these, moneyers' hands were cut off), they may indeed have been poor.[129] A number of men in the mid-twelfth century are known to have been moneyers even though no coins of theirs survive (there is a surviving coin from Eustace the moneyer of Norwich mentioned in the *Life*). All one can say for certain is that William's father had at least three sons, two of whom pursued occupations far removed from agriculture. This hints that their father's source of income may not have been primarily dependent upon farming. Moneying was a well-trod path to riches under Anglo-Norman kings.[130]

The Jews of Norwich may have taken an interest in William because of his skills as a leatherworker or because of his language skills. Brother Thomas puts forth various reasons for their patronage that appear contradictory: "They considered him highly suitable, either because they saw him as simple and skillful or because—led by miserliness—they reckoned they could pay him a lower wage."[131] Another reason this twelve-year-old apprentice was patronized by the Jews may have had something to do with his command of French. Jews in Anglo-Norman England would have spoken Norman French, written Hebrew, and possibly may have understood Latin as well; it is unlikely that they spoke much English and hence they were linguistically separated from the general population.[132] Likewise, it was exceptional for an Anglo-Saxon to speak Norman French: comprehension, even for an adult, was worthy to be recorded in a saint's *Life*. As the career of Wulfric of Haselbury demonstrated, it was socially advantageous for an Englishman to speak French.[133] Godric of Finchale, the other saint whose *Life* appears in the manuscript along with those of William and Wulfric, also spoke some French, but this Norfolk merchant had no formal education until his retirement from international commerce, when he joined the schoolboys at their lessons.[134] The apprentice William, in contrast, already knew his Latin letters and psalms at a young age.[135]

For a child of two Anglo-Saxons living in the countryside far from London, such bilingualism was noteworthy.[136] That William was able to converse easily with the Jews on more than a commercial level is indicated by Thomas's repeated mention that he frequented the Jews and by the assurance that William lived quietly with the Jews after his purported abduction.[137] It appears that William, like so many ambitious young men, moved to Norwich not only to learn a trade but also to gain some city polish, which included the acquisition of language skills his mother did not have.[138] In his long afterlife, William was to serve as a model not only for cloistered clerics but also for the urban bourgeoisie, who saw themselves reflected in his professional ambitions, class standing, and social networks. Someone like St. William was able to mediate the gulf that separated, for example, an unlettered Godric of Finchale from his educated biographer, Reginald of Durham.

William also served to bridge the divide between English and Norman clerics in Norwich. To authenticate and endorse their patron saint, members of the cathedral priory called upon well-known men of high status in the community with strong affiliations to the ecclesiastical hierarchy in Norwich and especially to the generation that grew up under the watchful gaze of Bishop Herbert Losinga. Among the most influential were the English priests Aelward and Wicman, and their older friends and colleagues of long standing who came from the families of the same Anglo-Saxon religious elite as William himself. Together with Bishop William Turbe, who succeeded Eborard, these men gave weight and credibility to a charge that might otherwise have been challenged. They were the least likely innovators in the city.

Wicman's name surfaces only intermittently, but his presence is sensed throughout Brother Thomas's *Life,* where he is identified as both monk and priest and is described as the bishop's confessor.[139] His office was a powerful one, because he heard confession on behalf of the bishop and assigned the appropriate penance.[140] Moreover, the confessor also had the power to interpret dreams when visions were mentioned in confession. Significantly, Wicman probably interpreted the initial visions of Brother Thomas when the latter arrived in 1150, as well as the many dreams that were later to give William's cult credibility.[141] Wicman also appears in the documentary record: he attested an early Norwich charter immediately after the first prior of Norwich. By the time of William's demise, therefore, he must have been of a certain age and eminence. He is also identified as a tenant in a Norwich document (ca. 1145) concerning St. Paul's hospital, in which a number of other people mentioned in the *Life* appear.

Wicman was responsible for the deathbed revelations of a leading citizen, Aelward Ded, "a certain burgess, one of Norwich's richest and most prominent men," who was enlisted to support William's claim to holiness.[142] Aelward's testimony was critical in linking the Jews with William, so his standing in the community would have been important to those who read or heard William's story.

Brother Thomas claimed that Aelward encountered the Jews of Norwich in the woods in the middle of the night, as they were attempting to dispose of William's body. According to Thomas, he laid his hand on the sack that they were carrying and knew immediately what had taken place. But Aelward never said anything publicly, and was compelled by a promise to Sheriff John de Chesney never to reveal what had happened. Only on his deathbed, after having received a vision of St. William (long after the sheriff himself had died) did Aelward reveal the story to his priestly confessor Wicman. The confessor then passed on the information to Brother Thomas.

This Aelward Ded, described in the *Life and Passion* as one who enjoyed the civic privileges of the new Norman borough, may be the Aelward who appears in Norwich documents as a wealthy priest of the church of St. Nicholas.[143] Aelward the priest's extensive holdings were repeatedly confirmed, first by Bishop Eborard, then by Bishop William, and finally by the archbishop.[144] The dates of these charters correlate well with those of the Aelward mentioned in the *Life*, who died around 1149.[145] Given his activity in the land market, it may be that Aelward the priest was one of the earliest to have had dealings with Jewish lenders in Norwich, but there is no documentation to that effect.

Brother Thomas's Aelward (spelled Aylward, Ailward, Agilward, Eylward, Eilverd, and Egelward) may be the well-known priest of North Walsham who appears repeatedly in Norfolk documents from this period, a man from a charitable family that is traceable in the area for many generations.[146] Aelward held land in Hoveton and North Walsham, and, like many other Norwich clergymen (such as Uncle Godwin), was a married priest and the father of a married priest, whose grandchildren were eventually to inherit some of his land, his church, and the rights associated with it.[147] The uncommon names of members of Aelward's family also occur in the family of Bishop Eborard of Norwich, who had a number of children for whom he provided, which may hint at some family connection.[148] Children attempting to inherit from their fathers who were priests had long been a source of contention in East Anglia.[149] On this issue the priests Aelward and Godwin shared a common interest.[150]

In various official documents, Aelward the priest is closely associated with the bishop and the promoters of the new cult of William in Norwich. These men with common interests include a monk named Elias, later the prior, and Henry the stableman (*de stabulario*), later the forester. In addition to these, others attesting a charter sometime between 1121 and 1135 include William Turbe (later the bishop), William de Novers, and William Peverel, all men subsequently connected with the cult of St. William.[151] Another charter for the same beneficiary records many of the same people, including, this time, John the steward (*dapifer*), whose son, according to Brother Thomas's account, benefited from St. William's intervention around 1151.[152]

In the *Life and Passion*, Aelward is described as the necessary "lawful witness" (*testis legitimus*), a status for which the others who came upon William's body in the wood would not qualify. "After already visiting that night the churches which are in the city, finally he was returning along the edge of the wood, with a single servant as company, from that of St Mary Magdalene."[153] It was on that journey that Aelward allegedly claimed to have seen the Jews with the body. Such activity reinforces the likelihood that this was indeed Aelward the priest and not simply a lay burgess. Before Aelward's death, there was no one to link the Jews to the body of the apprentice. But Thomas says that on his deathbed in 1149/1150 Aelward Ded confessed to two close colleagues, Wicman, and another man who was also a priest of St. Nicholas (whose name is left blank in the manuscript), telling them what he had seen. Accordingly, Aelward's contribution to Brother Thomas's ritual murder narrative was posthumous and third-hand.[154]

The monks who promoted the cult were members of the old establishment. They were men of stature, and, significantly, men who had been at the priory the longest and knew its earliest founders. Although the priory leaders were Norman, the other promoters were local men of English heritage of the same generation as Godwin, and the cult reflected many Anglo-Saxon values.[155] Even before they united in promoting a new patron of Norwich Cathedral, these men had worked together over decades.[156] Brother Thomas's account was a result of their joint interests, not the cause of them. The most fervent supporters of the cult were the most senior members of the convent, and in many ways the cult appears backward-looking, reflecting long-held Anglo-Saxon attitudes toward sanctity, innocence, and violence.[157]

The fault lines that appeared in the year of William's murder, 1144, are not simply those overarching conflicts between Normans and Anglo-Saxons, Christians and Jews, town and clerical gown. Rather, they are the fault lines typical of a twelfth-century city with strong institutional bonds and ecclesiastical partisanship: between monks of the cathedral priory and the monks of St. Michael's; between the monks of Norwich and the monks of Sibton priory, founded by the family of sheriff John de Chesney; between the mother church's initiatives and Godwin's attempts to establish a cult outside it; and, most strikingly, between the cathedral of Norwich and the abbey of Bury. The cult of St. William could offer an opportunity for reconciliation and harmony, but also a battlefield on which these various local rivalries were played out.

Interest in William's physical remains and the promotion of the adolescent from bumbling youth to esteemed holy patron took place only after the wrenching events of the five years that followed his death. "Saint" William was the product of a crisis mentality during a difficult period of economic, social, political, and religious uncertainty in the wake of a painful turn of events for the military. Quick-thinking churchmen turned his sad but unremarkable death to their own ends in an effort to explain and understand the critical events of the immediate past. In between the discovery of William's body and his promotion as a holy intercessor was the devastating conclusion to the Second Crusade. After the Crusade, new interpretations of past events turned the Jews into a more potent enemy, Norwich into a blessed city, and William into a wonder-working saint. To understand how that happened, we need to turn to another murder. This later murder of a Jewish banker who had lent money to Sir Simon de Novers became the immediate catalyst for the cult of St. William of Norwich and led to the earliest-known accusation of ritual murder. It is to the second murder that we now turn, and to the failure of the Second Crusade that lay behind it.

(a)

(b)

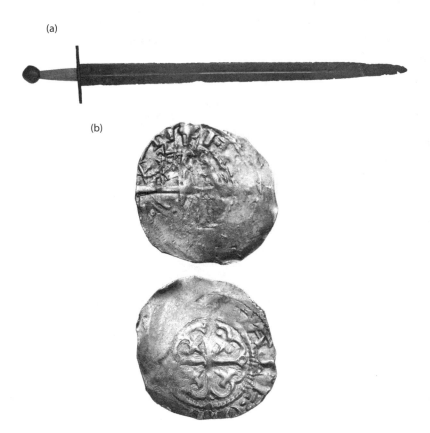

FIGURE 2.1A AND B To afford the equipment to venture on crusade, knights borrowed money. Pictured are a twelfth-century sword and a coin made by Eustace, a Norwich moneyer mentioned in *The Life and Passion of William of Norwich*.

CHAPTER 2   *The Second Crusade*

"MARVELLOUS MORE BY ITS START
THAN ITS END"—
ABBOT OF WERDEN, 1148*

The Second Crusade—and its ultimate failure—helps to explain why attention turned once again to young William of Norwich five years after his death and burial. The impact of this defeat was profound. It had widespread political, economic, social, and psychological repercussions and imprinted itself on the European consciousness. Following closely on the civil war that had devastated large areas of England, especially East Anglia, the failed Second Crusade saddled many of its participants with crushing debts and required great effort to explain the failure of what had seemed to be a divinely sanctioned enterprise. Such circumstances were ripe for exploitation and potentially dangerous for members of Jewish communities who were increasingly singled out as alien elements in the Christian body politic. The focus of this chapter is therefore on the impact of the disastrous Second Crusade on families and individuals in and around Norwich who were involved directly and indirectly in the creation and propagation of the cult of William of Norwich.

Many individuals who were involved in the veneration of William came from crusading families, including William de Warenne, the third earl of Surrey and a tenant-in-chief of the crown with holdings in thirteen counties, most clustered in East Anglia, who had gone on crusade to the Holy Land with his knights. In 1147 Warenne had set forth with an armed force from his seat in Norfolk, joining his family members in the French army, who accompanied their cousin King Louis VII through Europe.[1] Few soldiers from elsewhere in England are known to have joined the crusade heading overland to the East, but a sizable number from Norfolk and Suffolk sailed south on their way to the Mediterranean and joined in the capture of Lisbon. That victory would prove an important turning point in the Christian reconquest of the Iberian Peninsula and the only successful military enterprise of the Crusade.[2]

The counties of Norfolk and Suffolk were suffused with crusading zeal. From a great lord and his mounted vassals, to poor sailors— from fighting men with specialized technical skills, including use of crossbow and siege engines, to merchants, to a humble priest and at least one monk who went to Lisbon—East Anglian society in the middle of the twelfth century was on a war footing.[3] Very many common people, as well as two deaf mutes and some women, joined the effort to retake Lisbon, which suggests the broad extent of the crusade fervor in East Anglia and the enthusiastic response to local preaching.[4] Far less is known about those from England who headed directly to the Holy Land for what proved to be a military debacle of immense proportions.

Sometime around 1149, a few English soldiers straggled home from the East. Poor, empty-handed, and dispirited, they were not greeted as the conquering heroes they had hoped to be. After two years and catastrophic loss of life, the Second Crusade had failed. The French and English crusaders had not reclaimed the city of Edessa, in Asia Minor, the loss of which had spurred them to go in the first place. By the time they arrived in Nicaea, the German force they joined had already been decimated by flash floods and guerrilla attacks, and the combined armies had been forced to abandon the siege of Damascus near the coast of Syria after only four days.[5] Most crusaders gave up before making a pilgrimage to the holy sites in Jerusalem.

Having responded to the impassioned call of the saintly and eloquent monk Bernard, abbot of the monastery of Clairvaux in Champagne, these soldiers had risked life and limb but had little to show for it. Commissioned by a pope, Bernard famously preached at Easter 1146 in the presence of the king of France and his court. He delivered such a powerful message to the people lined up in the field at Vézelay in Burgundy that they immediately vowed to set forth on crusade. Having run out of fabric crosses to hand out, Bernard is said to have ripped up his own habit to distribute pieces of linen marked with the cross to indicate one's intention to go on crusade (crusaders were *crucesignati*, "signed with the cross"). "The event had been carefully planned and meticulously orchestrated."[6] The pope reissued a bull full of indulgences, spiritual and practical incentives to encourage participation, including a prohibition on the payment of interest on loans while borrowers were on crusade.

Embittered and impoverished, those who returned home arrived to find that they were blamed for the crusade's dismal conclusion. Far from securing a place in heaven, they were told that they had lost a holy war on account of their sins. At least two contemporaries characterized the disastrous events of the Second Crusade as the work of the devil. Henry of Huntingdon explained in his *Historia Anglorum*, which covers English history up to 1159, that the armies "came to nothing because God despised them."[7]

King Louis VII of France and Conrad III, the emperor of the Germans, returned unscathed, but their elite mounted forces, the flower of European chivalry, were destroyed on the way to Jerusalem. Many of the most eminent warriors from England, including William de Warenne, lay dead, killed in an ambush when crossing Asia Minor in the winter of 1148. The writer William of Newburgh (d. 1198?) blamed the disasters squarely on the crusaders themselves, concluding that "having achieved nothing of note they returned without glory."[8]

Historians usually focus on zealous crusaders, enthusiastically heading forth *en masse* to defend their church and make their fortunes under the direction of kings and princes. Little attention is paid to the individual forlorn fighter returning without his lordly leader, without his sworn comrades, without coins in his pocket, and without spiritual comfort, having pawned his armor and perhaps even having lost his horse.[9] The enhanced status of having gone on crusade was severely undercut by public failure on a grand scale. The "zeal for God's glory which burns in your midst," as Bernard had described it, was scarcely sufficient to make up for the lost years, the disillusionment, the high costs incurred, the deaths of friends, neighbors, and close relatives, and the great loss of blood.[10]

Numerous studies consider the varied motivations of the crusaders, the preaching and structure of the crusades, the timing and organization of the armies.[11] But almost none reflect on the demobilized crusaders who returned home and the debts they incurred. The monk William of Saint-Denis was not alone in demanding to know why "hardly anyone survived from so great a multitude of men and the army of two very powerful kings and [why] those who escaped the sword and famine returned without any result."[12] Many died from battle wounds, guerrilla attacks, shipwreck, disease, hunger, dehydration, drowning, or poison. So devastating were the losses on the march through Asia Minor that the crusade chronicler William of Tyre concluded that nine-tenths of the Germans died on the way.[13] An anonymous contemporary biographer observed that "many women were made widows and many little children were made orphans."[14] It was little comfort to be told that it had all turned out as God had intended. Bernard, after all, had given the assurance of security and victory if they went to defend Christ's own land from a wicked people in the places "where he was born, lived, crucified, and was buried."[15] Peter the Venerable, abbot of Cluny, had insisted that "victory was certain."[16] Many agreed with the bitter annalist of Rouen who noted that "most perished without the benefit of salvation."[17]

What a difference from the First Crusade fifty years earlier! The returning victors then were greeted with processions, careers were made, poems sung, family fortunes enhanced, good marriages contracted, and land ownership secured. The booming economy of East Anglia, with its administrative center at Norwich, gave King William Rufus of England the means to indulge his architectural tastes and his brother's military ambitions. The consciously elaborate and expensive palatial fortress the king built at Norwich, described as the most ambitious secular building in western Europe, testified to the wealth and strategic importance of the region and to his ability to extract and advertise its riches.[18] While William Rufus remained at home, piled up his treasure in Westminster, and grew fat off East Anglian sheep, his older brother Robert Curthose, who had inherited the duchy of Normandy, pawned it to William for 10,000 marks so that Robert could go on the First Crusade. By the end of the Second Crusade, the region was suffering from the effects of civil war and the country endured famine and disease.[19]

The crusaders returning at mid-century were not greeted by their religious communities in ceremonies of mutual respect. More often they ended up in disputes with their churches, which is how we learn the little we know of them. Once back home in 1150, four of the crusading companions of Bartholomew of Cicon, for example, were called to testify that he had reneged on his promise made in Jerusalem to restore property he had taken unjustly from his local church before his departure.[20] Alard of Esplechin in Flanders, on his return, became embroiled in a legal fight with the local abbey that had helped finance his departure on crusade.[21] There were legal disputes as well with the family over the financial arrangements made by the castellan of Lille, who apparently died on the Second Crusade.[22] Warriors returning from the Second Crusade failed to bring back valuable relics and souvenirs for their churches; not a single relic is known to have been donated by Second Crusaders. Yet at just this time, demand for authenticated holy relics increased, for the Holy See had determined that every altar must have relics. Nor was there literary recognition: the participants in the Second Crusade are known primarily from charters, not celebratory verse.

The Second Crusade was a public disappointment on all counts—military, religious, economic, political, and social. For the Anglo-Norman participants who had gone directly to the Holy Land, there was shame, anger, and humiliation, exacerbated by the success of their less eminent countrymen who had achieved a notable victory in Portugal (many of whom remained in southern Europe to reap the benefits). The soldiers returning in defeat (and their families, friends, and brothers-in-arms) looked to blame someone else, reassert their status, express their hostility, and receive spiritual consolation. Their crusade experiences suggested who that scapegoat might be.

William de Warenne, the French king's cousin, was among those who took the crusading vow with other leading French nobles at Easter 1146.[23] Like many Anglo-Norman magnates of the period, he held lands on both sides of the Channel. Warenne took the cross again the following year in a big Easter ceremony at Castle Acre, Norfolk. When a great English lord like Warenne took the cross at the seat (*caput*) of his vast estates (his *honor*), he would have done so before a crowd of friends, kin, supporters, his household knights (his *familia*), and his feudal tenants, just as he had done previously with his lord, the king of France. The earl took care to make donations and receive blessings from religious institutions with which he had local and family connections, leaving his younger brother Reginald, lord of Wormegay, in charge of his English lands when he went off to fight.[24]

The earl's knights, in turn, would begin their preparations, raise funds, organize loans, get family approval, and make grants, gifts, and donations to support local institutions and causes that their lord had endorsed. One of Warenne's knights, Philip Bassett of Postwick, explicitly stated his intention to go on crusade when he made his financial preparations in Norfolk.[25] He arranged for a loan with the abbot of St. Benet of Holme (a Norfolk Benedictine abbey closely allied to Bury St. Edmunds) in advance of the "departure for Jerusalem of the king of France and the barons and Philip himself."[26] Significantly, Philip, one of the few Anglo-Norman crusaders about whom we know, identified simply with the French and did not declare his interest in accompanying a group of Englishmen or Anglo-Normans.

The knight John de Chesney, a leading Norfolk man of arms and a tenant of Warenne, also made financial arrangements at the same time (this was a different John de Chesney than the sheriff who had died the previous year, and who was probably his cousin).[27] He appears to have prepared for the crusade by settling on the monks of Lewes some land in Brighton, half of which he had previously given them. The knight and monks made their agreement on St. Mark's Day, April 25, 1147, during the week-long celebration (*octave*) of Easter immediately after the earl and members of his household had taken the cross, and shortly before the English contingent left on crusade. The agreement was witnessed by Philip's wife and brothers and Odo the crossbowman (*arbalistarius*) and was confirmed by Earl William and King Stephen.[28] William of Oby, Norfolk, who made clear to the abbey his intention to assume the sign of the cross and visit the Holy Sepulchre, may have been another of the men at arms who went with Warenne in 1147.[29] Hugh de Gournay of Caister, Norfolk, another cousin of Warenne (whose family members also named Hugh de Gournay fought on the First and Third Crusades), may also have ventured with these men on the Second Crusade.

Anglo-Norman military custom suggests that another of Warenne's knights, Sir Simon de Novers, the knight who figures in this story of William of Norwich, may have joined this contingent from England serving with the French under the command of his lord, along with such fellow knights as John de Chesney and Philip Bassett.[30] Feudal bonds were a critical factor in recruiting for crusade, and *crucesignati* were often listed in groups simply by fiefs held directly from the crown.[31] Most crusaders set off with their neighbors.[32] Neighborhood pressure, the promise of pay, and ties of family, locality, and lordship were frequently as important as religious fervor in motivating men to venture to the Holy Land.[33] Simon de Novers came from the same locale and social circles as did John de Chesney and Philip Bassett, and they each held land from the earl and were bound to him by ties of loyalty and homage. English crusaders usually traveled and fought in clusters determined by familial and geographical alliances.[34] They were *coniurati*, sworn companions who traveled together and shared resources. Warenne's grandfather had been a famous crusader, and his half-brother, two cousins, and three uncles also took the cross.[35] At least one of Simon's grandfathers may likewise have gone on the First Crusade, and a possible relative, Clarembold de Noiers, was a Hospitaller who died in Jerusalem during the Third Crusade.

There is only circumstantial evidence to suggest that Simon ventured on crusade. What is known is that he took out large loans that he could not repay in 1150. Financing for the crusade was a critical issue in these years, and was one reason for a knight in the late 1140s to have borrowed extensive sums. Certainly there were other occasions on which a knight might be expected to come up with large amounts of cash quickly and might need to borrow money, such as to pay for fines, royal aids, feudal levies, perhaps a dowry for his daughter, to prosecute a law case, or to pay for a ransom contracted during the civil war.[36] But none of those is likely to have been as large, to have lasted as long, or to have made him so desperate as preparing to equip himself for the Holy Land. Crusade preparation and financing, as much as the crusades themselves, effected major changes in northern Europe on many levels: personal, institutional, and national.

The costs of crusading could be crushing.[37] Ecclesiastical and lay taxation were to emerge over the course of the twelfth and thirteenth centuries as it became increasingly clear that individuals could not bear the huge expense themselves. In 1188, to fund the Third Crusade, King Richard the Lionheart collected the "Saladin tithe," which was an early form of income tax. It consisted of 10 percent of revenues and movable goods throughout England, the largest tax ever collected in the country. Earlier in the twelfth century, broad taxes spanning the country were not yet established, and much of the Second Crusade was financed privately and locally.[38]

In mid-twelfth-century England the support system was limited to smaller geographic and social areas. Family and friends, kinsmen and lords were expected to contribute and were donors and lenders of the first resort for an ambitious knight.

As armed pilgrims, many of the crusaders expected to rely on handouts along the way, but there were still myriad expenses to meet before they left. Knights needed to equip themselves at a minimum with a war-horse, bridle, saddle, spurs, and arms, which included the long chain-mail shirt, the hauberk, helmet, shield, lance, and sword.[39] Crusaders also needed to ensure that their families were taken care of in their absence.

The First Crusade taught how expensive it was to set out on armed pilgrimage for the Holy Land but did not suggest how oppressive the total burden could be at the end of the day. Christian military victories at the beginning of the twelfth century suggested that for those who survived, these large initial outlays could be easily recouped with spectacular profits from the East. Aside from the calculable and incalculable spiritual reward of remission of sins, fighting yielded many potential prizes: land and lordships, the possibility of a wealthy wife, a new command, social prestige, the friendship and trust of powerful people, confirmation of contested holdings, bribes, ransoms of wealthy prisoners. There was also the alluring prospect of booty—gold, jewels, relics, household items, coins, fine fabrics, ships, and antiquities.

Financial gain was prominent among the many and complex motivations that induced knights to venture abroad. Many families deemed going on crusade a practical investment as well as a penitential act. It might have been a financial risk with high costs of entry, but there is reason to believe that economic motivation was a major, if not *the* major, consideration for many crusaders in the mid-twelfth century.

Undoubtedly, otherwordly spiritual concerns stirred a large number of crusaders and inspired them to tremendous sacrifice for their beliefs.[40] Some participants conceived of crusading as an act of love, and others went out actively seeking martyrdom, to be killed instead of to kill.[41] Some went for vengeance, motivated as much by hatred as by love.[42] But many crusading knights went primarily for booty and plunder: they sought to acquire treasure and were prepared to kill in order to secure it. A crusading priest in Lisbon, for example, whose exhortation to the English troops there survives, reflected the desires of his northern European flock, whose prime motive seems to have been acquiring plunder from sacking the city.[43] Those who had spiritual motives often demonstrated piety mixed with practical concerns. Crusaders were interested in confirming land grants, redeeming or enhancing a family's reputation, and traveling with a social group with which they wanted to be identified and accepted. All these considerations played a role in sending men and women on crusade. Economic motives did not conflict with religious ones; they were mutually reinforcing, for Christian victories confirmed God's path.

Warenne's knights, like most crusaders, would have been hard-pressed to pay for all the necessary equipment without borrowing. They turned, therefore, to institutions that could help them find the funds for equipment, horses, transport, and maintenance.[44] Financial arrangements could be complex, consisting of mortgages, loans, sales, or some combination. Most loans were for short terms, two or three years—rarely more than five.[45] Many crusaders chose to mortgage lands to wealthy religious houses, which were one of the few sources of ready cash in the twelfth century.[46] As a result, some of these houses made remarkable profits from their financial arrangements with crusaders.[47] Roger of Mowbray, for example, in his negotiations with local monks, sought to help build Newburgh Priory, finance his crusade, and simultaneously keep hereditary benefices in the hands of one of his kinsmen in a complex and ingenious arrangement to evade prohibitions on doing so.[48]

Wealthy monasteries were accustomed to provide both spiritual and financial assistance to local knights, and poorer houses were occasionally prepared to divest themselves of treasure to help crusaders. But many religious houses did not have available resources. English monasteries had been despoiled during the civil war, and by the late 1140s many were in no position to lend money. Just a couple of years earlier, both the bishop of Ely and the abbot of St. Albans had been compelled to strip the decoration of their shrines to fund King Stephen.[49] Moreover, because of the depredations of the civil war, even the eminent abbey of Cluny could no longer collect income from lands in England—and those included lands given by the king himself.[50] The abbey of Bury St. Edmunds was still able to commission stunning artwork in this period, but apparently arranged to pay on credit. The notion of "liquidized resources" was not entirely metaphorical: church plate was melted to make coin to pay soldiers during the civil war. Eastern England, the base for Stephen's resources, was particularly hard hit, as Stephen required constant infusions of funds to pay his army, much of which was composed of mercenaries.[51] The lack of available credit may have curtailed crusade enthusiasm in England as religious institutions, such as the abbeys of Ramsey and Ely, struggled to recover.

In their straitened finances, Norwich Cathedral and the Norwich Priory may have been in a comparable situation. There is no indication that Norwich offered loans or made financial arrangements with any crusaders; after completing an expensive building campaign, the church was likely in debt itself.[52] The civil war had cut revenues drastically, and monasteries were having a difficult time collecting income. After the war, recouping lost lands and rights became a primary focus.[53] Under duress, the bishop of Norwich had been compelled to hand over two manors to rapacious knights—for which he sought forgiveness from the pope—and by 1166 his successor had managed to reclaim only one.[54] Gilbert de Gant, earl of Lincoln, eventually compensated Norwich with lands in the north for excesses he had committed against church property in Lynn during the war.[55] Norwich was never a wealthy see, and most of the endowment of the cathedral priory had been given by the first bishop at its foundation, so its financial flexibility was limited.

If they had no land or other assets to offer as adequate collateral and could not get loans from ecclesiastical institutions, knights sought out one of the only other sources of funds: moneylenders, many of whom, though not all, were Jewish.[56] These men (and women) charged rates of interest to compensate for the high risks involved in lending to unreliable types. The very success of the First Crusade may have encouraged lenders to lay out more and borrowers to extend themselves beyond what they could reasonably be expected to pay back for the Second Crusade. If a knight took out loans and left with William de Warenne in 1147, the loans would have expired when he returned in 1149. Back in England, a knight was no longer protected by the church from his creditors, and the loans, both interest and principal, would be due.

The nature of the crusades as an intentionally violent manifestation of religious zeal was a complicating factor in relations between knights who borrowed funds and their Jewish creditors. The crusade preachers fostered a sense of righteous anger that led to vicious confrontations wherever soldiers mustered. Warenne joined the French contingent with his knights, and they in turn soon followed the Germans. In traveling with Continental crusaders, William de Warenne and his knights from eastern England adopted the prevailing values and prejudices of a tightly bound military clique—one that participated in violent attacks on Jews before departing for the East.[57] The Anglo-Normans were accompanied by Arnulf of Séez, bishop of Lisieux, who had preached and written against Jews earlier in his career.[58]

Throughout the preceding summer, while Warenne was getting organized in England, and before Bernard had embarked on his own preaching tour, a Cistercian monk Ralph (Raoul, Radulphus) was spewing propaganda against Jews throughout the Rhineland. "He set forth from France and travelled cross the entire land of Germany. . . . He went along barking and was named the 'barker,' . . . wherever he went, he spoke evil of the Jews of the land."[59] Although often described as a "renegade monk," Ralph was clearly well regarded, and

Bernard had an extremely difficult time hushing him.[60] Repeated letters failed to put a stop to his unauthorized preaching, and Bernard was compelled to track him down, a feat that took many months.[61] Despite Bernard's public censure, Ralph was recalled as a "splendid teacher and monk," full of humility and extremely effective.[62] Ralph's presence was recorded not only in Cologne, Mainz, and Strasbourg, but also in Franco-Flemish Hainault, where he appears to have had the support of Lambert, the well-connected abbot of Lobbes. Lambert's noble predecessor at Lobbes accompanied the count of Flanders on the Second Crusade.

It is conventional to suggest that at the time of the Second Crusade, Jews were persecuted only in one region of the Rhineland and that Bernard quickly put a stop to these "disruptions," which distracted from the crusade's main purpose. Jews are rarely mentioned in the sermons inciting Christians to attack Muslims in the Holy Land, so it is argued that they were not the intended victims. Assaults on local Jews, it is assumed, were marginal to the main crusading movement, and the participants in the violence are typically characterized as "hangers on."[63] But there is no evidence that these people were mere hooligans on the fringe of the crusading movement. The leader of attacks on Jews during the First Crusade, Emicho of Flonheim, was not a rootless vagabond, as he was often described, but a powerful local noble.[64] The participants in the assaults on Jews during the Second Crusade were similarly well regarded and well equipped—they were not the dregs of society. The men who attacked Jews at Clifford's Tower in York at the beginning of the Third Crusade in 1190, for example, were likewise members of the local elite, not on the margins of society.[65]

Even before the armies of the Second Crusade came together and set out from Würzburg, Jews were subject to vicious attacks throughout the German Empire, the Low Countries, France, and the French lordships. Secular and religious authorities were hard pressed to defend them. Bernard himself had little contact with Jews and promoted his own stereotypes. He is credited, for example, with coining the term *judaizare* (to act like a Jew), to mean "lending at interest."[66] For those less high-minded and spiritual than the saintly monk, it was easy to let crusade enthusiasm degenerate into physical aggression. Bernard was aware and concerned about such a possibility, to judge from a comment in his crusading letter to England: "the Jews are not to be persecuted, killed or even put to flight."[67] In his *Life and Passion of William of Norwich*, Brother Thomas writes as if it were well known that Jews were ready to be suddenly put to flight or expelled from their homes.[68]

Assaults on Jews in the mid-twelfth century were not limited to one area or to a small group of rabble-rousers. During the First Crusade, Christians intent on penitence assaulted Jews throughout Normandy and other centers, not just in the famous Rhineland cities where they had been long established.[69] Examples of attacks on Jews are legion in 1146 and 1147 throughout Christendom.

Ephraim of Bonn, thirteen years old at the time, experienced the attacks firsthand, and reported them in a memoir.[70] Simon the Pious of Trier was attacked outside Cologne, on his return from England, and was killed when he refused baptism. Two Jewish boys were attacked when they went to join Ephraim and other Jews of Cologne in the fortress of Wolkenburg. Mina of Speyer had her ears and thumbs cut off when she ventured outside the city. Two Jews from Mainz were killed while making wine, and their house and goods were seized. Jewish students originally from Bachrach were pursued by crusaders and killed when they sought protection in Stahleck. A tombstone survives today in Mainz for the (unnamed) daughter of Isaac who was martyred by drowning in April 1146.[71] Similarly, Ephraim writes of Gutalda of Aschaffenberg, who drowned herself in the river rather than convert. More than 150 Jews were killed in Ham (probably near Orléans in central France) and countless more in Carentan (probably in Normandy) and Sully.[72] A number of other Jews were killed in attacks along the crusade route in Cologne and Worms. Ephraim of Bonn concluded that contemporary Christians, like Jews, anticipated such attacks, and took it for granted that they might occur, even though some early crusade historians insisted that they were unusual, unforeseen, or isolated.

Attacks of this kind were not limited to urban moneylenders, who were often the objects of the hatred of poor knights. Crusaders went after young women, agricultural workers, children and students; they stoned them, burned them, tortured them, and decapitated them. Jacob Tam, the leading scholar of north European Jewry, who wrote glosses on the Talmud (*Tosaphist*), grandson of the famous Rashi, was seized and attacked in Champagne, where he lived.[73] Ephraim reported that the rabbi's attackers claimed that they were taking vengeance on the rabbi for inflicting wounds on Christ. Tam was rescued by a knight, who demanded Tam's horse for his good deed.[74]

Nor were these attacks centered on newcomers to towns who had failed to integrate: archaeological evidence confirms that the Jewish community in Cologne had a continuous presence since Roman times, possibly predating the Christian presence.[75] Their commitment to their local community was significant, as indicated by their willingness to dig many meters into sheer rock for their ritual pool, the *mikveh*. The Jews in Normandy had been settled there for generations, certainly more than a century; the Jews in Regensburg since before the year 1000.

In contrast, Jews in Würzburg first appear in the documentary record of the violence of the Second Crusade, but defaced Jewish tombstones recently unearthed from the wall of a convent indicate that they had settled there at least a decade or more earlier. The large number of tombstone inscriptions that read "slain" in Hebrew, discovered only in 1987, hint at the extent of the carnage.[76] While some of the Jewish communities that suffered crusade attacks were primarily mercantile, others were essentially educational and religious centers off the beaten path (Regensburg, for example, was a thriving metropolis with a large minority of Jews who regularly engaged with Christians on various levels). Some victimized Jews were prominent and successful, others were less well known. The mentions of deaths in Nuremberg and Aschaffenberg, among others, constitute the first references to Jewish communities in those cities.

The multiple locations in which attacks occurred and the varied circumstances in which Jews found themselves the objects of aggression from the crusaders suggest that crusade preparations led to this violence. King Louis VII of France's subsequent edict prohibiting forced conversion to Christianity may indicate the extent of the violence, suggesting that this issue was of immediate national concern. Yet he also issued an edict that mandated the death penalty for those apostates who wanted to return to Judaism. A great gathering of Jews around 1150 was called by Rabbi Tam, most likely to deal with the aftermath of the crusade—a time when Jews were under attack both by Muslims in Iberia and Christians north of the Alps.[77]

Even if they were not present among the German crusaders at Würzburg early in 1147, Earl Warenne and his knights were well situated to have learned of a widely reported account of a Christian whose death there was blamed on the Jews. In late February, according to both Christian and Jewish sources, Christian soldiers mustering in the city accused Jews in Würzburg of killing a Christian man and tossing him into the river.[78] In the aftermath of the discovery, twenty-one Jews were put to death, and the Christian corpse was seen to have performed miracles. The garden where the bishop left the Jewish victims was then purchased by the Jewish community and turned into a cemetery.[79] Having mustered in Metz, then crossed the Rhine at Worms in June, the French and Anglo-Norman contingent came through Würzburg shortly after the German imperial troops on their way to the Holy Land and likely heard the rumors. The survivors of Warenne's contingent could easily have passed on the story in Norwich once they returned. It is more plausible that the story of the miraculous Würzburg corpse informed the subsequent English ritual murder accusation in this way than that reports of the death of William of Norwich had quickly reached as far as Germany.[80]

Sudden brutal death on crusade, regardless of the precise circumstances, often prompted spiritual devotions. At least three examples are recorded of twelfth-century crusaders observing miracles associated with the violent death of one of their number. All three were deemed to have been killed by enemies of Christ—Theoderic of Würzburg and John of Stamford by Jews, Henry of Lisbon by Muslims. The Würzburg corpse, like that of Henry, the English crusader killed during the Lisbon crusade the same year, and later the corpse of John of Stamford, killed as he set off for the Third Crusade, were the objects of immediate popular piety.[81]

It is in this context of sudden violent death at an already emotionally charged period that the death of William of Norwich and the murder trial that ensued in 1150 should be understood. The backdrop was a disastrous crusade, spur-of-the-moment miracle cults emanating from mutilated corpses, animosity directed toward Jews and vigorously preached, crushing loans no longer able to be renegotiated or postponed, fears of sin and hopes for salvation by those committing violence. Whether or not he enjoyed the status of a crusader to the Holy Land, Sir Simon de Novers, a vassal of William de Warenne and also a vassal of the bishop of Norwich, was a warrior with no land, no money, and no hopeful future.

Simon de Novers (Noiers, Nodariis, Nod', Noyers, Noers, Nuers, Nuiers) was from a notable Norman family. One of Simon's ancestors had come over with William the Conqueror in 1066; a generation later, another ancestor, probably Simon's grandfather, was the largest tenant of the bishop of Norwich.[82] At the beginning of the twelfth century, he was in charge of vast acres, numerous "fees" or fiefs (*feudum*, the amount of land that could support a single knight, from which the word "feudalism" is derived), held from a lord in exchange for military service. By the end of the twelfth century, his family held next to nothing. In the thirteenth century the de Novers family name appears in East Anglian documents to identify land they had once held but which had since passed to others.

Simon, in short, was a member of a once-elite family that was rapidly losing status. During the reigns of Henry I (1100–1135) and his grandson, Henry II (1154–1189), "men raised from the dust," in the words of Orderic Vitalis, populated the court and administrative offices of the growing kingdom.[83] These "new men" were given administrative responsibilities, and benefited from lucrative marriages, tax exemptions, and other valuable privileges and duties. Simon was not so lucky or nimble. There is no mention of any marriage and dowry, no mention of debts forgiven, no indication that he had any abilities beyond that of fighting on horseback. Once called upon as a valued member of the inner circle of his lord, in later life Simon was no longer asked to witness documents or to attest to important acts.

Simon's family can be traced through administrative documents of the bishop of Norwich. The first ancestor recorded in England is William de Novers, a royal bailiff who was placed in charge of the estates that had once belonged to Stigand, archbishop of Canterbury. When the Conqueror's son confiscated ecclesiastical land in East Anglia, he turned the property over to one William de Novers, who appears repeatedly in the Domesday Book.[84] The last mention of William relates to land he sold to the bishop, a sale that is confirmed in the foundation charters of the priory of Norwich when the monastery was built. It is not known what happened to this man or why he held no land directly. There are various possibilities as to why he disappeared from the historical record.[85] He may have gone on the tail end of the First Crusade with participants who left England around 1101.[86] A departure on the "crusade of the faint-hearted," along with Stephen, count of Blois and Hugh of Vermandois (both of whom died on that crusade), might explain why he sold his land at that time.

The next documented member of the family is Hervey de Novers, who was almost certainly William's son. Hervey, in turn, had three sons, Simon, William, and Gervase, who succeeded their father, attesting documents at the bishop's court (either witnessing or subsequently authenticating documents). Hervey was still alive in 1130, for in that year he attested a document and his son Simon was included at the end.[87] In a series of charters dating between 1121 and 1135, a decade or more before the Second Crusade, Simon is found attesting charters along with members of the Norwich monastery, including administrators William Turbe and Elias (listed as *cellerarius*), Aelward *presbiter*, and Henry *de stabulo*—men who were to play an important role in the cult of St. William.[88]

By the mid-1130s Simon appears to have come into his inheritance. Late in the decade he was consistently identified as a "man of the bishop" and attested many documents. To judge from the episcopal *acta*, he was in frequent attendance on the bishop and was part of the episcopal court.[89] Simon also held a knight's fief (not previously noted) from William de Warenne (unlike ecclesiastical cartularies, no documents from the twelfth-century Warenne estates survive).[90] He briefly disappears from the documents at the beginning of the 1140s, most likely to support his lord the earl in battle. Around 1141 William and Gervase de Novers together attested a document, along with other men associated with the bishop of Norwich; Simon's name is nowhere to be found.[91] This is the only document in which Gervase's name appears.[92] He was the youngest de Novers brother and was likely drawn in because Simon was unavailable. The elder brother was perhaps away fighting with Warenne, one of King Stephen's most important supporters and a noted participant at the Battle of Lincoln (1141), where King Stephen was taken by the forces of Matilda and his earls fled. In a feudal assessment commanded by the crown (the "Return of Knights" of 1166), Simon de Novers is listed as holding a single knight's fief from the bishop, one not held by William de Novers at the beginning of the century.[93] After William Turbe ascended as bishop in 1145, Simon is again absent from the episcopal witness lists. He remained one of William Turbe's knights, but appears in few records of the diocese, as the new bishop preferred to have his clerical household, rather than monks and knights, attest his formal documents.

Simon's financial difficulties are only hinted at in the episcopal charters, but they are made explicit in Brother Thomas's *Life* of William, which describes the knight as desperate in 1150. He resurfaces in the book in the late 1160s as the master of an abused servant.[94] The Novers family had a long association with the cathedral chapter and its bishop. Simon may also have had family connections to the prior. Most of the lands that William de Novers had held at the beginning of the century—between twelve and thirty-three estates, according to the best estimate—ended up in the hands of the Ferrers (Ferrars) of Wormegay.[95] Although the Wormegays were not remembered as major benefactors of the priory or the see, at least one member of the family took holy orders and rose to become sub-prior and then prior (1150–1158). This Richard de Ferrar was one of the earliest supporters of Saint William; and in 1166 Richard's nephew, William Fitzwilliam, held ten knight's fiefs of the bishop. Simon may have been connected to Prior Richard de Ferrar and the house of Wormegay through the female line.[96] Reginald de Warenne, steward of his brother's estates, married Alice de Wormegay, later established Wormegay Priory, and built the motte-and-bailey fortifications at Wormegay castle outside King's Lynn.[97]

There may be an example here of the rise of one part of an extended Conquest family at the expense of another. Simon de Novers, with his one knight's fee, was a poor relation, clinging to his individual holding and his claim to consideration as a Norman knight. Although of disparate wealth, Simon and Prior Richard shared a common interest in promoting the cult of William. For Simon, it served to exculpate himself from a rightful accusation of murder. For the Ferrars, supporting a poor relation by promoting the cult of William might have been a relatively painless way to protect both family and institutional interests.

The disastrous Second Crusade lasted two long years. Hardly any of the Anglo-Norman crusaders who set off in the early summer of 1147 are known to have come home alive.[98] William de Warenne died in January 1148, in a Turkish ambush of the vanguard of the French army (leaving only a daughter to inherit), as did his brother-in-law Guy de Ponthieu and other knights from England, such as Stephen de Mandeville.[99] The last of the crusade's leaders, King Louis of France, returned home in the summer of 1149.

Warenne's half-brother Waleran de Meulan, Earl of Worcester, was shipwrecked near the coast of southern France on his return in December. Simon de Novers might have been one of those few who made it back to England. In any case, as noted, by late 1149 he was in Norwich and heavily in debt.

The one bright spot in the general gloom that enveloped medieval Christendom in the wake of the Second Crusade—the success of Englishmen of moderate means who helped take Lisbon, seamen, engineers, and merchants with no aristocratic leader—merely emphasized the debacle of those knights and their high-ranking lords who had answered the pope's call and headed directly to the Holy Land.[100] Simon de Novers would certainly have heard the glorious tales of martial valor, generous booty, and fertile acres as he sat warming his hands around the fire of peat from the Norfolk broads, in the winter of 1149, thinking of the hot sun beating down on men he probably knew from the neighborhood, men who had made a success of their lives and established themselves on the lush Mediterranean shores while he sat in damp Norwich in debt and despair, detained on a murder charge.[101]

FIGURE 3.1A AND B Bishop William defended his knight before royal officials. Pictured are a twelfth-century carving of a bishop of Norwich from Norwich Cathedral and Norwich Castle, the seat of royal government in East Anglia, where the first murder trial was held.

CHAPTER 3

The Trial

I n 1150, after five years of neglect, William of Norwich suddenly received the kind of attention merited by a saint. He appeared in numerous visions, was promptly moved inside a monastic building, and the following year was raised first to the high altar of the cathedral and then to a special chapel. William was provided with a carpet and candles on his tomb, as well as specially commissioned artwork. His teeth and bits of clothing were cherished. Miracles were duly noted around his tomb, the information about them collected, investigated, and carefully recorded. He was mentioned in chronicles. William's fame extended to Bavaria, where he was remembered on a list of martyr saints.[1] Virtually unknown in 1149 even in England, by 1150 William of Norwich was identified as a saint on both sides of the Channel.

This sudden transformation in William's reputation has been attributed to Brother Thomas, newly arrived in Norwich, who is said to have invented the ritual murder accusation for reasons that were personal, individual, and pious. He opens his work by telling readers of his "special devotion" and emphasizing his pious intention.[2] But the catalysts for William's striking transformation from local dead youth to internationally venerated holy martyr were political and legal as well, a result of common interest between secular and religious institutions, endorsed by authorities at the top of the ecclesiastical hierarchy in the immediate aftermath of the Second Crusade.

This transformation arose and took shape against the backdrop of a murder trial.

In 1149, Sir Simon de Novers, deeply in debt and unable to repay money he had borrowed from a Jewish creditor, arranged to have his creditor ambushed and killed in the woods outside Norwich. Even Brother Thomas, who sympathized with Simon's desperate circumstances, could find little good to say about the perpetrator. His attempt to exculpate the knight seems unconvincing:

> The knight [*miles*] was in dire straits, because he did not have the means to repay the debt and daily renewed his requests to defer payment. His men [*armigeri*], indeed, seeing their lord in such straits, took counsel among themselves in secret, as to how they might succeed in freeing him. After consulting together, one of them was sent to waylay the Jew—who was unaware of the ruse—as if he were to receive what was owed. . . . As soon as the Jew arrived, led by the squire, immediately he was seized by the others, dragged away and killed.[3]

The body of the victim was discovered and taken to London for burial.[4] Simon may have boasted of the deed, for his guilt was widely acknowledged, and later he appeared unrepentant. "He has become so insolent and obstinate that when we came to see him to settle the bond," a number of Jews in Norwich claimed (in the words of Brother Thomas, who did not dispute their assertion) "he hurled at us abusive curses and aimed at us a multitude of threats, which we do not deserve. So we consider the guilt of the murderous knight to be sufficiently demonstrated."[5]

The mass of native-born Englishmen would have relished the story of conflict between elites and followed with unfeigned interest the trappings and pedigrees of those involved. The story of the Jew's murder and Sir Simon's guilt quickly made the rounds in Norwich and its suburbs, "the news being commonly reported" (*necem . . . fama divulgante cognoverunt*). People were eager to seize upon some distraction after months of distressing news about the failed crusade.

Simon perhaps would have been remembered for the man he was in better days, witnessing important legal documents at the right hand of the bishop or on a military training exercise, or as a young man trailing his grandfather as he went about his duties managing the land of the archbishop. More recently, the perception of him was as a struggling fighter long past his prime.

Pitied, admired, or feared, Simon was in debt, and there is little wonder he would have blamed those who held power over him. Possibly inflamed by the preaching of men like Arnulf of Lisieux, Brother Ralph, and their colleagues, the aging knight may have felt he had little to lose by killing his creditor. In following the counsel of those ecclesiastical leaders who had spoken out fiercely against Jews and moneylending, he may have felt justified to take revenge. Certainly he judged, correctly, that if it came to trial he would be ably defended by his bishop and the local monks. His status as a knight (and possibly a former crusader) may have aided his social rehabilitation.[6]

Knights were often in debt. To pay for their costly equipment, as well as to keep up appearances and pay their retainers, they turned to moneylenders for cash. They were not supported during much of their time abroad and ravaged the countryside from necessity.[7] Should they fail to win booty from their military enterprises, they were forced to rely on the uncertain income from the seasonal agricultural produce of land cultivated for them by others and for which they owed services to their overlord.

Knights were inured to violence. The *Anglo-Saxon Chronicle* and the *Gesta Stephani* (1149) record that knights committed one atrocity after another, even and especially against church property. Many knights acknowledged their crimes when they attempted to make restitution at the end of their lives.[8] The profession of arms, for which they trained from adolescence, involved killing and intimidation. Chivalry and courtly love, just taking hold in the literature of the twelfth century, could not disguise the reality that medieval knights were brutal. Instances abound of knights attacking churches and monasteries, and committing rapes, arson, extortion, and other crimes. In East Anglia during the civil war, Hubert de Montchesney, for example, seized land from the abbey of St. Benet at Holme, John de Chesney and another knight seized manors from the Norwich monks, and William de Warenne brutalized neighboring abbeys.[9] Geoffrey de Mandeville's infamous attack on the abbeys of Ramsey and Ely, as noted, earned him fear and contempt in religious quarters (but on the earl's death in 1144 it did not preclude two religious institutions from fighting to keep and honor his mortal remains).[10]

Even more common than accounts of attacks on monasteries are accounts of knights attacking Jewish bankers in an attempt to destroy the records of their debts. The most famous instance occurred in York in 1190, following the coronation of Richard I in 1189.[11] The concerns of the barons expressed in Magna Carta (1215) also reflect knightly despair at mounting interest. In an effort to stop knights from attacking Jewish homes and burning documents of their indebtedness, at the end of the twelfth century the crown established chests (*archae*) in various English cities that held copies of loan documents under royal lock and key.[12] Much of our knowledge of Jewish history in this period stems from an analysis of surviving Jewish documents from the *archae* that the knights could not reach.[13] The establishment of the *archae* suggested that the crown was unable to protect Jews from attack. All that it could protect were the documents.

It was not surprising, therefore, that a Norwich knight would attempt to resolve his financial difficulties by murdering the banker to whom he was indebted, or that this crime would not have raised eyebrows among Simon's contemporaries in 1149.[14] Nor has this killing drawn the attention of scholars, since there is good reason to believe that there were many such assaults during the twelfth century. The Norwich murder was in many ways a typical crime of the period.

Even during the best of times, few were surprised when violence occurred. Jews, who usually settled close to each other in well-built houses, near the safety of a royal castle and market, were most vulnerable when in transit or when far from home.[15] Already by the twelfth century, kings viewed aggression against Jews as an assault on royal prerogatives. Perpetrators were prosecuted accordingly. The notion that the Jews were serfs of the king (*servi camerae*), effectively his chattel and subject to his protection, was in the process of formation. While this received formal legal recognition in the thirteenth century, the earliest intimation of it appears in England during the period in question. "Behold we run to you for succor, as to our sole and unique haven, secure in your patronage, and not doubting your justice," declared the Jews of Norwich to the king, in the words of Brother Thomas.[16] Repeated allusions to attacks on Jews, even if punished, suggest that such attacks occurred regularly.[17]

Individuals who traveled on public roads during the Middle Ages faced obvious risks. Travelers, merchants, strangers, Jews—all those who were thought to carry money—were frequently subject to attack. For this reason, whenever possible, merchants took pains to secure privileges for safe passage and often journeyed in convoy. Safety on the roads covered by the King's Peace was a sign of royal good government; its absence was an important measure of lawlessness.

For all these reasons, King Stephen could not let Simon's crime go unpunished. The king claimed to be in control of the country, and the prosecution of capital crimes was both necessary and profitable. It was important that the king be regarded as the fount of justice, mercy, and Christian rule. Justice must both be done and be *seen* to be done. Norwich and the region of East Anglia were the bases of Stephen's military support (his cousin Matilda had greater support in the western portions of the country). If Stephen had any hope of promoting the image of a competent government with authority anywhere in the country, it was here.

Nevertheless, the king was in a quandary because he could not afford to alienate any of the interested parties: barons like the Warennes, whose heiress daughter married Stephen's second son in 1150; knights, on whose military expertise he depended to uphold his claims to the throne; Jews, whose credit facilities appear to have provided cash to pay soldiers; and bishops, whose institutional and religious endorsement was critical to maintaining his legitimacy.

The trial against the knight therefore promised to be a fascinating one, a high-profile affair and a critical measure of Stephen's ability to govern. The very fact that there was a trial tells us that Stephen was able to master the machinery of government. The knight was held accountable before royal officials (*curia regis*) and eventually before the king himself (*coram rege*).[18] The king and his royal court heard the case first in Norwich and then in London, indicating the importance that the crown attached both to prosecuting high crimes and to protecting the Jews.[19] Brother Thomas, whose account of the trial is our only source for it, reported that "since the subject appeared to be of general interest to all Christians, the king commanded that it be delayed until the next council of clergy and barons was held in London. And so it was done."[20] When the court convened in the capital, therefore, all eyes were on Simon and his legal representative.

Before we turn to the trial itself, however, we need to consider the identity of those who acted for the prosecution and the defense, starting with the prosecution. The Jews of Norwich had appealed for justice in the death of their coreligionist and therefore effectively served as prosecutors, bringing evidence before the king himself, and pointing the finger at the perpetrator, an Anglo-Norman knight. As noted earlier, Norwich was a remarkably diverse and cosmopolitan city with close links to the Rhineland. It was also one of the first places outside London to which Jews moved, establishing permanent communities. Noblemen and churchmen in East Anglia were among the first in England for whom documentation survives of their dealings with Jews. The Jewish community of Norwich was one of the oldest, wealthiest, and most distinguished in all of Britain.[21]

Warenne claimed control over Jews at the same time he may have borrowed from them. Although no records survive, the earl himself may have contracted loans from Jews because Anglo-Norman noblemen like Warenne were the Jews' best customers, particularly in the period of the Second Crusade and civil war when they were eagerly searching for funds.[22] The earl was apparently one of the first in England to exercise direct lordship over Jews at Thetford, control he shared with Hugh Bigod, earl of Norfolk, who also welcomed Jews to his seat at Bungay.[23] Warenne would therefore have been acutely aware of the resources and services that "his" Jews could provide. The town of Thetford, thirty miles from Norwich, was one of the first Jewish settlements outside London (and the former seat of the bishop of Norwich).[24] King Stephen had granted Warenne lordship over the town around 1139. The earl's influence was sufficient reason for a local Jew to make a loan to Warenne's retainer, Simon de Novers, however risky. The lender could hope to please the earl by serving the needs of his entourage.[25]

Jews needed to appease their overlords: the risks to moneylenders were far greater from regulatory authorities than from individual recalcitrant debtors. Pope Eugenius III, in his bull *Quantum Praedecessores*, released Christians from their oaths to pay interest, effectively canceling income due to Christian lenders at the time of the crusades.[26] Bernard of Clairvaux demanded that this legislation apply to Jewish lenders as well, at least in "spirit," although popes had no direct authority to regulate Jewish moneylending. Bernard's influence prompted Louis VII to release crusaders from the obligation to pay interest owed Jews as well.[27] Some understood this ruling to go even further, supporting the notion that the king intended to cancel not only interest on loans but the principal as well. Ephraim of Bonn later noted that the Jews "did lose much of their wealth, for the King of France had proclaimed 'Whosoever volunteers to go to Jerusalem will receive remission of any debt he owes to the Jews.'"[28] Ephraim may have misunderstood the decree, or borrowers may have taken advantage of it to discharge their debts illegally.

Jewish financing of the Second Crusade was a fraught subject. The leaders of two of the great ecclesiastical centers of western Europe, the Cistercian abbey of Clairvaux and the Benedictine abbey of Cluny, urged that the crusades ought to be financed in part from Jewish funds. In 1146 Abbot Peter the Venerable of Cluny

attacked Jewish profits from usury and demanded that they be confiscated and used for a crusade.[29] Cluny was in debt to Jewish and
Christian moneylenders at this time, and had difficulty collecting
its own income; when Henry of Blois, bishop of Winchester, visited
Cluny in 1149, he discovered that the golden cross he had given earlier had already been stripped of its covering.[30] The attack on Jewish
financial activities at the start of the Crusade may have been a consequence of dissident views—Brother Ralph was summarily dismissed by a horrified Bernard of Clairvaux, and Peter the Venerable
was out of favor—but the opinions they expressed were not unique.
The financial realities following years of war may have made them
more widely accepted. Simon may have had reason to believe that
an attack on his Jewish lender would be tolerated, or would at least
appear justified.

Except for noting the names that appear in the sole surviving
account of the murder of the banker, so far no attempt has been
made to identify either the murder victim or his slayer.[31] Although
some of what follows is speculative, we can reconstruct important
parts of the network of social, religious, and economic interests that
informed the actions of both assassin and victim, and thereby cast
some light on the function that the ritual murder accusation served
in the community where the cult of Saint William of Norwich was
first recorded.

Brother Thomas wrote of the murdered Jew as "Deus-adiuvet"
("may God save"). For the past century this has been rendered as the
Hebrew name "Eleazar," although that is not a precise translation of
the Latin.[32] The name Thomas used for the murdered Jew may have
been chosen for ironic reasons, suggesting that it was the Christian
God to whom the victim must look for salvation. We cannot be certain of the given name of the murdered Jew, how he was known by his
friends and family, or how he signed documents—he may have gone
by different names. Norwich Jews did not use their Hebrew names
in daily parlance; most are recorded as having a religious name (*shem
hakodesh*) and a secular name (*kinnui*), and often more than two.

Although "Eleazar" is the name heretofore offered as a translation of *Deus-adiuvet*, it seems unlikely that the banker went by that name, for it was scarcely known in Angevin England. Far more likely is that Brother Thomas was referring to someone known by the French name Deulesalt (or Deulesaut, for *Dieu-le-saut*: "may God save"), quite a popular name for Norman Jews in this period.[33] Although it is not known how the banker was addressed by his contemporaries, "Deulesalt" will serve.

Brother Thomas offers other identifying characteristics of the victim: that Deulesalt was killed around 1149 but had been living in Norwich by 1144; that before his death he was the richest Jew of them all; that he was survived by a wife and relatives who were his heirs, likely children.[34] At the time of his death he carried a sword, and he was accustomed to moving among Christians and traveling without undue concern to distant houses on horseback with other mounted men.[35] At one time he argued with, or chastised, another Jew, who in turn denounced him to Christians.[36] He spoke confidently in front of the dean of Norwich. Many others owed him money, and the knight who arranged his death was not his largest debtor.[37]

Brother Thomas implies that Deulesalt was a wealthy and important man in Norwich. A horse and sword were expensive objects, and a horse was also costly to maintain, yet he had them for personal use, not merely as collateral.[38] Jews did not usually carry arms, which came to be forbidden to them by statute in 1181. In general they were classified as defenseless. That the Jewish victim had outstanding loans sufficient to inspire his murder by one of his lesser creditors—which description fits Simon, himself of elite status in the community—suggests that Deulesalt possessed unusually large resources for a moneylender in a provincial city. His influence among his coreligionists is clear: the monk attributes to Deulesalt the effective leadership of the Jewish community on a controversial matter; Thomas says he was "a person who had considerable authority among them."[39] Details of Deulesalt's argument with that individual Jew also imply that Deulesalt was a man of considerable political power as well as moral suasion. Lacking recourse within the Jewish community, the Jew had denounced Deulesalt to the Christian authorities, an act that would have been a last resort, and one traditionally frowned upon by medieval Jews as contrary to Jewish law (*mesirah*).[40] By 1144 Deulesalt is described as owning a centrally located house and having family close by. He was accustomed by this date to circulate in Christian society, and by 1149 he held outstanding loans long overdue, which suggests that he was not one of the Jews recently arrived from the Continent.

The years immediately surrounding the Second Crusade witnessed tremendous turmoil in the Jewish communities of Christendom, marked by forced conversions, exile, and violent attacks. The riots that accompanied the crusaders in French and German lands are well documented. No such attacks were recorded in England, however, and it is probable that European Jews moved into the lands of the Angevin rulers on both sides of the Channel. Most English Jews, though not all, came from the Norman and Rhineland territories.[41] Muslim military success had forced Jews out of old communities in what had been Christian Spain. Many settled in Toledo, while others moved further north.[42] With a change of ruler, still other Jews came north from the city of Narbonne, which was not yet under the jurisdiction of the crown of France.[43]

Before the turbulence of mid-century, however, Deulesalt was comfortably established in Norwich, and he almost certainly came by way of London rather than from abroad. So far as one can tell, Deulesalt is the first Jew to be mentioned by name outside the capital city. He thus appears to have been one of the pioneer Jews in Norwich and likely had received permission from King Stephen to settle there with his family.[44] Rights to leave London were generally not granted to Jews as a community, but rather to individual traders and lenders, and they were likely to have been costly. Deulesalt had adequate capital to make him attractive to the borrowers of Norwich, and was young enough to pick up and move away from his coreligionists and live a few days' travel from London. The likelihood that he had a personal royal grant implies that he was of some consequence.

Deulesalt was not an obscure provincial moneylender, but someone of more than local importance. In the financial records of the English exchequer, the one surviving pipe roll of Henry I, dating from 1130, includes mention of the Jews *Abraham* and *Dieu-le-Saut*, who render account of one mark of gold that they might recover their debts against one Osbert de Leicester.[45] We cannot be sure that this is the Norwich Deulesalt, whose ancestry is unknown. Still, it is possible to speculate about his heirs. One may have been the very wealthy Jurnet of Norwich who, by the 1150s, though still a very young man, already possessed national stature and international connections. Jurnet (c. 1130–1197) was the richest man in Norwich, and could trace his family in the city for three subsequent generations.[46] Jurnet and his brother Benedict engaged in high-risk lending, just as Deulesault did, as evidenced by their loans to the overextended abbey of Bury St. Edmunds. Jurnet probably loaned money to Norwich Cathedral for repairs after the disastrous fire of 1170. For work on his home, he used the same stonemasons who had previously worked on the cathedral buildings, which points to their close connections.[47] Brother Thomas completed his *Life* of William in the early 1170s, immediately before Jurnet built his house on a prime street in the center of town. If passers-by had taken to whispering and pointing out the purported bloodstains of the dead apprentice, as Thomas's text suggests, Jurnet's construction of a new and solidly masoned house would be understandable, especially if it meant destroying the foundations of the old one.[48]

The Jews who complained about the failure to prosecute the murderer of Deulesalt spoke confidently of their usefulness to the crown, and they had the initial sympathy of the court. The case seemed open-and-shut, and the outcome appeared obvious. King Stephen may have come to the Jews in search of funds and at their request; they were prepared to pay generously for justice. "We Jews are yours, your tributaries year in and year out, often required by you for your needs and always loyal and useful to your kingdom," Brother Thomas quoted them addressing the monarch.[49] King Stephen seemed already convinced of the truth of the charge against Simon. All agreed that "in so difficult a case the speech for the defense would have to be something very special in quality."[50]

The Jews laid out their case clearly:

> The debtor knight either wanted to pay and could, or wanted to and could not, or did not want to and could, or—the possibility which remains—did not want to and could not. If he wanted to and could why did he not pay? Or why did he remain so long in bondage? If he wished to, but could not, this inability doubtless gradually led to a desire in his mind to be free. If he did not want to and could pay, thus the inner voice of the evil mind already conceived the misdeed. But if—and we think this most likely—he neither wished to pay nor could do so, it is clear that diligent and careful thought gave birth to the plan of the crime. Again, if he did not want the killing of the Jew, with which he is accused; if he knew nothing of it, if he had not planned it, why did he not repay the debt to the widow of the dead man or his heirs in order to remove any suspicion of evil from himself??[51]

There was no answer to the prosecution. But Simon had a shrewd advocate to plead his case, and Thomas wrote admiringly of the bishop's courtroom tactics, reproducing his words to the best of his ability, like any well-trained medieval student, who was expected to take down verbatim the words of his master.[52] Although Thomas's recreation of the trial is said to be "imagined," the trial scene is the least likely part of the *Life and Passion* to have been invented. He could hardly pretend that the king had come to Norwich to preside over a trial if he had not. It was imagined because Thomas had not been there to hear the pleadings.

Bishop William Turbe was an experienced courtroom authority—sophisticated, well traveled, well read, mature, and a noted orator.

Thomas says his skillful eloquence "outstripped all others." He also took his local duties seriously. He presided over the large diocese and directed as well Norwich Cathedral Priory, which served his cathedral. Despite the vigorous objections of the sheriff John de Chesney, William had been consecrated bishop in 1146 (or 1147) and by the time of the trial had recently returned from the Great Council of Pope Eugenius at Rheims (1148) in the wake of the failure of the Second Crusade.[53]

Simon's trial was an opportunity for William Turbe to raise his profile throughout the realm.[54] Most of his fellow bishops had national stature and were members of aristocratic families, royal administrators, or theologians. William Turbe was none of these. Freely elected bishop by his fellow monks, he had spent his entire life in the Norwich monastery that he had entered as a child, dedicated by his family to monastic life (*oblate*).[55] Rarely did he attend the court. As a man who had worked his way up the monastery ranks (child oblate, brother, sub-prior, prior, bishop-abbot), Turbe had ample opportunity to ascertain Norwich's needs, learn church history, and gain experience as a legal advocate and ecclesiastical judge. Although not trained as a canon lawyer, he served frequently as a judge with powers delegated by the pope and archbishop.[56] Turbe was to be a remarkably long-serving bishop. Already described as "aged" in the 1160s (*iam centenarii*), he remained active until his death around 1174.[57]

A lifelong monk, Bishop Turbe was of a far different stamp than his predecessors, who had been royal nominees. He succeeded two married bishops, both of whom had numerous sons and relatives for whom to provide. In contrast, Turbe identified the priory as his family, and when times were difficult he retreated to the monastery attached to his cathedral.[58] One can presume that his closest interpersonal relations were with his fellow monastic officials.

The first trial was held in Norwich "after some time had passed, when the king visited Norwich and the Jews assembled in front of him" and made their case for the prosecution of the knight.[59] "And since the knight was, so to say, a vassal of the bishop, by the king's permission, Bishop William went forth to confer with them and to offer the knight advice."[60] The bishop "returned from taking counsel with his people and began to deliver his statement before the king."[61] It is not clear who exactly was present at this trial, most likely held at Norwich Castle; all Thomas tells us is "the minds of the king and those present were moved."[62] Stephen then decided: "since the subject of the speech appeared to be of general interest to all Christians, the king commanded that it be delayed to the next council of clergy and barons held in London." At that trial before the king's council, Bishop William "attended with many of his men and the accused knight," and "the wisest Jews from the various cities of England came together in London to deliberate" and both sides reiterated their arguments.[63] Thomas splits the speeches between Norwich and London, but because the defense was the same, we will treat the pleadings together as one. Not much time seems to have elapsed between them.

At the trial in London, the bishop knew he was addressing a group of aristocrats and churchmen who were predisposed not to believe his excuses for the indebted knight. Turbe therefore took a different defense tack, one that involved issues he knew would be immediately recognizable to his contemporaries, and that is what made him credible. He praised his knight's character, quickly passed over the knight's actions, and went on the offensive. As Thomas says, the bishop's speech "would be devoted to turning the accusation around." Turbe argued for a postponement of the trial so that officials could first investigate and prosecute a prior purported offense by the victim. "We think," the bishop said, according to Brother Thomas, "that we Christians should not have to answer in this manner to the accusation of the Jews, unless they are first cleared of the death of our Christian boy, of which they themselves are known to have been previously accused and have not been purged."[64] Bishop Turbe intended to charge the entire Jewish community with the death of William, a crime of which Deulesalt himself was purportedly the leader. "The rigor of justice should not be delayed too long," demanded the bishop, "we beg that it be deferred no longer," passing over the fact that he had done nothing to prosecute the crime since he had come to office four years earlier.[65] This was a new topic for the bishop. He apparently had not raised the issue with his ecclesiastical superiors, for example, when he was received by the archbishop of Canterbury in 1147.[66]

The bishop laid out the charge: Deulesalt had led the Jewish community in duping the boy and his mother with the offer of a job. The Jews then kidnapped him for three days, after which they inflicted upon him "all the tortures of the Lord."[67] Turbe further argued that Deulesalt and his fellows had gone to hide the body in the woods, where they had been accosted by a leading Norwich burgess, Aelward, who discovered what they were doing.[68] The only reason Aelward had not divulged this information for years was that he had been persuaded by Sheriff John de Chesney not to breathe a word of his encounter. He had confessed on his deathbed only after the sheriff himself had died (a death Thomas says was made extremely painful for his having protected the Jews).[69]

In a classic tactic, Turbe blamed the victim, framing the murder of Deulesalt as a justifiable revenge killing. In Brother Thomas's account of the trial, the bishop maintained that the real issue was the unresolved murder of the apprentice William in 1144, at the heart of which was the conduct and character of the Jews of Norwich. The principle of *mala fama*, their evil reputation or bad character, was sufficient to initiate proceedings. As was later made explicit in ritual murder trials of the fifteenth century, the material evidence was not important.[70] The character of the purported killing and the motivation of the alleged killers were of greater concern to the court than the facts themselves. It was the characterization of Jews as killers of Christ and William as a Holy Innocent that was of primary significance. The Norwich defense team emphasized that William was a type of Christ based on his physical suffering.[71]

In the courtroom, Bishop Turbe invoked ritual as well as rhetoric, combining his role as a legal advocate defending a layman in a secular court with that of a cleric who could invoke ecclesiastical rites. At the end of Book 2 of the *Life*, Brother Thomas juxtaposes the trial of Simon with the public recognition of William in the spring of 1150 (at the opening of Book 3), which suggests that the two events occurred close together.

According to Brother Thomas, Turbe offered the testimony of three witnesses and four pieces of circumstantial evidence. The witnesses were the aforementioned Aelward Ded the burgess, who had met the Jews carrying a body in the woods; Theobald the convert; and an unnamed Christian maid. Each of them was of questionable reliability. At the time of the trial the eminent Aelward was conveniently dead; Theobald was a monastic colleague who had probably not even been in Norwich the year William died; and the servant's part was likely a later addition to the story. The family members—William's mother, who supposedly met the man who had offered the job to her son, her brother Godwin, who proposed a trial by ordeal, and William's cousin, who supposedly followed the boy to the Jewish quarter of town—were not called upon to substantiate their stories.

The death of Aelward the burgess occurred around the time of the trial—which was now a double trial, having begun with the murder of the Jewish banker and now having been transformed into one involving William. Considering Aleward's wealth, he would have been among the elite of Norwich and possibly known to the royal court as well. His recent death probably diverted attention from the fact that his confessor, a priest named Wicman, would have had to have broken the seal of confession in reporting Aelward's deathbed revelation implicating the Jews in the murder of the young apprentice.

According to Brother Thomas, Bishop Turbe gave credit for information about William's murder to a Jewish convert identified as Theobald of Cambridge, one of the monks at Norwich.[72] Yet it appears that Theobald's testimony was not offered at the trial. His contribution may well have been made later, after the conclusion of the court case. Some scholars have questioned the very existence of Theobald, while others assume that he must have been known to the readers of Brother Thomas's *Life*. Although in Cambridge in 1144 Theobald described himself as a "Jew among Jews," there was no known Jewish community in Cambridge until a later date.[73] In fact, the contribution Theobald made reveals little about England; possibly he converted elsewhere during the turmoil of the Second Crusade.[74] There is no Theobald otherwise recorded among the monks of Norwich, but perhaps he belonged to Bishop Turbe's *familia*, the extended episcopal household: a *magister Teobaldus* twice attested charters for Stoke-by-Clare in the 1160s.[75] Whether Theobald the convert ever existed remains unclear; in any case, he was convenient but not necessary for the bishop's courtroom strategy.

As for the Christian maid, Brother Thomas does not mention her in the early part of his account. He subsequently argued that this was because she "held her tongue for a while" out of fear of retribution from her Jewish employers. She surfaces only later in the *Life*. It was probably when Brother Thomas was polishing his text that he added her "eyewitness" account, in which she told of peering through a chink in the doorway. Although fabricated, the scene is vivid and detailed:

> As she was preparing alone in the kitchen some boiling water, as ordered by them, not knowing what was going on, nonetheless heard clearly the noise of it . . . she happened to see through the open door—with one eye, since she could not with both—the boy fixed to a post. Having seen this she was horrified; she closed her eye and they shut the door. . . . While indeed she went busily about, hither and thither, she found part of a boy's belt and, hanging from the belt, a sheath with a knife in it, a needle and a purse. Next she looked around with more care and noted definite clues to what had happened.[76]

The figure of a peeping Christian maid in the Jewish household was to become a stock character in later blood libel accusations, someone who could testify to the "details" and precise circumstances of alleged events, and who could be easily influenced by ecclesiastical and governmental authorities. Christian wet nurses were commonly employed in Jewish homes. The Third Lateran Council in 1179 legislated against such employment, for fear that Jews would corrupt such simple souls. In later tellings of ritual murder narratives, the maid evolves into a "wicked woman," or *mauvaise femme* character, sometimes an old woman, but more often a young maidservant who cooperates with the Jews.[77] The Christian maidservant of the Jews appears prominently in the twelfth-century *Life* of Robert of Bury (discussed in Chapter 7). She often appears in later stories of alleged host desecration as well. The maid's late appearance in Brother Thomas's account suggests that personal testimony by the witnesses he originally invoked was not sufficient to convince people of William's sanctity.

To persuade the court, Turbe relied on what medieval Christians, or at least moderately educated and sophisticated ones, knew or thought they knew about everyday Jewish activities. These included the custom of rabbinical synods and communal gatherings, the practice of carrying a child to begin Torah study, the hiring of Christian maidservants, the choosing of lots, and the leadership of the *Nasi* of Narbonne, referring to the so-called Jewish king (*nasi* means "prince" in Hebrew). These were all enhanced by biblical interpretations. Images of Cain and the metaphors of innocent blood to cleanse unbelief were all in circulation when Bishop Turbe made his case at Simon's trial. The words and explanations that Brother Thomas put into the mouth of the convert Theobald reflect Christian views of Jewish behavior, not familiarity with actual Jewish practice.

Jewish identity was on trial, rather than any single individual perpetrator. A charge of murder directed only at the purported instigator would not have served the bishop's purposes because Deulesalt was already dead. For the logic of his defense to succeed, he had to blame the entire community. According to Thomas, Theobald the convert explained that the Jews assembled every year to choose a city where a sacrifice would take place.[78] The story of a large Jewish gathering picking a particular city in which to hold a sacrifice, it has been argued, was based on a comparable story from Late Antiquity, thereby implying the existence of some kind of continuous tradition. But few if any Christians in twelfth-century England would have known of this ancient story because no manuscripts recounting the earlier tale appear to have circulated.[79] Theobald needed no such distant source: he could refer to an unprecedented meeting of Jewish leaders that took place around 1150, the year of the trial. In that year, under the leadership of Rabbi Jacob Tam, more than one hundred rabbis convened to discuss Jewish law and matters of common concern (such as forced conversion) in the aftermath of the Second Crusade.[80] The efforts of French Jewry to act in concert in the twelfth century were remarkable, and were never to be repeated after the death of Tam. Rabbis came from many centers: Sens, Auxerre, Poitou, Paris, Melun, Étampes, Anjou, Normandy, and "the shore of the sea," a term that may refer to England. More than 150 rabbis attested the resulting decisions and agreed to abide by the conclusions of the synod. Such an important coordination of communal activity must have impressed Christian and Jew alike—whether or not all the rabbis were present at one time in one place.

The "choosing of lots" (*sortes ponunt*), which Brother Thomas claimed occurred at this meeting, would also have sounded familiar to contemporaries because of biblical precedents (including Matthew's account of Roman soldiers casting lots for Christ's robe). It also recalled the Jewish holiday of Purim, celebrated on the fourteenth of Adar, which usually fell in the month of March: the word Purim comes from the Persian word for "casting of lots." Some scholars believe that the communal horseplay around Purim, including the hanging of the enemy in effigy, could have led to the ritual murder accusation.[81] Christians might also have heard of Purim from the widespread Jewish tradition of observing "Second Purims" to celebrate escape from danger, a ritual that served as "the real vehicle of Jewish collective memory" during the Middle Ages.[82]

Theobald also indicates knowledge of the *Nasi* of Narbonne. This has led some scholars to believe that he must have had access to Jewish sources and significant Jewish learning.[83] William of Malmesbury, writing in the 1130s, made reference to the *Nasi* in the legend of the "Jewish Pope" of Narbonne (*summum papam*) and hints of a Jewish conspiracy.[84] Peter the Venerable testified to a general knowledge among Christians of the contemporary *Nasi* of Narbonne in his work "Against Jews" (*Adversus Judaeorum,* ca. 1148) and derided his importance. "I do not propose to accept that the king be one that some of you confess is from the city of Narbonne in Gaul, or others confess is at Rouen, which is ridiculous. . . . I will not accept any Jew as king of the Jews except one who lives and rules in the kingdom of the Jews."[85] The existence of the *Nasi* of Narbonne was an important element in crusade theology and of as much concern to Christians as to Jews in the years when the *Life and Passion* was composed.[86] It was not an obscure office, unfamiliar to educated Christians.

Although the office of the *Nasi* was popularly traced back to the early Middle Ages, extant references date only to the mid-twelfth century, and Jews and Christians had very different attitudes toward his status. According to the Jewish travel writer Benjamin of Tudela (d. 1173), Jews said that the right to settle in Narbonne had been granted to them for helping Charlemagne in the recovery of the city from the Saracens. The Christians, in contrast, looked at their defeat at the hands of the Muslims at the Battle of Fraga in 1134 (in which the viscount of Narbonne was killed) and saw Jewish treachery. The mention of the *Nasi* of Narbonne reveals that Bishop Turbe (or his source, Theobold) was a well-informed Christian but not someone in possession of recondite Jewish learning.

Another component of the ritual murder accusation based on contemporary notions about Jews was the belief that they needed to shed Christian blood in order to return to their homeland. This is a conflation of two myths that circulated in the high Middle Ages: the first was that Jews were cursed to wander until their conversion at the Second Coming of Christ; the second was that Jews needed Christian blood for medicinal purposes. These various elements were woven together. The myth of the Wandering Jew, which circulated widely in the Middle Ages (and again during the sixteenth and seventeenth centuries in Germany and England), was a piece of Christian folklore that has no parallel in Jewish culture.[87] It was first fully articulated by Roger of Wendover, a monk of St. Albans, in the early thirteenth century and was repeated by Matthew Paris, but it drew on St. Augustine's "Reply to Faustus the Manichean," in which he likened Jews to Cain, who must wander the earth in misery. Even earlier, Saint Ambrose, the archbishop of Milan whose works influenced Augustine, had asserted that Cain was the prototype for the Jews, and this association persisted for centuries: Peter the Venerable, for example, noted that because Jews bore the mark of Cain, they should be subjugated and oppressed.[88]

The idea that the application of innocent blood could cure unbelief and heresy as well as metaphorical or actual disease—especially Jewish heresy and Jewish disease—can be traced back to the early Middle Ages. Such ideas appear in contemporary Christian stories, such as that of the Emperor Constantine's baptism. According to this legend, Constantine was suffering from a disease and chose the Christian cure of baptism in place of a proposal, alleged to have been made by Jewish doctors, that he bathe in children's blood. The story of Clovis's baptism likewise portrayed this rite simultaneously as a cleansing of sin and disease. These ideas were current in the Parisian schools around 1170, and were alluded to by Rupert of Deutz (twelfth century) and Thomas of Cantimpré (thirteenth century).[89] They can also be found in the common visual culture of both Christians and Jews in northern Europe. Examples include representations of Pharaoh's infanticide, which show a diseased Pharaoh bathing in blood,[90] and dramatic performances, such as the twelfth-century *Jeu d'Adam*, in which the Jew inquires, "Look at me, am I sick?" He is told, "Yes, sick with error."[91]

Medieval Christians may also have been familiar with the practice of Jews carrying their children wrapped in a prayer shawl down to the river on the holiday of Shavuot. Aelward Ded's meeting with the Jews in the woods, who were allegedly carrying the body of the dead William, served as a model for later accusations. In a subsequent accusation (discussed in Chapter 6), Jews in Blois were alleged to have carried a wrapped body on horseback through the woods, near a river. One wonders if the original model was the actual carrying of a Jewish child wrapped in a bundle, so as to be shielded from the sight of Christians, on his way to the water for the traditional ceremony of a Jewish boy's rite of passage in springtime.[92] Knowledge among local Christians of a contemporary Jewish practice would confirm the ritual murder narrative in their minds more powerfully than, for example, the alleged influence of stories of Jewish martyrdom (*Kiddush ha-Shem*)—holy ones refusing to renounce their religion—witnessed by German Christians during the First Crusade half a century earlier, a parallel that is not mentioned at this time.[93]

It was anticipated that the court would find Simon guilty of killing Deulesalt, as everyone knew he had arranged for the crime. But Bishop William's counterattack was stunning in its effect. As Brother Thomas neatly summed it up, "On the knight's behalf, William, Bishop of Norwich, spoke effectively."[94] Turbe offered a masterful defense, dramatic and enthralling, emotionally satisfying, logically consistent, and theologically acceptable, if not entirely persuasive. He included familiar details, bits and pieces of contemporary "facts" on which to hang his story. Turbe was not laying out a legal brief for William's murder, merely demanding the postponement of the trial of Simon de Novers. He raised a procedural issue, one that was sure to gain sympathy with his audience.

The bishop's strategy produced a judicial stalemate. The "king, bishops, and barons all gathered" in London and the king, "exhausted by many speeches," concluded, "we cannot show this case the attention it deserves. . . . so let us postpone the case to another time and reserve it for a better opportunity."[95] Simon's trial for murder was adjourned *sine die* and the knight was free to go. Twenty years later he was still wreaking mischief in Norwich. Had he been found guilty, at the very least he would have had to leave the kingdom.

Nor were the Jews ultimately prosecuted for the alleged ritual murder, leaving the question of the guilt or innocence of each party open to question by later writers as well as contemporaries. Since the mid-twelfth century the alleged ritual murder has been regarded as a mystery or detective story that historians and religious observers have been attempting to unravel. But to contemporaries it was of less interest and was never fully investigated. The story had already served its intended purpose: raising sufficient doubt in the minds of the royal judges to defer the prosecution of Simon for homicide. There is no indication of any subsequent attempts to prosecute the knight for the murder of the Jewish banker, or the Jews for the murder of the Christian boy.

There never was a court case to prosecute William's killers. The example of William of Norwich, therefore, stands in marked contrast to most of the other famous medieval cases of alleged ritual murder, those of Hugh of Lincoln and Simon of Trent, in which one Jew after another was queried under torture to provide a coherent narrative in the search for "proof." The accusation of ritual murder would appear therefore to have originated as a clever legal tactic. Bishop Turbe and his legal team developed the argument in response to the contingencies of a particular trial. It has been argued that this trial indicated that the rule of law, and therefore justice, persisted under King Stephen during the civil war and after.[96]

Justice was not served. One cannot agree that the king made "a *de facto* ruling in favor of the Jews by making no ruling at all," as one scholar has termed it.[97] The postponement of the case against Simon, a postponement that proved permanent, allowed each side to claim victory. The failure to reach a conclusion—or to prosecute the Jews for the murder of William—demonstrated the king's irresolution in protecting the Jews, as in so many other things. Ephraim of Bonn has only heartfelt praise for Stephen: "In England the Most

High King [God] rescued [the Jews] through the instrument of the king of England, putting it into his heart to protect and save their lives and property."[98] Yet had Stephen and his court denounced the accusation of ritual murder, the libel would have been unlikely to have spread. By wavering, Stephen attempted to placate competing interests. The Jews of Norwich were proven correct when they stated (in words attributed to them by Brother Thomas): if the crime "be left unpunished in this way, we doubt not that there will be many future imitators of his audacity, and, indeed, that worse will follow."[99]

The first ritual murder accusation was not the result purely of personal piety from an individual monk or an outburst of violence— popular hatred barely reigned in by an exasperated bishop—but the well-considered judicial strategy created under pressure by a learned and sophisticated cleric and administrator faced with a difficult trial. Bishop Turbe's attempt to exculpate his vassal by asserting prior blame on the part of the Jews transformed what might have been thought of as the killing of an individual into a communal and religious act. It is this, above all, that raises the entire incident from a "simple homicide" to a "ritual murder." It was the educated bishop and his legal team, not Brother Thomas alone, who put together the story of William that was memorialized in the *Life*.

In the aftermath of William's death there are no records of real attacks on the Jews of Norwich. Brother Thomas writes of the extermination or scattering of the Jews and "the growing infamy of such a crime," but his foremost example is the murder of Deulesalt, so it is unclear whether he is referring to riots and expulsions that actually occurred, and if so, in what years.[100] As he did in other circumstances, Brother Thomas may have been exaggerating, elaborating from a single example. There is no evidence extant to suggest that the "scattering" which he mentions refers to something other than the upheavals of war, the vagaries of nature, and the voluntary dispersal of the community as peace was restored and opportunities for new business presented themselves.[101] The civil war and the Second

Crusade were over. What has been described as a "golden age of English Jewry" was about to begin.[102]

The monks and bishop soon realized what a treasure they had in the story of William the apprentice and began to embroider and enhance their story. They took to heart what the Jews had pointed out to them: that they, the Jews, had been able to create a saint when the Christians could not. The fiction enhanced the facts, and the facts gave credibility to the fiction. It was not long before the assertions made by Bishop William and Brother Thomas would form the basis of a master narrative of Jewish ritual murder.

FIGURE 4.1 Norwich Cathedral, the center of the cult of St. William of Norwich promoted by Bishop William Turbe and the monks of the cathedral priory.

CHAPTER 4

The Making of a Saint

The story of the trial involving the knight, the bishop, and the banker could have ended almost as soon as it started. The bishop's improvisation had served its purpose: the royal judges tossed out the murder charge, and the knight was free to go. The Jews, as so often in the Middle Ages, had no further legal recourse. Some chose to relocate, leaving Norwich and spreading throughout East Anglia and northward. Others stayed put. They assumed that the worst had passed, that better times were ahead. Norwich was their home and a good base for commercial and intellectual pursuits. There is no evidence that the Jews of Norwich suffered in the aftermath of the trial, despite Brother Thomas's claims that some endured prompt retribution for the crime and the assumption by some modern writers that there must have been a pogrom.[1]

The trial introduced the idea that Jews had murdered a Christian in a communal act. But it quickly became clear that the exculpatory account devised by the bishop could serve purposes beyond that of a criminal defense. If William had been killed by Jews in hatred of his faith (*odium fidei*), then he was a martyr.[2] Brother Thomas and his fellow monks filled in the details. Encouraged by Bishop Turbe, the Norwich monks attempted to benefit from the attention drawn to William's corpse by the knight's trial by leveraging ownership of his relics into a holy industry and a religious brand worthy of a major city, and they did so with zeal and energy. They elaborated upon the event, gave it characters and a narrative, incorporated its commemoration into the life and fabric of the monastery, and provided a corpus of miracles and other activities tied to the cult of a new saint. Their moving and memorable story explained the nature of William's martyrdom and the status of his body, and raised the stature of local figures, familiar sites, and concrete objects to gain attention in a crowded field. They organized a formal ceremony to move William's remains into the cathedral, distributed secondary relics to spread the word, commissioned one among them to write a *Life*, searched out and recorded miracles, and put together a dossier that served both to recount and to create the cult of a martyr. The Norwich monks had high hopes because other bishops and monastic communities had been effective in such endeavors. They promoted devotion to William in the manner of any successful capital campaign.

When Brother Thomas composed his story, his adopted hometown boasted all the accoutrements of a leading Anglo-Norman city but one. It had a cathedral, a castle, a market, an ancient heritage, and a diverse and growing economy. What it lacked was a patron saint. The cathedral was dedicated to the Holy Trinity and boasted the relics of many saints and martyrs, but it was not the final resting place, the eternal home, of a single holy individual. For it was a city's possession of a saint's body that linked it indissoluably to that saint.[3]

In this regard Norwich lagged behind comparable English cities such as Winchester, which had St. Swithun, or Durham, which had St. Cuthbert. The possession of a body that was intact, or at least that had once been intact, was the basis of institutional patronage and a primary source of significant social power in this period. A divine patron could defend property, encourage bequests and donations, draw attention to the community's strengths, and serve as a figurehead for a building campaign that in turn could spur other kinds of development, both religious and commercial. A suitable saint could also lay the groundwork for civic and regional independence. Norwich was conscious of competition from nearby communities that had been successful in harnessing religious devotion and building a cult center. The shrines of St. Etheldreda at Ely, of St. Edmund at Bury, and of St. Ives at Ramsey were all popular English pilgrimage sites not far distant, and Norwich was well aware of the benefits those towns derived from their patrons.

The elevation of William was not the first attempt the bishop and monks of Norwich had made to establish a claim to a corpse with stature, one that could bring aid and benefactions to their institution. Norwich had been searching for a suitable patron ever since the first bishop, Herbert Losinga, had moved the seat of the diocese from Thetford to Norwich in 1094 and had begun construction of the great Romanesque cathedral complex in the center of the city. Unlike other Norman churchmen, however, Losinga had not been able to build on or revive a native Anglo-Saxon saint. The monks had originally aimed higher than an apprentice leatherworker, seeking a patron with a national reputation. They employed legal and rhetorical tactics to lay title to venerable saintly men connected to the diocese who had already proven their efficacy: to St. Edmund, martyr and king of East Anglia, and to Felix, "Apostle to the East Angles." Norwich had the remains of Felix's stone throne, a good starting point for a relic cult, but not by itself sufficient.[4] Felix of Burgundy had first landed at Felixstowe, Suffolk, had been based in Dunwich, Suffolk, and then moved to Soham in Cambridgeshire, but eventually his bodily remains were successfully claimed by Ramsey Abbey, Cambridgeshire. The relics of St. Edmund were long established at Bury in Suffolk, so the bishop initially tried to move his seat there and claim control of St. Edmund's remains.[5] Failing to win Felix or Edmund, the Norwich monks then tried to make Bishop Losinga himself a saint on his death, but he was tarnished by accusations of simony. Norwich never earned a canonized bishop of its own.[6]

As Norwich Cathedral lacked an institutional focus and a powerful patron, its ecclesiastical authorities looked for a local saint whose body it possessed with good legal title, one whose intriguing story reflected the current fashion for young martyrs, an Anglo-Saxon heritage, and an ability to compete with popular regional cults.

When, in the wake of the murder trial, the monks and bishop of Norwich decided to endorse William as a possible patron saint, they moved with caution. They seem to have tried to assimilate William's cult to existing ones in two ways. First, the dates of William's celebrations coincided with those of other local saints; and second, the alleged martyr's veneration was bolstered with testimony demonstrating the approbation of others. Bishop Herbert—dead since 1119—was the first to vouch for William, albeit in one of Brother Thomas's visions.[7] The support of Norwich's most prominent ecclesiastical authority must have gone a long way to render the alleged youthful martyr acceptable to the community.[8]

In contrast to the stories of Felix and Herbert, William's offered some details especially attractive to his contemporaries; he was young, innocent, and violently martyred, all characteristics that had given powerful appeal to the cults of Saints Ethelbert and Ethelred, Edward, Kenelm, and Wigstan.[9] Felix and Herbert, on the other hand, had both lived long and productive lives and had died peacefully at home of old age.

During this period, stories of saints' miracles, especially those of the Virgin Mary, generally emanated from "monasteries with strong old English traditions, [told] by men united in admiration for the forms of Anglo-Saxon piety."[10] The same pattern would emerge in the miraculous doings attributed to the young leatherworker from Norwich. The monks and bishop sought a saint for Norwich who conformed to socially accepted customs and to the well-established expectations of a powerful spiritual patron. The aim was to recognize and empower local parishioners as much as it was to wring profits from pilgrims.

The first narrative of the alleged ritual murder served such a purpose. At the time of the trial it was enough for the bishop merely to point the finger and outline the charge. Back in Norwich, however, further details could emerge, the characters could be endowed with personalities and motivations, and local color could be added. Without the limitations and formalities of court proceedings, hearsay conversations could be recalled, expert testimony invoked, and circumstantial evidence provided to produce a well-rounded, convincing tale.

The first ritual murder accusation therefore was a literary creation, a story composed years after the alleged events. From the very beginning, it was designed to be read, possibly in the monks' school, or for instruction during periods of relaxation.[11] The vivid narrative of the alleged martyrdom was polished and enhanced with the addition of five books of miracles effected by the saint after his death (the text of Saint William's *Life and Passion*).

Before Brother Thomas put pen to parchment, however, the tale of William's murder was spread by word of mouth, gradually accruing details. It is possible, if unlikely, that at first, a version of just the first two books circulated. In the description of William's martyrdom by the first authorities, we find the seeds of the plot outline that would become standardized in the later Middle Ages. The account relies first on the testimony of male authorities of high religious and civil status who encounter the body and can testify to the innocence of the victimized boy and the reliability of his family. Characters are introduced, such as the suggestible Christian female servant, the distraught mother, and a son insistently and repeatedly described as innocent. Like the stereotypes who appear in later ritual murder narratives, these "witnesses" of the martyr's sufferings were effectively created by those promoting the cult of the martyr, with their stories elaborated upon from telling to telling.

Most of William's story emerged from an episcopal circle of influence. Cults take work, and members of the cathedral priory used what resources they had at their disposal. More important, perhaps, they relied on resources they *no longer had* in order to build an unassailable narrative. By 1150, when Brother Thomas commenced writing, the major protagonists were gone. Deulesalt, the purported Jewish ringleader, had of course been murdered in 1149. Aelward, the only Christian able to link the Jews to William's body, was dead by 1149; his testimony was reported third-hand. Bishop Eborard, who claimed jurisdiction and first investigated the murder, retired to France in 1145 and had died by 1147. Prior Aimery of Lewes, who first appreciated the importance of the martyr and sought to preserve his remains, died and had been replaced by 1147.[12] Sheriff John de Chesney, who had stalwartly refused to let the Jews come under the jurisdiction of the bishop, was dead by around 1146 (succeeded by his brother, who was himself out of power in 1154). Even the archdeacon William, whose name was invoked to entice the young apprentice William to his doom, appears to have died in the late 1140s, and William's own mother not long after.[13] That so many firsthand authorities were conveniently unavailable lends weight to the view that the cult commenced only after 1150: they were cited precisely because they were inaccessible to those who might have questioned the narrative.

The efforts of Norwich Cathedral Priory to acquire its own patron saint were the work of a number of individuals; contrary to the impression he wished to convey, Brother Thomas did not initiate the cult on his own.[14] Other members of the priory were instrumental, including the monks who commissioned Thomas to write William's *Life,* the chief means by which Norwich publicized its possession of the relics. They dedicated the book to their bishop and former prior with his evident approval.[15] There is no evidence that anyone within the cloister disavowed Brother Thomas's claims for William's sanctity; what criticism there was came from outside.

The assertion of William's sainthood appears to have had little or no support from the people of Norwich. There is not a single extant calendar from the vicinity, other than those from the priory itself, that includes a commemoration of William. William was not a "local" or "regional" saint in the sense that his adherents formed an identifiable geographic community. Few East Anglian notables were connected with his cult, and most members of the less-exalted classes who displayed an interest in him were connected with the monastery and its business.[16] In contrast, a saint such as Godric of Finchale appealed primarily to secular rather than clerical adherents and to those on the lower social rungs. The stories of Arthur and Guinevere, while promoted by monks of Glastonbury, were directed to a more elite lay audience interested in chivalric romance.[17] William's appeal, on the other hand, was within the cathedral close, "a village itself."[18]

Once given an impetus by the bishop, the Norwich monks attempted to foster awareness of the saint and garner attention by means of frequent reburials or "translations," around which miracles clustered. William's remains were moved four times in ten years: from the woods to the monks' cemetery near the cathedral (1144), to the priory chapter house (1150), to the high altar of the cathedral (1151), and then into a side chapel (1154). The relics were moved perhaps three additional times during the later Middle Ages, including once to the altar of the Holy Cross in the center of the cathedral.[19] Few other saints experienced such a peripatetic existence. The multiple transfers suggest repeated attempts to stimulate interest in a cult that apparently struggled to generate much enthusiasm. Medieval translations of saints' relics often coincided with construction projects, the dedication of a new shrine, the visit of honored guests, the celebration of a special feast day, or the composition of the official narrative of a saint's life, as did William's translation of 1154.

Notwithstanding the concerted efforts of the monks and the bishops, there is no evidence that St. William attracted significant sums or patronage to the community; his reputation rests entirely on the testimony of his biographer.[20] Brother Thomas claims that throngs flocked to the sepulcher, and subsequent scholars have taken him at his word. But there is no external corroboration of William's popularity, no record in the twelfth century of a single pilgrim to his site. Archaeological and literary evidence reveal no changes or expansion of the cathedral or chapter house; there is no independent mention of artwork dedicated to the saint, nor does any survive before the late Middle Ages. His first tomb was made of plaster and a recycled sarcophagus; a later sepulcher consisted of iron and lead. Comparable shrines were decorated with gold, gemstones, coral, and marble.

The nearby shrines of St. Ethedreda at Ely and St. Edmund at Bury were far more elaborate than any at Norwich. According to Brother Thomas, William's mother decided to provide enhanced accoutrements for the tomb when the sacrist of the monastery declined to provide them.[21]

Despite the claims of Brother Thomas and the priory's efforts, William was not the widely heralded, wonder-working saint who made Norwich famous in the decade after his death. This serves as a reminder that medieval men and women were not as gullible as many suppose. The hardheaded Norwich merchants, artisans, and aristocracy were not persuaded of William's sanctity, even after great effort on the part of the cathedral community and the local religious authorities. Brother Thomas complained bitterly that his neighbors ridiculed his composition.[22] Like many works of this genre of holy literature, it took time to find its audience and win approval.

The first of William's many translations began with a dream. On the first Tuesday in Lent in 1150, Brother Thomas, then a newcomer to the priory, learned of the slain apprentice in a vision and was instructed to protect his remains.[23] He waited for repeated confirmation of his vision before he told his superior, Elias the prior, who soon took action.[24] The first public acknowledgment of William's sanctity thus occurred in April, a time that corresponds closely to Simon's trial,[25] when William's remains were moved inside the chapter house, the focal point of monastic life. This was where monks met daily to listen to a chapter of the rule of St. Benedict, to hear sermons on feast days, to pray privately, and to have punishment meted out. William's first translation, on orders from Thomas's superiors, signified a cautious respect and a particular attachment to the brothers who gathered there.

Brother Thomas, for his part, declared that his fellow monks rejoiced in the discovery of a saintly presence in their midst, a declaration substantiated by the speed with which they moved William's remains—less than a fortnight after the monk first spoke of his vision. Thomas describes to his readers the details of an impressive translation, only to reveal subsequently that it was merely a dream.[26] By beginning his text with an imaginary account and then reporting concrete events, he manipulates his readers' perceptions and enhances the stature of the saint.[27] In the dream, the bishop preached a sermon demonstrating "the treasure that had been bestowed by the grace of God on the people of Norwich for their great veneration."[28] Together the bishop and prior welcomed the relics with all the members of the convent arrayed in white. After "the treasure" (i.e., the relics) had been censed, the remains were brought to the high altar. In the middle of the service, the bishop publicly announced that the saint should be carried to the chapter house. This was how a translation ought to unfold.

The actual translation of 1150, however, was far more modest: there was no grand entrance into the chapter house, no welcome by all the assembled monks, and no sermon by the presiding bishop. In the dead of night, without telling their brethren, who had retired to the dormitory, six monks raised and examined the body. This recalls analogous inspections, such as those of St. Dunstan, St. Edmund, and St. Cuthbert. In these other cases, the inspections established the status of the relics, confirmed the purity of the remains, and, as in the cases of St. Edmund and St. Dunstan, may have helped to silence doubters.[29] The exhumation also provided an opportunity to improve the preservation of the corpse.

The surreptitious examination of William's body was much like that of St. Edmund's body at Bury later in the century: the witnesses apparently stood at a distance, viewing the allegedly incorrupt remains only at night by candlelight, and the abbot alone touched the body.[30] Other bodies reputed to have remained uncorrupted after death were likewise inspected privately: in 1104 St. Cuthbert's body was first viewed at night by the prior and a few chosen monks, and the event was reported to the assembled community the next morning.

Only after the private nighttime inspection were William's remains moved into the chapter house. This occurred the following morning, with the whole convent solemnly in attendance.[31] Curiously, the relics were not placed in an altar, but, as the apprentice had requested in Thomas's vision, "under the seats of the boys."[32] Saints' relics were typically interred in altars, of which every chapter house possessed at least one. In no other documented case was a saint buried under the bench of a student. In the later Middle Ages, however, it was common for parishioners to request to be buried close to where they sat in church while alive, arranged according to their status.[33] Monastic leaders were interred in chapter houses, not as objects of lay veneration but because of particular affection for them by the monks. William's removal to the chapter house does not necessarily presage his veneration as a saint, although Brother Thomas calls it by the formal term *translatio*. What the move seems to indicate is William's close identification with the monks and boys of the priory, rather than his sanctity. The benches, too, may have been a compromise for those who did not think William worthy of interment at an altar.

The monks may have contemplated burial in the chapter house as an interim measure while plans were underway for a more elaborate entombment in the cathedral, which took place a year later. Those awaiting formal translation were often placed in a variety of temporary resting places within monastic precincts, and quite often in the protective environs of the chapter house. William's removal to the chapter house therefore seems to have been a temporary expedient to prepare the way for a more solemn and public ritual. Brother Thomas makes it clear that the translation to the chapter house was done in haste. He wrote that the site had been made ready, but in fact the sarcophagus did not fit the place appointed for it.[34] Bishop Turbe gave instructions for the disposal of the body but did not attend.

Considering Thomas's statement that "the commandment of the bishop was urgent," it seems possible that the translation occurred when the bishop was in London defending his knight.[35] This would explain Turbe's uncharacteristic failure to be present at an important occasion for the priory. The bishop's appearance in London before the royal court is the most plausible reason to explain both his zeal and his absence: his instructions to his successor and second-in-command, Prior Elias, to take appropriate action in Norwich supported his argument made before the king's court in London.[36] As lord and ecclesiastical authority, the bishop was able to use religious ritual in the provinces to support his argument in the secular court in the capital.

Brother Thomas writes that the prior and bishop carefully consulted about the day and date of translation.[37] Famous translations often coincided with the dedication of a church or shrine, but they could also provide the occasion for spectacular celebrations in their own right, such as those of St. Augustine at Canterbury (1091), St. Edmund at Bury (1095), St. Cuthbert at Durham (1104), St. Etheldreda at Ely (1106), St. Ethelwold at Winchester (1111), St. Frideswide at Oxford (1180), and St. Thomas Becket at Canterbury (1220). Becket's impressive thirteenth-century translation was planned more than a year and a half in advance, but even a century earlier, translations proceeded with due pomp and circumstance.[38] St. Edmund was translated to a new shrine on the completion of Abbot Baldwin's new church at Bury, in a solemn ritual over which Bishop Walkelin and Ranulf, the king's chaplain, presided. Ranulf, now bishop of Durham, also presided when St. Cuthbert was moved from the cemetery in the cloister into the recently completed cathedral of Durham. The Durham ceremony culminated with a visitation of the relics to verify their incorruption. Becket's translation occurred in the presence of the king, the papal legate, and most of the English bishops, each of whom authorized indulgences for those pilgrims present.[39]

In the case of William's translation to the chapter house, no special guests appear to have been invited, suggesting that this move was perhaps arranged on short notice. William may have been moved on Maundy Thursday, a day that was to have special associations with his cult. Maundy Thursday and Good Friday were two days of the year most closely associated with charges against the Jews.

Maundy Thursday was *dies salvationis*, the day the Church traditionally forgave its enemies, especially the Jews. It would also become the day that St. Edmund's tomb was opened annually for inspection.[40] During Good Friday services, two deacons sang reproaches (*improperia*) against the Jews, and the congregation responded to each with a refrain.[41] Before the end of the twelfth century, the congregation no longer kneeled when praying for the conversion of the Jews.[42]

It appears that in the twelfth century William's cult was tied to Holy Week celebrations.[43] William's relics may have been utilized as a means of bringing people to church at Eastertide. He was associated not only with the Christ-centered holidays calculated on a lunar calendar based on Easter, but also with the Marian-centered holidays calculated, as those of other saints, on a solar calendar.[44] William was closely associated with "Lady Day," March 25, the day of the Incarnation, tied chronologically as well as rhetorically with the growing veneration of the Virgin Mary, as were many subsequent purported victims of Jews.[45] Thomas reports that William was born on the feast of the *Purification* and died on the day of the *Annunciation*. The next time William's body was moved was on the feast day of the *Visitation*, the third of the great Marian feasts with which he was linked.

Devotion to Mary was to become a signal element of ritual murder accusations, often understood as a Christian response to traditional Jewish antagonism to the veneration of Mary and ridicule of the Virgin birth. Yet the Marian content of the Norwich narrative may have had more specific and local purposes. First and foremost, it appears in the context of the long-standing competition between Norwich and Bury, which was, as noted earlier, an important center of Marian devotion in the twelfth century. Norwich would appear to model its new patron saint on the cults of Becket and Edmund and also used elements of rising devotion to the Virgin Mary to welcome the new saint to East Anglia and win his acceptance. The *Life of St. William* reports a vision of Mary rejoicing with young William

in heaven and treating him affectionately; this offered a stark coun-
terpoint to the lamentations of William's mother and her sorrow on
earth, reflecting the hope and despair of many medieval mothers.[46]
William's cult was designed to appeal in large measure to lay mothers seeking healing for their families and to young boys entering the
monastery as oblates, choristers, and students, so Thomas's account
of Mary's concern for the young saint was both comforting and
instructive.

While Brother Thomas strove hard in his *Life* to portray the translation of 1150 as evidence of a strong and growing cult, his words
suggest the opposite. Each of the translations was an attempt to
make William seem increasingly worthy of veneration. Their purpose becomes more comprehensible when viewed in anticipation of
the grand ceremony of July 2, 1151, when William was moved to the
high altar near the founding bishop of Norwich, Herbert Losinga.
This public ceremony, held in the presence of Bishop Turbe, brought
William to the attention of a wider audience.

In the year that had passed since William's removal to the chapter house, leadership had changed at the cathedral priory. Elias
had died, and the new prior, Richard Ferrer, vigorously promoted
the new saint, having already demonstrated his active interest in
William by welcoming his aunt and uncle to the shrine for a cure.[47]
Under Ferrer's leadership, a carpet and light were placed once
again on William's sepulcher.[48] Prior Richard's patronage may have
enabled Brother Thomas to become custodian of William's shrine,
for the young man had already traveled with the new prior on monastic business to places like Ely, even though he had joined the priory
only recently.[49]

Like the move the previous year, the second translation of
William's body in 1151 was performed privately in the dark of
night: "The bishop, being anxious that the translation should come
under the notice only of a very few, bade me [Brother Thomas] and
the then sacrist Giulf to prepare the necessary instruments before-
hand, and so to manage the matter that it should be got over at

dawn in the presence of a few witnesses."[50] This covert operation enabled the brothers to confirm that the body was indeed incorrupt: "we found the saint in the same condition in which we had laid him there before."[51] Only after that inspection was the saint's presence in the cathedral widely publicized: "the bishop arose, and what he had arranged to effect with a few helpers was in fact carried out in the presence of many. For while the pre-arranged business was yet in hand, suddenly a number of people with eager devotion burst in from all quarters, being more desirous of being present at the service done to the martyr than with any idea of interrupting the proceedings."[52] The move to the cathedral was a well-orchestrated public relations event.

The translation of 1151 was public, even though it took place within the choir, the monastic part of the cathedral. Surprisingly, no visitors are mentioned, and it does not appear that an opportunity was taken at this time to distribute secondary relics to promote the cult of William in other locations. Brother Thomas, now the custodian and secretary of the shrine, may have begun taking notes, but the *Life* was not composed until 1154, on the occasion of yet another, and final, translation.[53] Thomas anticipated a subsequent translation, writing: "that reverend body of the martyr was laid up in a place sufficiently suitable for the time being, yet not with fitting honors; and his tomb was secured with iron and lead."[54]

Another motive for the translation of 1151, one that may have induced the new leaders of the Norwich Cathedral Priory to promote the cult of the child martyr, was temporary weakness at the abbey of Bury St. Edmunds. For nearly a century, the bishops of Norwich had attempted to wield authority over the wealthy and prominent Suffolk abbey and to move the episcopal seat there. Repeatedly foiled in their attempts to dominate Bury, Norwich's leaders welcomed the opportunity to boost its fortunes at this time. In 1150 Bury was going through a difficult period. A large part of its monastic buildings burned in that year, and the abbey began a period of extensive borrowing, which would effectively push it to the verge of bankruptcy in 1180. Moreover, Bury had recently commissioned a *Life of Edmund* focusing on its saint's childhood. This work was thoroughly in keeping with the new religious sensibility of the twelfth century, which centered on Christ's childhood.[55] This new sentiment was articulated by St. Bernard, who described contemporary attitudes toward Christ, noting *ante rex, modo dilecto* ("before he was king, now he is the beloved"), and argued for raising the status of the Holy Innocents, the young children murdered in Christ's stead. The success of Bury's new work of hagiography may well have prompted Norwich authorities to begin assembling notes about their own child martyr.

Norwich had a number of reasons to promote a cult that might compete with that of St. Edmund of Bury. As noted, William himself may have had family connections to Bury; so the priory might have wanted to emphasize the saint's choice of Norwich over Bury as his final resting place and the site of his miracles. Finally, a trial of Bury's knights for treason took place about this time in the garden of the bishop of Norwich, a trial that emphasized Bury's immunities from king as well as bishop because the knights evaded royal justice and were remanded to the abbot's own court for judgment. The trial thus laid bare the very real powers that contemporaries attributed to a patron saint, the presence of whose whole and incorrupt body was crucial to the abbot's power.[56]

However quietly it was conducted, the translation of 1151 drew international attention to William's martyrdom. Immediately afterward, William's name appears on a Bavarian memorial list, on the basis of which discovery it has been argued that knowledge of William and his story traveled widely and that the transmission did not depend on the intermediary role of Brother Thomas.[57] Based on the evidence, this is unlikely.

That Bavarian text, a martyrology, came from the Regensburg circle of Gregorian reformers. These polemically inclined prelates were acutely aware of Jewish-Christian religious issues, and they lived and worked in the home of one of the oldest, largest, and most active Jewish communities in German lands. Regensburg (*Ratisbon*), the capital of Bavaria, was also a staging point during the Second Crusade for both German and French crusaders. It should not be surprising that the Christian authors of the martyrology interested themselves in someone like William of Norwich: information about him had a direct, timely, and specific appeal.[58] The mere inclusion of William's name in the martyrology, however, does not prove that William's cult had spread widely from Norwich.

William's commemoration in Bavaria may have been the result of communication from an eyewitness to the translation of 1151.[59] Norwich had strong Germanic connections in commerce and in art, and it was a common stopping point for visitors from the continent.[60] A model for such a transmission by a single visitor existed close in time and place. Bishop Augustine of Norway visited Bury in 1181 and brought back veneration of St. Edmund to Norway (a considerable accomplishment given that Edmund was killed by Norsemen).[61] Similarly, Anselm of Bury was personally responsible for introducing St. Sabas to England, and Abbot Baldwin introduced St. Edmund to Lucca.[62]

Starting with the translation of 1151, the Norwich monks began to have increasingly ambitious hopes for William, envisioning the great multitudes who would come to venerate their chosen patron. Brother Thomas wrote that the crowds were getting so large, so frequent, and so irksome that Prior Richard suggested, and the monks entreated, that a more suitable place should be found for the martyr "where he could lay with greater decorum and the people thronging to the tomb could approach it without trouble."[63]

Bishop Turbe presided over the translation of 1154, which took place after a solemn dedication, when "a great multitude of people crowded together and the body of the martyr was carried with the greatest veneration" to the chapel of the holy martyrs in the north part of Norwich Cathedral. As Thomas writes: "There he rests, buried in body but alive in glory that shines in daily miracles."[64] Although Brother Thomas does not mention any special guests at the 1154 ceremony, the daughter of Reginald de Warenne, a leading magnate in the region and the brother of William de Warenne, was the first to be cured "a few days after the translation," suggesting that her father might have been present at the event.[65] The status of the other beneficiaries drops quickly: next was a moneychanger, then a fisherman, the young son of a knight, a peasant, and the daughter of a carpenter.

The move to a private chapel away from the monks' choir marks the true beginning of William's cult status, for it allowed pilgrims access and paralleled contemporary developments at other cathedral shrines.[66] The name of the chapel, however, was always associated with a number of different martyrs and relics, especially those of St. Stephen, so William was never the primary focus.[67]

Norwich had high aspirations. The translation of 1154 may have been prepared in part with an eye for a royal endorsement, for it took place just months before the death of King Stephen and the accession of Henry II Plantagenet in the fall. Bury proved a suitable model, for it had long wooed royalty and benefited from repeated royal visits.[68] Unhappily for Norwich, Henry II showed no interest in Norwich's new saint.

Nonetheless, late 1154 saw an urgent push for William's veneration, possibly in the hope that the new Plantagenet dynasty would endorse its new saint. Not only was there a solemn translation to a new chapel, but Brother Thomas's *Life* was composed after the death of Stephen, and books of miracle stories were quickly added.[69] To judge from the references in English chronicles, information about William cannot be shown to have been written before 1155.[70] This suggests that William's story was disseminated in 1154 only in conjunction with the composition of the *Life* and the translation of the relics to the martyrs' chapel.

For this important and seemingly final translation of William, Brother Thomas provides only the shortest description. Perhaps the monk was rushed, or perhaps he felt his readers were familiar enough with the event, which occurred on Easter Monday, April 5.[71]

Brother Thomas wrote of no more translations. When he revised his text around 1173, William remained in the martyrs' chapel, apparently having found a final resting place. Yet other altars and relic shrines may have contained his remains and offered an additional focus for his veneration.[72]

Of all the translations of William's relics, arguably the most memorable for the priory and its visitors was the one that went unrecorded in Brother Thomas's *Life*. Thomas tells of William's burial first in the woods, then in the cemetery, thereafter in the chapter house, then the high altar of the cathedral, and finally in the subsidiary chapel, but curiously, he never mentions William's translation to the center of the nave of Norwich Cathedral, at the altar of the Holy Cross.[73] Yet he was well known to have had an altar in that location, and maps of the cathedral repeatedly indicate that William's remains were there. As relics are divisible, this move to the nave may have accompanied one of the other translations about which Thomas writes.[74] It is unlikely to have taken place when the cult had gone cold, which it did by the later twelfth century. Nor is it likely to refer to a temporary resting place for the body when it was first brought to the cathedral.[75] Perhaps William was moved immediately after Brother Thomas revised his *Life* in 1173, as part of the refurbishment of the cathedral and its cult(s) following the fire of 1170. That might explain why this move is not mentioned in the narrative.

All the translations can be understood as attempts to initiate a cult, but they also suggest repeated attempts to appeal to different people and interests. The places mentioned by Brother Thomas were all protected by the monks, physically separated from areas open to the general public. The monks' cemetery, chapter house, and high altar were under their auspices, and access to these sites was restricted.[76] The altar of the Holy Cross, on the other hand, was open to laypeople and was the major focus of their devotion during confession on the days before Easter, exactly when William would have been on their mind. The translations make it clear that, despite all the monks's efforts, William did not quickly evoke widespread veneration.

The primary events responsible for the reverence accorded to saints were miracles. Stories of miracles reaffirmed faith in divine intervention in the affairs of ordinary men and women, provided models of behavior, and publicized the cults of sanctified individuals. They tied veneration of saints to the locations of their relics. In many cases, miracle stories suggested appropriate donations from interested disciples. As Brother Thomas explains to his readers, "It is worth the effort to make known to the devotion of believers the source from which it may always be increased. For while the little flame of our devotion often learns by listening to the pious deeds of the saints again and again, it flares up as a result, as if fanned by a breath of piety, and burns more strongly with love."[77]

The miracles of St. William have been treated in some detail on the basis of information drawn from the many closely written pages that describe his *post mortem* intercession in the human affairs of East Anglia.[78] For the most part, the recorded miracles are entirely conventional: healing cures of many kinds, threats, visions, safety at sea, and the like. William's list of miracles is comparable to contemporary collections, such as those of Thomas of Canterbury, Frideswide of Oxford, and Godric of Finchale in England, and those from Rocamadour and elsewhere in France.[79] Stories of wandering pigs, feverish children, and fearful and fearsome lords were treated with equal interest.

Perhaps the most striking feature of Brother Thomas's five books of miracles that follow the two books of William's passion is that the word "Jew" does not occur in any of them. One reads of no converting Jews, no blasphemous or wise Jews, no Jews debating William's merits or acknowledging the saint's power, as they do, for example, in the contemporary miracle stories of St. Frideswide or St. Nicholas. In fact, Brother Thomas's account indicates no concern with real Jews after William's death, nor any interest in their conversion. Whatever else William's miracle stories exemplify and reflect,

Jews, Judaism, and Jewish conversion are not among them.[80] Even the conversion of Theobald the monk is treated only in passing.[81] This stands in marked contrast to the miracle stories of almost all other purported victims of ritual murder from the thirteenth century onward; their discovery or intercession almost always culminates in a grand conversion, echoing the anticipated conversion of Jews at the End of Time.[82] Since the traditional Augustinian justification for the presence of Jews in Christendom was the hope and expectation that they would convert, this absence of emphasis seems noteworthy.

This lack of attention to Jewish conversion also diverges from the new literary genre of miracle plays, which emerged in the twelfth century. Medieval vernacular drama has been described by one scholar as "one of the most vehemently anti-Jewish genres in the history of English literature."[83] In those plays, "the Jew is made to embody an entrenched disbelief based on blind adherence to . . . reasoned doubt," which represented a profound threat to "the paradigm of salvation" that was at the core of the New Testament plays.[84] The miracles of St. William suggest none of this concern.

William of Norwich's miracles were traditional, even old-fashioned, and in some cases they were directly modeled on stories of St. Martin of Tours, composed five centuries earlier. The cult of William appears to have satisfied needs that were personal, local, familial, and pediatric. These needs were served as well, if not better, by other local cults and more familiar English saints. No evidence suggests that Christians in mid-century Norwich were plagued by doubts, and needed some new cult to reconcile experience and belief.[85]

The monks kept track of miracles at the shrine as they occurred. The original loose notes could then be copied into a more permanent and structured record.[86] Members of the priory were in a position to observe many of the miracles firsthand: When two local parents, Colobern and Ansfrida, watched their ill son kiss the sepulcher and be cured, Brother Thomas writes, "We also, who were present seeing such things, cried, pierced by compassion."[87] Later

Thomas describes seeing a man from beyond the Humber place a large amount of wax shaped into boots on top of William's tomb in appreciation for his cure from dropsy.[88] Brother Thomas details the saint's intervention on his own behalf, and also notes: "we have seen a certain peasant, Simon of Hempstead, who was vexed by a demon for many days, and after he tied himself hand and foot to that healing tomb of St. William, on the next day he was led home hale and healthy."[89] He continues, "we have also seen another possessed person who was cured by divine mercy at the tomb of St. William in the week of Pentecost."[90] That same week a poor woman from Bury had her prayers answered, "and after about an hour she rose up, sound and healthy, in our full view."[91] In his capacity as both custodian and secretary, Brother Thomas must have stayed close to the sepulcher, because he was frequently able to rush to the scene of a cure at the tomb. "As we rushed up to her and asked her with great care what had happened, we heard from the said Godiva and many others that they did indeed know the woman and had often seen that maiden bent and mute," who could now walk and talk in her maternal tongue (English).[92]

Other beneficiaries reported to the cathedral when their prayers were successfully answered elsewhere. Robert the Palmer "later told us that the flux of dysentery had ceased on the very day" his son had drunk some water with scrapings from the tomb.[93] Sailors of Yarmouth "as they themselves later told us, immediately, as they were calling the name of the holy martyr and offering him their vow, the whole tempest fell silent."[94] Ida Wrancberd told her father and mother about her vision, "which the father himself took care to inform us on the morrow. But what was even more amazing, before that hour the father, the mother and maiden—as they themselves said—did not even know the proper name of St. William."[95]

Not everyone immediately shared the good news of cures. Some had to be tracked down and persuaded. A man from Tudenham, suffering from dropsy, sought a cure from St. William. "When we carefully enquired into the affair, we learned from the account of his neighbors that he had been cured."[96] A letter from a monk of Pershore testifying to the power of the saint may also have been solicited in this way.[97]

Monks carefully investigated claims of cures and miraculous benefactions. Brother Thomas repeatedly writes of his efforts to scrutinize claims of William's intervention:

> Although the glorious martyr was becoming famous—as so many miracles took place around his tomb—we have not been able to take note of all of them, both because many have escaped our notice and because quite a few we have been unable to track down the full certainty of truth. Meanwhile, it has pleased us to insert into this book those we know for sure by sight or hearing.[98]

Brother Thomas assures his readers of his wariness in the case of a girl who had been born blind and dumb and was subsequently cured by St. William: "although we had learned the outcome as the mother described it, we wanted to know the truth more surely, and we placed a burning candle on top of a stick. We put it in front of her eyes and moved it from side to side."[99]

To underscore the veracity of the claims, Brother Thomas mentions people, places, and objects that his readers were likely to know. Disinterested eyewitnesses were also useful. A wine merchant of Cologne was called upon to authenticate the circumstances of the pilgrim Philip de Bella Arbore of Lorraine.[100] Another pilgrim required corroboration from those at home: "as we have learned from the account of those who were present when he was ill and when [he] got better."[101] At times, the testimony of the ill was not sufficient. In one instance, an epileptic peasant from Lothingland provided supportive testimony, and in another Thomas refers to other witnesses, most likely the parish priest who accompanied the sufferer.[102]

Brother Thomas was sensitive to criticism of his work, particularly from those who spread rumors "that we have struck the stamp of truth on untruths or have dressed up events with figments of the imagination."[103] This defensiveness occurs frequently. Writing of Philip de Bella Arbore's bursting iron fetters, he notes, "I do not think that we should believe those who attribute these events to the fraud of vagabonds, for whatever malicious wanderers might do for the sake of finding some food, we boldly testify to what our eyes have truly seen."[104]

Cures often did take place, as much perhaps from improved diet, change of scenery, hope, time, or care and attention, as from "miraculous" intervention. Yet in the case of St. William of Norwich there is an especially intriguing example of the medieval understanding of a miraculous cure. Adam, son of John, the bishop's steward (*dapifer*), had suffered a long and severe fever: "the disease had grown to such a degree that his skin was shriveled, marked by a certain wilted pallor, which looked to the eyes of witnesses like a sign of death." On the advice of relatives, he visited William's tomb and fell asleep there. "After two hours had passed," says Brother Thomas, "he then got up healthy and unharmed as if he had never before sensed any pain."[105] Adam *dapifer*, however, did not long survive his cure. He was soon replaced in the hereditary job by another man, who had acquired the office probably by marriage to Adam's widow and custody of his heir, suggesting that the improvement in his health was temporary at best.[106]

Many of William's miracles involve healing, demonstrating that his relics could accomplish what trained practitioners could not. Invalids came to the shrine after years of suffering, often after having consulted medical professionals to no avail. Thus Agnes, wife of Reginald the cowherd, after five years of suffering, "had spent no small amount on doctors."[107] An unnamed woman came to William's uncle Godwin saying, "I am so poor that I possess nothing more than what you see about me. I have spent all my earnings on doctors and I have benefitted not at all."[108] In the case of the son of William Polcehart, "the doctors were consulted about the boy's health and profited him not at all; at last the desperate parents took themselves to the help of St. William."[109] St. William and the Norwich monks are revealed as complementary to and even in competition with the local doctors (some of whom no doubt were Jews).[110]

In other cases, families brought relatives in need of discipline as much as cure. Gerard, the nephew of the knight William of Whitwell, escaped from fetters to come to William's sepulcher in Norwich, and other pilgrims came to be freed from bondage (either self-imposed or assigned as penance). Philip de Bella Arbore came in fetters, as did the brother of another man. Eborard the Fisher was brought by a number of men with "his feet tied up in shackles and his arms tied behind his back . . . he was taken up by the many people who rushed up to him, who secured him very tightly and placed him—as he resisted fiercely—next to the tomb."[111] We have seen, too, that Simon of Hempstead was also bound hand and foot to the tomb and on the next day was led home hale and healthy.

The fearfulness of some of William's pilgrims contrasts with the carefree attitude of Chaucer's merry band who "longed to go on pilgrimage." The son of Richard de Needham and Silverun, bound up, "was finally led to the oft-mentioned tomb by his parents, and as they approached suddenly he cried out in a horrible voice and said 'what do you want of me? Where are you leading me? I won't go there! I won't go there.'"[112] He was seized and bound and put down willy-nilly (*vellit nolit*) beside the holy tomb. "After an hour had passed, gently and humbly he asked to be released." Sieldeware of Belaugh was brought to Norwich by her relatives and dragged inside the cathedral by four strong men. "She demonstrated amazing strength and tried to escape from the hands of those who were holding her. She cried out in a loud voice, 'what do you want to do with me? Where are you dragging me? I will not go there.'"[113] Such anecdotes suggest that visiting a holy shrine could be as much a threat as a blessing. The monks upheld the social order and reinforced the authority of parents and guardians against children and servants.

William was considered especially beneficial to children, and many of his cures relate to standard childhood afflictions, fevers, and weaknesses. He appeared to serve as a local, approachable intercessor for people within the cathedral close. If he did "specialize," it may have been in pediatric cures.[114] Among the parents who brought sick children to the shrine of St. William were Albert Gressley, Adam de Croome, Bondo and Gunnilda Hoc, the aforementioned Colobern and Ansfrida, Aluric the tailor, Eustace the moneyer, Berengar of Norwich, Martin the Fisher, William Polcehart, Gurwan the tanner, and the fathers of both Huelina of Rocesburgh and Baldwin of Lincoln. Other parents, such as Lady Mabel de Bec, brought home water infused with the holy essence of the saint.[115] After more than two weeks in painful labor, Botilda drank a tincture made from a fern that had touched William's tomb, and delivered a healthy child.[116] William's non-monastic visitors were largely parents—both men and women. In contrast, the specialty of St. Cuthbert was men (he did not allow women in the church or near the shrine); perhaps to compensate, the majority of early pilgrims to St. Godric's nearby shrine of Finchale were women.[117]

As the collaboration of the monk, the bishop, and the knight demonstrates, clerical devotion and lay piety were closely intertwined and not easily separable. Knowledge was spread from monastery to lay circles by regular communication among relatives. A significant number of laypeople who supported William's sanctity were closely related to members of the Norwich Cathedral Priory and William's own family was connected with the monastery. As we have seen, the prior Richard de Ferrer welcomed his aunt and uncle to Norwich as adherents of the cult, and his predecessor Elias also introduced lay family members to St. William.[118] Peter Peverell spanned both worlds, leaving the active life of a courtier and knight to spend his later years as a monk.[119]

Veneration of St. William also spread in the other direction, from lay to clerical circles. Such a mode of transmission is exemplified by Lewin of Wells, a young man who knew of St. William and told his priest, who had been ignorant of the saint. Arriving at the synod in Norwich, the priest learned of St. William and "he rejoiced with no little happiness, because he recognized that the boy of whose death he had just heard talk was the same of whom at home the sick man was always speaking."[120] Equally significant, lay piety was interpreted by monastic confessors and priests. Thus the visions of Lewin and of the virgin of Dunwich were evidently refracted through the teachings and explanations of Wicman, the confessor appointed of the bishop, and then recorded by the monk Thomas.

Those who benefited from the miracles had a clear interest in supporting the cult, and in some sense they defined it. Grateful for healing, they often made donations to support the saint: cash, candles, or other goods. But those who supported the church first often later benefited from William's intercession. It is not clear, for example, whether Mabel de Bec's donation to the cathedral priory came as a result of her veneration of St. William and her gratitude for a cure, or whether William deigned to cure her children precisely because she had shown herself to be a loyal patron of the cathedral priory. "Whenever she or her sons incurred the trouble of any ill health," writes Brother Thomas, "immediately they ran for succour to the medicine which her faith had provided and on whose efficacy they relied. Calling upon the aid of the holy Martyr William they scraped the stone [from William's tomb] and dissolved it in holy water, then drank it, and soon they experienced relief."[121]

Mabel de Bec's dates are uncertain, but she made her donations to Norwich before William was moved into the cathedral, and it appears that her children were themselves adults by the time of William's death.[122] The daughter of Walter de Bec, Mabel was the wife of Stephen de Cameis (Chameys, Camoys), a tenant of the honour of Clare, who was active as a soldier in Wales in the 1130s.[123] Brother Thomas's phrasing suggests that Mabel was a young mother concerned about her ill infants, but two of her sons were attesting documents before King Stephen came to the throne, so she would have been an older woman by the time the monk knew her—perhaps seeking a cure for her grandchildren. Brother Thomas reports that she gave him a cupboard (or shrine, *scrinium*) for his private relics of St. William. However, her more generous benefactions had gone directly to the endowment of the Norwich monks even before Brother Thomas arrived at the monastery, apparently with no mention of the boy martyr.[124] Mabel's wealthy brother Walter II de Bec, who held land in three counties, gave the tithes from his holding in Harpley to St. Pancras at Lewes, not to Norwich; his son, Walter III de Bec, who became sheriff of Norfolk and Suffolk in 1167, did not make any known gifts to Norwich.[125]

The names of many of the supporters mentioned by Brother Thomas in the *Life* appear as well in the records of other Norwich religious institutions, but the gifts and endowments to others indicate that St. William was of only minor religious interest to these laymen and women. According to the *Life*, the wife of Bartholomew de Creak made a candle in the name of St. William and vowed to offer it for the recovery of her little daughter, who had been attacked by a burning fever. The mother duly offered the candle, and "that feverish heat suddenly ceased."[126] Sir Bartholomew, "very famous for both chivalry and nobility,"[127] held eight fiefs of William de Warenne and also land of Roger Bigod. He was generous in his benefactions to various religious institutions, but not to Norwich Cathedral Priory. Godiva, the wife of Sibald, also expressed gratitude to William. Godiva was in church on Maundy Thursday, and Brother Thomas's observation suggests that she was a prominent and regular churchgoer. Nonetheless, witnessing a miracle did not inspire her to endow the Norwich Cathedral Priory, nor to place her relatives there.[128] Her husband, Sibald, was sufficiently affluent to place his nephew Gregory in the monastery of St. Benet of Holme and give the abbey land at Conesford in Norwich, worth 16 pence yearly.[129] His contribution to Norwich priory on St. William's behalf appears paltry by comparison.

Young Albert de Gressley is another who benefited from St. William's intervention. His father, Robert Gressley, a nobleman and a knight, laughed with other knights when he observed his son Albert praying to St. William for the cure of an ill falcon. Nevertheless, St. William proved interested in trivial things, took pity on the boy, and cured the bird.[130] When the boy grew up, however, he did not make donations to Norwich Cathedral Priory, but instead to nearby St. Benet of Holme, to which he granted land and rights for the soul of his father, Robert, and his grandfather Albert.[131] The younger Albert was in a strong position to promote William's sanctity, if he had been interested in doing so.[132] The miracle of the cured falcon is the last miracle in Book 6 of Brother Thomas's text—a modest, not to say disappointing, culmination of the demonstration of William's powers. In these four elite families, moreover, the interested parties were young sons, daughters, or their mothers, suggesting that St. William appealed to those groups, rather than to the clans' wealthy and powerful heads.

St. William has often been characterized as an important pilgrimage saint of Norwich. That was the impression Brother Thomas was eager to convey. However, his miracles have been described as "scraping the barrel,"[133] and an examination of the saint's leading supporters suggests that his biographer was grasping for prominent endorsements. Even the knightly families that Brother Thomas mentions were hardly fervent in their support. There is little indication that the cult attracted pilgrims who journeyed to Norwich expressly to venerate William's relics, or that there was real enthusiasm for William among the secular society of Norwich. Since clerical endorsement alone was insufficient to build a cult, Brother Thomas supported William's credentials with testimonies from influential local laypeople. Those laypeople—often women and children from knightly families—were accustomed to charitable giving and were connected to prominent families and religious institutions, but they registered only mild approbation of William's cult.

The most energetic advocacy of William's sanctity came from individuals closely identified with the cathedral priory, especially those dependent upon the priory for their livelihood. Aluric, the monk's tailor; Alditha, the wife of Toke, the candle maker; Agnes, the wife of Reginald the cowherd; Botilda, wife of Toke the baker; Gilliva, daughter of Burchard the carpenter; Chole, the smith; the wife of Gurwan, the tanner, and their son; Robert the palmer—all worked in or near the monastic precincts and deferred to the monks on a daily basis. Three such women benefited from the saint's intercession on more than one occasion. The wife of Richard de Bedingham received help for a stomachache, and earlier their house guest Robert benefited from a vision of William.[134] Botilda, the cook's wife, relied on William for help during childbirth and later during a storm at sea. Ida, the wife of Eustace the moneyer, sought help from William to relieve the terrible pain of gout, and her daughter was cured of madness within an hour.[135] Uneducated women with sick children were especially open to the possibilities of alternative forms of medical treatment. Like many medieval saints, William specialized in therapeutic miracles—reducing fever, alleviating toothaches, reviving faints, and calming hysterics.

By repeating the names of the beneficiaries of William's miracles, Brother Thomas reinforces the impression that William's cult was not widespread. Lady Mabel de Bec's experience evokes the quotidian rather than the exceptional. This is not the sort of spiritual epiphany that resulted in valuable benefactions or encouraged great works of art or memorable devotional literature.

The promotion of William therefore took work. There may have been a *tabula* or board with basic information, much like a guidebook, located next to William's shrine, to announce to visitors to the cathedral the identity and importance of the shrine.[136] It is likely that such a board announced what the chronicles baldly record, "William of Norwich who was cruelly murdered by the Jews." Most important of all, however, was the composition of the *Life*. Volumes were available for consultation in the priory library or the cathedral, and the monks anticipated that these would be closely studied.[137] The monks were also conscious of the need to attract a less patient audience. Brother Thomas provided seven books in chronological order, detailed chapter divisions, cross-references, and a useful summary in the prologue.[138] His stated goal was to tempt "those who are interested in something new to read."[139] This concern with religious novelty remained typical of Norwich for centuries.[140]

As noted, the narrative account was composed quickly in late 1154, but was not completed, published, and distributed until after it was revised and the dedication was written in 1172. Brother Thomas wrote his version and packed it away in a cabinet (*scrinium*) next to the altar dedicated to the boy, where it apparently survived another fire and riots that consumed the cathedral library in the following century. But that literary creation by an individual author was made possible by group approval. It was not simply the product of one man's vivid imagination, an expression of his spiritual doubt during the long nights spent in his cold cell as the wind blew, far from his home on the other side of the country.

Brother Thomas's story was taken up, institutionalized, repeated, and abstracted. The illiterate learned about it in characteristic ways from preaching and ritual, memorialized on important liturgical occasions. The text of the *Life and Passion* was only one manifestation of an incipient cult centered on a literary text that few people can be shown to have read and on the rituals associated with the movement of William's relics from one site to another.

Above all, Brother Thomas sought to make his work accessible: "we have taken care to divide into seven small sections the quantity of our little book, small though it is, so that by taking breath at intervals the pious devotion of the reader may never stop running breathlessly through each section more than the previous one."[141] He was well aware that "too much prolixity most often vexes the good will of readers."[142] It was for just that reason that Hermann, the author of St. Edmund's miracles, and Goscelin, the author of the *Life of Saint Augustine,* each composed two versions of their miracles, a longer one for monks and a shorter one for the general public.[143] No shorter work about William ever appeared or was attempted; the monk's composition was intended for the edification of his fellow monks and not for an extensive lay audience. Accessible or not, only a few copies of the *Life* are known to have been made (one for Norwich, one for Sibton, and probably one for Bury). No will mentions bequests to an altar in his honor. He appears on no calendars outside the priory. No other saint's *Life* echoes his miracles, no one recalls anything about his existence. His relics (such as his shoes, clothing, and teeth) appear in the inventory of only a few other monastic relic collections, indicating that their distribution was limited.[144] No one else mentions miracles of St. William or cites them in the twelfth century, so one must approach Brother Thomas's enthusiastic claims judiciously if not skeptically: "the fame of the holy martyr was spread far and wide, and it became manifest to all in what mighty merit and virtue was his standing with God, no small crowd of sick people began to frequent the glorious St. William's tomb. More and more came ... a great multitude. ... ."[145] Brother Thomas nonetheless also reports that many of the beneficiaries only learned of William when they came to the shrine to report miracles, indicating that perhaps Wicman, the monk who heard confessions, may have introduced them to William's cult at that time.

William's veneration was therefore a product of local monastic interests, family maneuvering, and spiritual activity typical of mid-twelfth-century England. It was not particularly innovative, nor focused on social, economic, or religious competition between Christians and Jews. It did not culminate in religious riots, social upheaval, expulsions, or marked religious enthusiasm. There is no evidence of the religious fervor that was alleged to have engulfed Norwich at the time of William's death.[146]

St. William never had a significant reputation even within East Anglia, never became as important a saint as the monks and bishop had hoped, and never brought great riches to the cathedral. The motivation to promote him did not come from a single individual, nor was it a spontaneous outpouring of Christian fear of Jews. Many of the adherents of William's cult can be clearly located within that circle of overlapping interests and families already encountered in relation to the bishop and knight. William was never an important local or regional saint, but rather a representative of the extended interests of the bishop and of Norwich Cathedral Priory.

Some scholars have stressed the "popular" and "lay" origins of William's veneration, and suggest that the cult spread throughout East Anglia.[147] The cult of William attracted a small and focused community of believers with no obvious connection to the Jewish-Christian debate. These men, women, and children were not filled with doubt about the Eucharist but were conventional, orthodox believers, devout and impressionable. It was not the educated monks of the priory, as many seem to assume, who had misgivings about William's sanctity, and therefore about the charge of ritual murder, but the lay populace of Norwich and its surrounding area.

In his role as patron saint, William served the purposes of Norwich Cathedral Priory in its rivalry with Bury, through its cures of local tradespeople, and in its relations with secular society. Despite the claims of some historians, William was not a pilgrimage saint, nor was he a significant economic asset to the priory, or a focus of demonic outbursts against local Jews. It was abroad, not at home, that his story was to have its greatest and longest impact.

FIGURE II.1. Graffiti from Norwich Cathedral.

PART II *The Earl, the Count, the Abbot, and the King*

Far from spreading quickly, evenly, and widely in continuous waves, the accusation of ritual murder arose only intermittently in northern Europe in the next generation. When it did, the tellers repeated the basic plot from Brother Thomas of Monmouth's *Life and Passion of William of Norwich*, but with variations for their own, rather different, purposes. We will analyze these adaptations in the cases of four children regarded as martyrs: Harold of Gloucester, the unnamed child of Blois, Robert of Bury, and Richard of Pontoise. The charge resurfaced first around 1168 in Gloucester, on the other side of the country from Norwich and close to the Welsh border. It was leveled around 1170 in northern France, in 1171 at Blois, on the lower Loire River, and in 1181 at Bury St. Edmunds in Suffolk, as well as in Paris. Thereafter, another decade passed before the ritual charge was deployed again. No specific modes of transmission from Norwich to these other towns have been identified thus far; it is simply assumed that accusations of this type against Jews were quickly and widely shared and then imitated.

Because of a paucity of evidence, little attention has been given to the dissemination of the ritual murder charge and the "copycat cults" it engendered. The contemporary evidence that survives consists of a few lines of text for the events in Gloucester, a mere few pages for the events in Blois, and a single phrase for the events in Bury

St. Edmunds. Arguments based on such scant evidence must necessarily be suggestive rather than conclusive. For that reason, some ignore the evidence altogether. The issue of transmission is critical, however. Once again, the protagonists are typical characters from the period, people who appear in chronicles and charters, whose family trees are well recorded, who endow churches and fight in famous battles. With these later cases we move up the social ladder—from an impoverished earl to a struggling count, an ambitious abbot, and a resourceful king.

It soon becomes clear that the claim crafted by a bishop at a London homicide trial—to get the guilty man off the hook—had uses far beyond the courtroom and the cloister. In the ritual murder charge, the earl, the count, the abbot, and the king found a means to achieve their political goals. In each case a powerful lord used the charge to divide what seems to have been a relatively harmonious society of Christians and Jews in order to secure particular benefits. Each case was different, and none seems to have been motivated primarily by fear of Jewish aggression against Christians, or by a desire to find a pilgrimage saint who would bring penitents to a shrine, which is the reason most often adduced to explain the spread of Brother Thomas's story.[1]

In Gloucester, the murder accusation threatened new immigrants who were trying to find their place in a rapidly growing frontier society. Eager to avoid any taint of disloyalty, Jews moved expeditiously to accommodate the local lords (both religious and lay) by lending money to the earl and his followers for what appeared to be a foolhardy enterprise. As a result, they risked fines from the king and default from the borrowers. Once accused of ritual murder, and facing harsh and terrifying condemnation from their neighbors, some moved to establish a new community down the river Severn.

In Blois, central France, the count Thibaut V used the prosecution of his Jews to assert his independence from the king of France, who had otherwise successfully dominated the aristocracy, encroaching on the traditional powers of his nobles and turning a group of near-equals into resentful subordinates. Lacking the spiritual and economic resources of the French king, the count made use of legal powers he had at hand, manipulating political, sexual, and religious symbols to his advantage. The burning of more than thirty Jews of Blois should be seen as the count's attempt to lay claim to regal prerogatives. Appropriating elements of the Norwich story for his own purposes, the count enriched his coffers, raised his political stature, and reinforced his religious standing.

At Bury St. Edmunds, a monastic official who aspired to be abbot relied on the charge of ritual murder to build an infant martyr cult to compete with that of Norwich. He manipulated the accusation against Jews to provoke a dispute among the monks at the famous abbey, who were deeply divided over how to treat local Jews. The strategy succeeded. The resulting division swept him into elected office. Relying on financial maneuvering to garner institutional support in the wake of the accusation, the abbot then proceeded to use the expulsion of the Jews as a banner under which to promote and reinforce his abbey's independence from both the bishop and—more significantly—from the crown.

In Paris, the king of France, Philip II Augustus, used a revived charge of ritual murder to justify the expulsion of the Jews from the royal domain. He did so to unify and cleanse the city where he established his capital, as well as to eliminate conflicting and overlapping jurisdictions. He expropriated the extensive property of the Jews and used their funds to build a shrine to the alleged child victim. The king refurbished the parts of the city where Jews had lived so that he might profit from a growing commercial base, and he placed the merchant quarter under his dominion and protection. Shortly afterward, he expanded the city walls to include these new areas.

In each case, the charge against the Jews appeared to depart from conventional religious teaching, which had long argued for their protection in Christian society. But the original story of William of Norwich was not inherently improbable to Christians. It was supported by belief in the martyrdom of the Holy Innocents, whose cult expanded rapidly in the twelfth century. The cult of the Innocents had scriptural authority and the weight of centuries of veneration behind it, but it took on new meaning in a society where infancy—of Christ, John the Baptist, the Virgin Mary, St. Edmund, and other holy figures—was of significant concern to the general public. As important as was the focus on the perpetrators of evil deeds, attention was given equally to the victimized infant(s) and to their suffering mothers. These inconsolable mourners include Rachel of the Hebrew Bible, the mothers of Bethlehem at the time of Herod, Mary the mother of the infant Jesus, the *mater dolorosa* at the Crucifixion, and the image of the Church herself. In biblical exegesis these mothers were conflated, and contemporary medieval mothers were encouraged to identify with them. This framework of interpretation through which the purported martyrs of the twelfth century were viewed explains many elements of what was to become a pernicious master narrative of alleged Jewish atrocity.

As in Norwich decades earlier, devotional custom and local political and economic conditions combined to produce persuasive and useful stories. The more such accounts were repeated and the more reputable the people who invoked them, the more credible they became. By the time of the Third Crusade (1189–1192), accounts that had been considered unbelievable at the time of the Second Crusade were widely accepted. The stories of the earl, the count, the abbot, and the king illustrate how the story imagined by a bishop in a London murder trial came to be regarded as "truth"—how fiction became "fact."

FIGURE 5.1. Sheriff William de Chesney and Earl Richard de Clare (Strongbow), both deeply in debt, accompanied Matilda, the daughter of King Henry II, to her wedding to Henry the Lion in 1168 in Germany, depicted above, shortly before the blood libel was revived in England. Detail from the Gospels of Henry the Lion, Wolfenbüttel, Herzog August Bibliothek, Codex Guelf. 105 Noviss. 2°, f. 171v.

CHAPTER 5   *Gloucester*

In March 1168, fishermen pulled a body from the river Severn near St. Peter's Abbey, Gloucester. After an examination by some monks and others, the body was laid in state in the abbey church (now Gloucester Cathedral) with the claim that the victim, whose name was found to be Harold, had been killed by Jews. From the appearance of his wounds, it was concluded that Harold had been roasted and burned like an animal on a spit. The evidence of the injured corpse was deemed sufficient to charge the Jewish community with the killing. One paragraph explaining as much was recorded in a late-medieval history of St. Peter's, but nothing further is known of the charge or its outcome.[1] No other evidence, religious or secular, suggests that either Harold of Gloucester or his story was of any significant concern.[2]

Gloucester had suffered greatly as a result of the civil war between Stephen and Matilda and thereafter from the royal exactions that came with the restoration of peace and political stability. St. Peter's, in particular, had been hard hit. One of the leading Benedictine houses in Britain earlier in the century, the abbey had lost valuable landholdings, sold off precious art treasures, and was desperate enough to forge documents in an effort to recoup its losses. The preeminent lord in the neighborhood, Richard de Clare, was also urgently searching for funds to support his military adventures.

Gloucester sits at the lowest crossing point on the river Severn between South Wales and England; its strategic position at the time made it of critical interest to the kings of England.[3] The growing iron industry in Gloucestershire supplied armaments for forays into Wales and Ireland. The Gloucester mint was once the most important in England, and the royal castle there, rebuilt early in the century, was regularly maintained by Norman kings and was entrusted to hereditary castellans and sheriffs. Religious observance in Gloucester was reflected in its large number of churches.[4] As in Norwich, the accusation of ritual murder did not therefore spring up in some backwater, spurred on by uncontrolled mob violence among uneducated lower classes, but in a strategically and economically important center, under close scrutiny of the authorities. Gloucester was the gateway to Wales, an area the Normans had attempted to subdue since William's conquest of England by establishing "marcher lordships" on the Welsh-English border that gave extensive powers to the Norman lords, independent of the crown's legal control. The Clare family, leaders of the Norman advance on Wales throughout the twelfth century, were leaders of East Anglia as well, and as a result there were close relations between the two areas.[5] Like Norwich, Gloucester was booming, although it faced competition from Bristol, which was closer to the sea at the mouth of the Severn.

News of the accusation made in Norwich somehow reached Gloucester, although no plausible mode of transmission has been suggested.[6] St. Peter's was well placed to learn directly of events in Norwich, for it had a significant presence in Norwich—the monks owned a church, a market, and land in and around the city.[7] They also had received numerous small grants in East Anglia.[8] In addition, there were family, personal, and institutional connections between monks at Gloucester and influential individuals in Norwich. Gilbert Foliot, an abbot of St. Peter's (1139–1148), was a relative of John de Chesney and his brother William, as noted earlier, the successive sheriffs of Norfolk and among King Stephen's most loyal supporters, along with the Warennes. The Chesney family looked repeatedly to Gloucester as an easily exploitable source of funds in this period. William de Chesney, for example, the sheriff's Oxfordshire cousin, famously extorted money from his nephew Gilbert Foliot when he was abbot, and eagerly sought more.[9] Gloucester was especially vulnerable to such demands. In the 1140s the district suffered directly and indirectly; well into the 1160s, St. Peter's, like other houses, was trying to recoup losses it had endured during the civil war. As Stephen's stronghold and a significant source of his wealth, Norwich was better able to protect itself.[10] Gloucestershire, the base of Matilda, witnessed some of the worst fighting of the war, and St. Peter's paid the penalty.[11]

The difficult times St. Peter's faced, and the response of its monks, are revealed by a close scrutiny of later documents. The monks took steps to stake their claims to property of considerable worth. When they failed to find the necessary documentation, they acquired forged charters, more than twelve in all, giving them rights they believed they possessed.[12] The existence of these forgeries suggests that most of the disruption in St. Peter's holdings occurred during the civil war. Even after the war ended, however, man-made disasters continued to afflict the abbey. Sometime between 1163 and 1179, one of the western towers of the abbey collapsed (probably from poorly built foundations).[13] Rebuilding the edifice must have cost a significant sum.

There are indications that the abbey had to divest itself of valuable treasure and land in order to pay its bills. Gloucester's specially commissioned pair of silver altar candlesticks, of which only one survives, a masterpiece of Anglo-Norman metalwork, was probably sold around this time.[14] The abbey also surrendered one of its manuscripts to its daughter house of St. Guthlac, Hereford, possibly for a fee as well.[15] Still in need of funds, the abbot and monks borrowed £80 from a Christian moneylender, Robert fitzHarding in 1146, handing over for security the manor of Tregoff, their land at Penhow, and the church of Lancarvan.[16] It seems that they were unable to meet the original terms of the loan, according to which they were required to pay back the debt within five years, for fitzHarding acquired, at least temporarily, the Glamorgan properties belonging to St. Peter's.[17]

Not all of Gloucester's problems can be attributed to warfare and the disruption of civil society. Henry II took credit for re-establishing the rule of law and pressed the town and abbey for funds when he came to the throne in 1154—even more than his warring predecessors. St. Peter's abbey became a tenant-in-chief, holding its land directly from the crown, a status that initially gave it privileges but also imposed increased obligations.[18] Monasteries vigorously protested the obligations—most famously Bishop Herbert of Norwich to Henry I—but to no avail.

Coming on top of the ravages of the civil war, the new royal exactions left the town and abbey in urgent need of cash. The accusation of ritual murder against the Jews followed closely on the tax payment to the king of 1166 (*scutage*), which had followed on the arbitrary tax (*tallage*) levied on Jews and towns to pay for the king's expedition against Toulouse in 1159.[19] The people of Gloucester were also expected to pay another tax (*donum*). Moreover, in 1168, on the marriage of his eldest daughter, Henry II demanded a payment (*aid*) from his tenants-in-chief. In 1168 as well, the Jews were forced to make an additional payment (*tallage*) of 5,000 marks, somehow connected to negotiations with the German emperor Frederick; and on top of that, some rich Jews were expected to pay additional sums.[20]

The citizens and monks, knights and Jews of Gloucester were also pressured to finance the extravagance of local lords. In 1168 that meant the ambition of the earl Richard (fitzGilbert) de Clare to carve a foothold for himself in Ireland.[21] Richard, known to later admirers as "Strongbow," responded to the invitation of the king of Leinster, Dermot Macmurrough (*Diarmait mac Murchadha*), who had been banished from Ireland. Dermot promised Richard the hand of his daughter Eva (*Aiofe*) in marriage and offered to make him his heir if Clare would help him recover his kingdom.[22]

By 1167, when King Dermot came recruiting soldiers in Wales, Richard de Clare was not only penniless but already deeply in debt. William of Newburgh, the twelfth-century historian of English affairs, makes it clear that Strongbow embraced the Irish adventure to escape his loans.[23] The Norman-Welsh writer Gerald of Wales, closely connected with the expedition and eager to report favorably, described Strongbow with rhetorical flourish as one who "up to this time had a great name rather than great prospects, ancestral prestige rather than ability, and had succeeded to a name rather than to possessions."[24] In other words, "his pedigree was longer than his purse."[25] Strongbow's comrades were as bankrupt as he: the chroniclers relate that the leaders of both advance parties had equally poor prospects. Raymond le Gros, Strongbow's future brother-in-law, went to Ireland in 1168 and was obviously living hand to mouth; Strongbow's uncle, Hervey de Montmorency, who went in 1169, was, "another fugitive from Fortune, unarmed and destitute."[26]

The success of the Irish expedition has been attributed to dumb luck and superior military expertise, but historians tend to overlook how critical adequate capital was to Strongbow's venture.[27] The key to Strongbow's victory was not so much the skill and passion of his small band of Norman-Welsh and East Anglian vassals as the payments (*stipendia*) that supported his mercenary troops, which numbered in the thousands.[28] In 1173, when it looked as if the money would run out, Strongbow's warriors threatened to quit and join the other side.[29] While documentation is scarce, circumstantial evidence suggests that Richard de Clare turned to Jews in order to raise the necessary funds to mount his expedition.

It took two full years for Strongbow to collect the necessary men and arms to undertake the expedition, probably because few others shared his optimistic evaluation of the situation and the likelihood of success. Fellow adventurers needed to be persuaded that he had a chance—something the astute Henry II clearly doubted in 1168. This was a sorry band of desperate men, especially after Henry withdrew his permission for them to leave. What might have persuaded potential lenders to advance money to an impoverished knight heading off with the explicit disapproval of his king? The loans to Strongbow have never been related to the ritual murder accusation in Gloucester. Yet the charge of religious homicide and the implied threat to promote a cult would have been a strong incentive to compel Jews to underwrite a high-risk expedition. English Jewish lenders knew the risks of doing business with members of the Clare family. In 1130, another Richard fitzGilbert de Clare (Strongbow's uncle, d. 1136) owed the king 200 marks of silver for the crown's help in paying off his debt to Jews. Three Jews, in turn, offered six marks of gold to the king for further help in recouping their loans to Richard, all of which seems related not to aristocratic consumption but to the costs of subduing Wales.[30]

As demonstrated in the case of the Second Crusade, the financing of military expeditions and the funding of knights were complex processes in which religious institutions were intimately involved. St. Peter's was likely the first place Richard de Clare would have looked for help. If the abbey could not accommodate the earl directly, the monks and abbot may well have tried to help structure his debts to other lenders, just as the abbey of St. Benet of Holme, Suffolk, did for Philip Basset twenty years earlier and Tewkesbury Abbey did almost a century later for another Richard de Clare. Because "Strongbow" had no collateral, St. Peter's may have stood surety for his loans from the Jews of Gloucester, just as the prior of the Benedictine priory of Hatfield Peverel, Essex, did for someone who borrowed from the Jews of Norwich.[31] The Gloucester charters record some extremely complicated financial transactions, which would have been typical of the abbey's involvement as a source of local finance.

Although he was eventually successful, Richard fitzGilbert was a terrible credit risk. The Welsh resurgence from the 1130s through the 1160s had gradually chipped away at the once vast Clare holdings.[32] Without the threat of a ritual murder charge, therefore, it is difficult to understand what would have motivated anyone to lend to a man out of favor with his king, already bankrupt, and with no apparent prospects. Without Jewish financing, one Jewish historian claimed, "Strongbow would have found it extremely difficult, if it had been at all possible, to translate his ambition into action."[33] This Jewish support is mentioned only in histories of

Jews in England; it is not addressed in general histories of Ireland or Angevin England.[34]

English magnates and rulers knew all too well how to extract money and loans from Jews. During the civil war Empress Matilda demanded money from the Jews of Oxford. On reclaiming the town, Stephen threatened to torch Jewish homes in Oxford (and in 1141 actually did burn at least one, perhaps with its inhabitants inside) in order to raise more than three times as much as she had claimed.[35] In 1210, when King John levied another tax (*tallage*) on the Jews for his Irish campaign, Abraham the merchant refused to contribute. He was imprisoned in Bristol Castle, where his teeth were extracted, one each day, to induce him to change his mind. Abraham relented when he had lost eight teeth and parted with the enormous sum of 10,000 marks.[36]

This is the immediate historical context in which one should place the exhibition of the body pulled from the river in Gloucester. The primary motive for identifying Harold as a victim of calculated homicide, rather than of accidental drowning, was to exert pressure on potential Jewish lenders who had been settled there for little more than a decade. The Gloucester community was one of the most recent and smallest of the Jewish settlements in England and therefore more easily subject to intimidation and extortion.[37]

William of Newburgh and Gerald of Wales report that fitzGilbert had used up the limits of his credit. He had been compelled to approach Christian lenders, such as fitzHarding of Bristol, to offer good security, and to seek out a number of Jewish lenders as well, both close to home and further afield. The Christian lender seems to have driven a much harder bargain, for he won lands from the insolvent earl, while some of the Jews who are recorded as having lent money to the earl were never repaid.[38] Strongbow borrowed money from the Jew Josce of Gloucester, who was fined 100 shillings for lending "to those who went to Ireland against the king's prohibition."[39] He also borrowed from Aaron of Lincoln, the richest Jew in England, who had helped to finance the building of

St. Albans Abbey, Lincoln Minster, Peterborough Cathedral, at least nine Cistercian abbeys, and St. Peter's of Gloucester.[40] After his death in 1186, Aaron's outstanding loans escheated to the king; in 1191 fitzGilbert, identified as the "earl of Striguil" [Chepstow], still owed 80 marks, which were never repaid.[41] The debts of St. Peter's were paid off only in 1195. Richard fitzGilbert may have borrowed also from Moses of Gloucester, identified as the third-richest Jew in twelfth-century England, for in 1192 Moses's sons Abraham and Samuel paid 300 marks to the crown for the debts of their father. It is not unreasonable to propose that Strongbow may also have approached the second-wealthiest Jew in England, Jurnet of Norwich, who made loans in his native East Anglia; very few of Jurnet's loans are documented in surviving records, unlike those of others, such as Aaron.

Strongbow had the opportunity to learn about dealings with Jews from fellows he knew from East Anglia, men with firsthand knowledge of the situation in Norwich who were also pressed financially. In late 1167, immediately before his departure for Ireland, he joined the English contingent that accompanied Matilda, the eldest daughter of Henry II, for her marriage to Henry the Lion, duke of Saxony. Until that time, fitzGilbert had not received any signs of favor from Henry following his accession. He is not recorded in the royal presence during those fourteen years, nor was he, as son of the earl of Pembroke, accorded the hereditary title of earl (*comes*).[42] Indeed, fitzGilbert's inclusion on this embassy to Saxony is striking because of the low esteem in which he was held by Henry II (for reasons that are unclear). The privilege and signal honor of accompanying the princess may have come at fitzGilbert's request, for it entitled him to postpone repaying any debts while on royal business.[43] The party probably left England in September 1167.[44] Henry II likely acquiesced because he was eager to draw parallels and associate his reign with that of his grandfather by reviving some earlier traditions: Richard de Clare's great-uncle Roger de Clare had accompanied Matilda, the daughter of Henry I, to Germany for her marriage in 1110.[45]

The wedding of the younger Matilda took place in February 1168, with two English earls and many lords in attendance.[46] Sheriff William de Chesney, a Suffolk tenant of Clare, accompanied Strongbow to Germany, along with Reginald de Warenne, brother of the late Earl William, during which time the former sheriff was relieved from paying his debts to Jews.[47] Since Chesney received a royal reprieve from his Jewish creditors, it is likely that Strongbow did as well, and that may have been his motivation for going to Saxony. Deeply in debt by the time he was relieved of office in 1163, William de Chesney never managed to pay off his Jewish creditors.[48] After his death (by 1174), the debts were passed on to the next generation until they were canceled by royal fiat of King John in 1214.[49] Richard de Clare's Jewish debts were likewise kept on the royal books for decades and were passed down to the next generation until 1202, when King John canceled them.[50]

Had he not heard of it earlier, fitzGilbert could have learned of the accusation laid against the Jews of Norwich while traveling on royal business in the winter of 1167–1168. This leading noble of Gloucester and Suffolk, who had a vital interest in bringing pressure to bear on the Jews of that town, spent long hours in the company of William de Chesney and Reginald de Warenne, two men who played a role in the Norwich narrative of ritual murder and were motivated to endorse it; as noted, Reginald de Warenne's daughter had already benefited from a cure of St. William. Like Chesney and Warenne, the Clare family was predisposed to hear such charges. Richard's relatives were crusaders: his uncle Walter fitzGilbert de Clare took the cross for the Second Crusade with William de Warenne and other knights from East Anglia.[51] As noted above, another uncle, Richard fitzGilbert, appears in the 1130 pipe roll receiving the king's help for debts to Jews.[52] A cousin, Richard de Clare, died in 1190 on the Third Crusade, immediately on his arrival in the Holy Land. Into the thirteenth century, Jewish lenders considered the Clare family to be a grave credit risk: Richard, the earl of Gloucester and Hereford, the father of another Gilbert de Clare, was so untrustworthy that he could borrow money from Jews to venture on crusade in 1249 only with the help of the monks of Tewskbury.[53]

The problem of how to deal with crippling debts to Jews was likely to have been discussed by the knights and earls from East Anglia on the marriage trip to Germany. Immediately on their return, when they had to face their Jewish creditors, the story of Jewish ritual murder was suddenly revived. Such a sharing of information would explain the appearance in Gloucester of an accusation once fiercely contested but by then long forgotten in Norwich. The apparent lack of credibility of such a charge at this time would also explain why similar stories did not surface elsewhere in the British Isles. There is no evidence that anyone outside Norwich paid much attention to William between 1154 and 1168.

Neither is there evidence that anyone cared about the boy martyr of Gloucester. No contemporary chronicle outside Gloucester mentions Harold, and no artwork recalls his memory (the claim that a single image from the fourteenth century refers to Harold is based on a misreading).[54] Despite assertions to the contrary, no shrine was built and no saint was venerated. The story of Harold of Gloucester did not engage or enrage the Christian devout or inspire a holy cult or attacks on Jews. No blood was shed. There was no trial, no pogrom, apparently no mass conversion. Unlike William of Norwich, Harold of Gloucester played no role in the religious life of the county, either at the time of his death or centuries later.

Although clearly in the mold of Norwich, the events at Gloucester differed in important details. Both deaths allegedly occurred around Easter time, which coincided with the Jewish Passover. The Jews of Norwich came together to celebrate the *seder*; the Jews of Gloucester had the added festivities surrounding the birth of a Jewish boy, perhaps one of the first in the family to be born on English soil. Many Christians were afraid of Jewish groups, and sometimes suspected that some conspiracy was afoot when they observed Jews congregating in public. Brother Thomas's *Life*, as we have seen, included the story of an annual convention in Narbonne; events in Gloucester featured the celebration of a ritual circumcision (*brit milah*), perhaps even the special formalities for a firstborn son (*pidyon ha-ben*); the later ritual murder account of Hugh of Lincoln featured a wedding.

Knowledge of the accusation of ritual murder would come to make Jewish celebrations suspect. Later in the Middle Ages, the spread of stories on the theme of Jewish conspiracy was the apparent cause for Jews to include a ritual opening of the door in the middle of the *seder* celebrations. This practice survives in the Passover Haggadah as a ritual performed by children to welcome the prophet Elijah. The practice of opening doors is not documented before the end of the Middle Ages, but Brother Thomas apparently knew something of it.[55] He writes that the Christian maid reported that in the evening during the week of Passover, "the Jews threw open their doors, and free entrance was granted to any that came."[56]

Water is an important element in the Gloucester accusation: the victim was found floating in the river. To judge from later medieval legal and religious records, a number of children were discovered dead in wells and rivers. Often one hears of such children, who survived parental neglect only to be rescued by some saint. Many other children fell or were hurled into fishponds, rivers, and wells, in some cases by family members or other adults.[57] It is evident from miraculous stories of children's rescues that medieval families faced a hazardous world: children fell into wells, ponds, and buckets, and drowning is the accident most often noted by papal notaries.[58] The case of the ritual murder accusation at Blois in 1171 may also have been a drowning (Jews were accosted at the riverbank), as was that of Robert of Bury (the only known depiction of Robert shows him being cast into a well). Hugh of Lincoln was also said to have been found in a well.[59] The celebrated cases of the little girl of Valréas in the thirteenth century and Simon of Trent in the fifteenth century also concerned children found drowned.[60]

Childhood drownings were so common in the Middle Ages that the mere appearance of a drowned corpse should not attract undue attention from modern historians (whether in Gloucester, Bury, or Lincoln). Most often the explanation was mundane: accidental death. In rare cases, local pressures and circumstances, combined with the Anglo-Saxon tradition of honoring sudden and unexplained violent death, were sufficient to suggest that Jews were guilty. In Gloucester, as in Norwich, motives of this type provided a catalyst for the spread of the story.

Gloucester may have needed a saint, but there is no indication that Harold fulfilled its needs. He failed to perform miracles, inspire liturgical commemoration, or solidify Gloucester's corporate identity. The fact that he is not mentioned anywhere else in Gloucestershire—and does not appear ever to have had an altar or light in the cathedral, much less a shrine or chapel—suggests that he was essentially irrelevant to the devotional life of Gloucester's citizens, and that we should look elsewhere to understand his appearance. Harold's story did not inspire religious devotion.

But it did provide Richard fitzGilbert with the wherewithal to depart for Ireland. On the return of the indebted barons from the wedding of Matilda to Henry the Lion, the authorities immediately took action. At the same time as Harold was mourned as a martyr in Gloucester in the spring of 1168, the story of William of Norwich was revived back at his home on the other side of the country. Soon after Harold's body was fished from the river, the bishop of Norwich dedicated a new chapel to St. William at the site where his body had been discovered. This chapel long retained the euphonious tag of St.-William-in-the-Wood. Although the building was probably destroyed during the Reformation, the chapel appears on nineteenth-century maps, and its foundations could still be traced in the early twentieth century on Mousehold Heath. It must have been substantial: the walls were reputed to have been more than two and a half feet thick.[61] Today it is marked only by some stones at the edge of a soccer field, the overgrown site protected by the Ancient Monuments Act, first enacted by Parliament in 1882.

The Norwich building dedication of 1168 inspired a mere three miracles. For three years following, there is no indication that William performed any more. Rather than commemorating a budding cult, the resurgence of 1168 appears to have been inconsequential. The Norwich dedication may have been prompted by motives similar to those proposed for Gloucester—to persuade a major Jewish lender to accommodate the Clares. The altar display of the dead child, allegedly martyred by Jews, appears to have been a successful device to extract funds. In the wake of the accusations made in Gloucester and revived in Norwich, fitzGilbert received his money, recruited his troops, and secured the numerous ships to transport them as he headed for the shores of Ireland, fully equipped with the means necessary to conquer. After sending out some advance parties, he landed in August with an army of more than a thousand and proved successful. Later that month fitzGilbert obtained his prizes; he married Eva, gained lands in Leinster, and claimed the title of king.

None of the many books that treat the English advance into Wales and Ireland in the twelfth century discusses the delicate issue of financing thousands of soldiers to fight across the sea under the leadership of a dispossessed earl out of favor with his king. Yet the role played by Jewish lenders in Gloucester and East Anglia and the pressures that could be brought upon them to contribute to the enterprise were significant. Initially, even with the blessing of Henry II, King Dermot of Leinster could find no English soldiers willing to help him reclaim his throne; yet he had no trouble three years later. It is far more likely that lack of funding was the critical impediment, not that it was necessary to wait two years for the king's approval.[62]

Strongbow's striking and unanticipated success in Ireland brought King Henry of England up short. It led him to appreciate once again the financial power of the Jews of his kingdom and reinforced his insistence that they should come under his direct control. It is said that in anger at the role of Jewish finance in the invasion of Ireland, Henry demanded further extensive fines from English Jews.[63] Fearful that his underling was about to create a rival state, Henry arrived a scant year later to claim the conquest of Ireland for himself and to require the earl to acknowledge his overlordship.[64] Strongbow deferred to Henry, and Ireland then became subject to the English crown, ostensibly by grant of the pope, a result that was to be long contested.

The accusation of ritual murder against the Jews in twelfth-century Gloucester appears to have been a calculated effort to affect financial affairs. During this period, the blood libel was a tool for extortion, used by those familiar with Jews and Jewish money-lending practices. The charge of religiously motivated homicide does not appear to have been exercised on the spur of the moment or in the heat of religious frenzy; it was raised in relation to immediate political and economic circumstances. The accusation appears to have been remarkably effective in achieving its immediate purpose.

Although Harold did not inaugurate a viable cult of relics, the abbey in which his body was displayed may have been instrumental in the later dissemination of the ritual murder narrative in the context of devotion to the Virgin Mary and stories about her saving grace in the face of Jewish doubt. St. Peter's adopted new celebrations of Mary at an early date.[65] Shortly after Anselm of Bury circulated his legends of Mary, Dominic, prior of Evesham near Gloucester, borrowed at least one story and published an analogous collection in the 1120s.[66] The collections of Anselm and Dominic were soon combined by William of Malmesbury. These early collections of Marian miracles suggest patterns of circulation for new forms of religious lore. St. Peter's was closely allied with Pershore and Malmesbury, which were points of transmission for these new stories.[67] One of the earliest Marian miracle collections to include a version of the story of Jewish murder, the singing clergeon that features in Chaucer's Prioress's Tale, appears to have originated at the abbey of Llanthony Secunda, in the Gloucester area not far from St. Peter's, possibly as early as the twelfth century.[68] As recent studies have stressed, Marian miracles and characterizations of Jewish evil were developed in tandem during this period.[69]

The display of Harold's body in Gloucester and the attack on Ireland had effects both national and local. They led to Henry II's direct involvement in the settlement of Ireland—sometimes described as England's first colonial project—which he had previously rejected. They led also to the creation of the Jewish community of Bristol, where it appears that some Jews settled in the wake of the ritual murder charges. There was always a close connection between the Jews of Gloucester and Bristol, just thirty miles downriver. Throughout the Middle Ages, Jews from either town moved back and forth—voluntarily or not—up and down the river Severn, and they are identified with one city or the other at different times, and sometimes with both.[70] Yet there were significant differences between the two Jewish communities.

The settlement of Jews in Bristol was an anomaly in many ways.[71] It was, for example, a port town, during a period when Jews rarely, if ever, settled in English ports.[72] It was also the only significant English Jewish settlement that was not a county town, the seat of a sheriff, where Jews felt they would have better protection. Finally, in contrast to those in Canterbury, York, Lincoln, Cambridge, Norwich, and London, the Jews of Bristol had no stone houses. All of this suggests that Bristol may have begun as a temporary community, established by Jews who relocated from nearby Gloucester. As Brother Thomas claimed, "for some of them, unable to sustain the growing infamy of such a crime, were scattered to other regions and, as rumor has it, perished by a fitting revenge."[73] While such may not have been the case for the Jews of Norwich, it does seem to have been for the Jews of Gloucester, whose community in 1168 may have consisted of only a few families, later expanded by the opportunities of trade with Ireland.

Although Bristol does not appear in the 1159 *donum* tax list of Jewish communities, by the time of the Northampton *donum* of 1194 it figured prominently in the list, indicating the town's rapid expansion. Contrary to the suppositions of some earlier authors, there is no source that mentions Jews in Bristol before 1168: the so-called House of Converts (*domus conversorum*), for Jews who needed support after their conversion to Christianity, alleged to have been established in Bristol before 1147, never existed.[74] Jacob's Well, located on the outskirts of the city and at first thought to be a *mikveh* of the mid-twelfth century for Jewish ritual purification of many kinds, has been determined on further study to be a well associated with washing the dead that came into Jewish use only in the thirteenth century.[75] There is no evidence of Jewish trade between Bristol and Ireland before 1170.[76] The first recorded Jew of Bristol was Moses of Gloucester, the son of Rabbi Isaac, an immigrant from Mainz who came from a distinguished Rhenish family.[77] All that is known about Moses's time in Bristol is that he was there before 1170—exactly how long is uncertain—and that his family did not stay long before moving to Oxford. In Oxford, R. Moses's wife and sons took over the business, perhaps because he was already old and infirm.[78]

Bristol would have its own story of ritual murder, modeled on those told previously in Norwich and Gloucester—but only in the following century. The account of a ritual murder alleged to have been committed there in 1183, "Adam of Bristol," was written and performed a hundred years later, shortly before the expulsion of the Jews from Britain (1290), by which time there were no longer any Jews living in Bristol. This appears to have been intended for entertainment, a parish drama performed on a summer holiday in August for the Virgin Mary.[79] In the play, which is full of local detail, Adam, the son of William the Welshman, enters the house of Samuel the Jew, where he is tortured by Samuel, his wife, and son, and is eventually crucified. Labeled a "silly story" (*fabula ineptissima*), it offers moral instruction, comic relief, and satire rather than serving any evident political or economic purpose.[80] The interest in such stories was reciprocated: the sole surviving copy of the text of "Adam of Bristol" ended up in the hands of a fifteenth-century prior of Norwich Cathedral Priory, where it features a small picture of Samuel poking Adam hanging from a cross, the earliest known depiction of an alleged Jewish child murder.[81]

FIGURE 6.1 Church of St. Nicholas of the Benedictine abbey of Saint-Lomer de Blois on the river Loire.

CHAPTER 6   *Blois*

Scholars generally assume that the ritual murder accusation diffused easily through European society, but the evidence indicates that it took two decades for the libel to spread from Norwich. When it did, however, it proliferated quickly. The watershed year was 1170. By the following spring, accusations were documented in at least four towns in northern and central France. Before that, they were scarcely known.[1] In the interim, Jewish life flourished in Norwich, enjoying a halcyon period under Henry II.[2] Indeed, throughout northern Europe, Jewish communities were thriving, growing in size and complexity, and developing spiritually and materially.[3] Instead of a steady and inevitable decline in the wake of the violence of the First and Second Crusades, stable life re-emerged, punctuated only intermittently by violent outbursts.[4] In French lands, Jewish intellectual, cultural, and economic life prospered, apparently free from threats and persecution. Jewish communities blossomed in the county of Champagne in eastern France as well in the royal domain centered on Paris, lands under the direct control of the king. Jewish communities further west in the counties of Blois (under control of the count of Blois) and Le Mans (under control of the count of Anjou) could trace their stable, continued existence back centuries.[5]

Beginning in 1170, in a period of only twelve months, ritual murder accusations erupted across northern France at Loches-sur-Indres,

Éperney, Janville, and Pontoise. Few details survive about any of the charges except for that of Blois, where, at the behest of the count of Blois, more than thirty Jews were burned publicly. The communal response was rapid and far ranging. One wonders how and why all these northern French communities simultaneously came to accuse the Jews of child murder. One possible explanation is that the Norwich monastery made a conscious effort to publicize its story abroad. A devastating fire around this time had left the cathedral in major disrepair, and some of that burned stone is still visible today.[6] There was a pressing need to raise funds to reconstruct the fabric of the building, and Bishop William eagerly took on the job. The monks recalled him sitting outside the cathedral begging for contributions. According to the priory records, the bishop had "made a vow that he would not betake himself more than twelve leucas from his church *unless driven by necessity* [emphasis added] and he also had his Norwich church rebuilt. . . ."[7]

A fundraising tour with young William's relics would have been a conventional means of exciting interest in the new saint that Norwich Cathedral now possessed and could have served to draw visitors to support the damaged cathedral. Brother Thomas was clearly concerned with the spread of William's cult and acknowledged the importance of spreading his reputation abroad.[8] Early on he defended himself from the charge of presumption, and from critics who said William was scarcely known. He explains, "it can be said of few saints that knowledge of them is widespread in all the lands where the religion of the Christian name flourishes." A successful foreign tour would have given Brother Thomas ammunition against critics who questioned William's sanctity.

Those in charge of saints' relics were well aware of the benefits of travel and distribution of small pieces for publicity and fundraising purposes.[9] There was a long-standing custom of touring relics and reciting dramatic narratives about them to inspire and delight listeners, who would then open their pockets to offer contributions.[10] Relic tours combined entertainment, religious education, and a taste of the exotic.[11] In many cases, such as that of the trip made in the mid-twelfth century for Amiens Cathedral, relic tours followed upon fires.[12] Other tours took place at the commencement of building or rebuilding projects, such as the tour authorized through his domain by Louis VII when Senlis Cathedral was begun in 1155.[13] After a devastating fire in 1194, a successful relic tour inaugurated construction of the famous cathedral of Chartres.[14] Bishop William could have seen the results of a profitable relic tour in his own diocese when the monks of Stoke-by-Clare, Suffolk, on the recommendation of the earl, took their relics around the diocese to collect money to pay for new buildings.[15]

The usual destination of such tours was central northern France, and it is possible that Bishop William and his monks made a journey there in 1170 in pursuit of funds to rebuild Norwich Cathedral. Bishop Turbe raised money to repair the cathedral so quickly and effectively that his successor was able to cancel a tax imposed seventy-five years earlier to pay for construction. Yet the cathedral received no major donations of land or endowments at this time, suggesting that most of the benefactions were raised in cash or in kind.

A relic tour by the bishop of Norwich could also explain the sudden appearance of the charge of ritual murder on the Continent in precisely those places where Turbe would have been likely to have traveled and recounted the story of Norwich's relics.[16] If one does not consider some such form of direct transmission, another hypothesis must be found to explain why the charge of ritual murder arose so quickly in certain places and not others—for example, not in places where Jews were most densely distributed, perceived as most threatening, where Christian-Jewish tensions were of longest standing, or where clerics and theologians were most interested in questions of deicide.

Bishop William is a likely candidate to have spread news of St. William, for he was an enthusiastic traveler, as well as an avid fundraiser.[17] Among other trips to the Continent, he represented the English episcopate at the Council of Rheims in 1148, and in 1163 attended the papal Council of Tours.[18] Brother Thomas's praise of Turbe, "Rome itself has recognized your eloquence, and Gaul has discovered it, too, and the whole of England has very often also realized it," suggests that the bishop had recently delivered his sermons in France.[19] His comments argue against the notion that the long-serving bishop was too old by this date to take part in any important activities.[20]

In 1170, Bishop William needed to leave England not only to seek support for the cathedral, but also to escape the menacing attentions of Henry II. The bishop and king had long been at odds. Turbe was sympathetic to Thomas Becket, archbishop of Canterbury, and had become embroiled in the celebrated controversy between archbishop and king.[21] In 1164 at the Council of Clarendon, the bishop of Norwich was the object of royal bullying; according to at least one report, he was threatened with death.[22] In November 1169, Turbe further infuriated the king by excommunicating the Earl of Norfolk, who had sided with Henry.[23] Accordingly, crossing the Channel at this time would have been a safe alternative to staying home.[24] Late spring to summer appears to have been the usual time for relic tours, and carrying relics abroad in the spring of 1170 would have permitted Turbe to avoid one of the most important and contentious events in Henry's reign: the coronation of the king's eldest son in June, following a Capetian custom of crowning an heir during his father's lifetime.[25] Despite a papal ban, the king proceeded with the coronation in Becket's absence, calling on the Archbishop of York to perform the ceremony. When Becket returned to England in December 1170, he excommunicated those bishops who had participated in the coronation, a group that did not include the bishop of Norwich. The lack of punishment either by king or archbishop suggests that Bishop William was conveniently out of the country, and that his absence provided a plausible excuse for not taking a side on the merits of the coronation.[26]

In the spring of 1170, Turbe could have been in northern France and there related the story of William, whose sanctity he had embraced for a number of years, beginning with his defense of Simon de Novers at the murder trial in London. A relic tour introduced by visiting monks moving from town to town, headlined by an articulate bishop, communicated authority and conveyed important news. A professional organization of clerical collectors existed already by the second half of the twelfth century, indicating the institutionalization of the practice of sending relics on tour.[27] The typical routine for a relic tour (*delatio* or *circumlatio*) was to engage an influential sponsor (a king, bishop, abbot, earl) to endorse the campaign, receive permission from the necessary authorities, arrange safe conduct for the travelers, announce the trip in advance with letters to important clerics, engage a master of ceremonies (*prolocutor*), organize a welcoming reception of local notables, form a procession into town (an *adventus* perhaps with special chanting or banners), preach a sermon, hold up a reliquary box (*feretrum*), and announce special indulgences for those contributing alms. A successful itinerary was well planned and was based on clerical networks and personal connections.[28] It was customary for the owners of relics to hire a promoter who was particularly talented and experienced in warming up crowds. Such a master of ceremonies could summarize past miracles attributed to the relics or illustrate their continued efficacy with a practical demonstration of new cures.

By joining in a local procession, listening to the sermon, preparing for confession, saying prayers, seeking a cure, and making a donation, the urban residents of French towns actively endorsed the substance of an itinerant relic's history. If they had come to see the relics of William of Norwich, they would have been implicitly accepting the veracity of the accusation of ritual murder, whether or not they knew any Jews or had previously heard any inflammatory preaching on the subject.

Clerical promoters incited listeners to step up and contribute, emphasizing the dramatic elements of their stories and pointing to material objects to rouse enthusiasm. Skeptical contemporaries knew only too well, as Abbot Guibert of Nogent (d. 1124) put it in his essay on relics, that "greedy hearts of the vulgar mob can be fooled by phony deafnesses, affected madnesses, fingers cunningly bent back to the wrists, feet contorted back under buttocks." Abbot Guibert acknowledged, "I have heard these things worked out in whispers and I have witnessed ridiculous acts performed during relic tours and daily we see the very depths of some man's purse emptied by the lies of those men whom St. Jerome calls *rabulas* in mockery of their rabid eloquence."[29]

Bishop William had no need to engage an impresario. As we have seen, he was an impressive speaker and experienced legal officer devoted to his cathedral's new patron saint. Since so many of the cures attributed to young William of Norwich benefited his monks, Turbe could have brought a couple of the brothers along with him to testify to their own cures and describe those of their fellow monks. They could have held up the instruments of the alleged torture, the teazle gag that was allegedly found in the youth's mouth and preserved by his uncle, the pair of the saint's teeth squirreled away by Brother Thomas, scraps of the youth's bloody clothing, some of which were preserved at Reading, or one of his shoes that was stored at Norwich (or later, perhaps, at Wimborne).[30]

Half a century before Turbe visited the Continent on one of his documented trips, Abbot Guibert described in detail promotional techniques employed to energize the faithful and open their purses, telling of his embarrassment at one such brazen promoter whom Guibert declines to name. "After a long and exaggerated discourse on his relics, he brought forth a little reliquary and said, in my presence, 'Know that there within this little vessel is some of that very bread the Lord pressed with His own teeth; and, if you believe not, here is this great man'—this he said of me—'here is this great man to whose renown in learning ye may bear witness, and who will rise from his place, if need be, to corroborate my words.'" Abbot Guibert adds that he said nothing publicly to reprove and embarrass the speaker.

One can imagine Turbe and his monks standing outdoors, gesturing for extra effect at Jewish homes not far from the marketplaces of the towns they visited. Those who doubted the claims were unlikely to say anything, just as Guibert, doubtful of claims that the reliquary box held the very bread that the Lord chewed, did not speak up. He explained that he had been afraid to say anything for fear of being "obliged to show him up for the liar he was. But I respected their peace more than that of the speaker. What can I say?" So, too, when confronted with a determined promoter, there might have been few witnesses courageous enough to question the monk's story in the presence of the relics of William of Norwich, however much they may have doubted it.

Relic tours offered public, communal affirmation to the participants. The story of William's death at the hands of Jews would not have been a familiar legend read out in a monotone by some aged brother droning on at a sleepy Saturday lunch in the cloister's refectory, but a titillating tale of blood and horror with immediate relevance, likely to appeal to a distracted audience out on a spring day. To be successful, a relic tour had to attract people of all backgrounds and ages: canny merchants, careful artisans, shy peasants, impatient children, affectionate mothers, the irreligious who came to church only out of curiosity, and the devout who knew the liturgy by heart. The story of the death of William of Norwich would have served many audiences. It was well suited to theatrical flourishes.

Fabulous stories about Jews involving threatened innocence and bloody drama were fairly commonplace in this period. Miracle stories of all kinds surfaced, circulated, and faded to insignificance. The question, therefore, is not so much why and how the story spread, but under what circumstances it was taken seriously by the authorities who were in a position to take action, influence others, and prosecute purported evildoers. The other continental cases alleging ritual murder in 1170 were quickly quashed by the civil powers: Janville in France, under the lordship of the French king; Loches-sur-Indres in the county of Tours, under Henry II, king of England and count of

Anjou; and Épernay in the county of Champagne, under the count of Champagne.[31] In those places one hears of nothing more than that the charge was made.[32] There was apparently no investigation, no prosecution, no riot, and little lasting impact.

In Blois, however, a terrifying new pattern was established. This was no mere "incident," as historians repeatedly characterize it, one of a number of such attacks that were familiar to all the participants and of the type that occurred regularly in the fourteenth century.[33] The consequences of the accusation in Blois were new and frightening. The ritual murder accusation was given full faith and credit by Count Thibaut V of Blois, a close relative of the French king, who had many motives to do so. This was a time of economic hardship for him; he had a perceived need to express independence from an increasingly powerful and encroaching king; and he may have been inspired as well by developments in Christian spirituality that centered on the cult of relics and devotion to the Virgin.

French scholars have generally ignored the events in Blois—in part, perhaps, because most of the documents are in medieval Hebrew.[34] American scholars have tended to treat the burnings in Blois as a topic relevant solely to Jewish history.

As the Blois story is generally understood, Count Thibaut acted at the urging of his young, proud wife, Alix, the daughter of the king of France, who demanded that her husband spurn his mistress, Pulcellina, who was Jewish.[35] He did so by accusing the Jews of Blois of a child murder and condemning them to flames, apparently at the instigation of his wife, and perhaps reluctantly egged on by a crowd that was incited by the rabble-rousing preaching of some churchmen. The Blois story is usually framed in the context of a domestic spat: a jealous and humiliated young wife, a feckless count, and a spurned mistress, as if this were enough to result in the judicial condemnation and gruesome execution of more than thirty people, as well as public appeals to the king and an inversion of religious traditions. But the events at Blois are better understood in a political and economic context that relates directly to developments in the kingdom of France.[36]

Although Count Thibaut had a distinguished heritage, the ruling family of Blois was receding in importance by this date, and his
principalities were falling behind those of his neighbors. Modern
descriptions of the region and the house of Blois-Champagne focus
on its prosperous days under Thibaut IV "the Great" in the early
twelfth century, when the hereditary counts of Blois, with lands that
almost encircled the royal domain, posed a serious political threat to
the kings of France.[37] Eventually a settlement was reached, and two
of Thibaut IV's sons, Henri I "the Liberal," count of Champagne,
and Thibaut V, count of Blois-Chartres, each married a daughter
of Louis VII and his first wife, Eleanor of Aquitaine (whose marriage was annulled and who then married Henry II of England).
King Louis, in turn, took their sister Adèle as his third wife. On his
death in 1152, the lands of Thibaut the Great were divided among
his sons.[38] Henri, the eldest son, inherited the wealthy northeastern
county of Champagne, which benefited from the series of important
fairs that Thibaut the Great had established. The smaller, ancient,
hereditary lands of Blois and Chartres went to the younger son, who
became Thibaut V of Blois. A third son, Étienne (Stephen), became
count of Sancerre; a fourth son, Guillaume (William), became bishop
of Chartres and subsequently archbishop of Rheims. The assumption is that Alix and Thibaut V lived in similar cultural and financial splendor at their capital in Blois as did their siblings Marie and
Henri in Champagne.[39] Family members are often lumped together,
and the house of Blois-Champagne and its territories are treated as
a unity. But this masks striking differences between the individuals
and the lands the family ruled.[40]

Historians rarely consider the disparities between Blois-Chartres
(neighboring counties considered together in this period) and the
county of Champagne in the second half of the twelfth century
when they mention the celebrated "School of Chartres," the profitable Champagne fairs, and the count's extended family network.[41]
The two cities, Paris and Chartres, had been comparable in the
eleventh century but over the next hundred years Chartres failed

to keep pace; the School of Chartres may not even have survived past mid-century.[42] Overshadowed on either side by the towns of Tours and Orléans, which were backed by powerful kings and larger economies, Blois saw its fortunes decline rapidly. As Paris came to dwarf other cities and the Champagne fairs flourished, Blois (and to a lesser degree Chartres) gradually sank into relative obscurity. By the end of the twelfth century, Blois was small and fairly insignificant, considered a backwater. [43] It had no archives until 1196, so little is known of the county in the twelfth century.[44] Thibaut V ruled for forty years yet scarcely left an impression on his contemporaries before his death from disease on the Third Crusade.

There is much to indicate that the count of Blois and his wife had fallen on hard times. The literary and architectural works identified with Thibaut and Alix reflect the latest tastes but unrealized ambitions.[45] In contrast to the variety of texts firmly attributed to the count and countess of Champagne, for example, there are few artistic and literary commissions attributed to those of Blois.[46] Construction on the largest church in Blois, the abbey church of Saint-Lomer, a showpiece for the family, was halted in the middle of Thibaut's rule, probably for financial reasons.[47] For those projects they could afford to complete, they received little credit.[48] The intellectual reputation of Saint-Lomer also declined during the second half of the twelfth century.[49]

Rather than its generosity, the parsimony of the house of Blois was commemorated in a song intended to be performed at courts throughout Europe to raise money for the ransom of King Richard the Lionheart of England, who had been seized by Duke Leopold of Austria on his return from the Third Crusade. While writing poetry in captivity, Richard complained bitterly (both in Occitan and in French) about his predicament. In the song *Ja nus hons pris* he implied that, unlike his generous (half-)sister Marie de Champagne, his widowed (half-)sister Alix was not contributing to his ransom.[50] Queen Eleanor, the mother of Marie de Champagne, Alix de Blois, and Richard Lionheart, was the prime mover in collecting the huge ransom for her favorite child; she apparently condoned the poem criticizing her daughter's frugality, thus widely advertising the house of Blois's financial embarrassment.

There are also hints that the count and countess were making strenuous efforts to wring additional income from their existing rights and to pressure their vassals and townsmen to pay for privileges. Sometime soon after 1164, Thibaut and Alix made a promise to their burgesses not to debase the coinage, a development that suggests they had already engaged in some form of currency manipulation.[51] The importance of this promise for a stable currency made by both of them is reflected in the prominence with which it was displayed at the entrance to the city, where it was carved on a large rock at the bridge crossing the Loire.[52] The lost inscription indicates that they had instituted various new taxes, including one on cattle (the *cornagium*).[53] They were also careful to record their rights to seize featherbeds (*culcitras*) from the residents of the town of Chambord (which Thibaut surrendered, probably for a price, in 1180) and to take table linens from the inhabitants of Blois.

The role and the importance of the Jews in Blois and Chartres differed from those in the royal domain and in Champagne. As noted previously, King Louis had apparently encouraged Jewish settlement; the counts of Champagne welcomed Jews and were eager to have them attend the fairs. Jews were even more densely settled in Champagne than in the kingdom of France proper.[54] Blois and Chartres, on the other hand, had only small Jewish settlements; the community of Blois boasted scarcely more than one hundred Jews in a community of perhaps three thousand Christians.[55] The Jews of Blois appear less prominent and more vulnerable than others, a situation reflected in the political circumstances of their ruler and the declining status of their county.[56]

The weak position of the Jews and the relative impoverishment of the count and countess may help to explain the burnings in Blois as much or more than matters of domestic intrigue. Thibaut and Alix were stretched financially—buying food on credit, instituting new taxes, debasing the coinage, and surrendering future income for immediate sums. As a result, they turned their attention to the Jews, another obvious source of income. The "event" in Blois seems to have begun with the first recorded seizure (*captio*) of Jews in French territory, a practice that was to become common in the thirteenth century, when some rulers would abruptly round up all the Jews they could find and demand vast sums to release them.[57]

Thibaut was reportedly searching for an excuse to attack the Jews when a local cleric showed him the way. Ephraim of Bonn reported some of the details: "The ruler was revolving in his mind all sorts of plans to condemn the Jews, but he did not know how. He had no evidence against them until a priest appeared ... who said to the ruler 'come, I'll advise you how you can condemn them.'"[58] A circular letter from the Jewish community at Orléans explains that the servant of a nobleman who was watering his horse near the river came across a Jew carrying some hides, one of which unrolled and frightened the horses. The Christian then charged that the Jew had drowned a Christian child. This charge rested solely on the accusation of the servant, for no evidence was produced: no body ever surfaced, no missing child was ever reported, and no family mourned. The cleric suggested, therefore, that the count rely on a judgment of God as revealed by the results of an ordeal of water.[59] The ordeal was a Christian rite used to judge cases of guilt when there was no evidence, but Jews were rarely required to submit to such proof.[60] A local priest had similarly urged an ordeal of judgment in the case of William of Norwich, but under pressure from the sheriff, the bishop did not pursue it. At Blois, the cooperative witness submitted to an ordeal and unsurprisingly he was judged to be telling the truth, thereby proving the guilt of the Jews.[61]

Recognizing the danger that faced them, the Jews reacted swiftly and coordinated their activities. In the name of the highly regarded Rabbi Jacob Tam, neighboring Jewish communities sent circular letters describing the events, proposed penitential acts, and wielded what political and economic influence they could.[62] Despite the immediate and decisive action of the Jewish community at Blois and elsewhere around France, appeals to the king of France, and major bribes to interested parties and their relatives, more than thirty of the Jews of Blois were imprisoned in the dungeons of Blois fortress and shortly afterward were put to the flames in punishment for the alleged crime. Seventeen were women, some of whom were pregnant or holding their young children when they were locked in a building that was set alight. Three young Torah scholars were lashed to the stake and beaten with sticks and cudgels when they tried to escape after the fire burned the ropes binding them.

This horrendous punishment was not a result of uncontrolled passion or the frenzy of a crowd claiming popular justice when they first learned that the Jews were accused of murder. On the contrary, prior to the burnings there were a series of ongoing negotiations over the price of the prisoners' release. The Jews claimed to have had the sympathetic ear of the French king, which may have been excessively optimistic, but suggests that both sides believed that some agreement could be reached. Punishment by burning was not the anticipated result.

This outcome was sufficiently shocking and unexpected that Rabbi Tam called for a perpetual annual fast day on the twentieth of Sivan, the anniversary of the burnings. The eminent rabbi died almost immediately after, whether of old age, shock, or some combination of the two. The leaders of the Jewish community also called for penitential acts: for Jews to limit the size of wedding parties and for sumptuary laws that required women to forego wearing fancy silk cloaks and men to undertake rigorous fasts.[63] Many beautiful and heart-rending liturgical poems (*piyyutim*) survive to this day commemorating the Jewish martyrs of Blois.[64]

What happened in Blois is usually attributed to Alix's distress over her husband's relationship with Pulcellina. Whether this exacerbated the count's hard line toward the Jews is not clear, but Christians resented her and Jews themselves were not complimentary. According to Ephraim of Bonn, however, Pulcellina, "trusted in the affection of the ruler who up to now had been very attached to her."[65] It is possible that there never was a torrid affair of the type that historians have taken for granted, that the confident Pulcellina was not the count's lover but his moneylender, and that the relationship was one of loyalty and patronage.[66] Under the influence of contemporary court literature, an essentially feudal relationship was transformed into a romantic one and the haughty and proud businesswoman, described in the letter from Orléans, was subsequently transformed in later retellings into a spurned mistress and represented as a figure of Esther. The affective element has been highlighted and embraced by historians to the exclusion of both political and financial considerations.[67]

That Pulcellina might have offered Thibaut financial aid rather than sexual favors is in keeping with what we know of Jews in this period, when many Jewish widows plied their trade as bankers. It does not negate the possibility of an intimate element to the relationship as well.[68] Pulcellina seems to have matched the count in years and in self-assurance. That Alix was under twenty and the count over forty years of age suggests one reason that Thibaut might have been attracted to this "arrogant" Jewish woman, who was already the mother of two and probably widowed by the time of her death.[69] Once imprisoned with the others, Pulcellina was forbidden to see the count, intimating that their relationship was not simply financial: "All the Jews had been put into iron chains except Pulcellina," wrote Ephraim of Bonn, "but the servants of the ruler who watched over her would not allow her to speak to him at all, for fear she might get him to change his mind."[70]

Fears that Thibaut could not produce a healthy male heir may have exacerbated local misgivings over his contact with a Jewish woman. As the counties of Blois and Chartres were coming into the orbit of King Louis, the lack of a male heir would have had significant political implications.[71] By 1171, Henri and Marie de Champagne had two children, but it seems that Alix and Thibaut did not have a healthy male heir. Nonetheless, on hearing of the burnings at Blois,

King Louis cursed his son- and brother-in-law with the words, "May he and his descendants be barren throughout the entire year"—a harsh malediction from a king who had waited twenty-three years for a son.[72] Thibaut had only managed to produce a daughter, Marguerite, born in 1170, the year before the burnings, but finally had a son, Louis, born in 1172, who eventually succeeded his father.[73] If the charge of an affair were raised against the count, perhaps because he had just produced a daughter and not a male heir, Thibaut may have felt compelled to establish his religious orthodoxy in a brutal and public manner, to demonstrate that Pulcellina had not bewitched him. The concern of the countess and the elite of the city was less likely to have been irritation at a possible extramarital fling than fears about the future independence of the county.

The source of animosity against the Jews in Blois does not appear to have been exploited farmers but a small group that possessed power and social standing, so-called "fellow-citizens."[74] The Hebrew term *b'nei ha'ir* ("sons of the town") probably refers to the political elite of the county, not simply merchants; this group may coincide with the Latin "men of the homeland" (*hominibus istius patriae*) addressed in the concession of Thibaut and Alix.[75] These would have been Thibaut's barons and the families who provided his seneschal, butler, treasurer, marshals, chamberers, chancellor, provost, and castellan.[76]

Another influence was Alix's closest advisor, her nursemaid or guardian, an important source of animus against the Jews and a member of that elite. The person in question was apparently not a wet nurse or nursemaid (*nutrix*), but a respected tutor from a knightly family (*nutricius*)—an important position used in the education of the children of the nearby counts of Anjou in the same period.[77] Her identity is not known, but she was likely a member of the county aristocracy, probably a nun in the convent where Alix was likely raised after her childhood engagement, the abbey of Saint-Lomer of Blois, endowed by Thibaut's grandmother Adela, the daughter of William the Conqueror.[78] The countess and her tutor might have borrowed money from Pulcellina, who was "harsh to all who came to her," in the words of the letter sent from the Jewish community at Orléans.[79] Religious women were especially likely to have faced a shortage of funds in this period.[80] If Bishop William and the monks of Norwich brought the relics of their young patron William on tour to France in 1170, Saint-Lomer would have been a likely site for a visit.

The secular and religious courtiers who surrounded Alix and Thibaut had the means, motivation, and opportunity to raise a charge of murder against the local Jews. The story of William would have provided them with an example of how to do so. In any case, it seems clear that financial considerations were at the forefront of what happened in Blois, both at the abbey and at the court. Alix and Thibaut were living beyond their means and were seeking new sources of income; the countess's childhood home was likely piling up debts. Thibaut expected to hold the Jews for ransom and, according to Ephraim of Bonn, he was furious at the paltry funds he was offered. "At the outset the count had begun by discussing money. . . . When the count heard [the offer], he was angry, and ceased speaking with [the Jewish negotiators]. Because of his anger, he did not listen to them. He turned only to the priest and did all that he ordered."[81] Later, in exchange for a lump-sum payment, Thibaut agreed not to raise the ritual murder charge again, which suggests that the accusation was a pretext for financial extortion.[82]

Thibaut's reaction suggests that he was naïve, unaware of the amount he could realistically expect to receive. The Jews of Blois have been criticized for not being willing to pay sufficient sums, but those negotiating with Thibaut had consulted widely "with their Christian friends and also with the Jews in the dungeons."[83] It was well known that Jews were willing to pay for justice and to assure their safety. In Norwich the Jews had paid the sheriff, had offered to pay the bishop and the brother of the victim, and were willing to pay for justice from the king.[84] In later years, at least one leading Jewish scholar refused to let his friends pay the exorbitant ransom demanded for his release because, as he explained, it would merely encourage further violence and exploitation. He remained in prison for seven years and died there.[85]

In Blois the Jews were willing to pay. Thibaut's two brothers accepted the amount that was offered by the Jews and did not pursue prosecution.[86] But neither brother may have been as needy as Thibaut, who had more to gain. The burning of the Jews proved extremely profitable for the rulers of Blois. They appropriated the chattels and loans from the Jews who were killed, demanded large sums to ransom the bodies and books of those who survived, received payment for exculpating Jews from such charges in the future, and tried to extract yet more money from the Jews for the right to bury their dead. If the count and countess had owed money themselves to Jewish lenders, they were freed from any obligations to pay back capital or interest.

As noted, the count's burning of the Jews of Blois staked a claim to power as well as money, and can be taken as a measure of his frustration with his weakening position in relation both to his fellow lords and to his father-in-law King Louis.[87] All his brothers seemed to have surpassed him in honors and advancement. Thibaut had inherited the family's ancestral lands of Blois, but his elder brother Henri had received the wealthier lands of Champagne that had come from an uncle. Although Thibaut had been named seneschal of France in 1154, the position was more symbolic than powerful.[88] Thibaut's younger brothers were also moving ahead. Guillaume (William of the White Hands) became archbishop of Sens in 1168 and was allowed to keep the bishopric of Chartres as well; the following year he became papal legate (later he would be named archbishop of Rheims and a cardinal).[89] An even more galling event occurred in 1169, when Étienne, count of Sancerre, was offered the hand of the daughter of the king of Jerusalem, and was therefore in line to become king in right of his wife. He departed for the East around 1170 with a substantial subvention from the king.[90] Given that his brothers were wealthy, powerful, and princely in manner and expectations, Thibaut likely felt he needed to take action to improve his status.

Like many other counts in western Europe, Thibaut tried to leverage the antiquity and power of his house by the use of elevated titles, claiming, for example, that he was count by the grace of God, but in this he was not as successful as the Capetians.[91] Thibaut's father-in-law was more adept. King Louis changed his royal title from "king of the Franks" to "king of France" and added the designation "by the grace of God" (*dei gratia*). This claim to royal status was expressed in the famous boast attributed to Louis's young contemporary, Thibaut's brother-in-law King Richard of England: "I am born of a rank which recognizes no superior but God." Louis thus laid the groundwork for Capetian dominance by asserting the distinctiveness of the French kingdom, and he began by insisting on moral, not only legal, superiority.[92] It was during his reign that the French aristocracy changed from a political confederation of equals into vassals of their liege lord.[93] The king of France successfully leveraged symbolic and practical powers in the domination of his ambitious vassals. Lords such as Thibaut could not compete and soon abandoned their claims to rule *dei gratia*.

The decision to condemn the Jews of Blois to the flames made Thibaut appear powerful, kingly, ritually pure, solicitous of his people, and capable of independent action in his lordship (*dominium*). The count's actions signal a change in political realities and national consciousness. Thibaut tried other ways to raise his status and assert his independence from the crown. It is not coincidental that increasing attacks on the Jews correspond to the growing pressure on powerful barons by the French kings. Execution by burning was a particularly royal gesture.[94] The count's actions in 1171, especially in the face of his ruler's indignation, constituted a claim to share in royal power.

Thibaut was not only financially pressed and losing political power; he lacked religious authority as well, and sought a means to buttress his claim to spiritual prestige by publicly demonstrating his piety. Other princely families celebrated their crusade activity in the new chivalric literature that was rapidly becoming popular, while both of Thibaut's grandfathers, Stephen and Hugh, were still ridiculed for deserting the First Crusade (both died on a later expedition to the Holy Land); unlike his elder brother Henri, moreover, Thibaut had missed the Second Crusade.[95] Participation in the crusades was an important family claim to fame.[96] Meanwhile, not only had King Louis gone on crusade, his political support for the pope earned him the coveted title Most Christian King (*rex christianissimus*) and the present of a golden rose from Pope Alexander III for his extraordinary devotion to the Church.[97]

Thibaut's actions in Blois should therefore be placed in the political context of competition for prestige and power on a national and international scale. The burnings of Jews at Blois can be linked with notable public burnings before and after by members of the same family, such as those in Orléans and Sens. Burning became an acceptable punishment for heretics in western Europe only after King Robert II "the Pious" of France burned ten convicted heretics at Orléans in 1022.[98] Thibaut was a direct descendant of Robert through his powerful grandmother Adela of Blois, and the count was placing himself squarely in that royal tradition. As a result of the burnings he orchestrated, Thibaut earned the designation "the Good" (*le Bon*), a title comparable to encomia of the French kings (*le pieux* or *christianissimus*), or his father's occasional designation as *le saint*.

A notorious case of burning comparable to that of Blois was the later dramatic "holocaust of heretics" in Champagne, five weeks before Thibaut's younger relative, Thibaut IV the troubador (*le chansonnier*), count of Champagne, set off on crusade in 1239. The event was horrifically spectacular, involving 180 victims. Widely reported, it made a dramatic religious statement, emphasizing Thibaut of Champagne's piety and the penitential purpose of his crusade. Almost all the important clergymen of the principality attended the event, which was termed "a holocaust pleasing to the Lord."[99] The confiscation of the heretics' goods also provided Thibaut of Champagne the resources to depart.[100] Like the executions of Jews at Blois, the burning of Christian heretics in Champagne had a strong political as well as a religious element. Thibaut of Champagne's departure on crusade came not long after he had ceded Chartres, Blois, and Sancerre to the French crown, and may have been a belated statement of independence.[101] Piety was practiced and was seen to be practiced. Just as the younger Thibaut's public act of violence in Champagne served two immediate needs, spiritual purification and capital accumulation, so too did his great-uncle's immolation of his county's Jews in 1171, which appears to have functioned as the same kind of cathartic and dramatic statement, reverberating through Christian as well as Jewish society.

The Blois burnings therefore served multiple purposes: they reinforced Thibaut V's hold on a county that was overshadowed on all sides by wealthier towns with competing loyalties; they served to raise urgently needed funds for the count and his wife; they eliminated a contentious source of power (Pulcellina) in the small county; they celebrated and reinforced Thibaut V of Blois as a most Christian count, silencing any rumors involving his ritual impurity and as a result his failure to produce a male heir.

The public nature and function of the burnings cannot be overemphasized. Although they were charged with homicide, the Jews of Blois were treated as heretics rather than as murderers, perpetrators not of felony but of sin. The public punishment was intended to be educational both for the viewers and for the victims: burning offered people a taste of the hellfire to come. The audience could hear the agonized groans and watch the suffering, vividly bringing home to them the torments that awaited if they persisted in sin. When, where, and how the guilty were punished is essential to understand the meaning that the punishment had for Christian viewers and participants. The date, time, place, and manner of the execution were carefully considered. Thibaut's judgment was meant to be public, pedagogic, and pious as well as political and punitive, but only the latter considerations have drawn attention.[102]

By considering medieval attacks on Jews primarily in relation to Jewish history, rather than to Christian religious and European political history, the importance of the events in a broader context has been underestimated or lost. For Jews, the events of 1171 could be placed in a straightforward and coherent tradition that was familiar: as the Passover Haggadah explains, "in every generation they rise up against us to destroy us." In that sense the Blois burnings were part of a continuum that began long ago and was to continue far into the future. They were shocking but not exceptional, and the tools used to address them were conventional ones: political activism, bribes, rational argument, and penitential practices, all of which had been employed before and would be used again.[103]

For Christians, however, the Blois affair was a turning point. By ordering the burnings, Thibaut V was formally assimilating Judaism to heresy and thus indicating that Jews were subject to all the punishments intended for those who willfully denounced Christ.[104] Previously, Judaism had been a licit but subordinate religion. Under Roman law, Jews were citizens of the empire, and in St. Augustine's formulation Jews were to be tolerated as a witness to the truth of Christianity. In *De civitate Dei*, he explicitly referred to Psalm 59:12, "slay them not, lest my people forget," an opinion reiterated in the mid-twelfth century by Bernard of Clairvaux.[105] In Christian eyes, Jews testified to the truth of Christianity, for it was believed that they preserved in their ancient writings prophecies that predicted the coming of Christ, to whose meaning they were blind. Prior to the religious developments of the later twelfth century, Judaism was not a heresy. Heretics came under the sway of the Church and were to be persecuted. Jews were not subject to the canons of the Church. They lived under their own laws, and it was expected that at least some Jews would still be present in Christian society to convert at the End of Days. The condemnation of the Jews of Blois, therefore, indicated that those beliefs and traditions had changed. Jews were not to be tolerated in Christian society, but rooted out and killed.

At the time of Thibaut V, judicial death by burning was not the usual penalty, even for heresy. Before this, medieval Jews had never been sentenced to the flame, and heretics were generally condemned to severe punishments other than death (King Robert's action was the exception). After the events of 1171 in Blois, however, burning became widely accepted as a suitable punishment for heretics; by the time of the Fourth Lateran Council in 1215, death by fire was almost a routine punishment. Earlier in the twelfth century, it was more common to burn relics and test them in the fire, than to burn people.[106] The holy remains of saints were placed on hot coals to prove their authenticity. If they emerged unscathed—as they always did, according to the judgment of those witnessing the test—they were truly sanctified. Burning Jews and heretics was an inversion of this practice, meant to prove the contrary, that they were not sanctified, but unholy.

To those who witnessed the execution, the ordeal by fire proved that the Jews of Blois were guilty, just as the ordeal of water immediately preceding it had done. The fire confirmed religious guilt; it was not the obvious, natural conclusion to a typical case of medieval homicide. There was little likelihood that young children and nursing babies had participated in any murder, yet they too were condemned and consigned to the flames, as were many women.[107] The count thereby blamed Jews collectively not merely for the kidnap and killing of a neighbor, but for refusing to recognize the Incarnation and for participating in the death of Christ. Thibaut's punishment referred implicitly to Jews everywhere, even those born long after biblical times. This decision reflects the feeling that Christ was continually and repeatedly at risk and that contemporary Jews were implicated in an ongoing effort at deicide.[108] Thibaut's actions reflect the ideological conflation of Jews past, present, and future into one threatening, suspect group. Such a view was later represented pictorially in depictions of medieval Jews in contemporary dress observing and participating in Christ's Crucifixion. Burning the Jews of Blois eliminated any challenges to religious orthodoxy and removed sources of conflict; it created a homogenous holy community united by bonds of faith. To condemn sages, students, pregnant women, and children to the flames both symbolized and resulted in the end of the Jewish community in Blois far more effectively than any expulsion or forced conversion.

The Jews of Blois were not all executed in the same way or at the same time. As noted, more than thirty victims were locked in a building that was then put to the torch. But three young Jewish scholars of Blois—R. Judah ben Aaron, R. Yehiel ben David ha-Kohen, and R. Yekutiel ben Judah ha-Kohen—were singled out for a particular and public punishment. They were tied to a stake with ropes and set afire, after they were selected for symbolic reasons rather than traditional judicial concerns. There were three such reasons. First, these young men recalled for Christians such figures as the Three Young Men of the Book of Daniel who were compelled to bow down to idols by the Babylonian king, Nebuchadnezzar; second, the Jewish Boy of the miracle tale who was rescued by the Virgin Mary; and perhaps most obviously, the three students rescued by St. Nicholas in one of his popular miracle tales, the Three Clerks. All three stories reinforced the lessons of contemporary Christian orthodoxy: martyrdom, baptism, salvation, and the saving grace of Mary and the saints. The youths in these three stories told by medieval Christians did not die (or if they did die, they were revived), and they never rejected the opportunity to embrace Christianity. All three stories undercut Jewish claims to an independent religious identity and social space in medieval Europe. The outcome in Blois was meant to reinforce the message that the best Jew, the only tolerable Jew, was a converted Jew.

At one level, the burning of 1171 fit into a traditional pattern. Three young men engulfed in flames routinely turned to Christ for salvation in the liturgical dramas performed in the churches of central France. The three men condemned for refusing to bow down and worship an idol and cast into a fiery furnace were miraculously preserved. In the Book of Daniel these boys (named Hananiah, Mishael, and Azariah in Hebrew and in the Vulgate; Shadrach, Meshach, and Abednego in the King James translation) are Jews who refuse to worship idols. Thus, according to Jewish commentators and exegetes of northern

France, they were martyrs who willingly performed Sanctification of the Name (*Kiddush ha-Shem*) because the three Jewish boys were prepared to die rather than submit to idolatry. Their unyielding faith in Judaism meant that they emerged unscathed from the flames (just as the Jewish scholars were to explain that the Blois martyrs were not consumed by the flames either).[109]

According to medieval Christian exegesis, however, the Three Young Men in Daniel adopted Christianity because they saw an angel in the fire, who rescued them. They were not consumed by the flames because a cool breeze blew over them. Ironically, while simultaneously celebrating the steadfast religious faith of the boys in biblical commentary, drama, the plastic arts, and manuscript illustration, medieval Christians denied the ancient youths their Jewish identity.

Medieval Christians knew this story of religious fortitude in fire from sermons, scholarly commentaries, works of art, and early church dramas. In the Loire Valley during the twelfth century, Christians were accustomed to seeing the three boys burn every year when cathedrals and monastic schools staged the Procession of Prophets, the *Ordo Prophetarum*, as part of their Christmastide celebrations. The theatrical *Ordo*, in which a series of Old Testament prophets testified to the truth of the Incarnation and came to preach about the foreshadowing of Christ's sacrifice on the cross, was the oldest dramatized part of the Christian liturgy.[110] In the drama, a hut-like furnace large enough to hold several actors was built in the middle of the church nave and was bound with tarred rags so that when it was lit on cue, it went up in flames while the boy actors snuck out the back.[111] Over the years the technical effects grew more elaborate and expensive and the stage business more complicated and stereotyped, especially to the delight of the young and less sophisticated viewers in the audience whom the drama was intended to educate.

The *Ordo* was presented as a disputation whose purpose was to confute the Jews from the mouths of their own prophets. The prophet tradition is related, therefore, to the well-documented polemical tradition of the *Adversos Iudaeos*. Indeed, Peter the Venerable of Cluny begins his famous *Adversos Iudaeos* sermon of 1146 with the opening words of the Late Antique sermon that was the basis for the *Ordo Prophetarum*, and concludes with the witness of Daniel, whose lesson should be evident to the Jews.[112] At least five versions of the *Ordo Prophetarum* are known to have circulated in the twelfth and thirteenth centuries, and depictions inspired by the Prophet Play appeared prominently on church walls, especially in the sculptural programs of Romanesque cathedrals. Even with no Jews in the audience, the play was seen as an important tool, both to reinforce Christian belief and to convert non-believers. In Riga on the Baltic, the Prophet Play was performed at the opening of the thirteenth century in order that pagans and neophytes "might learn the rudiments of the Christian faith through ocular assurance (*gentilitas fide etiam disceret oculata*)."[113]

The Prophet Play was open to theatrical elaboration and exaggeration. Foolish Balaam and his recalcitrant ass, for example, were portrayed by a wooden hobbyhorse, or, as at Rouen in the thirteenth century, by an actor hiding underneath the horse's trappings.[114] Parts were soon spun off into separate plays, especially during the Christmas season. By the early twelfth century, Daniel starred in his own play (*Ludus Danielis*), of which various versions survive. The Play of Daniel only alludes to the fiery furnace, but the *Jeu d'Adam* from the mid-twelfth century (*Ordo Representacionis Adae*) culminated in a procession of the prophets and the burning of the three boys, which was comprehensible by the general public, for it was delivered in vernacular Anglo-Norman, rather than Latin.

The audience observing the burnings of the Jews in Blois would have recalled not only the Daniel story, but also its analogue in the Marian tales beginning to circulate widely in the mid-twelfth century. Christians viewed the three young men burned at Blois in the context of the growing cult of the Virgin Mary and in explicit opposition to Judaism. In the popular miracle story known as the "Jewish Boy of Bourges," Mary rescues a boy from a furnace in which he has been tossed by his furious Jewish father when the boy had dared to take communion with his school friends.[115] The Virgin's protection of the boy in the midst of the flames was compared explicitly with Christ's protection of the three young men in the fiery furnace. For Christians, the story had a happy moral ending: the Jewish boy is baptized, the mother converts, and the father is thrown to his death in the furnace in the boy's place.[116] The story of the Jewish Boy reinforced the idea that a Jewish parent was prepared to obstruct conversion and to kill young Christian children.[117] But in the twelfth-century retelling, it is not only the father who is guilty of the attempted murder of his son, but all Jews. In the version Bishop Herbert Losinga preached on Christmas day in Norwich, "they who would not believe the Incarnate word were all alike burned in the aforesaid furnace," which he termed "a most just vengeance on the heads of the Jews".[118]

The story of the "Jewish Boy of Bourges" was profusely illustrated, especially in Romanesque cathedrals and in a variety of media—stained glass, sculpture, manuscript painting. In its barest outline, it told the same story as Daniel and was modeled on it: a young Jewish boy condemned to the flames through no fault of his own found religion in the fire and emerged as a dedicated Christian. This is perhaps what Christian observers hoped would happen to the young Jewish scholars of Blois: that they would play the role in salvation history in which the Christians cast them.[119]

Above all, when Christians saw three young scholars suffering torment, they brought to mind the three young clerks (*tres scholari, clerici, literati*) from the miracles of St. Nicholas, which was another analogue to the Daniel story.[120] In this story, three students enter the house of an innkeeper or butcher who, at the urging of his wife, plans to steal their purses, cut up the boys, cook them, and serve the meat.[121] St. Nicholas arrives in time to uncover the innkeeper's plans and to rescue or revive the boys. Once again, three innocent youths condemned to death and at the point of dying are saved by simple faith and the intercession of a Christian saint. Even more than the three youths in the furnace, or the Jewish boy, the story of the three clerks in the oven was a common subject in medieval art, appearing on baptismal fonts, in stained glass, and in illuminated manuscripts.[122]

Like the three young clerks of St. Nicholas, the three youths burned at Blois were identified as young scholars: all three were called rabbis, two were of priestly descent, but none appears to have been married, which suggests that they were quite young.[123]

The Christians of Blois were particularly attuned to the St. Nicholas story: the Loire Valley was a center of veneration of St. Nicholas beginning in the early twelfth century, and the central church in Blois, the focus of Thibaut's family patronage, was dedicated to the saint.[124] Performances of the "Three Clerks" (*Tres Clerici*), like other plays of St. Nicholas, most likely took place on the site where the burning of the Jews probably occurred in Blois, outside the Church of Saint-Nicolas, attached to the abbey of Saint-Lomer. Four St. Nicholas plays were composed in this period, and to judge from internal evidence of the play, at least one was performed directly outside a church dedicated to St. Nicholas. The four plays appear in the so-called "Fleury" Playbook, which is a manuscript of ten plays dating from about 1200 but based on earlier originals and dedicated to St. Lomer.[125] This playbook is usually attributed to the abbey of Fleury, near Orléans, where it was discovered, but many scholars are now reluctant to assign the composition to a particular location in the Loire region and conclude that the contents may have been collected from various places and authors.[126]

As those who argue for locating the playbook in Blois pointed out long ago, Saint-Lomer's reputation as an important intellectual center has been overlooked.[127] The playbook must have been compiled, however, at a center "where literary and musical activity flourished over a considerable period and where associations with France, England and the empire were extensive."[128] The more that is known about Blois at mid-century, the more plausible appears an attribution of the playbook to the abbey of Saint-Lomer. Further attention, for example, to the patronage of Adela of Blois (as noted above, Thibaut V's grandmother) and to the career of Peter of Blois (ca. 1135–1203), the author of "Against the Perfidy of the Jews," who began his studies at Saint-Lomer before moving to Tours, Paris, and Bologna and making his career as a diplomat and theologian in Sicily and England, may suggest the rich cultural environment of the town and neighboring abbey. If the playbook was put together at Blois, as seems possible, the manuscript may soon have gone to Fleury in the wake of the community's political and economic decline following a fire at Saint-Lomer in 1204.

The St. Nicholas verse music-dramas copied in the playbook were likely composed by students or minor clergy, possibly as a school exercise. Musical references from the Nicholas plays can likewise be found influencing the eponymous hero of the Daniel play, which was a production of the choir clerks and subdeacons.[129] The writing, composing, and performance of these dramas were intended to inculcate values among the minor clergy, oblates, young scholars, and students in monastic schools. These dramas, neither obscure nor truly popular, but introductory, summarizing and simplifying complex concepts, were made to appeal to an audience much like that of the families and participants in the Blois burnings, not a mass audience of the unlettered, nor an especially educated and sophisticated one.[130]

The story of the Three Clerks and St. Nicholas does not include any mention of Jews, but many of the other St. Nicholas stories do, most notably one of the other dramas in the playbook, the "Image of St. Nicholas" (*Iconia Sancti Nicolai*), in which a leading character, formerly portrayed as a pagan, is transformed into a Jew. In this play, the Jewish protagonist, likely a merchant, leaves his goods to the protection of an image of St. Nicholas, admonishing the saint to guard them.[131] When the man returns and finds that all his goods have been stolen by thieves, he takes his revenge on the image of the saint by beating and berating it. Nicholas then appears to the thieves and commands them to return the goods, at which point the thieves repent and the Jew, suitably impressed, converts to

Christianity. Like the Daniel and Jewish Boy stories, this, too, ends happily with a conversion. In the fifteenth century, school children from Saint-Lomer performed one of the dramas of St. Nicholas in the cemetery of Saint-Lomer,[132] possibly the same *Iconia* that was written down in the aftermath of the Blois burnings, and performed it on the site where the martyrs likely were interred.

Saint-Lomer is in close proximity to the castle but was located outside the walls of the town; its land extended up to the banks of the Loire. Significantly, this abbey fits the description of the site of the burnings in 1171. According to Jewish reports, the victims were immolated, under religious auspices, "outside the town, at the place of the fire."[133] The burned bodies were never returned to the Jewish community, but were left on land that became a *de facto* cemetery. According to a Jewish account, "those burned at Blois were not accorded burial, as a result of our great sins. But the site of the burning was a low area, and Thibaut ordered that the bodies be covered with dirt and stones."[134]

There are additional associations of the place and the plays. Another miracle story of St. Nicholas found in the playbook, "Son of Getron" (*Getronis Filium*), begins with a procession to a church dedicated to the saint, at which a young boy is kidnapped by heathens, and taken from his family to serve a foreign ruler. He is eventually returned to his mother when she beseeches St. Nicholas for aid. Like *Iconia*, scholars have found this play a "site of struggle" in which the dominant culture stigmatizes a minority group and acknowledges its existence.[135] The implied connections between homosexuality—it seems clear the boy will serve the foreign ruler sexually—and Jewishness are clear. Although not explicitly about Jews, "Son of Getron" features characters and music heavily influenced by the anti-Jewish liturgical dramas of Herod (portrayed as a Jew at this time) and the Slaughter of the Innocents (discussed in the following chapter). The foreign ruler "hungry" for the young Christian is modeled on Herod, and the boy's mother displays many parallels ("figural resonance") with mourning biblical mothers—Rachel weeping for her sons, the mothers of the Holy Innocents, and Mary seeking Christ in the Temple.[136]

St. Nicholas was a patron saint of children, so it may have been deemed appropriate that the church of St. Nicholas at Saint-Lomer should be the site to punish Jews, the alleged enemies of Christian innocence. A new abbey church begun by Thibaut V's father in 1138 was completed with an elaborate dedication and translation of relics from the old church to the new in 1186.[137] Thibaut and Alix celebrated there, along with their son Louis.[138] St. Nicholas's patronage of children may also suggest that young Louis participated in the festivities of 1186 not merely as the future count of Blois, but as an especially appropriate young acolyte. It has been argued that an ecclesiastical drama of St. Nicholas was performed at this celebration of dedication and translation of relics.

The timing of the Blois burnings may hint at competing feasts of Christians and Jews, in this case both emphasizing the protection and education of the young: the Christian Feast of St. Nicholas and the Jewish festival of Shavuot. We know from the Jewish circular letter that the date of the Blois burnings was a Thursday, the twentieth of the Hebrew month of Sivan (May 26). Exactly two weeks earlier, the sixth of Sivan, was the Jewish holiday of Shavuot. This feast celebrating the gift of the Torah on Mount Sinai was a holiday centered on Jewish boys and their introduction to formal education.[139] In later years the Shavuot ritual became a celebration self-consciously constructed in response to Christian symbolism.[140] In 1171 Shavuot fell on May 12, thus coinciding with the week-long observance of the major Christian celebration in Blois, the feast of the translation of the relics of St. Nicholas beginning on May 9.[141] That Saint-Lomer celebrated May 9 as an important feast (the date of the translation of the relics of St. Nicholas, rather than the better-known feast of the anniversary of his death, December 6) is indicated by a grant of Count Louis in the early thirteenth century of certain privileges on the "evening, day, and day after Saint Nicholas of summer."[142]

The St. Nicholas plays may have been performed on this spring feast of Nicholas, most likely outside a church, with an audience of laypeople, rather than in the nave during matins in the middle of the night. There was also a strong tradition of merrymaking and playing on the feast of the Ascension and on Pentecost ten days later (which in 1171 fell on May 6 and May 16). This playmaking tradition survived most vigorously on Whitsunday in England (the English name for Pentecost). Pentecost was also the traditional day for the baptism of new converts, and it may be that those Jews of Blois who survived and were persuaded to convert did so on Pentecost (it is assumed that a few did, although how many is unknown). The Jewish accounts mention a Holy Thursday, most likely a reference to Ascension, forty days after Easter.[143] The overlapping celebrations of Christians and Jews provided an opportunity to reinforce boundaries, celebrate the arrival of spring, and advertise competing interpretations for the biblical Feast of Weeks, Shavuot/Pentecost.

The dating of the accusation and punishment may thus have been consciously tied to the liturgical year, and not simply to the vagaries of the judicial calendar. Indeed, the date of the punishment perhaps drew more attention than the date of the alleged crime. In Blois, the initial accusation of ritual murder may have been dated to Easter.[144] The likelihood of a connection with the Easter holiday is enhanced when one recalls that a crusade planned to include the kings of England and France had originally been called to depart at Easter 1171.[145] As is well known—and as we have seen—crusade preaching in the twelfth century often provoked attacks on Jews. The date of May 25 may have had some particular meaning in Blois because it was shortly to become the day of the translation of the relics of St. Lomer to the new abbey church. As noted above, such dates were carefully chosen and often became a signal day in the life of the community. The fact that the Jews were burned on that day sixteen years previously hints that it may already have been a date associated with the abbey at Blois. The fact that the same day was chosen to dedicate the building as to burn the Jews suggests that the execution by fire was viewed in the guise of a foundational myth for the establishment of the church in Blois, a physical enactment of Christian replacement of Jews as the Chosen people ("supercessionism"). Killing or expelling Jews was closely tied in the later Middle Ages to the dedication of churches, often on the site of former synagogues where miracles occurred.

In sum, the burning of Jews in Blois in 1171 was a formal, carefully stage-managed affair, perhaps with a procession to the site of the burnings, which took place in more than one location, in keeping with the arrangements for an *auto-da-fé* typical of the late medieval Inquisition.[146] Such a procession would also have been in keeping with the tradition on Ascension Day ("Holy Thursday") of an outdoor procession to celebrate the final victory of Christ over the devil, when he ascended into heaven, forty days after Easter. There is no indication that in Blois a mob got out of hand or that the populace rose up, as was so often the case during crusade preparations. The affair at Blois had all the trappings of ritual formality and procedure. There must have been many witnesses, for the burnings would have been comparable to the ceremony of a donation charter: a public assembly presided over by the count at Blois, attended by his barons, townspeople, and religious advisors.[147] The surviving letters state that the event took place before dawn, most likely after matins. The witnesses may have been limited to a select group of clerical and administrative authorities.[148]

The burning embodied and enacted the judgment of God. Each religious group interpreted it differently. Christians emphasized the iniquity of the alleged perpetrators. Jews identified those who died as martyrs to their faith, and they responded to Christian teaching by clarifying their own interpretations.[149] They emphasized the adult manhood of the victims, not their youthful innocence. They focused on two of the martyrs, rather than three, in order to draw out biblical parallels other than the boys in the furnace from Daniel. They insisted that the Torah scholars and holy men were not consumed by fire and developed the motif of the "fireproof martyr." For Jews, the burnings served not only to idealize a form of martyrdom, but also to counter the Christian view espoused by the chronicler Hariulf of Saint-Riquier (d. 1143) that "[the relics of the saints] were not in anyway harmed by the effects of fire or able to be burned." This contrasts with the views of the Christians, who thought they saw Jews actually subjected to the fires of purgatory.[150]

The Blois burning was widely publicized by both Jews and Christians, but for different reasons. The Christians organized a public exhibition, trial, and punishment to advertise Thibaut V's orthodoxy and independence. The Jews wrote to their co-religionists to alert them to what had happened and to warn them of incipient danger. Both had an interest in spreading the word as far and as wide as possible. The attention generated by the murder accusation in Blois far surpassed the modest enthusiasm recorded for William of Norwich or Harold of Gloucester. It is one of the few actions by this count of Blois that merits mention in French reports by Christians; it obviously made a great impression in Paris as well as in the Loire Valley. For Jews, the poetry composed in the wake of the burnings became an influential model for much later writing about martyrs.[151]

The public audience of Christians was important for medieval Jews who celebrated the dead at Blois as religious martyrs, not victims of civil prosecution. Earlier Jewish legislation reflected an indifference to the presence of Gentiles, but in this period martyrdom "was deliberately and pointedly directed at the Christian world."[152] Everything was put to the service of interpretation—the site, the smells, the sights, and even the sounds. The *Alenu l'Shabeah* prayer praising God, which the martyrs sang as the flames rose around them, became a daily memorial in Jewish liturgy.[153] It explicitly gives thanks to God for not having made the Jewish people like those of the other nations of the world, who do not know the true God. According to Jewish reports, the Christians who attended the burnings of the Jews commented on the glorious music. "As the flames rose, the Jews sang together; they lifted their voices sweetly. Indeed the Christians came and told us of this, asking: 'What is your song that is so sweet? We have never heard such sweetness.'"[154]

On another level, that question posed about the music in the Jewish accounts of Blois reflected Jewish awareness of Christian apochryphal texts not found in the Hebrew Bible. Between Daniel 3:23 and 3:24 in Christian Bibles was to be found the prayer of Azariah and a Song of the Three Boys, *benedictus es domine* and *benedicite laudamus*, which became canticles.[155] In a medieval clash of songs, the Jewish *Alenu* is thus implicitly contrasted to the Christian *benedictus*. In response, perhaps, to Jewish claims of exceptional qualities of the song and the faith of those singing it, Christian drama very soon after the horrific event integrated the Jewish *Alenu* to represent the opposite. Within a decade or two at most, Christians who may have seen and heard the *auto-da-fé* in Blois heard the melody of the solemn Hebrew *Alenu* echoed in the music of a Latin lament (*planctus*). In a kind of "lyrical logic" in which "melody and character cohere," the Jew in the *Iconia* St. Nicholas play was given "Hebrew" music.[156] It is a remarkable—and unusual—melding of words and music, "one of the most memorable solos in the corpus of church drama."[157]

For Jews, the burning at Blois was initially an act of political outrage against which rational forces could be called upon. After the burning, when the smoke still lay on the breeze and babies' bodies were crushed in the collapsing house, the remains of the scholars lay smouldering on the ground and the books destroyed, the event was regarded differently. It was a matter of Jewish sin, not political willfulness. The response, therefore, was penitential. The Jewish communities of France instituted immediate fasts for themselves, an annual perpetual fast to remember the victims (a fast as important as the Fast of Gedaliah), they adopted sumptuary guidelines limiting the decoration on their clothing and the size of their celebrations, and they urged Jews in Lotharingia to do likewise.[158] Half a millennium later, all of Polish Jewry adopted the fast on 20 Sivan in memory of the Blois victims in order to recall their own victims of the Chmielnitzky massacre of 1648. For that reason, the prayers (*selichot*) written after the Blois burning in 1171 were recited up until World War II.[159]

It was the punishment, not the alleged crime of ritual murder, that was remembered by Christians and Jews alike. Few details survive about the charge because what was important for Count Thibaut of Blois was not the accusation but the penalty. In his eyes, by their very existence, Jews were already guilty of the sin of deicide, of heresy. He would see to it that his county remained religiously orthodox, and he, like his ancestors, would be the guarantor of its orthodoxy. Putting people on the pyre satisfied his need for money and advertised his pious purposes in public.

The accusation of ritual murder in Blois and the punishment by fire of the alleged perpetrators was a striking event in Christian-Jewish relations, and it also signaled changing relations between the king of France and his vassals. So much historical attention has concentrated on tracing textual influences that there has been a tendency to overlook the effects on those who watched. Well before the composition of any text about ritual murder, the sights, sounds, and smells of the burnings in Blois impressed themselves on the minds of French Christians and confirmed for them the truth of the accusation. Although the events at Blois were ostensibly civil and secular in origin—the alleged murder of some local child—it was their ecclesiastical commemoration that made them significant. In Blois, as in Norwich and Gloucester, the religious and secular were intimately and inextricably linked.

FIGURE 7.1. *Scenes from the Life of Saint Robert of Bury,* illumination of c. 1490, illustrating the late twelfth-century *Life* by Jocelin of Brakelond (no longer extant), the only known image of the saint.

Los Angeles, J. Paul Getty Museum, MS 101, fol. 44r.

CHAPTER 7   *Bury St. Edmunds*

As news of the burnings of Jews in Blois rippled through northern France after 1171, the monks of Norwich put the finishing touches on a major promotional campaign for their purported child saint. Its greatest impact seems to have been at the nearby ecclesiastical center of Bury St. Edmunds, Suffolk, where a ritual murder accusation was made in 1181. Almost a decade later, more than fifty Jews were massacred in riots at Bury that followed the accession of King Richard I. With the first mention of a child murder in Norwich in 1150, the composition and circulation of the text of William's *Life* in the 1170s, the accusation in Bury in 1181, and the massacres in 1190, notions of Jewish involvement in ritual murder gradually percolated through Anglo-Norman society. At Bury, as in Norwich, the accusation of ritual murder served to unite the monks in common purpose and to enhance their common institutional identity.

Contemporary evidence of the ritual murder accusation made against the Jews of Bury St. Edmunds in 1181 consists of only one sentence in a chronicle by Jocelin of Brakelond, a local monk who also wrote a *Life and Passion* of the supposed victim, Robert of Bury; but the text of this *Life* has never been discovered. Beyond that, there is only one illustration of the child martyr that dates from the late Middle Ages. Very little, therefore, has been written about young Robert of Bury. For these reasons, we have to examine the setting in which the purported events took place, consider their immediate historical, social, and economic circumstances and look closely at the people involved to understand what happened and why and how it was important. As we shall see, the local circumstances differed considerably from those of Norwich, Gloucester, and Blois. Although little is known about Robert of Bury, his story was in some respects more important to the promoters of the charge at Bury than those of any of the other purported victims we have considered.

The first context—and the best known—is the financial difficulties in which the abbey of Bury found itself during the late twelfth century, and which come into focus against the background of its long-running competition with Norwich in the same diocese. The second is the potentially important role of the Jews at Bury at this time, particularly in relation to the profitable mint at the abbey. A third, equally significant factor, however, relates to the implications that this charge of homicide had for Bury's legal and feudal relationships.

The monks of the great abbey of Bury St. Edmunds, a mere forty miles from Norwich, may have heard of William's story by word of mouth, they may have read the newly completed *Life*, or they may have witnessed liturgical celebrations connected with his cult. Certainly the monks of Norwich had tried to spread word of their saintly patron (and with it the story of ritual murder) with elaborate ceremonies, which included everything mentioned thus far: moving William's remains around the cathedral, establishing a substantial suburban chapel, recording miracles, identifying secondary relics the saint had touched, possibly taking them on tour, interpreting visions that featured the holy youth, encouraging candles to be lit in his name, and honoring him with a decorative carpet on his altar. Bishop William had raised funds to repair the church after the fire of 1170, but after more than a quarter-century in office—and twenty years after his spirited defense of his knight—he was nearing the end of his time. With his encouragement and approval, therefore, the Norwich monks decided to honor him and advertise Norwich's new patron by composing an authoritative *Life* from the notes of William's miracles that Brother Thomas had so assiduously collected. This was the culmination of a two-decades-long effort to enhance the dead youth's stature and share his story. The monks were pleased and proud that their bishop, who had first welcomed "their great treasure," would be able to see and endorse their work and also contribute to it.

Despite all their efforts, William's story did not travel widely. As far as one can tell, knowledge of the text remained within a small area of East Anglia. The sole surviving manuscript appears to be from the Cistercian house of Sibton Abbey in Suffolk, and was donated to a local parish library in the eighteenth century.[1] Norwich at the time still had its own copy, which eventually disappeared.[2] The extant volume, which is a collection of the lives of twelfth-century saints, all of whom have spring feast days (Godric of Finchale, Wulfric of Haselbury), is a typical East Anglian product of the fourth quarter of the twelfth century, apparently intended as a work of reference.[3] The other texts in the volume were composed between 1169 and 1180. The abbey of Bury St. Edmunds in Suffolk was one of the few ecclesiastical institutions that may have made an effort to copy William's *Life*, for it had a large and up-to-date scriptorium and frequently lent out books to other houses. The extant manuscript was once thought to have come from Bury.

It was at Bury that the story of William prompted the cult of a young boy, Robert of Bury, comparable to that of William of Norwich. As noted, Norwich and Bury had a long tradition of cooperation and competition. From the eleventh century onward, Bury had successfully escaped Norwich's repeated attempts to dominate the nearby wealthy abbey.[4] Bury had been remarkably successful in parrying those attempts, most recently in 1175, when Norwich boasted a new bishop in great favor with the king, and Bury managed to maintain its independence by means of a grant from Pope Alexander III that gave it the enhanced status of a "mitred abbey." The bishop's mitre worn by the Bury abbot made it clear to all that he was not subject to the jurisdiction of Norwich. The subsequent abbot had to renew that episcopal exemption, which was so important that he insisted he be portrayed with his mitre clearly carved. By the 1180s the abbot of Bury was exempt not only from the control of the bishop of Norwich but also from that of the archbishop of Canterbury and the papal legate.[5]

Bury's celebration of its own boy martyr, Robert, has been attributed to the abbey's ongoing competition with Norwich. The presumed popularity of William, together with Bury's desire to establish a rival center, appeared to be sufficient explanation for the promotion of an infant found tossed in a well into a wonder-working saint. But Bury and Norwich did more than compete with one another; they were also close. The two leading Benedictine institutions of East Anglia had much in common and willingly shared many texts. Their separate cults of twelfth-century boy martyrs may have been mutually reinforcing as well as competitive.[6] Robert served far more important purposes for the monks of St. Edmunds than as a mere weapon in its competition with Norwich (which it appeared to have won).

Although it drew on Norwich's story of William, and presumed that townsmen and pilgrims knew of the young apprentice, the cult of the child martyr in Bury arose in markedly different circumstances and served different purposes for its creators. Far less well known today, in the Middle Ages veneration of little Robert of Bury appears more continuous and more important than does that of his predecessor in Norwich. The role of Jews, who were deeply involved not just in making loans but also in exchanging and minting coin, appears to have been a critical element at Bury.

Robert is first mentioned by Brother Jocelin of Brakelond, a monk of Bury who left a lively contemporary account of the period, including a famous profile of his abbot, Samson of Bury. In his *Chronicle*, Jocelin offers no details about the purported child martyr, directing readers to his separate *Life* of the saint, a work that has never been found.[7] Brother Jocelin's *Chronicle*, on the other hand, is easily accessible. It was recopied at Bury and has been frequently reprinted, excerpted, and translated from the Latin, making Robert's name, if not his story, widely cited.[8]

Few people have paid attention to Robert because very little is known of him, and nothing that might distinguish him from later victims. The context of the accusation seems straightforward from Jocelin's account. Bury was close to Norwich, and the accusation occurred during an interim period when there was no head of the abbey and when debts to local Jews had been growing. Within a decade, the new abbot, Samson, received royal permission to expel the Jews from Bury, the same year as vicious massacres of Jews occurred throughout England, most notably in York and London, but also in Bury, where fifty-seven Jews were killed. In such a context, historians have seen the ritual murder accusation as anticipating the harsh policies of the future abbot Samson, so they do not question the monastic endorsement of Robert's cult and the establishment of a chapel in his name. The frequent association of the debts and accusation of 1181 with the massacre and expulsion of the Jews from Bury in 1190, a full century before their expulsion from the kingdom of England (and the confusion of the two dates by scholars), indicates that these two examples are treated as aspects of the same impulse, effectively occurring at the same time and reflecting the same circumstances. Scholars conclude that the motive for attacks on Jews—at Blois and at Bury—was purely or primarily financial and reflected an outbreak of mob violence. The same story would be told throughout much of Europe during subsequent centuries and is therefore not worthy of close examination. But as in Norwich, Blois, and Paris, the issue was as much about power and rights as it was about economics and short-term debt.

To the extent that he has been mentioned at all, Robert of Bury has been relegated to the religious history of Jews. He is not included in histories of popular devotion, the history of Bury or East Anglia, or histories of medieval civic identity.[9] It is frequently stated that medieval chronicles "provide insufficient context for the analysis and interpretation" of earlier accusations of ritual murder.[10] Brother Jocelin's latest translator shows no interest in Jews in Bury, nor have other scholars who focus on the twelfth-century cult of saints and popular devotion as expressed in art and liturgy thought Robert worthy of further consideration. But Robert was of far more importance to the history of Bury and of England than he was to the history of Jews, and the sparse surviving evidence suggests that in this period his cult was more closely related to local power and politics, than to popular religious devotion.[11]

By assimilating Robert to William of Norwich and other purported victims of ritual murder, historians imply that Bury, like other monastic foundations, must have been in "need of a saint." But this was not the case. Bury was one of the wealthiest and most powerful abbeys in England, and its patron, St. Edmund, enjoyed international stature.[12] Until his eclipse by St. George under the influence of King Edward III, St. Edmund was effectively the national saint of England. Edmund's reputation was such that even without the influence of an abbot in 1181 (when the office was temporarily vacant) the saint could impress the power of his cult upon a visiting bishop and induce him to transmit it abroad.[13] Bury had many friends in high places. The chief political and judicial officer of the crown, the justiciar Warin fitzGerald, for example, commended the monks of Bury to the king's care and made a generous donation to them on his deathbed in the 1160s.[14] Edmund, king and martyr, received significant patronage from English royalty. Henry I vowed to visit St. Edmund if he avoided a perilous sea crossing. Henry II visited Bury as he planned for the Third Crusade shortly before his death in 1189; Queen Eleanor donated some precious jewels to the abbey.[15] Their son Richard the Lionheart was especially devoted to the royal warrior saint. In 1190 he visited Bury before departing for the Third Crusade and did so again immediately upon returning; and while abroad he sent the abbey a golden banner that he had captured.[16] With Bury's immunities from episcopal interference recently confirmed by the pope, and with young William of Norwich's short-lived popularity ebbing, a minor child-saint such as Robert would seem to have added little either to Bury's prestige or to its spiritual and financial resources.

The institutional promotion of Robert's cult seems all the more striking in light of the previously comfortable position of the Jews of Bury as well as the few previous allegations of ritual murder, which, as demonstrated above, were often greeted with skepticism, not enthusiasm. The nine-year gap of time between the accusation in 1181 and the expulsion of the Jews from Bury in 1190 is also curious.[17] Nor was an alleged martyr necessary to provoke an attack on Jews and the cancellation of debts: there was no mention of ritual murder when Jews were massacred in York tower and other towns in England in 1190 and their bonds burned. Robert's alleged martyrdom should be viewed in relation to political, judicial, legal, and local history, not just Christian–Jewish relations. It fits well with recent studies about the political maneuvering of Bury's abbot.[18]

So little is known of St. Robert that one must consider the position of the Jews in the Liberty of Bury at this time in greater detail and press hard on the few sources that exist. Because Brother Jocelin's *Life* of Robert is lost, all that can be adduced of the charge against the Jews that resulted in Robert's claim to martyrdom derives from late medieval sources. These consist of a single manuscript page with a full-page illustration of four scenes that accompanied a short prayer to the young martyr (see Figure 7.1 at the beginning of this chapter) and a five-verse poem composed by one of the most popular of all Middle English poets, John Lydgate, a monk of Bury in the fifteenth century.[19]

The poem includes information about Robert derived directly from Jocelin's *Life*, "lyk as thy story makyth mencyoun."[20] Lydgate explains that Robert, a "sucking" child (a nursing infant), was scourged and nailed to a tree (line 12). He was "slain in earth" (line 21) but is now in heaven. There is much mention of blood: his veins bled (line 18), and his clothes were sanguinous (line 20).[21] Lydgate's poem also suggests that Robert's nursemaid was in league with his oppressors: "Suffering death [n]or you could complain, / your purple blood allayed with milk white / Oppressed with torment, [you] could not say a word / for from your nurse, found no respite."[22] Robert's nursemaid is an early literary model of what was later stereotyped as the Wicked Woman (*mauvaise femme*), a Christian who serves as an intermediary for Jews in such narratives.

The four pictures of the martyrdom offer little additional information. The first frame shows a child held over a well by a woman, presumably the nursemaid, with a Latin scroll that says, "She wished to, but was not able to hide this light of God." In frame 2, an archer discovers Robert's body on a hillside, its sanctity revealed by the divine light of the sun, which is a medieval commonplace (as in William's *Life*). In frame 3, a richly attired man, depicted in a typical contemporary donor portrait, invokes St. Robert, whose tiny soul ascends to heaven in a sheet drawn up by the hands of God. The words on the man's speech scroll reach directly from his mouth to Robert's soul: "Have mercy on me by the merits of St. Robert, now and forever."[23] Frame 4 is entirely taken up by a sealed charter with a large and clear picture of a bird on it. Instead of any text or writing, the large robin apparently refers to the boy's name (Robin is the diminutive of Robert).[24] In English folklore the robin with his red breast was associated with Christ's sacrifice and the theme of murdered innocents.

From the pictures one can deduce that many of the themes in the Bury martyrdom story correspond to those of Norwich: the concealed death, the discovery in the woods, the divine light, the emphasis on the boy's youth and innocence. A new element is the treatment of the body after death. Robert was said to have been cast into a well, a motif that was to become a common element in ritual murder accusations for centuries. Other stereotypes familiar from later accusations are missing: the protagonists consist only of the baby boy, his nurse, the archer, and the patron of the manuscript. No picture portrays the boy's family, or the Jews who were his alleged persecutors.

The prominent placement of the charter, taking up a full quarter page, its association with Robert's sanctity, and the absence of any Jews suggest that the cult was not focused on Jewish malevolence but on chartered rights. The large, unusually shaped vellum document probably represents the important charter of immunities and privileges granted by Edward the Confessor to the abbot of Bury. That valuable royal charter gave the abbot and monks control of the "Liberty of St. Edmund" and associated royal rights, including the right to enjoy royal revenues there, the profits of justice, and the right to run a mint.[25] This remarkable grant of extensive lands by King Edmund the Confessor (the Eight and a Half Hundreds), about a third of the county of Suffolk once controlled by his mother, the queen, was the basis of Bury's considerable wealth and power.[26]

The Liberty of St. Edmund was maintained with great energy and effort for centuries, even in the face of the murders of the prior and abbot by the townsmen in later years. "At several points in Jocelin's chronicle, Abbot Samson is heard insisting on the importance of his responsibility to administer royal justice. . . . Samson sometimes speaks as if St. Edmund died in order to win these rights."[27] The charter was frequently invoked and confirmed by popes and king; when necessary, the abbots would wave the document in the face of authorities—not merely metaphorically. This power was emphasized and reinforced in 1150, when two men accused of treason were not prosecuted by the royal courts but were remanded to the abbot's court because they were "men of St. Edmund."[28] The abbot's own jail is documented from the 1160s, when it was jealously maintained.[29] In the 1180s, immediately after the ritual murder accusation, the monks went so far as to forge a document maintaining the abbot's privilege to try cases of homicide.[30]

Bury's right to high justice was of critical importance to the abbot, monks, and Jews of the Liberty. For Jews, the primary concern when facing a possible prosecution for homicide was access to justice. As we've seen, if an accused were Jewish, he would almost certainly have appealed to the crown, just as Jews successfully did to King Stephen in Norwich, to King Louis VII in France, and later to Emperor Frederick in German lands. A charter of Henry I apparently promised that English Jews could be tried only in royal courts, and this was repeatedly confirmed by Henry's successors.[31] Yet in the Liberty of Bury, the royal justice was administered by the abbot.

Even some Christians were so fearful of the abbot's court that they preferred to maintain silence rather than appeal its judgments.[32] The archbishop of Canterbury was so wary that, according to one scholar, in the 1180s he "preferred to suffer his monks to be done to death without redress rather than to allow his tenants to plead in the abbot's Court."[33]

The Jews apparently avoided the Bury court with some success. It appears that no prosecution for Robert's murder took place, and there is no mention of a trial. Had the Jews been prosecuted successfully, one might expect Jocelin to have repeated the details in his chronicle. Readers could learn there of Bury's success in prosecuting King Sweyn; in prosecuting the treasonous knights; in poisoning the rampaging king's son; and in outwitting the archbishop of Canterbury by prosecuting a homicide.[34] But, surprisingly, there is no mention in any of the voluminous Bury documents of a trial of Jews whom the abbey believed guilty of murder. There may have been no trial because of the actions of royal authorities—just as the sheriff protected the Jews of Norwich from a trial by the bishop in 1144. This apparent defeat must have come as quite a surprise to the monks, who had reason to believe that the charge against the Jews would be taken seriously and that they were within their rights to prosecute them. St. Edmund's power had been repeatedly confirmed, and the position of the Jews in Christendom had steadily eroded.

Events in the years immediately preceding the accusation disposed the monks of Bury to view Robert as the innocent victim of a violent religious crime rather than an unfortunate infant who died in an accident. In 1180 Abbot Hugh of Bury went on a pilgrimage to Canterbury, fell off his horse in September, and despite the best efforts of doctors, died in the middle of November.[35] This led to protracted maneuvers concerning his successor. Brother Jocelin wrote pages weighing the advantages of prospective abbots. Sides formed around Walter the sacrist and Samson his sub-sacrist. Samson, the eventual winner, blamed Walter for allowing Jews free access to

Bury, permitting them to walk around the altars even while Mass was celebrated, and protecting them in an abbey building during the troubles of 1173.[36] Brother Jocelin reports that Hugh had borrowed money repeatedly from various moneylenders and that Bury's finances were desperate:

> Before Hugh died, everything was pillaged by his servants so that nothing was left in his house but three-legged stools and tables that they were unable to carry off. The abbot himself was scarce left with his coverlet and two old torn blankets that someone had placed over him after removing those that were whole. There was nothing worth a single penny that could be distributed to the poor for the benefit of his soul.[37]

Twelve years later Samson had eliminated the debts and had begun to construct and enhance a series of buildings, the remains of which dominate the town to this day. Samson's abbacy was a rejection of everything Abbot Hugh and his sacrist Walter had represented. Samson's fight for leadership of the abbey and the need for funds for his ambitious building plans have been put forth as the primary motive for the ritual murder accusation at Bury.[38]

Equally important, however, were the decisions of the Third Lateran Council in 1179, the Assize of Arms in 1181, Henry's attack on the moneyers in 1180, and Philip Augustus's attack on the Jews of France the following year—events that do not appear immediately relevant to the veneration of a dead child. Coming on the heels of one another, these events were as important for the endorsement of Robert's sanctity and for the revival of charges against the Jews as were other issues related to the abbey's debts to Jewish (and Christian) moneylenders, such as an ambitious and expensive ecclesiastical building program, Christian spiritual insecurity, or Jewish fantasies of revenge. These documented events provided timely support to notions coalescing around Jews, for they offered a series of immediate, specific, and authoritative indications that Jews were pernicious.

The Third Lateran Council sent an unequivocal message to clerics that Jews were not only inferior, but also harmful to the body of Christendom. The horrific actions of the nursemaid at Bury (one can deduce from the picture and poem that she was regarded as having acted on behalf of the Jews) served a pedagogical purpose, reinforcing the decrees of Lateran III, which forbade Christians to work for or to eat, drink, or have intercourse with Jews.[39] In contrast to Lateran IV (1215), which famously required that all Jews wear distinguishing garments, it could be said that Lateran III did not significantly affect Jews. Yet exactly one year before the death of Robert of Bury, the monks learned that the highest religious authorities were reinforcing spiritual and cultural boundaries and insisting that socializing with Jews presented some danger. For the insolvent monks of Bury, hearing the news from their aging and bankrupt abbot, the legislation concerning Jews would have seemed highly relevant.

The following year, English secular authorities conveyed a similar idea about the marginal position of the Jews in contemporary society. The Assize of Arms in 1181 forbade Jews to carry military weapons.[40] In theory, medieval Jews had no need to carry arms, for they were under the protection of the crown. In practice, the message indicated that Jews had to surrender their arms because they were capable of causing harm—or were at least not suited to defend the nation. In the secular urban world, as well as the spiritual one, Jews were therefore clearly ostracized from the social body. This decision left Jews unable to defend themselves, a practice followed in many European countries and well understood by subsequent regimes eager to denigrate and marginalize them.[41] Jews were thrown back on the protection of the crown and the crown alone. The pipe rolls reveal that the legislation was enforced.[42]

The importance of the Assize of Arms should not be underestimated. During the riots of the First Crusade, Jews were occasionally able to protect themselves with their own arms; without weapons, they were at the mercy of the rioters of the Third Crusade.[43] The massacres at York and throughout England less than a decade after the Assize indicated just how unreliable royal protection could be.[44] The danger of relying on the crown for protection became self-evident the same year that Robert of Bury died. In one of his first acts of state, the newly crowned Philip Augustus of France, aged fifteen, attacked Jewish synagogues of the Île-de-France on the Sabbath and then expelled Jews from the royal domain (actions discussed in the following chapter). The meaning of such royal expedients would not have been lost on the insolvent monks of Bury.

Another important element in the triangular relationship among the Bury authorities, the crown, and the Jews in 1180 is usually overlooked: Henry II's attack on the mints in 1180, of which the abbey of Bury boasted one and in which Jews may have played a key but unacknowledged role. King Henry took action throughout his realm. He suppressed mints, radically redesigned the coinage, and imported advisers and practices from the Continent.[45] These reforms of 1180 followed the mint reforms of 1158, when Henry "removed from office almost the entire body of moneyers, many of whom had held office for generations," as part of "an overall plan to extend royal authority over the mints, to unify their administration, and to increase the king's share of the moneyers' profits."[46] The attack on the local mint in 1180 was not unique to Bury, but it must have been dramatic, for Bury was the last ecclesiastical institution that had the privilege of a mint, a highly profitable endeavor usually reserved for royalty. Bury successfully reasserted its privileges in 1205 and continued to mint into the fourteenth century, so many have overlooked the fact that the Bury mint was closed for some decades in the late twelfth century.[47]

The suppression of moneying at Bury would have been a financial blow to the fortunes of the already hard-pressed abbey and a psychological blow to the cherished powers of abbot and monks. Among the generous and unusual grants Edward the Confessor made to the abbot of Bury was the right to strike coins. The abbey clung to this right as a special mark of favor and a source of profit. Bury expanded production and produced numerous varieties of coin after 1158 that brought a large profit to the abbey and made the Bury fairs particularly attractive. The abbey had the right to employ its own moneyer and to operate an exchange for coin or bullion brought to the mint.[48] The suppression of the mint in 1180 was thus a serious business, and the cost to the abbey must have been substantial. Although both King Richard and King John confirmed the abbot's minting right, and Samson insisted that the grant to the abbey be read out in the chapter house on his installation as abbot, no coins minted at Bury survive from this period. The crown took the responsibility for exchange away from the minters (i.e., the *cambiatores* now came under direct royal purview) and the mint ceased to operate. It appears that the Bury mint did not "fall into abeyance," but that it was actively suppressed.[49] As has been noted, "the changes in 1180 seem to have been designed mainly to divert profits on coinage from the moneyers more directly to the king."[50]

From the beginning of his reign, Henry II had tried to assert royal control, and he enjoyed great success in bringing the ecclesiastical mints under his authority. On the death of an abbot, minting privileges were suspended and had to be renewed. It was precisely at such times that the king took the opportunity to close ecclesiastical mints indefinitely and, on the death of a lord, to close baronial mints.[51] From fifty-two mints operating at the time of Stephen's death in 1154, Henry reduced the number to ten in 1180; by the time of his death, there were no ecclesiastical mints operating in England.[52] Bury was the last of the privilege mints to operate, and Abbot Hugh's death in 1180 was just the excuse for which Henry had been looking since Hugh's election as abbot in 1157.

The closing of the Bury mint from 1180 to 1205 struck at the heart of the power of the monks and abbot. The monks fought bitter battles throughout the thirteenth century to reclaim their right to mint coins, making these rights a top priority in discussions with the papal legate and raising them in meetings of the full convent.[53] At the end of the century, when the mint had been closed once again, after a showdown at court during which the abbot entered waving the abbey charter from Edward the Confessor (and after the king had a bad dream about the saint), another king acquiesced when Edward I restored Bury's minting privileges in 1291, ruefully admitting, "St. Edmund had raised his banner for them all."[54] This focus on moneyers may have drawn new attention to the role of Jews in Bury in minting, exchanging, and lending money.

Evidence is growing that Jews played a leading part not only in lending money, but also in minting and exchanging money throughout Europe at this time. The full extent of Jewish involvement in minting and monetary exchange remains unclear, but indications are that it was far more important in the twelfth century than has previously been thought. "The Jewish mintmaster was a key figure in the transformation of the barter economy of medieval Europe to a money economy. The twelfth and thirteenth centuries show Jewish mint lessees in almost every European country: in Aragon, Castile, Catalonia, Austria, many German states, Moravia, Hungary, Poland, and possibly England."[55] It is possible, although unproven, that Jews were involved in the Bury mint as well. Five individual Jewish moneyers have been tentatively identified as working in England in this period from their names on coins.[56] The names of another two Jewish moneyers are documented, but their coins have not yet been found.[57] In Canterbury, "the *monetarii*, moneyers, or workers in the mint, lived in the Jewish quarter, and it is interesting to note that one of these workmen was Nicholas, a converted Jew, who is mentioned as early as 1181."[58] Some English Jews, identified as goldsmiths, may have been craftsmen, mint officials, or both.[59] But even if in England Jews were not minters or moneyers themselves—a risky but high-status profession traditionally passed down in Anglo-Saxon families—Jews were closely associated with mints as exchangers and then moneylenders.

The rise and decline of some twelfth-century Jewish communities may be explained by the loss of mint and exchanging rights rather than, as often assumed, by a decline in aristocratic borrowers.[60] The beginning of the decline of the Jewries of Thetford and Bristol, for example, like that of Bury, coincides with the suppression of the mints in 1180, a decade before the debilitating attacks of 1190.[61] Jews may have had relative advantages in minting and exchanging, and they may also have amassed capital by arbitrage.[62]

In the 1140s it was taken for granted that Jews operated the financial exchanges. When Empress Matilda occupied Oxford during the civil war, she demanded that the Jews pay one "exchange." Upon Stephen's reoccupation, he demanded three and one-half times as much.[63] Although the precise meaning of the term "exchange" remains unclear in this context, it referred to a substantial sum related to an important occupation. Having been accused of some crime of exchanging (*cambivisse*) under Henry II, three Jews paid a fine to be quit of the charge, a term that may refer to minting rather than exchanging money.[64] The repeated use of such terms suggests that Jews in England were closely involved in the production, distribution, and exchange of coin. Christians who exchanged money in the twelfth century were often "financiers of considerable wealth."[65]

Jews first came to Bury exactly when the mint there was expanding its production. They are not mentioned in Bury before the time of Henry II and are not listed as contributing to the Northampton *donum* of 1159. Yet in the third quarter of the century, Bury Jews were actively involved with the sacrist and were protected by him. It is possible that they were employed by him: the sacrist had complete responsibility for the Bury exchange, and he "supervised the mint, claiming dies, presenting officials at the exchequer and accounting for profits."[66] By 1190, when the Jews of the Liberty were massacred during the riots, Bury had a very large community and one that had grown quickly.

The mint closure occurred at the worst possible time for the abbey, which was already facing a serious crisis of liquidity. If the Jews were indeed involved in minting and exchanging, the closure would have exacerbated tensions between monks and Jews.

The appropriate context for considering St. Robert's cult is not simply that of an abbey between abbots, a divided convent, or one squeezed by Jewish debts—circumstances that occurred frequently in this period at monasteries throughout England. The relevant backdrop was a sudden attack on well-defended privileges that threatened further to deplete the abbey's finances and to assail its vast array of royal grants. The Jews were used as convenient scapegoats in a bid to fend off the legal and financial encroachment of the crown. The discovery of a victim allegedly martyred by Jews allowed members of the abbey to unite in support of its ancient charters. Among the important privileges under attack at the time of Robert's death were those connected to the mint and to the prosecution of homicide.

In 1181 at Bury there was a conflict between rights claimed by abbot and king in which the Jews were targets of convenience. At that time the abbey was unable to prevail over the more powerful claims of the king, as Jocelin's failure to mention a successful prosecution suggests. A decade later, within a year of the accession of a new king to the throne, issues raised over the right to prosecute the Jews for homicide prompted Samson to request the expulsion of the Jews. The time was then ripe. Earlier, Henry II would never have granted permission for an expulsion; he was far more effective at protecting "his" Jews than was his son Richard.

King Richard the Lionheart was in a weaker position in 1190 than his father had been in 1181, and his own position on Jews was further compromised by the riots and massacres in London that accompanied his coronation in September 1189. Richard needed Samson's support.[67] In the fall of 1190, six months after the spring massacres of Jews across England, the government therefore allowed Samson to expel the Jews throughout the Liberty of Bury St. Edmunds, the first such expulsion in medieval Europe. Samson returned the favor shortly afterward by personally carrying the treasure of Bury St. Edmunds to Germany in an effort to free Richard from captivity on his return from the Third Crusade.

Brother Jocelin reports that Samson received permission from the government to expel the Jews, but even then Richard's representatives declined to give Samson free rein:

> Leave was therefore given him to expel them, but on this condition, that they should keep all their chattels and have the value of their houses and lands as well. And when they had been sent forth and conducted under armed escort to other towns, the Abbot ordered that all those who from that time forth should receive Jews or harbour them in the town of St Edmund should be solemnly excommunicated in every church and at every altar. Nevertheless afterwards the king's justices ordained that, if Jews came to the Abbot's great pleas [court] to exact the money owed them from their debtors, they should under those circumstances have leave to be lodged in the town for two nights and two days, and on the third day should depart in freedom.[68]

The alleged ritual murder case of 1181 concerned the rights and privileges embodied in Bury's charter. After decades of battle, Bury's rights had been repeatedly confirmed by pope, king, and bishop. These remarkable privileges, embodied in the royal charter, included minting and exchanging privileges and the prosecution of crown pleas, high justice for felony crimes, immunity from supervision by the bishop of Norwich, and later from interference by papal legates as well.

Whatever spiritual purposes the interpretation of Robert's death may have served, it was also used in an attempt to reinforce the power of the abbey, the abbot, and the convent as a whole at a time of crisis. Brother Jocelin, who entertained second thoughts about Samson over the long years of his chronicle, evinced no doubts about "Bury and the Jewish question." His composition of Robert's *Life* indicates that he wholeheartedly believed the ritual murder accusation to be true, and he states proudly that Samson's expulsion of the Jews from Bury nine years later was among the abbot's most significant accomplishments. In Norwich, Brother Thomas suggested that

William's cult was a divisive issue. In Bury, the cult of young Robert provided a rallying point for the entire convent, not just the party of the wily Samson.

It is easy to be misled by the claims for St. William's popularity and to overlook devotion to St. Robert. Ironically, illustrations of William's martyrdom are more widely reproduced now than they ever were in the Middle Ages.[69] In contrast, until its recent sale to the Getty Museum, the manuscript page depicting St. Robert was reproduced only once in black and white, more than sixty years ago. Practical considerations go some way toward explaining this fact, but there are aesthetic and stylistic reasons as well. The Bury manuscript of Robert, (fig. 7.1) with its depiction of donor and charter taking up a half page and no illustration of Jews, does not overtly illustrate notions of marginalization, hatred, crucifixion, and deicide, which the ritual murder accusation supposedly represents and reinforces. The fifteenth-century picture of William of Norwich that hung in Loddon Church, (fig. C.1), showing him grossly splayed and suspended from a wooden crossbar, in contrast, is suitably violent and threatening, reaffirming modern views of the Middle Ages. It accords well with our idea of the content and meaning of the twelfth-century accusation. The Bury manuscript illumination, with its emphasis on rights and privileges, does not.

As Brother Jocelin and his abbot were keenly aware, St. Robert of Bury addressed some of the most pressing concerns of their day: he was as important in his own way as the celebrated St. Edmund in defending their jealously guarded liberties. It is not surprising, therefore, that an altar in Robert's name was maintained in Bury centuries after Harold of Gloucester, a similar sort of victim, was forgotten. The monks' insistence on the importance of their charter from Edward the Confessor and its apparently prominent placement in the depiction of Robert's martyrdom suggest that the twelfth-century ritual murder charge at Bury was largely legal, constitutional, and ecclesiastical in nature.[70]

The next charge of ritual murder, which was made across the Channel, likewise reflected concerns about the role of the king, royal power, civic identity, and local juridical authority that were embodied in civic legislation and manifested in an ecclesiastical shrine. The abbot of Bury, like the count of Blois, the earl of Gloucester, and the bishop of Norwich, realized that charging Jews with homicide raised issues about the use and manipulation of power. This supposed "irrational," "bizarre," "literary trope" was the product of lucid, cogent arguments, thoughtfully and carefully debated in executive councils, judged in detail by sober men who were not reacting under pressure to thoughtless mob violence. In both Blois and Paris there were real consequences for Jews and Christians that extended far beyond the veneration of an individual saint.

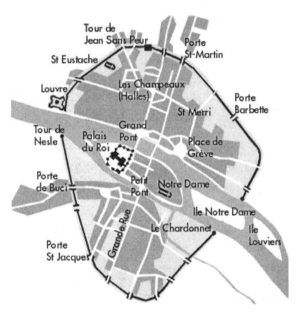

FIGURE 8.1A, B, AND C King Philip expelled Jews from the royal domain, seized their land, and included it within the new walls he erected to enlarge the city. Parts of the walls survive today; the tower of the cemetery of the Holy Innocents where Richard of Pontoise was buried has not survived.

CHAPTER 8 *Paris*

Around the same time that the monks of Bury believed that they had found a victim of ritual murder to follow upon that of William of Norwich, the young king of France, Phillip II Augustus, recognized a similar victim in Paris. In both cases, the purported martyrs were put to practical, immediate, strategic uses while they also helped to promote and make credible a more general belief about Jewish animosity toward Christians. The accusation against the Jews was employed to serve local interests, to underscore conventional religious teaching, and to accord with contemporary and earlier biblical exegesis.

As with Robert of Bury, little is known of the purported victim Richard of Paris. All that survives is a paragraph in the royal chronicle Rigord composed sometime in the 1180s, after the Jews were expelled from the royal domain, the part of France under direct control of the king rather than that of his feudal lords, like Blois and Champagne. Rigord suggests that stories of Jewish malefactors were current around the palace where Philip grew up. He famously wrote that

> Philip had heard many times from the boys who were fostered with him in the palace—and commended to memory—that the Jews who lived in Paris slit the throat of one Christian in the hidden underground caverns every year on Maundy Thursday or during the Holy Week of penitence, and that they did so as a kind of

sacrifice in contempt of the Christian religion, noting that many who had long persevered in this kind of wickedness by diabolical seduction had been burned in his father's time.[1]

The burnings were those of Blois in 1171 and the "youths" from whom Philip heard stories of alleged Jewish atrocities may have been an exaggerated reference to his young cousin Louis, the son of Alix and Thibaut V of Blois.[2]

Further details of the Parisian accusation are known only from a brief funeral oration composed in the late fifteenth century.[3] The Jews were said to have abducted Richard, a twelve-year-old boy from Pontoise, a town in the north Paris suburbs. They were accused of hiding him in a cave, demanding that he deny Christ, and then crucifying him.[4] The adolescent was acclaimed a martyr and was laid to rest in the cemetery of *les Innocents* at Paris, where Rigord reported that many miracles occurred.[5] Few other customary elements of a popular holy cult are recorded—no artwork, pilgrimages, notes in liturgical calendars, prayers, donations, invocations, or inscriptions. Like William of Norwich, Richard of Pontoise (or "Richard of Paris") appears to have been recognized as a saint only years after his death, and like Harold of Gloucester he may initially have been an unidentified corpse, buried in the cemetery of the Holy Innocents for that reason.[6] As with William of Norwich, Robert of Bury, and the earlier cases, we will examine the local political circumstances and the immediate religious context in which this incident of blood libel was promoted.

Whether he believed the accusation or not, Philip took an active role in spreading it and used it as the centerpiece for his long-term strategy of building up Paris and cementing and centralizing royal power.[7] As in Norwich and Bury, it provided a common focus and linked religious devotion with secular ambition, neatly combining the practical and the spiritual to the obvious advantage of the king.

Both boys—that in Bury a babe in arms, the one in Paris an articulate youth—were identified with the biblical child martyrs of

Bethlehem, the Holy Innocents. In Paris, as in Bury and in Norwich, the association of local contemporary children with Gospel precedents served to tie medieval Europe to the Holy Land and lay worshipers to the life of Christ and the history of salvation. It elevated their existence from the humdrum to the holy.

It is therefore worthwhile to digress for a discussion of the cult of the Holy Innocents, which was revitalized and took new shape in the middle of the twelfth century, before we return to the final ritual murder accusation we shall consider in this chapter, one vigorously promoted by the king of France in his capital city. This ritual murder accusation became the occasion or pretext for the expulsion of the Jews from the royal domain and it thereby spread knowledge of the charge throughout Europe. Only after the charges made in Bury and Paris, and the expulsions and dispersion that followed, did the ritual murder accusation become a familiar part of the landscape of Christendom, but it was the widespread veneration of the Holy Innocents that laid the groundwork and helped to make the charge credible.

The accusations made against Jews in the twelfth century were closely aligned with the medieval celebration of the cult of the Holy Innocents, infant boys said to have been killed in place of the Christ Child. The Gospel of Matthew recounts that King Herod flew into a rage when told of the birth of Christ and ordered his soldiers to seek out the male infants in Bethlehem and slay them. Joseph, Mary, and Jesus escaped to Egypt while the soldiers massacred the children of Bethlehem in an effort to kill Christ.[8] Herod was known to have had mad rages and to have killed his wife and two sons out of jealousy, as reported by the Jewish historian Flavius Josephus.[9] Medieval Christians, therefore, had little trouble believing that the Slaughter of the Innocents occurred and that many thousands of infants were killed, possibly 14,000 or as many as 144,000, a number mentioned in the Book of Revelation (14:3).[10]

The Bethlehem infants, Jewish children of Jewish mothers, were transformed in medieval Christian interpretations to become

Christian children of Christian mothers, while their putative Roman murderers were understood as Jewish perpetrators who threatened all Christian families, not just that of Christ the Savior. Jews, therefore, were not only implicated in killing the adult Christ at the time of the Crucifixion; they were also singled out as a collective menace to the young children of unexceptional families at the time of the Nativity. Attributing the death of the Holy Innocents to Jews placed them under the suspicion of seeking the death of all Christian children, even when Christ himself, for whom the Innocents died, was absent. Fervent belief in the cult of the Holy Innocents underpinned belief in the medieval accusation of ritual murder.

The cult of the Holy Innocents began early, but the twelfth century saw a marked rise in the devotion and a new emphasis on the cult's importance.[11] A number of factors contributed to the spread of the devotion. The population surge of the twelfth century may have led to a greater focus on the needs of children. Historians now argue that concern for the welfare of children may have been greater in the twelfth century than previously, countering an earlier notion that high infant mortality contributed to a hardening of parental hearts and a lack of emotional involvement with their offspring.[12] A growing sentimentality in European culture and an increased interest in the humanity of Christ also drew attention to the story of the massacre, and the victims often figure prominently in artistic cycles depicting Christ's infancy. Fascination with the *innocenti* also paralleled growing interest in the childhood stories of other holy figures such as St. Edmund and the Virgin Mary.

The narrative of ritual murder also evoked the only biblical story from Christ's childhood: Mary searching for her son and finding him after a three-day absence among the doctors of the law in the synagogue (Luke 2:41–52), an incident featured in the very popular and influential work from the 1150s by Aelred of Rievaulx, *On the Boy Jesus When He Was Twelve Years Old*. The anguished mothers in later medieval ritual murder stories search fruitlessly for their sons and imagine finding them, as Mary does, among the rabbis.

The twelfth-century narrative also recalls the genre of the *Planctus Mariae*, lyric poetry and drama that imagines Mary's lament over the crucifixion of her son and that was developed into an elaborate liturgical performance over the course of the twelfth century.[13]

Before the mid-twelfth century, the feast of the Holy Innocents was a sad occasion, an opportunity for parents who had lost children to indulge their grief. Paulinus, the fifth-century bishop of Nola, and his wife lost a child in infancy; his poem to other parents who had also suffered the loss of a child suggests that they "would find comfort in the cult of the Holy Innocents."[14] Amalarius of Metz pointed out that the liturgy was intended "to have us sympathize with the feelings of the pious women who wept and sorrowed at the death of their innocent children."[15] There must have been many, like the Anglo-Saxon nun Richtrude who, on the feast day of the Holy Innocents, explicitly compared her pain on the death of her daughter to that of the mourning mothers of Bethlehem.[16] For Pope Gregory the Great, the feast of the Innocents was a day of mourning.[17]

The early feast of the Innocents was a sorrowful occasion because the children suffered and were not redeemed. Augustine of Hippo, for example, thought they were damned because they had died unbaptized. Other theologians were less confident. Aelfric concluded that they would arise at the Last Judgment. By the twelfth century, attention focused on the children, and there was a new emphasis on rejoicing rather than sorrowing. The children, it was thought, were baptized with their blood; the grieving mothers were baptized with their tears. Dressed in the white gowns associated with baptism and sexual purity (*in albis*), the Innocents would rejoice in heaven, not languish in hell.[18]

The Slaughter of the Innocents therefore became a popular story in the twelfth century and was widely disseminated. Relics of the Holy Innocents were easily obtainable, and with so many purported victims, many churches could plausibly boast of having some without fear of duplication. Not only did twelfth-century Christians see relics of the young victims (such as the shoulderbone of an Innocent in

Peterborough), they could look at depictions of their death whenever they went to church. From the middle of the twelfth century there was a significant proliferation of representations of the Massacre of the Innocents. Depictions of this subject appeared on everything from a metal altarpiece in Denmark and the doors of Novgorod Cathedral, to illuminated English psalters, the portals of a cathedral in Pisa, and a Swiss furniture bench. The subject was especially popular on the exterior of Romanesque and early Gothic cathedrals in France, prominently placed on doorways and the tops of columns. The story of the Innocents appears on three-quarters of the known twelfth-century French cloisters.[19]

In the mid-twelfth century two notable French patrons raised the profile of the Innocents and endorsed their cult, setting an example for others. Royal figures seemed particularly drawn to the Innocents, perhaps because the catalyst for the massacre was Herod's fear of a newborn king (*rex novus*).[20] King Louis VII encouraged veneration of the Holy Innocents, building a prominent church to them in Paris and frequently swearing *per sanctos de Bethlehem*.[21] Bernard of Clairvaux, Louis's spiritual advisor and friend—the influential abbot of Clairvaux who encouraged him to venture on the Second Crusade and consoled him on his return—famously endorsed the sanctity of the Innocents as well, as did other leading clerics, such as Peter Abelard, who wrote a dramatic hymn to them.

The cult of the Innocents was prominent among Benedictines in the early twelfth century; it is likely for that reason that Gregorio Papareschi (d. 1143) took the unusual name "Innocent" in 1130 when he was elected pope. The choice of this name drew distinctions as well between him and his opponent, Peter Pierleoni, who was also elected pope the same year. Although his election was more "regular," Pierleoni is now remembered as the antipope Anacletus II, the grandson of a Jewish convert to Christianity.[22] Pierleoni, a Benedictine monk educated in Paris and having the support of the majority of cardinals and the Roman clergy, was never allowed to forget his origins. Taking the name Innocent drew parallels not only between Papareschi and the martyred child saints, but also to the Jewish heritage of his adversary, which Papareschi's supporters took pains to demonize. Among those leading the charge against the eminent Pierleoni, and one of the most vicious, was Arnulf of Séez (bishop of Lisieux from 1141), who was later to accompany Louis VII on the Second Crusade, as noted above. Arnulf denounced Anacletus's perfidy, gluttony, sexual desires, and Jewish appearance, and associated those characteristics with the Antichrist.[23] The successful pope Innocent II was strongly backed by Bernard, who acquiesced to having Pierleoni's name disparaged during the schism that lasted until Pierleoni's death in 1138.

Bernard's vigorous public support of the Holy Innocents occurred in the context of his attacks on heresy, especially against dissidents who denied the efficacy of infant baptism. While preaching against heresy in his *Sermons on the Song of Songs*, Bernard spoke directly to the parents in his audience. He compared the Innocents killed by Herod's soldiers to contemporary children of the twelfth century. He further equated the crown of martyrdom earned by the Innocents "with the salvation bestowed by baptism on any child who died before the age of discretion."[24] For Bernard, the Innocents were baptized by the blood of martyrdom, which was as effective as the water of baptism. Although they could neither assent to martyrdom nor articulate their faith, he suggested that the babies were also baptized by desire, as indicated by their wailing.[25]

Earlier theologians were enthusiastic about the Innocents but less sure about the theology. There was some question about exactly where the Innocents went after death and about the state of their souls *post mortem*.[26] The children lacked cognition and articulation, and they died before Christian baptism was instituted and before Christ's Resurrection, all of which presented a challenging theological problem. They died not only for Christ, as did other martyrs, but, uniquely, in his stead. This interpretation of the Holy Innocents as the first martyrs of the Church was open to challenge by heretics and Jews, for did not Christ die to save the world? How then could one justify the deaths of those who died for Christ and in his place? This difficult issue provoked disagreement among devout and learned Christians. The late eleventh-century *Micrologus*, a treatise on the liturgy of the Mass, for example, explained that the Holy Innocents went down to the underworld, not to Paradise.

By the twelfth century, parents were instructed that the Innocents were specially blessed, and the emphasis of the cult shifted perceptibly from the sorrow of the mothers to the happy fate of their children, who were soon to be reunited with Christ. Parents in the twelfth century were assured that their children, and the Innocents on whom they were modeled, would not be deprived of the holy vision by an early death. In fact, as the first martyrs of the Church, the Innocents did not have to wait for the Second Coming. But to the extent that twelfth-century Christian parents were encouraged to see their children as innocents, their fears coalesced around a perceived threat to them.

The veneration of the Holy Innocents is rarely, if ever, considered in the context of Christian–Jewish relations, but it had a profound impact on how the Christian faithful viewed nonbelievers. The newfound popularity of the cult of the *innocenti* required a dramatic inversion so that Jewish babies killed by Roman soldiers were regarded in medieval Christian exegesis as Christian boys killed on the command of a Jew. Herod, the authoritarian madman who gave the horrific orders, the learned but evil advisors who recommended killing innocent babies, and the bloodthirsty soldiers who dispatched the nursing infants—all were portrayed in the High Middle Ages as a wicked network of Jews intent on murder.

In contrast, the mourning Jewish matriarch Rachel, inconsolable with grief over the death of Jewish children, explicitly recalled by Matthew, and the mourning mothers of Bethlehem, were regarded as Christian mothers rejoicing in the heavenly future of Christian children. This belief was expressed visually: in works of sculpture, manuscript paintings, and, above all, in drama, where Jews were portrayed as scheming murderers intent on killing Christian youths.

Much of the theatrical documentation dates from the late Middle Ages, but there are indications that most of the traditions described here began by the twelfth century. In viewing performances of the Slaughter of the Innocents, Christians "saw" dramatized Jews murdering young children on account of their hatred of Christ, exactly as was alleged in the contemporary ritual murder accusation.

To demonstrate to the Christian faithful that the Innocents went to heaven, church drama was enlisted to bring home the lesson to the pious in vivid and arresting scenes using every form of media—sound, sight, action, and audience participation. The Slaughter of the Innocents was one of the first biblical stories to be dramatized. These early dramas express a distinctive religious theology: the *innocenti* are portrayed as sentient children, not helpless infants. In Renaissance art, nursing infants are ripped from their mother's breast, but in medieval church drama they willingly proceed to their doom, intoning both before and after their sacrifice, indicating their acquiescence to the grand plan of salvation. In the earliest dramatized representations of the massacre, they seem to die quickly and do not indicate what then takes place, but in slightly later versions, also of the twelfth century, they arise and walk to the choir of the church.

Changes in performance were spurred by developments in theology, not just by the emerging demands of dramatic art, as some critics imply. In an early Church performance, when the boys sang, "why do you not defend our blood?" an angel explained that they must wait to join their brothers in heaven. The new theology was manifested when, at the end of the liturgical drama, the boys were resuscitated. They do not wait but immediately rise to their feet, making clear the theological explanation that the Holy Innocents went directly to heaven. Scholars credit the resuscitation to the creativity of the dramatist, but the producers may have been motivated by pedagogy as well as by theatrical art.[27]

The emerging drama highlighted the identification of contemporary adolescents, such as William of Norwich, with the Innocents of ancient times. The medieval performers were active youths (*pueri*), not inarticulate infants (*infanti*), and were portrayed by young monks processing from the monastery to the nave of the church, arrayed in white to reinforce the notion of their sexual purity. These young actors were oblates or scholars and choristers at the local monastery, dedicated by their parents to the Church for the good of their souls and that of their families. The music and drama in which the boys participated served to fuse the two types of innocents.[28] The Benedictine monasteries had large numbers of oblates at this time, and the cult of the Holy Innocents and the practice of child oblation among the Benedictines were consciously linked. Orderic Vitalis (d. ca. 1142), for example, who was sent abroad to a monastery in France at the age of nine, was assured that "if I became a monk I should taste of the joys of heaven with the Innocents after my death."[29] It is in the Benedictine context that the ritual murder accusation first arose.[30]

Later medieval Christians could have learned of the ritual murder accusation from the mouth of a young cathedral student in connection with celebrations of the Holy Innocents, when a boy playing the role of bishop took on the instruction of his elders. Veneration of the children of Bethlehem was closely associated with the cult of St. Nicholas, whose feast day in winter, December 6, inaugurated a season of festivity. On that day, a boy bishop was elected by the choristers and began his preparations to take office on Holy Innocents Day (December 28), when he first preached before the public and began his "rule."[31] The feast of the Holy Innocents was the most likely occasion when a story of ritual murder, or an *exemplum*, was recited; the boy bishop would have been the appropriate candidate to deliver it. Chaucer, for example, probably heard a story of Jewish ritual murder at an Innocents' mass, which he then included in the Prioress's Tale.[32] His mention of "another Hugh" suggests that it was delivered in proximity to Hugh's shrine in Lincoln Cathedral.[33]

The parallels between the purported child victims of the twelfth century and the infants of Bethlehem described in Gospel accounts of the Nativity were implicit and explicit. They were connected visually, rhetorically, musically, and spatially. The visual associations, for example, were established by the style and placement of their pictures. William of Norwich was depicted as part of the story of the Infancy of Christ. At Loddon, for example, William appears on the late medieval rood screen among scenes of the Annunciation, Nativity, Presentation in the Temple, and Adoration of the Magi. The text of his passion is full of allusions to the Holy Innocents, and its author, Brother Thomas, made explicit comparisons between the twelve-year-old victim of the twelfth century and the biblical infants.[34] Subsequent accusations of Jewish ritual murder were consciously created in the context of veneration of the Holy Innocents. The only surviving picture of the infant Robert of Bury, for example, in the late medieval English manuscript of the Life of the Virgin described above, placed him squarely between the death of Herod and the Flight into Egypt, thus making him a Holy Innocent.[35] In Fulda in 1235, the alleged perpetrators of a ritual murder or blood libel were burned on Holy Innocents Day. When a mass was celebrated in memory of St. Andrew of Rinn (usually remembered by the diminuitive Anderl), who was believed to have been killed by Jews in 1462, it was a votive mass of the Holy Innocents.[36]

This link between a purported victim of Jewish ritual murder and the Holy Innocents was made especially powerfully in Paris, where the new young king associated himself both with the cult of the Innocents and the persecution of Jews. In Paris, the shrine to a new child saint, Richard, was erected in the Church of *les Innocents*; references to the biblical Innocents, the pope Innocent I (d. 417) to whom the church had originally been dedicated, and the new boy martyr were frequently confused. Each cult buttressed the other and situated Richard, the dead medieval child, squarely in the embrace of the institutional Church, not at the margins of some uncontrolled popular piety.

Philip Augustus was fifteen when he ascended the French throne in 1180. Philip was supposedly so scared of the animosity of the Jews in his kingdom that one of his first acts as king was to raid the

French synagogues under his protection and hold Jews hostage until they paid vast sums to be released. Fearful of the stories he had heard as a child about Jews kidnapping and torturing young boys, he endorsed the sanctity of one purported Christian martyr, Richard of Pontoise, who was said to have been held captive in the caverns of the Paris suburbs before his murder.

The following year, Philip decided that more action was needed to counter the purported criminality of the Jews.[37] For the first time since Jews were recorded in Gaul under the early Merovingians, they were expelled. More than one thousand Jews were given less than three months to leave the French royal domain, in the first of many national expulsions to come.[38] A reversal of that policy by Philip, a more mature and experienced monarch sixteen years later, brought Jews back into the kingdom and underscored the hasty decisions of the teenage ruler.

Such is the common explanation for the actions at the opening of Philip's reign, which receive far less attention than his successes in state building during his forty-year rule—accomplishments that, aside from his actions concerning Jews, are regarded as modern and forward-looking. The accusation that Jews had committed ritual murder was well known, and the idea of a Jewish threat was so generally accepted by the time of Richard of Pontoise, we are assured, that the young king was compelled to act quickly and respond to the public outcry.[39]

Contrary to conventional interpretations, it seems clear that the accusation of ritual murder was not widely known, as Rigord is at pains to suggest (but did build on the previous cases previously discussed), that the cult of Richard of Pontoise was not a cause but the result of the expulsions of 1182, and that Philip's support of the cult was not anomalous but central to his vision of kingship. As with the later actions of the mature ruler, we see Philip leading his subjects rather than reacting to a popular outcry. In this interpretation, Philip manipulated the charge of ritual murder, a charge publicly dismissed by his father, to enhance his power and standing.[40]

Philip deployed the charge of ritual murder to unify a diverse urban community in ways that both reflected and reinforced royal power. At a time of potential weakness, when the young king was facing an uprising from his barons, Philip's exploitation of Richard's cult enabled him to be seen as leading the charge against an undisputed external enemy. By successfully harnessing religious animosity for civic purposes, the king drew attention away from a serious military menace and internecine family squabbles. His actions cast him in the role of his nation's chief defender at precisely the time when its leading magnates were assembling in opposition to the crown and when conflict with England loomed.[41] Promoting the cult also enhanced Philip's support from the Church: it is in the context of his actions with regard to the Jews that he is described as *christianissimus* by his clerical biographer.

Philip learned from the actions of his uncle Thibaut V of Blois in the provinces and emulated them. He had seen how the count and countess of Blois, without any evidence of a crime, had benefited by accusing Jews of killing a Christian child, executing the alleged evildoers, and seizing the pledges made to them. As a result, the Blois rulers enjoyed enhanced political status, the appearance of religious piety, and financial advantage (as discussed here in Chapter 6).

The timing and sequence of Philip's attacks on the Jews seem straightforward—rumors, specific accusation, *captio* extortion, expulsion—extending over the course of more than a year—but the chronology is much more complicated than the sources would have us believe.[42] Writing about two decades after the events, Rigord is vague about the exact year the events took place and often rearranges chronology for dramatic effect.[43] He mentions that the young king was advised by a hermit, by which one might presume an unwordly man of the cloth. But the monk in question was Bernard de Boschiac, the well-connected fifth abbot of the austere order of Grandmont, an experienced administrator from an illustrious French family. Bernard was no country bumpkin, but one of the king's most trusted counselors, who supervised the establishment of eighty new foundations of his order.[44] Although often portrayed as the sudden whim of an excessively pious and severe teenager, the expulsion of the Jews was part of a calculated political effort endorsed by the king's eminent advisors.

Like his uncle Thibaut, Philip used the story of ritual murder to achieve political goals and acquire land, to clean Paris literally as well as figuratively, to replenish royal coffers, to break decisively with the rule of his father, and to enhance the commercial capabilities of his capital. In 1171 Thibaut had used the accusation against the Jews of his domain to stake his claims to power, independence, and religious orthodoxy. Philip, following in the footsteps of Thibaut, the royal seneschal of France, availed himself of the opportunity to make a dramatic and profitable statement of piety and power. Philip and Thibaut both placed themselves in opposition to the policies of King Louis VII.[45]

Philip rebuilt and endowed the church where Richard was interred, most likely blessed it with his presence, and may have contributed a valuable reliquary.[46] Richard's cult was the center-piece of a major reconstruction project. It was initiated and supported by the king, and his largesse was everywhere apparent. The site of Richard's shrine was carefully chosen for maximum symbolic impact. The old church apparently possessed relics of an individual saint, Pope Innocent I.[47] By the late twelfth century, with the growth of interest in holy children, the long-forgotten singular St. Innocent was assimilated to the plural Holy Innocents, Herod's infant victims.[48] The date of celebration, the location, and the architecture of the shrine emphasized Richard's spiritual affinities with the biblical Holy Innocents, the crown's connection to the young martyred boy, and the association of both with the murderous intentions of the Jews of Paris. The apparent threat to civil harmony was quickly dispatched by the newly crowned young king, who was himself a kind of Holy Innocent, a royal type of Christ.

The location of the church where the alleged martyr was interred had strong associations with Parisian Jews and the king. The church was attached to the large cemetery of *les Innocents* that at the time received perhaps half the corpses of Paris, including bodies from hospitals, plague victims, and cadavers found on public thorough-fares.[49] The cemetery abutted a Jewish residential and commercial district. When Philip II expelled the Jews from France in 1182, he confiscated their property and thereupon established the market-place of *les Halles du Rois*. The young king used Jewish resources to clear the area and to build the stalls, and he established them on or near Jewish buildings that he had destroyed and Jewish land that he had expropriated.[50] Les Halles was in the area of Champeaux (*cam-panelli*) to which Philip's grandfather Louis VI had moved the large Paris market. Louis VII expanded the market, and Philip Augustus transferred to it the fair his father had established and originally granted to the leper hospital of Saint-Lazare (*St. Ladre*) on the major road north from Paris out to Saint-Denis and toward Pontoise.

The king constructed two long arcades with walls and covered stalls as a shelter for merchants who congregated there, replacing the open booths.[51] In 1186 the king enclosed the ancient and unsavory cemetery of *les Innocents* with a wall and directed that the gates to *les Halles* be locked at night, clearing the area of prostitutes and highlighting the permanence and stability of his commercial enter-prise.[52] Encouraging merchants to leave their goods at *les Halles* pro-moted trade in large and expensive items, luxury goods and bulk produce, cloth, and grain. The new market was held on Saturdays, when Jews traditionally did no business. To further urban develop-ment, the king also required the citizens of Paris to pay to enlarge the major roads and to have them paved with flagstones cut to pre-cise measurements (*carreaux des Halles*), which could still be found in early modern Paris.[53] The paving began directly in front of the Church of *les Innocents*, defining the city's major north-south com-mercial artery.

Shortly thereafter, beginning in 1190 as part of his preparations for the Third Crusade, Philip constructed new city walls, and this part of town, once outside the walls (*extra muros*), was incorporated into the city. It was the expansion of *les Halles* that first gave the Right Bank its economic importance.[54] The speed of its development is suggested by the notably straight roads in the *quartier*, which contrast markedly with the old sinuous streets of Saint-Germain, and testify to the planning and attention it received.[55] The work, like the construction of the city walls (*enciente*), was carried out in record time (*brevi temporis elapso spatio completum*).[56]

By seizing the old Jewish commercial and residential area and incorporating it into the city, Philip set the stage for the expansion of Paris from the 25 acres enclosed by the walls of the old Roman city to the 625 acres enclosed by his new walls, which were enhanced with gates and towers, including the new palace fortress of the Louvre.[57] Clearing the site and clarifying the overlapping and conflicting claims to lordship spurred the development and growth of the city, which was one of Philip's signal accomplishments. His transformation of Paris from what had been a relatively small town to the greatest city north of the Alps within little more than a decade was a remarkable feat.[58] The expulsion of the Jews on the pretext of an alleged ritual murder proved central to Philip's long-term strategy.

To signal his intentions, Philip immediately embarked on a major construction project that explicitly linked the ritual murder accusation and the solicitousness of the new king for his people. As one of his significant urban improvements, Philip erected a fountain (first recorded in 1186) on the external wall of the Church of *les Innocents*, facing the main road to central Paris that later offered a prime expression of royal and religious symbolism.[59] The fountain next to *les Innocents* was regarded as the oldest in Paris; access to water was critically important for the health and welfare of the new *quartier*.[60]

The centerpiece of Richard's cult may have been the tall slim octagonal tower erected exactly in the middle of the cemetery of *les Innocents*, which was likely a tumulary shrine.[61] Although nothing certain is known of its origin or use, the style and dates for the construction of the tower (sometime between 1155 and 1186) and its likely purpose accord well with the death date attributed to Richard of

Pontoise and the intentions of the promoters of his cult.[62] The tower may have alluded architecturally to the chapel dedicated to the Holy Innocents in Bethlehem and would have connected Richard both to the Christ Child and the Holy Innocents. The octagonal shape of this "enigmatic" little tower is analogous to other twelfth-century bell towers that were intended to recall the octagonal *martyrium* Constantine built over the Grotto of the Nativity in Bethlehem (which was restored by Frenchmen in the 1160s).[63] A warning bell (*tocsin*) rang out regularly from the little tower in the cemetery. Although the reason for the sound was long forgotten, it should be noted that alarms rang out from other chapels dedicated to the Holy Innocents.[64] The bell that rang from the tower in the cemetery of *les Innocents* in Paris may have had a similar purpose.[65]

Other structures around *les Halles* and *les Champeaux* served to remind visitors of the dangers of an ongoing Jewish threat that had been averted by the French king. The walls and gates to the cemetery and merchants' halls had carvings, pictorial illustrations, and derogatory inscriptions that referred to Jews, either in Hebrew or in mock-Hebrew lettering.[66] The entrance portal to *les Halles* was reportedly inscribed, "Beware the friendship of a lunatic, a Jew, or a leper," or in another version, "Beware of a Jew, a lunatic, and a thief."[67] Many of the district's residents continued to be closely identified with the expelled Jews; some had converted to Christianity rather than leave the kingdom.[68] In the seventeenth century, old-clothes dealers in this location were still derided for their Jewish associations.[69] The placement of a warning on this entrance gate advertised the enclosed area as free of Jews. The warning also reinforced the rationale for Philip's action and justified the expropriation of Jewish businesses, boutiques, ateliers, and shops in that part of town, quelling any doubts about the legitimacy of the king's initiative.

The exact financing and purpose of the twelfth-century structures around *les Innocents*—the church, fountain, cemetery, walls, gates, tower, even the roads and paving—are poorly documented and not well understood. But the expenditure of significant resources by the crown over a short period of time is amply attested. For centuries, residents retained a memory of a Jewish presence that was publicly and decisively erased by the actions of the young king in the late twelfth century, on the grounds that the Jews had participated in a ritual murder.

Although the popularity of the cult of Richard of Pontoise has been attributed to a widespread animosity toward Jews in the capital, there is little evidence of Richard's appeal to the general public. He does not appear in any Parisian liturgical calendars, and no contemporary depiction of him is known to have been made. His tomb does not appear on any plan of the church.[70] By the fifteenth century, the cult of the twelfth-century martyr was assimilated into that of the Holy Innocents, which received renewed attention from early humanists and the royal patronage of Louis XI.[71] In the late twelfth century, however, it seems that the cult of St. Richard flourished only briefly and was advanced by the authorities for political ends, rather than in response to popular piety. Once the monarch lost interest, Richard's cult did not retain any hold on the popular imagination. One of the Capetians donated a valuable gift in Richard's honor. It seems likely that the silver reliquary in which the partial remains of Richard's skull were contained was a gift of King Philip, not that of his fifteenth-century descendents, by which time the reliquary may already have been lost.[72]

Philip's endorsement of the cult of St. Richard is comparable to Edward I's patronage of the cult of Little St. Hugh of Lincoln a century later. Having expelled the Jews from the kingdom in 1290, Edward, like Philip before him, had a strong interest in documenting both the alleged criminality of the Jews and defining the crown's position as a staunch defender of the Christians of his nation.[73] Philip, like Edward, endorsed the cult, built the shrine, and authorized the translation of a purported victim of ritual murder immediately after he had organized the expulsion of the Jews from his territories.[74] The cult of Richard of Pontoise, what there was of it, seems, like the early cult of Hugh of Lincoln, to have been of royal origin and to have been deployed expressly for political purposes.

Many authorities held sway in twelfth-century Paris, none more prominent than the bishop of Paris, who controlled vast swaths of land in *culture l'évêque* and the area called the *villa episcopi*. Other feudal lords also held land and wielded significant power in the city, and many monasteries and churches had their own grants of rights and privileges over land, people, and taxes. Philip's grandfather, Louis VI, for example, had ceded his rights over Jews in Paris to the abbot of Saint-Denis.[75] By invoking Richard of Pontoise and taking on the role of the city's defender, Philip regularized and formalized his rights and control. As royal patron of the young saint, Philip legitimized his domination of Paris. By framing the expulsion of Jews as a religious issue (just as the abbot of Bury did), he limited the secular prerogatives of the bishop, undercutting ecclesiastical claims over land. At the same time, the king increased and extended the bishop's spiritual authority by establishing the parish of *les Innocents*, which was the first of several parishes created by Philip. This new relationship between the bishop and the king was later confirmed by charter.[76]

Philip's actions enabled him to cut through overlapping and conflicting claims to authority within Paris, especially those of the count of Meulan and the bishop of Paris. The king secured the bishop's cooperation by handing over one of the most important pieces of real estate in the city, the site of the ancient Jewish synagogue at the edge of *villa episcopi*. It had been a Jewish house of worship for more than six hundred years when Philip confiscated it and permitted Bishop Maurice de Sully to consecrate it as the Church of *la Madeleine*. It quickly became one of the city's principal churches and a focus of royal patronage.

The support of Christian merchants, tradesmen, and artisans was assured by grants of Jewish property seized by the crown. The recipients of these grants may have included Jewish converts to Christianity who continued to practice the same industries and crafts after the expulsions of 1182 as they had previously. But some property went to Christians who may have been competitors as well as colleagues of the expelled Jews. The king granted eighteen houses to the skinners or furriers (*pelletiers*) for a rent of 73 livres and twenty-four houses to the drapers for a rent of 100 livres.[77] One part of town became a butcher's quarter; another was associated with bakers (*pannificorum*).[78] The king leased four acres of vines that had belonged to the Jew Abraham to a goldsmith for a rent of 30 sous. It appears that Jews had also been active in areas that became known for "fripperie" and "tacherie," garment fastenings closely allied to the arts of goldsmithing, which they were forced to abandon when they left the city.[79] In 1217 Philip transferred a market once owned by Jews, this one limited to wheat from Beauce (*halle au blé*), to his steward (*échanson*) Renaud l'Archer with a rent of only 12 deniers.[80]

The various locations and their subsequent names suggest that in the twelfth century the Jews of Paris were involved in a wide variety of occupations of importance to the city—the production of and trade in wool and cloth, leather goods, decorative and ornamental objects, garments, grain, wine, and some foodstuffs. Moneychanging, which was carried on under close royal supervision on the Grand Pont, was only a part of their activity, although one that drew the most attention.[81] In applauding the expulsion of the Jews, Rigord claimed that they had owned half the city.[82] His statement suggests the importance of Jewish claims on property, and although regarded now as an exaggeration, it should not be dismissed lightly. Few, if any, records survive of the vast majority of transfers of Jewish buildings to Christians.

When the Jews were permitted to return to Paris in 1198, they installed themselves primarily on the Left Bank and created new or expanded settlements in poorer neighborhoods and less desirable locations.[83] They limited themselves primarily to moneylending, not participating, as before, in a variety of trades, and were no longer part of an economically diverse community.

The repercussions of the king's decree were felt far beyond the capital. Philip bought loyalty throughout his domain with Jewish properties he had appropriated and debts seized from the Jews.

Confiscated synagogues were reconsecrated or torn down and rebuilt as churches, not only in Paris, but also in Bourges, Orléans, Étampes, Melun, and Corbeil, with explicit approval from archbishop and pope, who referred to "the divine intervention" that made such things possible.[84]

Contemporary historians tend to focus primarily on the confiscation of Jewish religious buildings and the money seized by the king. In an effort to explain the unprecedented expulsion and the seizure of goods and debts, they emphasize the modest geographical extent of the royal domain (far smaller than modern-day France) and Philip's strict piety. Philip's actions are described as a short-term solution to pressing financial problems, justified or motivated by religious concerns. But much of what was seized was secular property, not kept by the king but turned over to courtiers and officials for political advantage. For Philip this was a cheap and easy way to spread bounty at no cost to himself, especially in areas where he could benefit from additional support, such as Château Landon, the "cradle" of the Angevins and the capital of the Gâtinais region. Under Philip Augustus, Hugh, the abbot of Château Landon, was able to complete a major expansion project of the royal abbey of Saint-Severin (now recently restored) without repaying his loans to the Jews. Instead, on their expulsion, he surrendered to the king only 20 percent of his debt of 225 pounds, as the king had demanded, announcing that it was for the protection of the realm. The "money porch," where loans were contracted close to the old market, survives today in what was the Jewish part of the town. In the capital of Berry, the first marshal of France, Matthew of Bourges, one of the leading officers of the realm, was awarded the property of the Jew Isaac of Uradis on the payment of seven pounds. This is the first documentation of the important office of marshal, and the account suggests that he gained a prestigious house in the center of town.[85]

Philip spread the booty seized from the Jews to his court officers—his marshal, his steward, his clerical advisors—tying them to his side and rewarding his own men (men who did not come from the ancient aristocracy, which was both wealthy and resentful). In a move comparable in some ways to Henry VIII's dissolution of the monasteries, Philip played an active role in the ongoing land transfers. By emphasizing Jewish perfidy, the king received the public approbation of pope, archbishop, and chronicler.

Philip's actions on becoming king are often seen as both forward- and backward-looking: modern in his determination to establish Paris as the center of culture, finance, education, court, and government, and backward in his relations with Jews of his domain, which included seizing their property, endorsing a dubious child saint, expelling them in 1182, then reluctantly bringing them back in 1198. These apparently contradictory impulses should be considered as parallel embodiments of the king's efforts to impose his will.

As at Bury, the catalyst for the expulsion of the Jews was claimed to be an accusation of ritual murder. At this date the king's control was not sufficiently secure for him to expel Jews solely on his own authority. He needed an excuse of criminal behavior on their part, and he framed the accusation in the terms of a continuous, ongoing criminal enterprise that represented a spiritual as well as a physical threat.[86]

The advantages were both financial and ideological. As in Blois (and probably in Bury and Gloucester), in Paris the accusation of ritual murder led to great profits from beleaguered Jews. This was not a "windfall" of unexpected good fortune, but a fortune carefully calculated.[87] Philip gained immediate funds totaling more than the entire annual royal budget, as well as property, productive assets, and rights and privileges that were to produce income for many years to come.[88] Described as tantamount to "slaughtering the profitable milk cow," Philip's attack on the Jews is often characterized as an unwise short-term expedient.[89] Those few historians who consider the profitability of the expulsion focus on "the golden egg" of 1182, but the king had his eye on larger goals.

Conventionally treated by historians separately from the political issues of his reign, Philip's endorsement of the ritual murder accusation in the person of Richard of Pontoise and his attacks on Jews of the royal domain should be seen in the context of the rebuilding of the Church of *les Innocents*, the walling off of *les Champeaux*, the building of critically needed fountains (by 1186), the purchase and removal of the fair of Saint-Lazare (1181), the creation and extension of *les Halles du Roi* (1183), the confiscation of the synagogue and its reconsecration as *la Madeleine* (1183), the paving of roads, the building of new city walls (1190), the commencement of the Louvre fortress, the splitting of feudal and commercial dues with the bishop of Paris (confirmed 1222), and the establishment of the University of Paris. These acts were all part of his creation of the capital, which quickly and effectively established his royal persona.

Rarely, if ever, are Jews mentioned today in connection with the urban redevelopment of Paris, but they played an important role.[90] The money seized from Jews did not simply go into royal coffers for war and royal luxuries; it underwrote the very fabric of the city that Philip cherished and which, for the first time, the king made his permanent residence. It apparently paid for the famous walls.

The timing of the expulsion of the Jews hints at themes that were both religious and financial. The decision was made around Eastertide, the most common period of the year when Christian–Jewish tensions came to the fore.[91] The final expulsion was ordered for the feast of St. John the Baptist, the end of the most important commercial fair in Paris, the Lendit fair of Saint-Denis, which lasted for two weeks, thereby providing a final occasion for Jews to dispose of their goods and settle debts. The feast was also that of Midsummer Day, a traditional opportunity for processions and for the performance of plays of the Holy Innocents. Richard of Pontoise, the supposed catalyst for the expulsion, was closely identified with the Holy Innocents, and they, in turn, were linked to notions of appropriate punishment for Jewish blindness and failure to recognize the Incarnation. Church dramas of the Nativity reinforced the contemporary drama of expulsion.

The king's endorsement and promotion of the martyr saint Richard of Pontoise provided a powerful justification for the actions he took against the Jews of his kingdom and coincided with other of his actions concerning the Jews when he assumed the crown. It expressed in concrete terms an alleged reason for expelling the Jews from homes, workshops, and gardens that they had long inhabited. Here, as elsewhere, religious motives served as a justification for economic extortion. Belief in the ritual murder charge was not the cause of the expulsion, but the pretext for it.

FIGURE C.1 All surviving images of William of Norwich date from the fifteenth century, when the cult was revived. St. William appears here on the rood screen of Holy Trinity Church Loddon, Norfolk.

Conclusion

The accusation of Jewish ritual murder was created and developed in northern Europe in the second half of the twelfth century. It was invented, as we have seen, in the context of a homicide trial in 1150. Thereafter, through the lens of contemporary biblical exegesis, it was enhanced, disseminated, and altered over the course of the following decades, spurred on by immediate political and economic pressures.

Although the fame of the first purported victim, William, languished, the structural framework of his passion endured and proved easily adaptable to other situations. The accusation gained power and resonance from typological associations between the purported victims and the Christ Child, as well as from the growing cult of the Holy Innocents and the increasing popularity of miracle stories of the Virgin Mary. The accusation served to link the familiar contemporary provincial medieval landscape directly with the awesome holiness of the biblical story, to tie mundane existence to sanctified time and space. It also proved a practical and efficient tool to extort funds from Jews. Once the charge was accepted by the king of England, and was endorsed and advertised by the king of France, it was available to be widely utilized in multiple ways by different individuals and groups.

Other than William, the purported victims of ritual murder in the twelfth century are rarely studied. Historians refer to the "small, sad pantheon" of martyrs, observe that "next to nothing is known of them," agree that "they were little more than names" and conclude that there is "insufficient context for analysis."[1] Embarrassment and ignorance seem to trump historical curiosity. The real victims of the accusation are mentioned in passing, if at all, while the purported martyrs are dismissed, ignored, passed over, relegated to "discourse," or summed up with the term "bizarre." The very existence of the martyrs is considered marginal to what are deemed significant issues during the Middle Ages, such as state building, cultural formation, and national identity—in short, to many important questions of medieval history.

Yet one can discover a great deal more about these earliest cases, and studying their circumstances reveals issues of central importance to medieval society. The paucity of documentation, however, requires that any conclusions are necessarily tentative.

These circumstances would change in the late Middle Ages and thereafter, when many more accusations of ritual murder were amply documented and widely publicized, especially when disseminated through the media of printed images and movable type. By that time, and in marked contrast to the early examples of the twelfth and the thirteenth centuries, accusations of ritual murder were closely linked to riots, violence, and judicial condemnation. The later episodes contributed to the popular acceptance of such accusations and to the pernicious outbreaks of hysteria and brutality that accompanied them or that they provoked. The endurance and wide dissemination of ritual murder accusations have in turn contributed to some of the principal historiographical pitfalls of studies of the phenomenon. Foremost among these has been the tendency to search for common elements and universal explanations of the accusation (a "one size fits all" explanation), and the concomitant problem of interpreting all instances, including the earliest ones, through the lens of what is known about the later tradition, despite significantly different cultural and social forces at work in those periods.

Although the early examples I have treated in this book spanned a period of less than four decades, they established precedents of signal importance both for the later history of the ritual murder accusation and for the more momentous questions of how Jews might be viewed and treated in a Christian universe. One of the most damaging features of the first account of the blood libel crafted by Brother Thomas is the manner in which it assigns guilt for an alleged murder of a Christian youth to the Jews as a people, rather than to individual perpetrators. In this first telling, that idea was embedded in the defense of a Christian knight for the murder of a Jewish banker. Later accounts of the blood libel took over the notion without the need of narrative complexities, developing it into the assertion that Jews organized such murders in mockery of Christ and the Christian religion, and did so regularly and in different locales. The idea of communal blame adopted in the first cases traced in this study had profound implications, for it helped to prepare the way for later and eventually modern condemnations of the Jewish people.

A second key development in the early examples appeared at Blois, where, in the wake of a new accusation of ritual murder, Count Thibaut V condemned Jews of Blois to the flames. This act represented a radical reinterpretation of the status of Jews in Christian society, for it contradicted traditional views of Judaism as a divinely ordained stage in the evolution of sacred history and the notion that in their sacred writings they predicted the coming of Christ and testified to the truth of Christianity; on these grounds, Jews were to be tolerated in Christian society in the expectation that they would convert at the End of Time. The condemnation of Jews at Blois overturned the notion of toleration, replacing it with a determination that for their perfidy, Jews could now be rooted out and killed.[2] In Paris, Philip Augustus chose to expel the Jews (a form of eradication), rather than kill them, thereby providing a variant exemplar. Both precedents had tragic aftermaths in later attempts to banish Jews or to destroy the Jewish people. These two assumptions, about the communal nature of Jewish responsibility for the murder of Christian children (and before that, of Christ) and the punishments they merited, were embodied in and rapidly developed in the earliest accounts of the blood libel.

The story that began with a monk, a knight, a bishop, and a banker metamorphosed into what one might call a master narrative that became the basis of expulsions and murders, tortures and mass conversions. It provided the outline of a story that could be reimagined and repurposed in every generation. Financially advantageous, politically useful, ethnically and socially bonding, the ritual murder accusation united community, reinforced borders, and reassured medieval Christian believers about God's salvific plan. It was—and is—a powerful story that retains its capacity to fascinate, provoke, disgust, and repel.

Acknowledgments

I have been fascinated by this topic for so long that during my childhood I recall discussing it with Cecil Roth. I am indebted to all those who inspired me to pursue the topic and corrected me along the way. Janet Allison first introduced me to the history of Anglo-Norman England and demonstrated a "hands-on" approach to education by making me sew part of a Bayeux tapestry replica; her colleagues Ruth Carpenter, Julia Schiefflin, and Judith Hurwich exhorted me and my classmates to "worship at the shrine of text."

I offer thanks to many friends, colleagues, and teachers for guidance, encouragement, and criticism: Anna Sapir Abulafia, Martin Allen, Elizabeth Archibald, Anthony Bale, David Berger, Heather Blurton, Anne-Marie Bouché, Martin Brett, Peter Brown, the late Olivia R. Constable, Adam Davis, Marilyn Desmond, Yaacob Dweck, John Gager, Shoshana Goldhill, Simon Goldhill, Anthony Grafton, Dietlinde Hamburger, Jeffrey Hamburger, William Chester Jordan, Berthold Kress, Hillel Levine, Olga Litvak, Robert Lopez, Gregory Lyon, Ivan Marcus, John McCulloh, Harry Miskimin, Leslie Mitchell, Alexander Murray, David Nirenberg, Mark Pegg, Rick Rubens, Vasily Rudich, Kimberly Schwing, Jerry Singerman, Rebecca Sokolovsky, Alan Stahl, Deborah Steiner, George Steiner, Zara Steiner, Nicholas Vincent, Andrea Worm, and Israel Yuval. Many others kindly shared their expertise and responded to questions, among them Robert Bartlett, Kathleen Biddick, Christopher Brooke, David Dumville, Antonia Gransden, Joan Greatrex, Paul Anthony Hayward, Willis Johnson, Anthony Julius, Janet Martin, Nigel Morgan, and Zefira E. Rokéah. Even when we disagreed—perhaps most especially when we disagreed—I learned from them.

I acknowledge other colleagues in the notes, but scholars and librarians have given me so much generous help over the years that it is impossible to mention all to whom my thanks are due. Sometimes even ostensibly offhand comments proved as useful and thought-provoking as in-depth discussions. Invitations to deliver papers based on this study at Cambridge, Oxford, Johns Hopkins, Harvard, the Institute for Historical Research in London, Queen Mary, and the Institute for Advanced Study in Princeton offered precious opportunities to try out ideas and receive critical feedback.

For their enduring friendship, support, and astute suggestions over many years, I am deeply grateful to Giles Constable, Miri Rubin, and Gabrielle Spiegel. I appreciate having had the opportunity to discuss my work at length with Gavin Langmuir, Jaroslav Pelikan, and Yosef Yerushalmi before their deaths. Cordelia Grimm, Elizabeth Leiman Kraiem, Joanna Semel Rose, Lauren Osborne, Elaine Bennett, and Janet Rogan read parts of the manuscript in draft and offered perceptive comments. For close critical readings of the text I thank Hugh Thomas, Charles Dibble, and Timothy Bent, my enthusiastic editor. I am most appreciative of the efforts of the team at Oxford University Press—especially Prabhu Chinnasamy, Alyssa O'Connell, and Dorothy Bauhoff.

James H. Marrow has contributed immeasurably and in multiple ways at every stage of the work. My thanks to all the members of my family are as heartfelt as they are inadequate.

E. M. Rose

Appendices

A Note on Terminology

Some scholars distinguish between "anti-semitism" and "anti-Judaism," seeing the latter as "rational" and having originated early in the history of Christianity, and the former as "irrational" and dating from the twelfth century.[1] The cult of William of Norwich is taken as the significant turning point. Although thought-provoking, this distinction has not found widespread acceptance. Other scholars, in contrast, consider it anachronistic to use the term "anti-semitism," which was coined in the late nineteenth century to characterize pre-modern religious sentiment, preferring to reserve it for racial hatred of the modern era. The appropriate uses of the terms "anti-semitism," "anti-Judaism," "Judeophobia" (and such alternatives as "Jew-hatred," "anti-Jewish sentiment," etc.), are still disputed.[2] While acknowledging a debt to those scholars who have raised the issues of terminology, in the present study I do not use any of these terms to characterize the behavior and thoughts of the monk, the knight, the bishop, and the other medieval protagonists I discuss. The word "anti-semitism" does not appear elsewhere in these chapters.

Some scholars also differentiate the "blood libel" from the accusation of "ritual murder," and maintain that the two accusations originated in different times and places. "Ritual murder" is described as a uniquely English creation, centered on the accusation of a ritual crucifixion modeled on the death of Christ on the cross, an innovation for which Thomas of Monmouth is given credit.[3] According to this view, the "blood libel" first appeared on the Continent in the thirteenth century, when Jews were accused of using the blood of children for medicinal and magical purposes, and it sometimes included the charge of "ritual cannibalism" as well.

Malevolent child murder laid at the feet of the Jews during the Middle Ages was always understood as a type of or a referent to the killing of Christ, irrespective of whether it was said to have taken the form of a crucifixion or not. The purported use of blood was interpreted sometimes in practical terms and at other times in allegorical ones. Both charges can be related to an interpretative tradition that viewed the death of the Holy Innocents recounted in the New Testament as a foreshadowing of the death of Christ on the Cross, and Jews as continuing perpetrators of deicide. Many scholars debate the relationship of one charge to the other, or conclude that one was a subset of the other. But it remains to be demonstrated conclusively that the two medieval accusations were separate and distinct. In this study, I use the terms "blood libel" and "ritual murder accusation" almost interchangeably.[4]

One might take issue with the use of the term "banker" to characterize the Jewish lender. Although perhaps considered anachronistic, the term "banker" is not loaded with the conceptual freight and pejorative connotations of "medieval moneylender," and I employ it here for that reason. In the mid-twelfth century, Jews were not the only moneylenders, nor even the major lenders. Absolute prohibitions on Christian lending at interest developed in canon law only in the late twelfth century. Medieval Jewish businessmen, such as Jurnet of Norwich in the later twelfth century, performed the activities of bankers, collecting capital on behalf of others, making loans, exchanging foreign currencies, investing their capital in other debt, developing real estate, and dealing in commodities, specie, pawnbroking, and mortgages.

To avoid confusion, Anglo-Norman names are given here in the familiar English form (Henry, Stephen, William, Theobold) and continental names in French form (Henri, Étienne, Guillaume, Thibaut), even though they appear identical in Latin records.

Likewise the forms Alix, Alice, Adèle, and Adela are used to differentiate individuals who shared the same name in contemporary documents. Although Simon was a knight, he was not referred to with the honorific "Sir" (*dominus*), a practice that came into effect in the fourteenth century. Also for clarity, the bishop of Norwich is sometimes referred to here as Turbe, although he is correctly called Bishop William. In contemporary documents, "William of Norwich" more often referred to the sheriff William de Chesney or to the bishop than to the murdered young apprentice whose cult the bishop championed. In some cases, geographic designations became proper family names, as with Chesney, Novers, and Warenne, so I occasionally use them that way; in most other cases, they did not. Thus, for example, Earl William de Warenne is occasionally referred to simply as Warenne and the "de" is not used.

A Note on Chronology

The present account of the cult of William of Norwich departs from the conventional chronology, which dates it to 1144, the year of his death, and links it to the beginning of the Second Crusade. Moreover, most scholars place the death of Deulesalt the Jewish banker (previously identified as "Eleazar the moneylender") in 1146, and the trial of Simon de Novers for his murder in 1148.[5] I argue that the banker's death and Simon's trial occurred in late 1149 or soon after, possibly on Simon's return from the Second Crusade, and that they immediately preceded and played a role in the development of the cult of William, which began to take form only after 1150.

There is some disparity in the estimates of when important events occurred. Jessopp and James, *Life and Miracles*, Chronology, xc, suggest (with question marks) that the death of Deulesalt/Eleazar took place in 1146 and the trial in 1148. Cronne, *Stephen*, 262–263, states these dates confidently, followed by King in *The Anarchy of Stephen's Reign*, 131. Harper-Bill, "Bishop Turbe," 143 n., maintains that the murder and trial took place sometime between 1146 and

1150. Further down, on page 143, he implies that the trial was over by 1148 because he considers that Turbe's eloquence at the trial influenced his appointment to represent English bishops at the Council of Rheims. Langmuir assumes that the indebted knight Simon de Novers murdered Deulesalt/Eleazar before Thomas of Monmouth arrived in Norwich, around the year 1146, the year Turbe became bishop (*Toward a Definition*, 230). He notes parenthetically that Deulesalt/Eleazar "was safely dead by 1149" (*Toward a Definition*, 222); two pages later, he adds that Deulesalt/Eleazar had died about 1146. McCulloh, "Early Dissemination," 39, does not mention Deulesalt/Eleazar's death and simply notes that after William's death, "several years later," the bishop told the king that William's uncle Godwin was still prepared to bring his case, but the king postponed the hearing indefinitely. Yarrow, *Saints and Their Communities*, 129, says that Simon de Novers was brought before the royal court in 1146.

Anderson, *A Saint at Stake*, 137–144, devotes an entire chapter to "The Trial of Simon de Novers." She asserts that Deulesalt/Eleazar was killed in the supposed uprisings that immediately followed Turbe's election as bishop of Norwich (1146/1147). To support this assertion she offers no date for the trial, but implies it took place some time after the murder, 139. She concludes, on page 143, however, by considering that Turbe may have defended Simon de Novers in order to prosecute his quarrel with John de Chesney, who had opposed his election. As John de Chesney died ca. 1147, shortly after Bishop Turbe's election, this would place the murder and trial very close together in time, about 1147.

Other historians do not address these questions.

Notes

Part 1

1. See the Appendix, "A Note on Terminology," for a discussion of the terms "blood libel" and "ritual murder."

2. Among the famous denunciations are those of Emperor Frederick II, Pope Innocent IV in the encyclical *Lachrymabilem Judaerorum Alemanniae* of 1247, and the (future) Pope Clement IV in 1758, for which see Cecil Roth, *The Ritual Murder Libel and the Jew: The Report by Cardinal Lorenzo Ganganelli (Pope Clement XIV)* (London: The Woburn Press, 1935). Suleiman the Magnificent issued a *firmam* denouncing the blood libel in the sixteenth century.

3. The best-known, Simon of Trent and Werner of Oberwesel, were dropped from the Roman (Catholic) calendar in 1965 in the liturgical reforms implemented in the wake of Vatican II. The cult of Andreas (Anderl) of Rinn was suppressed by the bishop in 1984 and forbidden in 1994. Many cathedrals that once featured shrines to boy martyrs are now rethinking how they should memorialize purported victims of ritual murder. Some have eliminated all mentions in guidebooks and buildings; others now post prayers for victims of prejudice or to holy innocents.

4. Thomas of Monmouth, *Liber de Vita et Passione Sancti Willelmi Martyris Norwicensis*, Cambridge University Library, Add. Ms. 3037, first edited and translated by Augustus Jessopp and M. R. James as *The Life and Miracles of St. William of Norwich by Thomas of Monmouth* (Cambridge: Cambridge University Press, 1896). Thomas's work is hereafter cited as *Vita*; Jessopp's and James's editorial comments are cited as Jessopp and James, *Life and Miracles*. Miri Rubin has produced a new English translation and has posted a fresh transcription of the Latin manuscript at http://yvc.history.qmul.ac.uk/passio.html. The English quotations here and corresponding page references are to Thomas of Monmouth, *The Life and Passion of William of Norwich*, ed. and trans. Miri Rubin (London: Penguin Books, 2014) unless otherwise noted. Rubin's editorial comments are cited as Rubin, *Life and Passion*.

5. Thomas says the Jews hanged William from a tree by a flaxen rope (*Vita*, I, vii, 21) after they had tortured him and placed a wooden teazle in his mouth (a teazle was a prickly tool used to raise the nap on woolen cloth), but he was found at the foot of an oak (*Vita*, I, x, 24), his head shaven and pierced.

6. John Shinners, "The Veneration of Saints at Norwich Cathedral in the Fourteenth Century," *Norfolk Archeology* 40: 133–144, discusses the late medieval revival, which is not treated here.

7. Anthony Bale, *Feeling Persecuted: Christians, Jews and Images of Violence in the Middle Ages* (London: Reaktion, 2009), 50ff.

8. Rubin, *Life and Passion*, xvii, emphasizes how difficult is any historical reading of Thomas's work when it is virtually the only source for the events he recounts.

9. This is in marked contrast to the protagonists of the supposed *martyrdom*, most of whom were conveniently dead when Brother Thomas began his work.

10. Alex J. Novikoff, *The Medieval Culture of Disputation: Pedagogy, Practice, and Performance* (Philadelphia: University of Pennsylvania Press, 2013), traces the increasingly performative aspect of Jewish-Christian disputation in this period.

11. Rubin, *Life and Passion*, xx.

12. It is worthwhile to compare this text to the work of Geoffrey of Wells in the same years. Geoffrey's obviously false facts became fixed elements in the hagiographical tradition of the Life of St. Edmund, for which see Paul Hayward, "Geoffrey of Wells' *Liber de infantia sancti Edmundi* and the 'Anarchy' of King Stephen's Reign," in *St Edmund, King and Martyr: Changing Images of a Medieval Saint*, ed. Anthony Bale (York: York Medieval Press, 2009), 63–86 at 75.

13. The vibrancy of the age is discussed in Charles Homer Haskins, *The Renaissance of the Twelfth Century* (Cambridge, MA: Harvard University Press, 1927). See also Robert L. Benson, Giles Constable, and Carol D. Lanham, eds., *Renaissance and Renewal in the Twelfth Century* (Cambridge, MA: Harvard University Press, 1982).

14. See most recently Thomas N. Bisson, *The Crisis of The Twelfth Century: Power, Lordship, and the Origins of European Government* (Princeton, NJ: Princeton University Press, 2009) and R. I. Moore, *The Formation of a Persecuting Society; Authority and Deviance in Western Europe, 950–1250* (Malden, MA: Blackwell Publishing, 2007).

15. J. J. Cohen, "The Flow of Blood in Medieval Norwich," *Speculum* 79 (2004), 26–65, especially 49 and 56, reprinted in Jeffrey Jerome Cohen, *Hybridity, Identity and Monstrosity in Medieval Britain: On Difficult Middles* (New York: Palgrave MacMillan, 2006), 139–174, which argues that focusing on bloody Jews temporarily alleviated the twelfth-century racial crisis in Norwich by displacing anxieties about the "irresolvability" of the divide between Anglo-Normans and Anglo-Saxons. Simon Yarrow, *Saints and Their Communities: Miracle Stories in Twelfth-Century England* (Oxford: Clarendon Press, 2007) 167, likewise emphasizes that the cult of St. William "articulated and exploited the social anxieties of Norfolk's commercial establishment." Langmuir in "Historiographic Crucifixion," discusses the many modern writers who begin their work by considering Jews guilty in William's death.

16. James Campbell, "The East Anglian Sees before the Conquest," in *Norwich Cathedral, Church, City and Diocese, 1096–1996*, ed. Ian Atherton, Eric Fernie, Christopher Harper-Bill, and Hassell Smith (London: The Hambledon Press, 1996), 3–21 at 19–20.

17. Elizabeth Rutledge, "The Medieval Jews of Norwich and Their Legacy," in *Art, Faith and Place in East Anglia from Prehistory to the Present*, ed. T. A. Heslop (Woodbridge: Boydell and Brewer, 2012), 117–129. V. D. Lipman, *The Jews of*

Medieval Norwich (London, The Jewish Historical Society of England, 1967), is the classic treatment.

18. Lipman, *Norwich*, 4, based on calculations taken from H. G. Richardson, *The English Jewry under Angevin Kings* (London: Methuen and Co., 1960).

19. See, for example, the thirteenth-century manuscript that alludes to Arabic loans in Malachi Beit-Arié, *The Makings of the Medieval Hebrew Book: Studies in Paleography and Codicology* (Jerusalem: Magnes Press, Hebrew University, 1993), and the frequent uses of the term "Ha-Nadib" (intellectual patron) in Hebrew charters cited by Lipman, *Norwich*, 150.

20. See, for example, the uproar over use of the term "blood libel" in 2011 by the former vice presidential candidate Sarah Palin; recent debates about the visual imagery of blood libel motifs in political advertising in the United Kingdom, Hungary, and Israel; and the discussion of contemporary poetry in Anthony Julius, *Trials of the Diaspora: A History of Anti-Semitism in England* (Oxford: Oxford University Press, 2010). For a recent case study on the role of the media, see Raphael Israeli, *Poison: Modern Manifestations of a Blood Libel* (Oxford: Lexington Books, 2002).

21. Christopher Ocker, "Ritual Murder and the Subjectivity of Christ: A Choice in Medieval Christianity," *Harvard Theological Review* 91 (1998), 153–192 at 155 n. 4.

22. See most recently on Damascus, Julie Kalman, "Sensuality, Depravity, and Ritual Murder: The Damascus Blood Libel and Jews in France," *Jewish Social Studies* 13, no. 3 (2007), 35–58; Ronald Florence, *Blood Libel: The Damascus Affair of 1840* (Madison: University of Wisconsin Press, 2004); and Jonathan Frankel, *The Damascus Affair: Ritual Murder, Politics, and the Jews in 1840* (Cambridge: Cambridge University Press, 1996). On the Mendel Beilis case, see most recently, Edmund Levin, *A Child of Christian Blood: Murder and Conspiracy in Tsarist Russia: The Beilis Blood Libel* (New York: Schocken Books, 2014), and Robert Weinberg, *Blood Libel in Late Imperial Russia: The Ritual Murder Trial of Mendel Beilis* (Bloomington: Indiana University Press, 2013).

23. Covers of the notorious tabloid *Der Stürmer* published by Julius Streicher that vigorously promoted the blood libel were featured in "Stürmer-kasten," display cases distributed throughout Nazi Germany.

24. Subtitles of recent books on the topic include such phrases as "the longest hatred," "a lethal obsession," and "the pinnacle of hatred." See Anthony Bale, "Some Blood and a Lot More Ink," *Journal for the Study of Antisemitism* 3 (2011), 782.

25. *Encyclopaedia Judaica*, "Blood Libel: Origins," in *Encyclopedia Judaica* (first ed. 1971; second ed., Jerusalem: Macmillan Reference USA in association with Keter Publishing House, 2007), 3:774–776.

26. On circumcision, see *Jewish Encyclopedia*, 3:263; Abraham Gross, "The Blood Libel and the Blood of Circumcision: An Ashkenazic Custom That Disappeared in the Middle Ages," *The Jewish Quarterly Review* 86 new ser., no. 1–2 (1995), 171–174; and Joshua Trachtenberg, *The Devil and the Jews: The Medieval Conception of the Jew and Its Relation to Modern Antisemitism* (Philadelphia: Jewish

Publication Society, 1983), 149, for the first association of ritual murder and circumcision in the fifteenth century. See also David Biale, in his response to Israel Yuval, "Blood Libels and Blood Vengeance," *Tikkun* 9, no. 4 (1994), 39–40, 75. About Purim violence, see Cecil Roth, "The Feast of Purim and the Origins of the Blood Accusation," *Speculum* 8 (1933), 520–526, reprinted in Alan Dundes, ed., *The Blood Libel Legend: A Casebook in Anti-Semitic Folklore* (Madison: University of Wisconsin Press, 1991), 261–272, and Elliott Horowitz, *Reckless Rites: Purim and the Legacy of Jewish Violence* (Princeton, NJ: Princeton University Press, 2006), 220–226. Horowitz has traced the invention of the accusation that Jews used blood in Purim *hamentashen* to Ernst Ferdinand Hess, a Jewish convert to Christianity in the late sixteenth century (Horowitz, *Reckless Rites*, 226).

As Kenneth Stow has noted, the association with the ritual murder charge of the red wine in Passover *haroset*, a mixture of fruit and nuts, was first made in the early fourteenth century in Savoy. See also Israel Yuval, "Jews and Christians in the Middle Ages: Shared Myths, Common Language," in *Demonizing the Other: Antisemitism, Racism and Xenophobia*, ed. Robert S. Wistrich (Jerusalem: Vidal Sassoon International Center for the Study of Antisemitism, 1999), 88–107 at 102, and David Biale's comments on Ernst Bischoff's 1920s analysis of the *haroset* charge, David Biale, *Blood and Belief: The Circulation of a Symbol Between Jews and Christians* (Berkeley: University of California Press, The S. Mark Taper Foundation Imprint in Jewish Studies, 2007), 133. The charge that Jews used blood for *matzah* is first recorded in the late fifteenth century.

On homicide see *The Jewish Encyclopedia*, 3:263. Israel Yuval, however, traces the accusation of "ritual cannibalism" back at least as far as the early thirteenth century. The Jewish *Sefer Nizahon Vetus* alludes to Christian accusations "that we eat human beings and the blood of Christian children," a claim which he notes closely parallels a liturgical poem (*piyyut*) from 1221. See Israel J. Yuval, "'They Tell Lies: You Ate the Man': Jewish Reactions to Ritual Murder Accusations," *Religious Violence Between Christians and Jews: Medieval Roots, Modern Perspectives*, ed. Anna Sapir Abulafia (New York: Palgrave, 2002), 86–106 at 90ff. On the crusade, see Israel J. Yuval, "Vengeance and Damnation, Blood and Defamation: From Jewish Martyrdom to Blood Libel Accusation" [Hebrew] *Zion* 58 (1993), 33–96, and Israel J. Yuval, *Two Nations in Your Womb: Perceptions of Jews and Christians in Late Antiquity and the Middle Ages* (Berkeley: University of California Press, 2006), 164ff.

On kosher butchering, see Robin Judd, "The Politics of Beef: Animal Advocacy and the Kosher Butchering Debates in Germany," *Jewish Social Studies* 10, no. 1 (2003), 117–150, especially 124–125, expanded in Robin Judd, *Contested Rituals: Circumcision, Kosher Butchering, and Jewish Political Life in Germany, 1843–1933* (Ithaca, NY: Cornell University Press, 2007). On child abandonment, see John Boswell, *The Kindness of Strangers: The Abandonment of Children in Western Europe from Late Antiquity to the Renaissance* (New York: Pantheon Books, 1988), 352, and Diane Peters Auslander, "Victims or Martyrs: Children, Antisemitism, and the Stress of Change in Medieval England," in *Childhood in the Middle Ages and the Renaissance: The Results of a Paradigm Shift in the History of Mentality*, ed. Albrecht Classen (Berlin: Walter de Gruyter, 2005), 105–135 at 125–129.

27. In "Thomas Monmouth, Detector of Ritual Murder," *Speculum* 59 (1984), 820–846, and then in two books published in 1990, Gavin Langmuir claimed that Thomas of Monmouth invented the ritual crucifixion accusation in order to reinforce his religious security. See Gavin Langmuir, *Toward a Definition of Antisemitism*, a book of essays and *History, Religion and Antisemitism* (both Berkeley: University of California Press, 1990). Although three of Langmuir's main conclusions have been challenged—that Thomas of Monmouth invented the ritual crucifixion charge; that the ritual crucifixion charge is inherently different from the blood libel; and that the ritual crucifixion charge of the twelfth century represents the emergence of "antisemitism"—his pioneering work remains an important consideration for anyone addressing this material. See Langmuir, *Toward a Definition*, 11–12, 235, and Moore, *Persecuting Society*, 139–140.

28. In addition to Langmuir's work noted above, see Magdalene Schultz, "The Blood Libel: A Motif in the History of Childhood," 273–303, and Alan Dundes, "The Ritual Murder or Blood Libel Legend: A Study of Anti-Semitic Victimization Through Projective Inversion," 336–378; for these and other essays, see Dundes, *Blood Libel Legend*.

29. See especially the chapter "Historiographic Crucifixion" in Langmuir, *Definition*. For a discussion of the most recent studies of the ritual murder accusation and the various methodologies used by those writing about it, see Hannah Johnson, *Blood Libel: Scholarship and Ethics at the Limits of Jewish History* (Ann Arbor: University of Michigan Press, 2012), and Darren O'Brien, *The Pinnacle of Hatred: The Blood Libel and the Jews* (Jerusalem: Magnes Press, 2011) for a focus especially on the early twentieth century. Rubin, *Life and Passion*, vii–xi, neatly summarizes the historiography.

30. Rubin, *Life and Passion*, li–lxiii, discusses the provenance of the manuscript and the correspondence of its first editors.

31. See, for example, *Vita*, III, xiii, 94.

32. Most recently, the editor of *Folklore* concludes, "we will never know." See Gillian Bennett, "Towards a Revaluation of the Legend of 'Saint' William of Norwich and Its Place in the Blood Libel Legend," *Folklore* 116 (August 2005), 119–139, and "William of Norwich and the Expulsion of the Jews," 311–314, both of which ignore all historical scholarship of the past two generations on William of Norwich and on ritual murder.

33. Indeed, one editor has opined that "one might despair of being able to say anything about the legend that has not already been said before" (Dundes, "Ritual Murder," 336). Much of the detailed scholarship on the subject was prompted by contemporary accusations of the late nineteenth and twentieth centuries, not by disinterested historical investigations into the past but by avowed partisans.

34. See the forthcoming work of Hillel J. Kieval, *Science and Blood: The Strange Career of the "Ritual Murder" Trial in Modern Europe.*

35. Some cases whose texts have survived may be written versions of stories that first circulated orally, but many others appear to be later constructions with a focus on displaying appealing material objects to visitors. For examples, see Caroline Walker Bynum, "The Presence of Objects: Medieval Anti-Judaism in Modern Germany," *Common Knowledge* 10 (2004), 1–32, discussing fifteenth-century Sternberg in North Germany; Anderl of Rinn in the Italian Tyrol, whose cult was created in the seventeenth century and "backdated" to the fifteenth; and the alleged site of the martyrdom of Hugh of Lincoln in 1255, a shallow pool created by a homeowner in 1910 to benefit from the growing English tourist trade. The mid-thirteenth-century account of Adam of Bristol that describes an allegation of ritual murder a century earlier appears also to be a case of conscious backdating. An alleged case of 1250 in Zaragoza, Spain, is first mentioned in the sixteenth century, and the "remains" of the purported victim were discovered a century after that. The charge in late fifteenth-century Endingen occurred more than eight years after the alleged homicide. Such "backdating" suggests that quite often an accusation against local Jews was *not* prompted by news of a recently missing child.

Chapter 1

1. Since the time of William the Conqueror, it was immediately assumed that any dead man might be Norman and the perpetrators English, unless the community could prove otherwise. The word "murder" comes from the *murdrum* fines King William employed to punish the killing of his men in secret manner. Not until the royal charter of 1194 were the citizens of Norwich exempted from paying the *murdrum* fine. See Bruce R. O'Brien, "From Mordor to Murdrum: The Preconquest Origin and Norman Revival of the Murder Fine," *Speculum* 71 (1996), 321–357. By the late twelfth century, there was a special officer of the crown, the coroner, to investigate and prosecute deaths. See R. F. Hunnisett, *The Medieval Coroner* (Cambridge: Cambridge University Press, 1961).

2. *Vita*, I, xi, 34.

3. Ibid.

4. Hunnisett, *Medieval Coroner*, 9.

5. For the important role and high status of Anglo-Norman foresters, see Dolores Wilson, "Multi-Use Management of the Medieval Anglo-Norman Forest," *Journal of the Oxford University History Society* 1 (2004), 1–16. Sprowston was a manor held by the bishop of Norwich about three miles north of the center of town: in 1086, at the first mention of Sprowston, the Domesday inquest revealed a small run-down village; it is now a luxury golf course and spa.

6. Oak was not the only forest product. Various woods were used to make tables and stools. Willow was used for baskets and eel nets; beech was used for charcoal and firewood; yew was used for the famous English longbows. Elm trees were

hollowed for use as water pipes; hazelwood was used for medieval tally sticks issued to sheriffs by the royal exchequer as receipts for payment (such as those from the thirteenth century now at the National Archives, Kew, E 402/2); and carpenters sought flexible ash wood for plows, axles, and oars. Woodchips and twigs were burned to smoke fish and meat, and in desperate times, acorns could be ground for flour and bark could thicken stews.

7. Information in this paragraph follows Everett Crosby, *Bishop and Chapter in Twelfth-Century England, A Study of the Mensa Episcopalis* (Cambridge: Cambridge University Press, 1994), 179ff.

8. Despite the existence of a formal agreement, disputes between bishop and monks about rights in Thorpe Wood continued until the early thirteenth century.

9. *Vita*, I, xi, 34.

10. *Vita*, I, xiii.

11. *Vita*, I, iv.

12. *Vita*, I, iv.

13. *Vita*, I, xiii.

14. Langmuir, *Definition*, 218–219, 220.

15. Michael Goodich, *Violence and Miracle in the Fourteenth Century: Private Grief and Public Salvation* (Chicago: University of Chicago Press, 1995), 98.

16. The "inordinate support" and "ardent local veneration" of St. William claimed by Cohen, "Flow of Blood," 28, following Ronald Finucane, *Miracles and Pilgrims: Popular Beliefs in Medieval England* (New York: St. Martin's Press, 1995), 119, are not apparent.

17. Since Wulfric of Haselbury, the hermit whose *Life* appears in the same manuscript with that of William, was certain to become a saint, even before his death his abbot sent someone to record the details of his life and secure his body. See *Wulfric of Haselbury* by John, Abbot of Ford, ed. Maurice Bell (Somerset Records Society, vol. 47, 1933). Wulfric died in 1154. A summary of the life is printed in H. Mayr-Harting, "Functions of a Twelfth-Century Recluse," *History* 60 (1975), 337–352. So, too, Godric of Finchale, the other saint whose *Life* appears in the same manuscript, was acknowledged a saint before his death in 1170. A version of Reginald's Latin *Life of St. Godric* was printed by the Surtees Society in 1847, ed. Joseph Stevenson. Benedicta Ward, *Miracles and the Medieval Mind: Theory, Record, Event, 1000–1215* (Philadelphia: University of Pennsylvania Press, 1982), 76–82, offers an accessible summary of Godric's life in English. His posthumous miracles, largely centered on medical cures, have much in common with those claimed for William. For the context of twelfth-century miracle collections, see Rachel Koopmans, *Wonderful to Relate: Miracle Stories and Miracle Collecting in High Medieval England* (Philadelphia: University of Pennsylvania Press, 2011), especially 119–122 for Thomas of Monmouth.

18. Bale, *Feeling Persecuted*, 53, demonstrates how the mother's dream encapsulates the entire story of William and his martyrdom.

19. *Vita*, II, iii: rose blossomed in winter; II, iv and v: visions; I, vii: easy labor during pregnancy; II, vii: virgin delivered from succubus. Close parallels to these phenomena can be found in the influential miracle stories of Gregory of Tours.

20. *Vita*, I, ix.

21. King Stephen, the nephew of Henry I, had to defend himself in battle against the claims of Matilda, Henry's daughter and the widow of the Holy Roman Emperor, whom Henry had publicly declared his heir. See H. A. Cronne, *The Reign of Stephen, 1135–54: Anarchy in England* (London: Weidenfeld and Nicolson, 1970); R. H. C. Davis, "What Happened in Stephen's Reign," *History* 64 (1964), 1–12; E. J. King, "The Anarchy of Stephen's Reign," *Transactions of the Royal Historical Society* 34, 5th ser. (1984), 133–153; and Jim Bradbury, "The Civil War of Stephen's Reign; Winners and Losers," in *Armies, Chivalry, and Warfare in Medieval Britain and France*, ed. Matthew Strickland (Stamford, UK: Paul Watkins, 1998), 115–132. Volume 6 of *Albion* (1974) offered a number of articles on Stephen's reign by Callahan, Hollister, and Patterson. See also Graeme White, "Were the Midlands 'Wasted' during Stephen's Reign?" *Midland History* 10 (1985), 26–46. By the time Brother Thomas had completed the first five books of his *Life* of William, the conflict had been settled in favor of Henry, Matilda's son by her second husband Geoffrey of Anjou, who succeeded Stephen on his death in 1154 as King Henry II; indeed, William's *Life and Passion* may have been composed with an eye to Henry's endorsement.

22. Hugh M. Thomas, "Violent Disorder in King Stephen's England: A Maximum View," in *King Stephen's Reign (1135–1154)*, ed. Paul Dalton and Graeme J. White (Woodbridge, UK: Boydell, 2008), 139–170, includes a number of maps that display the distribution of violence, the wasting of land, and recorded instances of killing, famine, and depopulation, with references to recent bibliography. For some earlier treatments of the destruction wrought by the civil war, see King, "Anarchy"; Thomas Callahan, "A Reevaluation of the Anarchy of Stephen's Reign, 1135–1154: The Case of the Black Monks," *Revue Benedictine* (1974), 338–351; Davis, "What Happened"; and H. W. C. Davis, "The Anarchy of Stephen's Reign," *English Historical Review* 18 (1903), 630–641.

23. Whitelock, *Anglo-Saxon Chronicle*, 200; Swanton, *Anglo-Saxon Chronicle*, 265.

24. *Vita*, I, i, 10, for the reference to the wealth of William's parents. See Thomas, "Violent Disorder," 151–154, for the killing of non-combatants, the overwhelming evidence of kidnapping for ransom, and widespread use of torture to extract money.

25. William of Malmesbury, *Historia Novella*, in Joseph Stephenson, *Contemporary Chronicles of the Middle Ages* (Felinfach, Dyfed: Llanerch Enterprises, 1988), nos. 34, 32.

26. Translation from Whitelock, *Anglo-Saxon Chronicle*, 199, Scribe E, entry for the year 1137. Swanton, *Anglo-Saxon Chronicle*, 264, includes "common men" [*carlmen*] in his translation and adds, n. 5, the torture term *crucet-hus*, from the Latin *cruciatus* with a suffix made by "popular etymology." Whitelock notes, xvi, that the scribe who wrote of events from 1132 to the early part of 1155 "can only rarely assign them to their proper year." The year in which this scribe situates the tortures is the same year in which he includes mention of the death of St. William.

27. William of Malmesbury, *Historia Novella*, trans. K. R. Potter (London: Thomas Nelson and Sons, 1955), 40ff.: "under-tenants, peasants any who were thought wealthy, they kidnapped and compelled to promise anything by the severity of their tortures." See also William of Malmesbury, "Historia Novella," in *De gestis regum anglorum libri quinque and Historiae novellae libri tres*, ed. William Stubbs (London, 1887–1889), ii, 560ff. Whitelock, *Anglo-Saxon Chronicle*, 199 n. 3, makes the comparison.

28. Davis, "The Anarchy," 637: Philip Gay, the castelan of Bristol, "began the practice of kidnapping non-combatants and holding them to ransom. His plan of operations is described in the *Gesta Stephani*. His men sallied out into the highways, often in disguise, and mixed in public gatherings until they had found a suitable and unsuspecting prey. The victim was then carried off by force to Bristol with his eyes blindfolded and a gag in his mouth; when once in the castle he was tortured or starved into paying down his last farthing in ransom. In Bristol such a panic was created by these proceedings that whoever saw a stranger approaching him on the high road took to the woods or any other convenient hiding-place until he was sure the coast was clear."

29. Thomas, "Violent Disorder," 152–153, refers to the description of the kidnapping ring in the *Walden Chronicle* and confirmation in other records by testimony of the victims.

30. James W. Alexander, "Herbert of Norwich, 1091–1119: Studies in the History of Norman England," *Studies in Medieval and Renaissance History* 6 (1969), 115–232 at 182.

31. Graeme J. White, "Royal Income and Regional Trends," in *King Stephen's Reign (1135–1154)*, ed. Paul Dalton and Graeme J. White (Woodbridge, UK: Boydell Press, 2008), 27–43 at 37.

32. *Vita*, I, xvi, 43.

33. Paul Hyams, "Trial by Ordeal: The Key to Proof in the Early Common Law," in *On the Laws and Customs of England: Essays in Honor of Samuel E. Thorne*, ed. M. S. Arnold (Chapel Hill: University of North Carolina Press, 1981), 90–126.

34. Shlomo Eidelberg, "Trial by Ordeal in Medieval Jewish History: Laws, Customs and Attitudes," *Proceedings of the American Academy for Jewish Research* 46, Jubilee Volume (1979–80), 105–20.

35. *Vita*, I, xvi.

36. The theme of trial by ordeal is treated by Heather Blurton, in "Narratives of Ritual Crucifixion in Twelfth-Century England," a paper delivered at the conference *Antisemitism and English Culture* (Birkbeck College, University of London, July 9–11, 2007).

37. See Willis Johnson, "The Myth of Jewish Male Menses," *Journal of Medieval History* 24 (1998), 273–295.

38. *Vita*, I, xvi.

39. The king profited from court cases involving homicide, and for those found guilty, well-known formalities procured his pardon. Naomi Hurnard, *The King's Pardon of Homicide before 1300* (Oxford: Oxford University Press, 1968).

40. Capital crimes were traditionally a royal matter, as were cases dealing with Jews. John McCulloh, "Jewish Ritual Murder: William of Norwich, Thomas of Monmouth, and the Early Dissemination of the Myth," *Speculum* 72 (1997), 698–740 at 735, says that Thomas hints that William's brother was pursuing prosecution in secular courts as well. As a priest, Godwin would naturally have sought justice in an ecclesiastical court; Colin Morris, "From Synod to Consistory: the Bishops' Courts in England, 1150–1250," *Journal of Ecclesiastical History* 22 (1971), 115–123 at 116.

41. Suicide, now considered a serious public health problem, is the third leading cause of death among adolescents today, often caused by depression and family turmoil, according to statistics from the Centers for Disease Control. In New York City, hanging is the most common method of teen suicide, far surpassing jumping, poisoning, and use of firearms. For a study of medieval adolescent suicide in this period, see Ephraim Shoham-Steiner, "*Vitam finivit infelicem*": Madness Conversion and Adolescent Suicide among Jews in Late Twelfth Century England," in *Jews in Medieval Christendom: "Slay Them Not,"* eds. K. T. Utterback and M. L. Price (Leiden: Brill, 2014), 71–90.

42. See Alexander Murray, *Suicide in the Middle Ages* (Oxford: Oxford University Press, 1998), and Georges Minois, *History of Suicide: Voluntary Death in Western Culture* (Baltimore, MD: Johns Hopkins University Press, 1999).

43. That the Chesneys were apparently out of shrieval office when the *Life* was composed is a point drawn to my attention by Hugh Doherty, University of Oxford. Doherty considers the power of the Chesneys in a forthcoming work on the government of Angevin England.

44. The evidence for his seizure of a manor from the Norwich church is discussed below.

45. *Sibton Abbey Cartularies and Charters*, ed. Philippa Brown (Woodbridge, Suffolk: Boydell Press for the Suffolk Records Society, 1985–1988), vol. 1, 17.

46. Rubin, *Life and Passion*, lvi.

47. Helen Cam, "An East Anglian Shire-Moot of Stephen's Reign, 1148–1153," *English Historical Review* 39 (1924), 568–571.

48. There is much speculation about Bishop Eborard's departure because resignation was usually regarded as an abdication of duty. Christopher Holdsworth says "he was deposed" by the papal legate; cited by King, "Anarchy," 213. He died within two years, but regardless of his age or state of health, Eborard's resignation is striking. John H. Druery, "On the Retirement of Bishop Eborard from the See of Norwich," *Norfolk Archeology* 5 (1859), 41–48 is interesting but unreliable. The challenges of episcopal retirement are discussed in Marylou Ruud, "'Unworthy Servants': The Rhetoric of Resignation at Canterbury, 1070–1170," *Journal of Religious History* 22, no. 1 (1998), 1–13.

49. *Vita*, I, xvi, 31.

50. *Vita*, II, vii, 56.

51. Patrick Geary, *Furta Sacra: Thefts of Relics in the Central Middle Ages*, 2nd ed. (Princeton, NJ: Princeton University Press, 1990).

52. It is worth noting that, according to Brother Thomas, the bishop first went to prior Aimery for advice on the correct legal procedure, before the prior went to the bishop to request the relics (*Vita* I, xvii). As St. Pancras was already endowed with a famous child martyr, the abbot may have intended the saint for a local East Anglian house for which he was responsible.

53. His predecessor, Hugh of St. Margaret, died in 1143, and Aimery's name occurs only in 1145. David Knowles, C. N. L. Brooke, and Vera London, eds., *The Heads of Religious Houses: England and Wales, 940–1216* (Cambridge: Cambridge University Press, 1972), 119: this publication does not mention Aimery's appearance in the *Life* of St. William. Mention of the next prior of St. Pancras, William I, occurs in 1147.

54. According to a charter of Bishop Herbert Losinga, the monks received mortuary and burial fees, something they could not claim for the informal burial of the victim in Thorpe Woods. See Christopher Harper-Bill, ed., *Norwich Episcopal Acta* (London: Oxford University Press for the British Academy, 1990), no. 1, 9.

55. Barbara Dodwell, ed., *Charters of Norwich Cathedral Priory* (London: Pipe Roll Society, 1974), no. 18, 12 (1107–1108); Alexander, "Herbert," 143.

56. Harper-Bill, *Norwich Episcopal Acta*, no. 120, 99.

57. Contemporary examples of what a priory ["poor and most obscure"] could expect to receive for a simple burial in East Anglia are suggested by some Sudbury charters. Robert, *magister*, son of Godric of Acton, granted two and a half acres to St. Bartholomew's, together with his body for burial (no. 59, 10); Ivo gave two parts of the tithes of his demesne at Thorpe, along with his body for burial, a donation that was confirmed by Henry I and Henry II (1155–1162) (no. 103, 78) in Richard Mortimer, ed., *Charters of St. Bartholomew's Priory, Sudbury, Suffolk Charters* (Suffolk Records Society, 1996). See M. J. Franklin, "Bodies in Medieval Northampton: Legatine Intervention in the Twelfth Century," in *Medieval Ecclesiastical Studies in Honour of Dorothy M. Owen*, ed. M. J. Franklin and Christopher Harper-Bill (Woodbridge, Suffolk: The Boydell Press, 1995), 57–82 at 68: "The issue of the right of burial in monastic houses became critical in the religious atmosphere of the twelfth century; 72, "the potential losses for a monastery that was dilatory in these matters could be considerable."

58. See the discussion of his family below.

59. *Vita*, V, xxi, 142.

60. *Vita*, I, xviii, ff.

61. Robert Dinn, "'Monuments Answerable to Mens Worth': Burial Patterns, Social Status and Gender in Late Medieval Bury St. Edmunds," *Journal of Ecclesiastical History* 46 (1995), 237–255 at 240.

62. Elizabeth Valdez del Alamo, "Lament for a Lost Queen: The Sarcophagus of Dona Blanca in Najera," *Art Bulletin* 78 (1996), n. 22, citing Serafin Moralejo, "La reutilizacion e influencia de los sarcofagos antiguos en la Espana medieval," in *Colloquio sul reimpiego dei sarcofagi romani nel medievo* (Marburg-an-der-Lahn, 1984), 189–190.

63. Bishop Walkelin and Ranulph, the king's chaplain, attended the translation of St. Edmund in 1095, to which Bishop Herbert Losinga of Norwich was pointedly not invited. He preached instead at the translation of St. Etheldreda at Ely in 1106. Ranulph, who became bishop of Durham, in turn presided over the translation of St. Cuthbert in 1104 at Durham.

64. Paul A. Hayward, "The Idea of Innocent Martyrdom in Late Tenth- and Eleventh-Century English Hagiology," in *Martyrs and Martyrologies*, ed. Diana Wood (Cambridge: Ecclesiastical History Society, 1993), 81–92.

65. Stephen Lay, "Miracles, Martyrs and the Cult of Henry the Crusader in Lisbon," *Portuguese Studies* 24.1 (2008), 7–31.

66. The national outpouring of emotion surrounding the death of Princess Diana in an auto accident in Paris in 1997 suggests that English culture retains such a reaction to sudden violent death.

67. *Vita*, II, xii, 96.

68. Guibert of Nogent, *De sanctis et eorum pignoribus, Patrologia Latina* 156 (1853), col. 607–680, at col. 621. The English translation is taken from G. G. Coulton, *Life in the Middle Ages* (Cambridge: Cambridge University Press, 1928), 1, 15. See also Colin Morris, "A Critique of Popular Religion: Guibert of Nogent on the Relics of the Saints," in *Popular Belief and Practice* (Cambridge: Ecclesiastical History Society, 1972), 55–60.

69. *Vita*, II, I, 60–61.

70. Hayward, "Innocent Martyrdom," 82, 90, discussing Saints Ethelbert and Ethelred of Ramsey, Ethelbert of Hereford, Edward the martyr, Kenelm, and Wigstan, most of whose stories seem to have been composed between 1050 and 1130, noting that the youth of martyrs seems to have been deliberately emphasized.

71. See, for example, Richard Utz, "The Medieval Myth of Jewish Ritual Murder: Toward a History of Literary Reception," in *The Year's Work in Medievalism* (1999), 23–36, who mistakenly describes William as seven years old. J. J. Cohen, "Flow of Blood," notes, 46, "this poor ragged little lad was picking up a precarious livelihood at his tanners' business" and, 61, "the indigence of William's family is continually underscored in Thomas's text." Yarrow, *Saints and Their Communities*, 161, in contrast, notes William's connection to the urban and commercial establishment of Norwich.

72. Jessopp and James, *Life and Miracles*, lxv.

73. *Vita*, I, i, 10. Jessop and James translate it: "they passed their lives as honest people in the country, being somewhat well supplied with the necessaries of life and something more."

74. *Vita*, I, i, 10.

75. Brother Thomas uses the word "rustic" (*rustici*) when he is describing peasants (*Vita*, I, xi, 34, and IV, xii, 203), with the added sense of "ignorant." The "rural" character of the family contrasts here with families from the city of Norwich. See also Michael Richter, "*Urbanitas-Rusticitas*; Linguistic Aspects of a Medieval Dichotomy," in *The Church in Town and Countryside*, ed. Derek Baker (Oxford: Ecclesiastical History Society, 1979), 149–157 at 155: in the twelfth century, the inhabitants of towns "enjoyed special privileges which set them apart from the rural population and may have given rise to a feeling of superiority of the townspeople over the *rustici*."

76. *Vita*, I, ii, 13. Jessopp and James, *Life and Miracles*, lxv. The area is still rural and undeveloped, described as charming, bleak, isolated, and one of the prettiest villages in the county before the construction of an airbase during World War II. In the most recent census, it still boasted fewer than seventy households.

77. *Vita*, I, iii, 15.

78. *Vita* I, iii, 16.

79. *Vita* I, xv, 41. See also *Vita*, V, xxi, 13ff.

80. *Vita* I, iii, Jessopp and James translation, 14–15.

81. Yarrow, *Saints and Their Communities*, 216, rightly points out that "William's willingness as a young entrepreneur to deal with the Jewish community in Norwich may ironically make him a more fitting representative of the Christian economic community of Norfolk than the martyred status invented for him by the monks of Norwich."

82. *Vita*, I, ii, 14. *Litteras, psalmos et orationes discebat.*

83. *Vita*, I, iv, 17–18.

84. *Vita*, I, v, 19–20.

85. *Vita*, I, xiii. 27.

86. Maryanne Kowaleski, "Town and Country in Late Medieval England: The Hide and Leather Trade," in *Work in Towns, 850–1850*, ed. P. J. Corfield and D. Keene (Leicester: Leicester University Press, 1990), 57–73 at 68 and *Norwich: The Growth of a City* (Norwich: The Norwich Museums Committee, 1963), 14.

87. Shinners, "Saints at Norwich," 136.

88. See most recently, Tom Licence, "Herbert Losinga's Trip to Rome and the Bishopric of Bury St. Edmunds," *Anglo-Norman Studies* 34 (2010): 151–168.

89. Jessopp and James, *Life and Miracles*, lxv; *Vita*, I, i, 10–11. The Latin text says *Wlwardo presbitero famoso quidem illius temporis viro*, a far cry from Jessopp's and James's translation of "a well-known man in the neighborhood."

90. D. C. Douglas, ed., *Feudal Documents from the Abbey of Bury St. Edmunds* (London: British Academy, 1932), nos. 107, 109.

91. William appeared on a screen that featured scenes from the Infancy of Christ. Ann Eljenholm Nichols, *The Early Art of Norfolk, EDAM Reference Series* (Kalamazoo, MI: Medieval Institute Publications, 2002). See now C. A. Bradbury, "A Norfolk Saint for a Norfolk Man: William of Norwich and Sir James Hobart at Holy Trinity Church in Loddon," *Norfolk Archaeology* 46, no. 4 (2013), 452–461 and

Julian Luxford, "The Iconography of St William of Norwich and the Nuremberg Chronicle," *Norfolk Archeology* (2015 forthcoming). I thank the authors for sending me copies of their work which dates the painting to the first quarter of the sixteenth century.

92. Douglas, *Feudal Documents*, nos. 108, 109, charter of Abbot Albold making Maurice of Windsor steward of the land of St. Edmund, 1114–1119. *Wlwardus presbiter* attested to an addendum. The second charter: Douglas, *Feudal Documents*, nos. 109, 111, charter of Abbot Albold to Maurice of Windsor granting him all the land which Ralph, his predecessor as steward of the abbey, held of the abbey. Wlward once again appears in the addendum. These charters appear to have been prepared close in time.

Douglas, *Feudal Documents*, nos. 123, 121–122, a land confirmation by the abbot to Richer of Troston (Suffolk) and his heirs. Rodney M. Thomson, "Early Romanesque Book-Illustration in England; The Dates of the Pierpont Morgan *Vitae Sancti Edmundi* and the Bury Bible" *Viator* 2 (1971), 211–225, notes that most of Anselm's charters in Douglas's *Feudal Documents* need to be redated. This is eagerly anticipated in the final volume of Suffolk Charters Society publication series.

93. *Wlwardus presbiter* disappears from the records at this point, and his place in the witness lists is taken by *Wlwardus clericus*. Wlward was not a common name, and *clericus* was a generic title that often referred to a younger person, of more junior status than a priest, generally someone in minor orders, possibly the elder Wlward's son. *Wlwardus clericus* appears in Douglas, *Feudal Documents*, no. 113, 114–115; no. 114, 115–116, 1121–1238; no. 121, 119–120, grant of land by Abbot Anselm to Leo, 1121–1148; no. 122, 120–121, where he is occasionally associated with Lemerus de Westlea.

94. Christopher Harper-Bill, "The Struggle for Benefices in Twelfth Century East Anglia." *Anglo-Norman Studies* 11 (1989), 113–132 at 126.

95. The story is broken off by Hermann but taken up and continued by Abbot Samson. Hermannus archdiaconnus, *"De miraculis Sancti Eadmundi,"* in *Memorials of St. Edmund's Abbey*, ed. Thomas Arnold, Rolls Series (London: 1890–1896, repr. Kraus Reprint, 1965), 26–92 at 92, no. 3: "Some travelers returning by sea from Rome are in danger of shipwreck [May 17, 1096]." The rest of this story is found in Samson abbatus, *"Opus de Miraculis Sancti Eadmundi,"* 107–208, beginning on 162; Wlward (Wulfward) the priest is named among the passengers on 163.

96. Bale, *St Edmund*.

97. *Vita*, I, i, 11: *Pater itaque plurima exponendarum visionum peritiam habens.*

98. Hermannus, *"De miraculis Sancti Eadmundi,"* 91–92, no. 52.

99. Ibid.

100. There is more to suggest that William's mother and aunt (with two similar names, Elviva and Levive, *Aelfgifu* and *Leofgifu*) remained familiar at Bury St. Edmunds. Later Norfolk records describe land "which the widow Alviva held of the abbot of St Edmunds at 12 pence yearly." The description is a way of identifying

the land. Since William's mother, Elviva, died in the 1150s after more than a decade of widowhood, it is possible that the notice refers to property that she held.

101. William of Malmesbury in *De gestis pontificum anglorum* (London: Rolls Series, vol. 52, 1870), 424.

102. This is the context in which Yarrow, *Saints and Their Communities*, places William.

103. Harper-Bill, *English Episcopal Acta*, no. 153, 120–121. The ancient settlement of Acle boasts a round tower church of Saxon origin whose surviving nave is Norman stone.

104. Coslany was originally a hamlet in the old Saxon part of town that developed rapidly in the eleventh century with the Norman occupation. For the altar to William, see Francis Blomefield, *Blomefield's Norwich* (Fersfeld, 1741), 846. St. Michael's was founded before the Conquest but was later rebuilt. From at least 1304, authority over the church of St. Michael was connected with a half acre of land in Acle; that connection between land and church authority may well date back earlier to the settlement between *Wlward* and *Rainald*. In the mid-fifteenth century the *advowson*, the right to present the holder of church office, for St. Michael Coslany along with a half acre in Acle, was turned over to Gonville and Caius College, Cambridge.

105. Harper-Bill, *Norwich Episcopal Acta*, index, 419, s.n. "Timsworth," raises the possibility that Wulward was the *persona* (i.e., the person entitled to the income of the greater and lesser tithes), but the concord states that the issue in question is Wlward's ownership (*dominium*). The actum is the "notification of a settlement in the presence of the bishop" (March 29, 1155–1163), no. 53, 120–121.

106. The names are similar enough that they may even refer to the same person: the Latin spellings of *Radulfus* and *Rainaldus* are easily confused, and the abbreviations could be identical. Ralph the priest "had bought [the psalter] for three pence, but after hearing that it had been stolen and often inquired for in the church, he delayed to return it—whether from shame or because he was corrupted by the desire of keeping it, I know not. It was indeed a precious and dear book and not unworthy of being coveted." *Vita*, V, xi, 201–202.

107. Godwin's son Alexander was a deacon in 1144 (*Vita*, I, xiii, 38), an office for which one had to be over the age of 25, so he was born before 1119, the date of Bishop Losinga's death.

108. Jessopp and James, following Thomas of Monmouth, accept these final honors as Elviva's due for having produced a martyr son, but this too is unlikely. Jessopp and James, *Life and Miracles*, xiii and xiv.

109. It is unclear why the dead boy's family and the Norwich ecclesiastical establishment should be considered "unlikely allies" in promoting William's cult, for which see Cohen, "Flow of Blood," 26.

110. Dinn, "Burial Patterns," 241, suggests that in medieval East Anglia "like funeral ritual, the site of their burial locations was used by wealthy townspeople to assert their status to the living, and that this status remained important after

death." If his findings for late medieval Bury are applicable to Norwich, it would complement other hints that William's family was part of the local elite (243): "A third of those buried at the abbey [Bury] were members of the town's clergy who, since the abbey held the rectories of both parishes, had close links with the monks. The lay people asking to be buried there tended to be members of Bury's social elite which, although in dispute with the abbey over the town's administration, maintained close social and kinship ties with the monks." There are many comparable examples from the twelfth century. E. Mason, "A Truth Universally Acknowledged," *Studies in Church History* 16 (1979), 171–186 at 181: "From the early twelfth century onwards, Westminster abbey offered a whole range of spiritual services to the laity in order to attract donations. . . . Burial within the precincts of the abbey was one such option available from the early twelfth century, and the monks were surprisingly open-minded about whom they accepted."

111. *Vita*, I, iii, 16; I, xiii, 38; I, xvi, 43.

112. Losinga writes, "your father is safe and sound and has his every wish gratified." E. M. Goulburn and H. Symonds, *The Life, Letters, and Sermons of Bishop Herbert de Losinga* (Oxford: Parker and Co., 1878), vol. 2, letter XXVII, 87–88.

113. Decades before the *Vita* was discovered, the nineteenth-century editors and translators of Losinga's letters suspected that deacon Godwin was also addressed in this letter. Goulburn and Symonds, *Losinga Letters*, letter LV, p. 100, and appendix G, 414.

114. Dodwell, *Norwich Cathedral Charters*, i, no. 106, 57; printed in Goulburn and Symonds, *Losinga Letters*, i, 415; noted in Harper-Bill, *Norwich Episcopal Acta*, appendix I, no. 11, p. 359, confirmation by subscription for the monks of Norwich of the gift of Godwin the deacon of the church of Cressingham with its appurtenances and whatsoever he held there [1101–1119]; H. W. Saunders, ed., *The First Register of Norwich Cathedral Priory* (Norfolk: Norfolk Record Society, 1939), 46–48.

115. Dodwell, *Norwich Charters*, i, no. 106, 57.

116. Mason, "Truth" notes, 182, that confraternity "did not automatically include burial within the abbey."

117. Dodwell, *Norwich Charters*, i, no. 106, 57.

118. Godwin's own son, William's cousin Alexander, made a career in the church like his father. In the 1150s Alexander appeared as a monk at Norwich among the witnesses to an episcopal charter about a mill in Pedham (the only Alexander to appear in any of the extant Norwich charters). See Harper-Bill, *Norwich Episcopal Acta*, no. 128, p. 105, ca. 1150–1159. He may have become a monk later in life, between 1144, when Thomas records him as a deacon, and ca. 1159, when the attestation apparently occurred. A deacon, he expected to take over his father's benefices and position as priest, according to *Blomefield's Norwich*, 19. He was therefore at the abbey along with his first cousin Robert, William's brother, who also joined the priory sometime after 1144. *Vita*, II, x, 91. Thomas of Monmouth also mentions William's second cousin Hathewis, daughter of Edwin, priest of Taverham: "deformed and weak in her limbs, she, prompted as I rather think by the

fact of her relationship, came to the tomb of the holy martyr as to a kindred refuge, and instantly obtained the longed-for cure." *Vita,* VII, xv, 275.

119. *Vita,* I, ii, 12.

120. The Norwich school offered not just preparation for young oblates who intended to become monks, but formal instruction for thirteen boys with a school-master, *Losinga,* 70; Joan Greatrex, *Biographical Register of English Cathedral Priories* (Oxford: Clarendon Press, 1997), 470: "An almonry school was certainly maintained before 1272, and the monks themselves believed that it dated back to their founder, bishop Losinga, who himself had donated books for the library." A large number of Bishop Losinga's letters reflect his concern with the education of young boys.

121. Blomefield, *Topographical History,* 5.19 n.4. Matthew appears on the Pipe Roll of Henry I holding land in Essex and Norfolk; his service for four knights was awarded to Geoffrey de Mandeville in King Stephen's famous charter of 1141, printed in David Douglas and George W. Greenaway, eds., *English Historical Documents* (London: Routledge, 1966), 466–467.

122. Greatrex, *Biographical Register,* 508; see also Jessopp and James, *Life and Miracles,* 142.

123. J. R. West, ed., *St. Benet of Holme, 1102–1210* (London: Fakenham, 1932), 203.

124. The list of tenants is found in the Feudal Book of Abbot Samson, for which see Douglas, *Feudal Documents,* viii, 27. William's mother was widowed sometime between 1135 and 1144. The original document from which the manuscript was copied was clearly drawn up at a much earlier period, Douglas, *Feudal Documents,* xlvi. The dating of Aelfwine and his father, Wenstan, would be in keeping with the age of William's father and one of his elder brothers, whose names we are not told.

125. R. P. Mack, "Stephen and the Anarchy, 1135–1154," *British Numismatic Journal* 35 (1967), 38–112, table of moneyers, mints, and types.

126. Ian Stewart, "Moneyers in the 1130 Pipe Roll," *British Numismatic Journal* 61 (1991), 1–8 at 4, among moneyers known from the 1130 pipe roll: "Spelring was a London alderman and Algar a canon of St. Paul's." See also Ian Stewart, "The English and Norman Mints, C. 600–1158," in *A New History of the Norman Mint,* ed. C. E. Challis, 1–82. (Cambridge: Cambridge University Press, 1992), 1–82 at 71: "seven of the eighteen forges listed in [the Winchester survey] of 1115 were held by Robert, son of the presbiter Wimund, who himself had been a moneyer since the 1080s."

127. Stewart, "Moneyers," notes a number of moneyers who worked at more than one mint. For example, Edric coined at Stafford, Bristol, and Hereford; Tovius, an engineer, who was excused from taxation, and the moneyer Tovi signed coins at Oxford, Stamford, Twynham, Winchester, and London.

128. *Vita,* I, iii, 13. Michael Adler, *Jews of Medieval England* (London: Edward Goldston, 1939), 65: "The *monetarii,* moneyers, or workers in the mint lived in the Jewish quarter, and it is interesting to note that one of these workmen was

Nicholas, a converted Jew, who is mentioned as early as 1181... and this *monetarius* may have been a member of the monastery also. The mint was property of local Cathedral authorities."

129. Pamela Nightingale, "Some London Moneyers, and Reflections on the Organization of English Mints in the Eleventh and Twelfth Centuries," *Numismatic Chronicle* 142 (1982), 34–50 at 34, 48; Stewart, "The English and Norman Mints," 69. See also John D. Brand, *The English Coinage, 1180–1247: Money, Mints and Exchanges, Special Publication No. 1* (British Numismatic Society, 1994), 21.

130. Norwich was the second-largest city in the country and had a number of active mints and named moneyers. Known moneyers in Norwich from whom coins survive include one Edstan, who owed money for taking over the work of Ulchetell, according to the 1130 pipe roll. See William Farrer, *Honours and Knights' Fees*. 3 vols. (London: Spottiswoode, Balantyne and Co., 1923–1925). 1:360 for speculation on his family connections. Some moneyers worked for the city and for the bishop, who had the rights to his own ecclesiastical mint, Brand, *English Coinage*, 22 and n. 39. A number of men in the mid-twelfth century are known to have been moneyers for whom no coins survive. Stewart, "Moneyers," 2: "The Lincoln hoard added no fewer than 15 new moneyer/type combinations for the Lincoln mint from type VII to XV [these were coins minted under King Stephen]. Any discussion of the careers of individual moneyers can therefore be only of the most provisional kind, and is liable to major revision in the light of subsequent discoveries."

131. *Vita*, I, iii, 13.

132. Robert C. Stacey, "Jews and Christians in Twelfth-Century England: Some Dynamics of a Changing Relationship," in *Jews and Christians in Twelfth-Century Europe*, ed. Michael Signer and John Van Engen (Notre Dame, IN: University of Notre Dame Press, 2001), 340–354 at 341. Paul Hyams, "The Jewish Minority in Medieval England, 1066–1290," *Journal of Jewish Studies* 25 (1974), 270–293 at 273, concludes that Jews were usually bilingual at least, based on the translation rather than the transliteration of their names in contemporary Christian sources. No manuscripts survive that demonstrate any knowledge by Jews of English: Beit-Arié, *Medieval Hebrew Book*, 132. No manuscripts known to have been made in England survive before the Valmadonna Pentateuch. It is worthwhile noting here that Beit-Arié refutes Roth's claim that the Hebrew manuscript dictionary now in Cambridge, St. John's College, Ms. l.10, came from Norwich Cathedral Priory, since it was written in a Sephardic, probably Provençal script.

133. Mayr-Harting, "Recluse," 341. The English parish priest who served the hermit of Haselbury despaired when Wulfric blessed some stranger with the ability to speak French: "All these years I have served you, and today I have clearly proved that it was for nothing. To a stranger, whose tongue it would have been enough to open, you have kindly given the use of two languages, while to me, who am forced

to remain dumb in the presence of the bishop and archdeacon, you have never imparted a word of French."

134. He began to learn his letters among the schoolboys, years after a successful international trading career. Virginia Tudor, "Reginald of Durham and St. Godric of Finchale: Learning and Religion on a Personal Level," in *Studies in Church History: Religion and Humanism*, ed. Keith Robbins (Oxford: Ecclesiastical History Society, 1981), 37–48 at 43: "one suspects that while he knew the alphabet, he used his knowledge to decipher the first few words of, for example, a prayer and then relied on his memory for the remainder of the text. Thus, if Godric was not illiterate, it seems likely that he never rose much above this level."

135. Mayr-Harting, "Recluse," 341, assumes that Godric could speak French because he had lived in Walter Fitzwalter's household. William's ability to speak (or to learn) the language of the archdiaconal household may have made him an attractive potential employee.

136. It is difficult to assess how widespread bilingualism was during this period. Abbot Samson of Bury, for example, knew sufficient English to preach in it. For a discussion of bilingualism, see Giles Constable, "The Language of Preaching in the Twelfth Century," *Viator* 25 (1994), 131–152. The beneficiaries of William's miracles, such as the girl observed in the cathedral by Godiva, the wife of Sibald, spoke English. *Vita*, V, xvi, 207. Godiva herself understood both languages: she explained to Brother Thomas in Latin what she had heard in English. To judge from her husband's contribution to the abbey of St. Benet of Holm, noted above, Godiva must have been fairly well off and of relatively high status in the English community.

137. *Vita*, I, iii, 13; I, v, 16.

138. Jessopp and James, *Life and Miracles*, xvii, direct the readers' attention to the fact that "there was much more education of a certain kind among all classes than one would have expected." If William's mother or aunt was buried with the monks as a *confrater*, then she may indeed have spoken French. Mason, "Truth Universally Acknowledged," 182, observes: "It was presumed that *confratres* were French-speaking, a social class which ranged upwards from the urban bourgeoisie."

139. *Vita*, I, viii, 23; II, vii, 55.

140. Yarrow, *Saints and Their Communities*, draws attention to Wicman's importance.

141. *Vita*, III, i, 77. Thomas is here recalling the Vision of Lucian, which circulated as one of the miracles of St. Stephen the Protomartyr. The *Revelatio Sancti Stephani* and the subsequent success of Stephen's relics, most notably in converting Jews, played a significant role in persuading St. Augustine of the importance of relic cults. In the early Middle Ages, the cult of Stephen was linked to conversions of Jews to Christianity; it may not be surprising, therefore, to find Stephen invoked in the first accusation of ritual murder. In the early twelfth-century musical tropes, and soon after in liturgical drama, the virtue of St. Stephen is contrasted with the perfidy of the Jews. See Daniel F. Callahan, "Ademar of Chabannes, Millenial Fears and the Development of Western Anti-Judaism," *Journal of Ecclesiastical*

History 46 (1995), 19–35 at 32. It is not known where, when, and under what circumstances Wicman (or perhaps Thomas) came to read the *Revelatio*, as no copy of
this vision is known to have been in England in the twelfth century.

142. *Vita*, I, vii, 20.

143. Aelward attested a document concerning a donation to Thetford priory
in the mid-twelfth century. One of the East Anglian churches dedicated to St.
Nicholas was in Thetford, very near Warenne's foundation of the priory of the Holy
Sepulchre. Lewis C. Loyd and Doris Mary Stenton, eds., *Sir Christopher Hatton's
Book of Seals*, vol. 15 (Oxford: Clarendon Press, 1950), 230, no. 334. David Knowles
and R. Neville Hadcock, *Medieval Religious Houses: England and Wales*, 2nd ed.
(London: Longman, 1971). The church is gone, but St Nicholas Street has retained
its name.

144. Perhaps as early as 1121, Bishop Eborard of Norwich had confirmed
Aelward's holding in North Walsham, Harper-Bill, *Norwich Episcopal Acta*, 359,
no. 18, confirmation by Bishop Everard of Calne "for Eilward [*sic*] the priest of
the church of North Walsham with its tithes and appurtenances" [1121–1145];
mentioned in confirmation of Archbishop Richard of Dover, citing an actum of
Archbishop Theobald (archbishop, 1139–1161); 360, no. 29 confirmation by Bishop
William Turbe in the confirmation of Archbishop Richard of Dover. There is no
record of any later confirmation. His land in Smallberg and Antingham was in the
hands of St. Benet of Holme by 1147–1149, but whether by sale or gift is unknown.
West, *St. Benet*, 37 no. 68 (1147–1149) general confirmation by Pope Eugenius III
of the abbey's possessions and liberties. But if Aelward or his heirs were compelled
to sell some land in the late 1140s, his sons were able to maintain and recoup their
wealth. Aelward's son Adam the priest gave land to the priory at Binham, his son
Ebrard inherited the lay fee of his father in North Walsham, and his grandchildren
inherited the church at North Walsham, which was presented to Thomas archdeacon of Norwich for the yearly fee of twenty shillings while they were probably still
minors. For Adam's donation to Binham, see Harper-Bill, *Norwich Episcopal Acta*,
55–56, no. 62. Pope Lucius III included the church and appurtenances of North
Walsham among the possessions of St. Benet's in a general privilege of July 28,
1183 (*St. Benet* i, 39, no. 69). See C. R. Cheney and Bridgett E. A. Jones, eds.,
Canterbury, 1162–1190, English Episcopal Acta 2 (London: British Academy, 1986),
113 no. 13 for the earlier confirmation.

145. Ailward's son Adam had managed to expand his holdings by adding land
to them from Ailmer, the son of Mosse, West, *St. Benet*, vol. 1, 152–153, no. 285.
In his index, 281, West seems to imply that *Almerus* and *Ailwardus* are the same
man, i.e., the son of Mosse, husband of Leviva, and father of Adam and Ebrard.
Yet this is not the case: the original grant to "Aylmer" (*Ailmero filio Mosse*),
98–99, no. 176, is attested by *Ailwardus presbiter*. West gives the date of this
charter as sometime between 1153 and 1168, based presumably on the abbati-
ate of William of St. Benet. Knowles, *Heads of Religious Houses*, 68, gives Abbot
Willliam II dates of ca. 1154–1168. William succeeded the controversial Abbot

Daniel (ca.1141–1146, ca. 1150–1153), who was deposed and reinstated and who may have been out of office earlier than 1153. The list of abbots of St. Benet, giving the dates on which they died, was compiled in the fourteenth century (see West, *St. Benet*, appendix C). If Ailward *presbiter* attested the charter of William II as late as 1153, he presumably could not be the *Aelward presbiter* of Norwich who died around 1149, but he could have died before Thomas began the *Vita* of St. William.

146. Compare, for example, Humphrey de Criketot, indexed in the published Leiston cartulary as Hemfrid, but whose name is variously spelled as Hamfrid, Ennfrid, Heynfrey, Homfrid, and Amfrid, R. H. Mortimer, ed., *Leiston Abbey Cartulary and Butley Priory Charters, Suffolk Charters* (Suffolk: Suffolk Records Society, 1979), 10. In the following citations I use the English spelling of Aelward, as indicated by the author or editor quoted. The dates are those suggested by the editor. Cecily Clark, "Women's Names in Post Conquest England: Observations and Speculations," *Speculum* (1978), 223–251 at 250 notes "Ellwardus, although probably representing the English Aethelweard, might possibly stand for the continental Agilward."

147. Aelward was married to Lefleda and their names appear in documents of the Norfolk abbey of St. Benet of Holme, West, *St. Benet*, vol. 1, 72, no. 125, grant by Abbot Conrad for the food and farm of the monks of St. Benet, of the land which Aylward [*Egelwardus*] and his wife Lefleda held in Hoveton and North Walsham. (October 1126xFebruary 1127); 96–97, no. 172, grant by Abbot William Basset to Peter the Chamberlain [*camerarius*], of the land that Aylward had held in Hoveton and North Walsham, for eight shillings annually (1127x34). From later documents the sons of Aelward the priest of North Walsham can be identified as Adam the priest and Ebrard; West, *St. Benet*, vol. 1, 148, no. 275, and vol. 2, 270. Adam, in turn, had sons Elias and John, who inherited from their father. West, *St. Benet*, vol. 1, 148, no. 276.

148. I thank Martin Brett for bringing this to my attention. Eborard was married, and one of his sons witnessed a document in Bury in 1135. It is likely that Eborard was widowed when he was named bishop of Norwich. See L. Landon, "Everard Bishop of Norwich," *Suffolk Institute of Archeology Proceedings* 20 (1929), 2: 186–198 at 190.

149. Augustus Jessopp, "On Married Clergy in Norfolk in the Thirteenth Century," *Norfolk Archeology* 9 (1884), 197. See also West, *St. Benet*, vol. 1, 41 no. 70: letter of Pope Lucius III to the abbot and monks of St. Benet condemning the practice of allowing sons of priests to have the churches of their fathers in the latters' lifetime, and so creating a kind of hereditary succession (1181–1185). See also Harper-Bill, "Struggle for Benefices,"126.

150. *Blomefield's Norwich*, 19.

151. Barbara Dodwell, ed., "Some Charters Relating to the Honour of Bacton," in *A Medieval Miscellany for Doris Mary Stenton*, ed. Patricia M. Barnes and C. F. Slade (London: Pipe Roll Society, 1962), 147–165 at 158, no. 2.

152. See below for a discussion of this miracle. Henry *de stabulario* appears in a number of St. Benet documents later in the twelfth century. He may have retired and become a monk.

153. *Vita*, I, vii, 21.

154. *Vita*, I, viii, 30. Jessopp and James, 303, indicate that they consider Wicman to have been the priest of St. Nicholas at Aelward's bedside. It is evident, however, that Thomas is referring to someone else who was with Aelward along with Wicman, thus the plural *quibusdam... dignos* would refer to both Wicman and the unnamed priest.

155. In the Bavarian account in which William first is mentioned outside Norfolk, he appears in the context of Anglo-Saxon saints, McCulloh, "Early Dissemination," 728.

156. For a contrary view see Cohen, *Hybridity*, Epilogue.

157. See Paul Hayward, "Innocent Martyrdom," 1993, and idem, "The Idea of Innocent Martyrdom in Medieval England, c. 700 to 1150 A.D.," Ph.D. thesis, University of Cambridge, 1994.

Chapter 2

* The quotation in the subtitle of this chapter is from a charter of the Abbot of Werden in 1148, in Giles Constable, "Medieval Charters as a Source for the History of the Crusades," in *Crusade and Settlement: Papers Read at the First Conference of the Society for the Study of the Crusades and the Latin East and Presented to R.C. Smail*, ed. P. W. Edbury (Cardiff: University College Cardiff Press, 1985), reprinted in Thomas F. Madden, ed., *The Crusades: The Essential Readings* (Oxford: Blackwells, 2002), 73–89 at 74.

1. William III de Warenne went on crusade with his half-brothers Waleran de Beaumont, count of Meulan and earl of Worcester; Robert de Beaumont, earl of Leicester; his mother's brother Simon of Vermandois, the one-time bishop of Noyon; his wife's brother Guy, count of Ponthieu; and his cousins Roger of Mowbray, Drogo II of Mouchy-le-Chatel, and Hugh de Gournay. Of those, only Roger of Mowbray had spent much time recently in England. For the possible influence of Warenne's mother, Isabel de Vermandois, see J. S. C. Riley-Smith, "Family Traditions and Participation in the Second Crusade," in *The Second Crusade and the Cistercians*, ed. M. Gervers (New York: St. Martin's Press, 1992), 103. See also Jonathan Phillips, *The Second Crusade: Extending the Frontiers of Christendom* (New Haven, CT: Yale University Press, 2007), 100, for a discussion of Second Crusaders whose forebears had gone on the First Crusade.

2. Scholars continue to debate whether the Second Crusade was focused solely on the Holy Land or should be understood to include the attacks on the Muslims in southeastern Europe and on the pagan Slavs in northwestern Europe. For an overview and context, Philipps, *The Second Crusade*, is a magisterial undertaking. See now Janus Møller Jensen and Jason T. Roche, eds. *The Second Crusade: Holy*

War on the Periphery of Latin Christendom, Outremer: Studies in the Crusades and the Latin East, 2 (Turnhout: Brepols, 2015 forthcoming).

3. See Matthew Bennett, "Military Aspects of the Conquest of Lisbon, 1147," in *The Second Crusade: Scope and Consequences*, ed. J. Philips and M. Hoch (Manchester: Manchester University Press, 2001), 71–89 at 79, for details on the technical skills required to lay siege effectively and for the English names of those who settled on the Mediterranean coast after the crusade.

4. Charles Wendell David and Jonathan Phillips, eds., *De Expugnatione Lyxbonensi* (New York: Columbia University Press, 2001). See Susan Edgington, "Albert of Aachen, St Bernard and the Second Crusade," in *The Second Crusade*, ed. Phillips and Hoch, 54–70 at 61, for the "common people." See Giles Constable, "A Further Note on the Conquest of Lisbon in 1147," in *The Experience of Crusading*, ed. M. Bull and N. Housley (Cambridge: Cambridge University Press, 2003), 39–44, for references to the deaf mutes and women. Susan Edgington, "The Lisbon Letter of the Second Crusade," *Historical Research* (1996), 328–339, emphasizes the response to local preaching.

5. Graham A. Loud, "Some Reflections on the Failure of the Second Crusade," *Crusades* 4 (2005), 1–14 at 14, argues that attacking Damascus was not "incredibly stupid," as many historians have concluded, but "all but inevitable."

6. Christopher Tyerman, *Gods' War: A New History of the Crusades* (London: Allen Lane/Penguin, 2006), 279.

7. Henry of Huntingdon, *Historia Anglorum*, ed. Diana Greenway (Oxford: Clarendon Press, 1996), 752–753.

8. William of Newburgh in *Chronicles of the Reigns of Stephen, Henry II and Richard I*, ed. R. Howlett, 4 vols. (London: Rolls Series, 1884–1889), Book 1, chap. 20, 67.

9. Elizabeth Siberry, "The Crusader's Departure and Return: A Much Later Perspective," in *Gendering the Crusades*, ed. Susan Edgington and Sarah Lambert (Cardiff: University of Wales Press, 2001), 177–190, discusses the attempts of nineteenth-century artists to portray returning crusaders.

10. For the most recent interpretation of the Second Crusade, see the comprehensive treatment and up-to-date bibliography in Phillips, *The Second Crusade*, which replaces Virginia G. Berry, "The Second Crusade," in *A History of the Crusades*, ed. Kenneth M. Sutton, 2nd ed. (Madison: University of Wisconsin Press, 1969) 1: 463–512. See also Martin Hoch, "The Price of Failure: The Second Crusade as a Turning-Point in the History of the Latin East?" in *The Second Crusade*, ed. Phillips and Hoch, 180–200, and the classic essay by Giles Constable, "The Second Crusade as Seen by Contemporaries," *Traditio* 9 (1953), 213–279. For the English context, see Christopher Tyerman, *England and the Crusades, 1095–1588* (Chicago: University of Chicago Press, 1988). The most extensive recent treatment of broader issues is Tyerman, *God's War*. Shorter accessible overviews include John France, *The Crusades and the Expansion of Catholic Christendom, 1000–1714* (London: Routledge, 2005); Helen Nicholson, ed., *Palgrave Advances in the Crusades*

(Basingstoke: Palgrave, 2005); and Nikolas Jaspert, *The Crusades* (New York: Routledge, 2006). Much important scholarly work on the Second Crusade appears in essay collections such as the two-volume Festschrift in honor of Jonathan Riley-Smith: Bull and Housley, eds., *Experience of Crusading.*

11. See, for example, John France, "Logistics and the Second Crusade," in *Logistics of Warfare in the Age of the Crusades,* ed. John H. Pryor (Aldershot, UK: Ashgate, 2006), 77–93, and Penny J. Cole, *The Preaching of the Crusades to the Holy Land, 109–1270* (Cambridge, MA: Medieval Academy of America, 1991). See Marcus Bull, *Knightly Piety and the Lay Response to the First Crusade, the Limousin and Gascony, c. 970–1130* (Oxford: Clarendon Press, 1993) for additional material relevant to the Second Crusade.

12. Giles Constable, "A Report of a Lost Sermon by St Bernard on the Failure of the Second Crusade," in *Studies in Medieval Cistercian History Presented to Jeremiah F. O'Sullivan,* ed. Joseph F. O'Callaghan (Spencer, MA: Cistercian Publications, 1971), 49–54 at 52.

13. Runciman accepts that figure; Loud, "Some Reflections on Failure," 6–8, questions it.

14. Cole, *Preaching,* 52.

15. Ibid., 48–49.

16. Dominique Iogna-Prat, *Order and Exclusion: Cluny and Christendom Face Heresy, Judaism, and Islam (1000–1150)* (Ithaca, NY: Cornell University Press, 2002), 281.

17. Cole, *Preaching,* 52.

18. T. A. Heslop, *Norwich Castle Keep: Romanesque Architecture and Social Context* (Norwich: University of East Anglia, 1994), 11.

19. David Crouch, "King Stephen and Northern France," in *King Stephen's Reign (1135–1154),* ed. Paul Dalton and Graeme J. White (Woodbridge, UK: Boydell Press, 2008), 44–57 at 55.

20. Constable, "Medieval Charters," 142.

21. Jonathan Phillips, "The Murder of Charles the Good and the Second Crusade: Household Nobility, and Traditions of Crusading in Medieval Flanders," *Medieval Prosopography* 19 (1998), 55–75 at 56.

22. Ibid., 56.

23. Brian Golding, "The Coming of the Cluniacs," *Battle Conference on Anglo-Norman Studies* (1980), 65–77 at 72. William (III) de Warenne and Louis VII were second cousins: they both were great-grandsons of King Henri I of France.

24. As part of his preparations for crusade on his return from France, Warenne founded the Holy Sepulchre priory of Thetford, Norfolk, and made contributions to the Cluniac house of Castle Acre, Norfolk (founded by his family in 1089). He also made a donation to the family foundation of St. Pancras of Lewes, Sussex, which his grandparents had established in 1077. See Freda Anderson, "St. Pancras Priory, Lewes: Its Architectural Development to 1200," *Anglo-Norman Studies* 11 (1989), 1–35 at 6.

25. G. Constable, "The Financing of Crusades in the Twelfth Century," in *Outremer: Studies in the History of the Crusading Kingdom of Jerusalem Presented to Joshua Prawer*, ed. B. Z. Kedar, H. E. Mayer, and R. C. Smail (Jerusalem: Yad Izhak Ben-Zvi Institute, 1982), 72. Most of the detailed examples that Constable discusses are continental. Christopher Tyerman, *England and the Crusades*, 197, calculates that the abbey made a profit of over 133 percent, spread over seven years, "not a bad return for an age and an institution which frowned upon usury and for a deal with a man supposedly immune from it."

26. West *St. Benet of Holme*, 1: 87, charter no. 155. Constable notes that this charter is the only evidence for Philip's participation in the crusade.

27. There were two related men by the name of John de Chesney in East Anglia at this time—probably first cousins. One was the sheriff of East Anglia, whose death in 1146 is reported by Thomas of Monmouth (but questioned by J. H. Round); his brother William succeeded him as sheriff. These brothers were sons of Robert fitzWalter, who had been sheriff of East Anglia from 1115 to 1128 and had shown his strong loyalty to Stephen as an undertenant on the honor of Eye. The other John de Chesney was the son and grandson of men named Ralph. It now appears that brothers Ralph and Walter de Chesney both received land as rewards for aiding the Conquest.

28. Farrer, *Honours and Knights' Fees*, 3: 315.

29. West, *St. Benet of Holme*, 1: 205.

30. Riley-Smith, "Family Traditions," 101–108. Hubert Hall, ed. *Red Book of the Exchequer* (London: Public Record Office, 1896), 744.

31. Tyerman, *England and the Crusades*, 178, 70.

32. Corliss Konwiser Slack, ed. *Crusade Charters 1138–1270* (Tempe: Arizona Center for Medieval and Renaisance Studies, 2001), 46.

33. Tyerman, *God's War*, 280.

34. Jonathan Riley-Smith. *The First Crusaders, 1095–1131* (Cambridge: Cambridge University Press, 1997), 94: "crusading interested only a minority of those arms-bearers qualified to go." Tyerman, *England and the Crusades*, 182: "In the process by which crusade armies were forged, the influences of lordship, kindred, and locality were complementary and mutually supportive." For recent bibliography on kinship networks and personal links among noble and knightly families and ecclesiastical institutions, see Jochen Schenk, *Templar Families: Landowning Families and the Order of the Temple in France, c. 1120–1307* (Cambridge: Cambridge University Press, 2012). Much of what Marcus Bull writes about in *Knightly Piety* for a slightly earlier period is relevant for the Second Crusade.

35. Riley-Smith, "Family Traditions," 103.

36. See Richard de Anstey's repeated recourse to some Cambridge Jews in the 1160s for loans to finance his pleadings in various court cases, in R. B. Dobson, "The Jews of Medieval Cambridge," *Jewish Historical Studies* 32 (1990–1992), 1–24, and P. M. Barnes, "The Anstey Case," in *A Medieval Miscellany for Doris Mary Stenton*, ed. Patricia Barnes and C. F. Slade (London: J. W. Ruddock and Sons, 1962), 1–24. For ransom payments, see Thomas, "Violence."

37. See Christopher Tyerman, "Paid Crusaders. 'Pro Honoris Vel Pecunie'; 'Stipendiarii Contra Paganos'; Money and Incentives on Crusades," in *The Practices of Crusading: Image and Action from the Eleventh to the Sixteenth Centuries*, ed. Christopher Tyerman (Farnham: Ashgate Variorum, 2013), 1–40.

38. Berry, "The Second Crusade," 471, concludes that the king of France "employed something like a forced loan or an extension of feudal aids" to augment his resources before leaving on crusade, which foreshadowed the Saladin tithe.

39. Marjorie Chibnall, "Mercenaries and the *Familia Regis* under Henry 1," in *Anglo-Norman Warfare*, ed. Matthew Strickland (Woodbridge, Suffolk: The Boydell Press, 1992), 84–92, citing R. W. Southern and F. S. Schmitt, eds., *Memorials of St. Anselm* (London: Oxford University Press for the British Academy, 1969), 97.

40. It is now fashionable to point to how expensive crusading was and to consider what sacrifices were expected of the extended family of a crusader. Jonathan Riley-Smith, himself a knight of Malta and a knight of the order of St. John, argues that economic motivation could not have been the primary attraction. See his "Early Crusaders to the East and the Cost of Crusading, 1095–1130," in *Cross Cultural Convergences in the Crusader Period: Essays Presented to Aryeh Grabois on His Sixty-Fifth Birthday*, ed. Michael Goodich, Sophia Menache, and Sylvia Schein (New York: Peter Lang, 1995), 237–258, where he concludes, "Crusading was not profitable. It did not relieve a family of cost but added to them."

41. Jonathan Riley-Smith, "Crusading as an Act of Love," *History* 65 (1980), 177–192, makes the point that crusaders were encouraged to express their love of neighbor as well as love of God and were exhorted to fight by thinking of the Holy Land as Christ's patrimony, their father's inheritance. This widely cited essay is reprinted in Constance Hoffman Berman, ed., *Medieval Religion: New Approaches. Rewriting Histories* (New York and London: Routledge, 2005), 44–61, and in Thomas F. Madden, ed., *The Crusades: The Essential Readings* (Oxford: Blackwells, 2002). In much the same way, Christopher Ocker argues in the "Subjectivity of Christ" that the ritual murder accusation stemmed from a theology of love and empathy as much as a theology of hate and violence. According to Etienne Delaruelle, "For Bernard, one went on crusade not to kill but to be killed." See Constable, "Report of a Lost Sermon," 52.

42. Susanna Throop, *Crusading as an Act of Vengeance, 1095–1216* (Farnham, Surrey: Ashgate, 2011).

43. See, for example, Bennett, "Military Aspects," 75–77.

44. See Tyerman, *England and the Crusades*, 187–228, for a discussion of crusade expenses.

45. Emperor Frederick II expected crusaders to be able to finance themselves for at least two years; if not, they were to remain at home. Tyerman, *England and the Crusades*, 219: in 1188 the crusader's obligation was specified as three years.

46. Constable, "Financing," 74.

47. West, *St. Benet*, 205: "The wording of the lease of a marsh to Geoffrey, son of Master Nicholas, leads naturally to the conclusion that Philip of Postwick had

granted the marsh to the Abbey . . . but Phillip's charter and an episcopal confirmation tell a different story. . . . Philip granted the lease of the marsh and obtained three years rent in advance in order to raise the funds necessary to enable him to set out on the second crusade. Apparently the business deal was more on the abbot's mind than the encouragement of the crusaders."

48. Christopher Brooke, review of *Religious and Laity in Western Europe, 1000–1400: Interaction, Negotiation, and Power*, ed. E. Jamroziak and J. Burton (*Reviews in History*, no. 608), http://www.history.ac.uk/reviews/paper/brooke.html. As Brooke rightly warns, "the complex processes of foundation and endowment cannot be understood by taking charters at their face value: many disguise as much as they reveal about the tortuous paths by which rights and privileges were genuinely established." The notion that Mowbray recouped on the Second Crusade the fortune he lost during the years of the Anarchy and used it to establish Burton Lazars priory may be true, but there is little evidence to support it.

49. Henry Thomas Riley, ed., *Gesta Abbatum Monasterii Sancti Albani* (London: Longmans, Green, 1867–1869), 1: 94.

50. Giles Constable, ed., *Letters of Peter the Venerable* (Cambridge, MA: Harvard University Press, 1967), letter 60, 1:190–191, 2:138–139.

51. Judith Green, "Financing Stephen's War," *Anglo-Norman Studies* 14 (1991), 91–114, offers useful background.

52. The construction of the cathedral was completed only around 1145, and archaeological studies of the site suggest that the next phase of building, the infirmary, in the 1170s, involved Jewish moneylenders.

53. Harper-Bill, "Bishop Turbe," 149ff.

54. Saunders, *First Register*, fol. 13.

55. Eric Stone, "The Estates of Norwich Cathedral Priory 1100–1300" (Unpublished Ph.D. thesis, Oxford University, 1956), 1:70.

56. Tyerman, *England and the Crusades*, 196, points out that Jews were theoretically excluded from lending for the Second Crusade under the provisions of the papal bull *Quantum Praedecessores*.

57. Norman Golb, "New Light on the Persecution of French Jews at the Time of the First Crusade," *Proceedings of the American Academy for Jewish Research* 34 (1966), 1–45 at 25, 33–35, emphasizes French aggression toward Jews during the crusades.

58. Mary Stroll, *The Jewish Pope: Ideology and Politics in the Papal Schism of 1130* (Leiden: Brill, 1987), 159ff.

59. Ephraim of Bonn, *Sefer Zekhirah*, 121–122. The German variation of the monk's name Radulph that Ephraim consciously uses is similar to the Hebrew *radof*, "to persecute." The best recent efforts to contextualize Ralph's crusade preaching are Tyerman, *Gods' War*, 282ff and Philipps, *Second Crusade*.

60. The term "renegade" is used by Loud, "Some Reflections on the Failure," 4, and Jonathan Philips, "Saint Bernard of Clairvaux, the Low Countries and the Lisbon Letter of the Second Crusade," *Journal of Ecclesiastical History 48* (1997),

485–497 at 489. Thomas Madden, "Crusade Myths," *Catholic Dossier* 8 (2002), in an essay widely reproduced online, elides preacher and crusaders: "during the opening phase of the Second Crusade a group of renegades killed many Jews in Germany before St. Bernard was able to catch up to them," likening them to "a large band of riffraff, not associated with the main army," who descended on the Rhineland and attacked Jews during the First Crusade.

61. Bernard *Opera*, ed. J. Leclerq and H. M. Rochais, vol. 8: *Epistolae* (Rome: 1977), letter 365, 320–322.

62. Edgington, "Albert of Aachen," 58–61.

63. For a summary of recent scholarship on this topic, see Daniel P. Franke, "The Crusades and Medieval Anti-Judaism: Cause or Consequence?" in *Seven Myths of the Crusades*, ed. Alfred J. Andrea and Andrew Holt (Indianapolis: Hackett Publishing, 2015 forthcoming). I thank professor Franke for letting me see his work before publication.

64. Kenneth R. Stow, *Alienated Minority, The Jews of Medieval Latin Europe* (Cambridge, MA: Harvard University Press, 1992), 110.

65. See the essays in Sarah Rees Jones and Sethina Watson, eds., *Christians and Jews in Angevin England: The York Massacre of 1190, Narratives and Contexts* (Woodbridge, Suffolk: Boydell and Brewer, 2013).

66. David Berger, "The Attitude of St. Bernard of Clairvaux Towards the Jews," *Proceedings of the American Academy for Jewish Research* 40 (1972): 89–108 at 104, follows Salo Baron in noting that Bernard's neologism *judaizare* (to lend at interest) "lent authoritative support to the stereotype of the Jew as usurer."

67. *The Letters of St. Bernard of Clairvaux*, trans. Bruno Scott James (London: Burns Oates, 1955), letter 391, 460–463.

68. *Vita*, I, vi, 19.

69. Norman Golb, "New Light on the Persecution of French Jews at the Time of the First Crusade," *PAAJR* 34 (1966), 1–45.

70. Ephraim of Bonn, *Sefer Zekhirah* or the Book of Remembrance, in Shlomo Eidelberg, ed., *The Jews and the Crusaders: The Hebrew Chronicles of the First and Second Crusades* (Madison: University of Wisconsin Press, 1977), 121–133.

71. The tombstone is pictured in Eidelberg, *Jews and Crusaders,* 126.

72. The present-day locations of places Ephraim writes about in Hebrew are unclear, and the locations of Ham, Sully, and Carenton have not been identified satisfactorily, as noted by Chaviva Levin, "Constructing Memories of Martyrdom: Contrasting Portrayals of Martyrdom in the Hebrew Narratives of the First and Second Crusade," in *Remembering the Crusades: Myth, Image, and Identity*, ed. Nicholas Paul and Suzanne Yeager (Baltimore, MD: Johns Hopkins University Press, 2012), 50–69. See also Eidelberg, *Jews and Crusaders*, 175–176 n. for a discussion of the possible sites.

73. Norman Golb, "The Rabbinic Master Jacob Tam and Events of the Second Crusade at Reims," *Crusades* 9 (2010), 57–67, makes the case that Tam was attacked in the city of Rheims (Hebrew RMRW = Romeru, for *civitas Remorum*), rather than Rameru, the village in southern Champagne where he supposedly lived.

74. Eidelberg, *Jews and Crusaders*, 130.

75. Documented since 312, Cologne is the oldest known Jewish community north of the Alps. Remains of the medieval *mikveh* have been dated to 1170, but archaeological study suggests that it may have been rebuilt from centuries earlier. Unearthed in 1956, the *mikveh* can be viewed through a skylight in the park facing city hall.

76. See, for example, Karlheinz Müller, Simon Schwarzfuchs, and Abraham Reiner, eds., *Die Grabsteine vom Jüdischen Friedhof in Wüzburg aus der Zeit vor dem Schwarzen Tod (1147–1346)* (Wüzburg Veröffentlichungen der Gesellschaft für fränkische Geschichte, Reihe IX: Darstellungen aus der fränkischen Geschichte, Band 58, 2011).

77. Gérard Nahon, "From the *Rue de Juifs* to the *Chemin de Roy*: The Classical Age of French Jewry, 1108–1223," in *Jews and Christians in Twelfth-Century Europe*, ed. Michael A. Signer and John Van Engen (Notre Dame, IN: University of Notre Dame Press, 2001), 311–339.

78. Julius Aronius, *Regesten zur Geschichte der Juden im fränkischen und deutschen Reiche bis zum jahre 1273* (Berlin, 1902; repr. New York: G. Olms, 1970) no. 245, 113–114. See also Ephraim of Bonn, *Sefer Zekhirah*, 127.

79. Karlheinz Müller, "Würzburg—The World's Largest Find from a Medieval Jewish Cemetery," in *Culture, Mobility, Migration and Settlement of Jews in Medieval Europe*, an international symposium in Speyer, October 2002, and published in Christoph Cluse, ed., *The Jews of Europe in the Middle Ages (Tenth to Fifteenth Centuries): Proceedings of the International Symposium Held at Speyer, 20–25 October 2002*, Turnhout, Brepols (2004), 379–390.

80. Israel Yuval follows John McCulloh in observing that the ritual murder charge appeared in Germany in the late 1140s. He concludes therefore that the charge appeared in Bavaria almost at the same time as it appeared in Norwich and that it is difficult to determine which libel occurred first; channels of communication went both ways, but in either case "they retained the image of the First Crusade and the behavior of the Jews at that time," Yuval, *Two Nations*, 168–169.

81. The marked similarities between "John of Stamford" described by William of Newburgh and the Würzburg corpse are noted in Heather Blurton, "Egyptian Days: From Passion to Exodus in the Representation of Twelfth-Century Jewish-Christian Relations," in *Angevin England: The York Massacre of 1190, Narratives and Contexts*, ed. Sara Rees Jones and S. C. Watson (York: York Medieval Press, 2013), 222–237 at 226–227. For the crusader killed in Lisbon in 1147 and treated as a holy relic, see Lay, "Henry the Crusader."

82. K. S. B. Keats-Rohan, *Domesday People: A Prosopography of Persons Occurring in English Documents, 1066–1166* (Woodbridge, Suffolk; Rochester, NY: Boydell Press, 1999), vol. 1, 476, suggests that Willelm de Nuers came from Noyers, Eure, arr. Les Andelys, Cant. Giros, and notes him as a tenant of William de Beaufour. "Possibly he was also a tenant of Robert de Tosny of Belvoir at Hose in Leicestershire though this does not appear in Domesday."

83. William de Chesney was one of the men on the rise. The careers of such men are discussed in Ralph Turner, *Men Raised from the Dust: Administrative Service and Upward Mobility in Angevin England* (Philadelphia: University of Pennsylvania Press, 1988).

84. William de Novers was at one time responsible for the largest amount of land in East Anglia. It is not clear under exactly what arrangement he held most of the land; he probably served as a temporary steward rather than a settled tenant.

85. Perhaps William de Novers returned to the Continent to look after property there, as did Waleran of Meulan, earl of Worcester, or he may have died young. It is also possible that he is not documented because he was a tenant of Roger Bigod (future earl of Norfolk in the 1140s), whose vast collection of estates in East Anglia included lands confiscated from Stigand, the disgraced archbishop of Canterbury, and turned over to the de Novers family decades earlier.

86. The family name is not listed in Riley-Smith, *First Crusaders* but the names of many crusaders listed there are known only from a chance mention in a single extant document.

87. Dodwell, "Bacton Charters," charter no. 6. See also charters nos. 35, 36, and 37, confirmations for Robert of Homersfeld, the cook.

88. In the charters relating to Bacton and the transfer of land from William of Bacton to his uncle Roger de Valognes, Simon de Novers (Nuiers) attested on behalf of William, along with others of the Norwich monastery. Dodwell, "Bacton Charters," 158–159, charter no. 2, dated between 1121 and 1135. William de Peverill (Pellevill) attested on behalf of Roger. Another charter of the same time and for the same cause also includes Simon attesting with many others, not with those just listed, but with the household officials of the bishop, *capellanus, dapifer,* and *camerarius* (chaplain, butler, etc). Ibid., 159, charter no. 3, dated between 1121 and 1135.

89. The order in which knights witnessed or attested charters may be indicative of their status, to judge from later documents and from ecclesiastical parallels. (The order may, however, simply reflect convenience and the availability of those attesting.) If this is the case in twelfth-century Norwich, then over the course of the decades the de Novers family dropped successively lower on the rungs.

90. Hall, *Red Book*, 744.

91. Dodwell, *Norwich Charters*, 64, charter no. 115.

92. Robert the Cook, the beneficiary of many of the charters that Simon's family attested, appears to have been exceptionally cautious about gaining episcopal confirmation of his son's lands at a time of uncertainty, and he asked that a number of sons and brothers of his friends and colleagues join in the attestation he desired.

93. Barbara Dodwell, "The Honour of the Bishop of Thetford/Norwich in the Late Eleventh and Early Twelfth Centuries," *Norfolk Archeology* 33 (1962–1965), 185–199. For context, see also Thomas K. Keefe, *Feudal Assessments and the Political Community under Henry II and His Sons* (Berkeley: University of

California Press, 1983). Simon de Novers was a knight (*miles*), that is, a mounted horseman who made vows of fealty and homage to his lord, not a "citizen" (burgess, *civis*).

94. *Vita*, VI, xviii, 258.

95. This paragraph follows the argument of Dodwell, "Honour of the Bishop," 195.

96. Dodwell, "Honour of the Bishop," 192. Dodwell traces the Noers of Swanton Noers, Norfolk, to Simon but it appears that Ralph de Nuers who held Swanton Noers of the bishop and Ralph's son Milo were a separate branch of the family.

97. In a settlement of 1153, Reginald inherited ancestral estates of Bellencombre and Mortemer in France when the rest of his brother's estates went to William (III) de Warenne's daughter Isabel and her husband William. That husband, King Stephen's son William ("of Blois"), then took the title William "IV de Warenne" through his wife, although he was not descended from William III (d. 1148).

98. The only two Anglo-Normans living in England who can be confidently named survivors of the Second Crusade to the Holy Land are Roger of Mowbray and Hugh Tirel, lord of Poix and, significantly, a Clare tenant.

99. It is reported that Stephen de Mandeville went on the Second Crusade with Baldwin de Redvers (d. 1155); see *Charters of the Redvers Family and the Earldom of Devon, 1090–1217*, ed. R. Bearman (Devon and Cornwall Record Society ns. 37, 1994), 10. See also Robert Bearman, "Baldwin de Redvers, Some Aspects of a Baronial Career in the Reign of King Stephen," *Anglo-Norman Studies* 18 (1985), 19–46 at 19, for their associations.

100. The basic source for the conquest of Lisbon is Charles W. David and Jonathan Phillips, eds., *De Expugnatione Lyxbonensi* (New York: Columbia University Press, 2001). Important work on the Iberian expedition includes Matthew Bennett, "Military Aspects,"; Giles Constable, "A Note on the Route of the Anglo-Flemish Crusaders of 1147," *Speculum* 28 (1953), 525–526, and idem, "A Further Note"; Edgington, "Lisbon Letter"; and Alan Forey, "The Siege of Lisbon and the Second Crusade," *Portuguese Studies* 20, no. 1 (2004), 1–13. For the most recent scholarship see Susan Edgington, "The Capture of Lisbon: Premeditated or Opportunistic?" in *The Second Crusade. Holy War on the Periphery of Latin Christendom*, ed. Jason T. Roche and Janus Møller Jensen (Turnhout: Brepols, 2015 forthcoming). I thank professor Edgington for letting me see her essay in advance of publication.

101. Nikolas Jaspert, "*Capta est Dertosa, Clavis Christianorum*: Tortosa and the Crusades," in Philips and Hoch, *Second Crusade*, 90–110, discusses the many Englishmen on the Iberian crusade expedition who participated in the conquest of Tortosa; they were awarded land by Ramon Berenguer and soon established themselves as part of a wealthy elite. The success of the southern contingent would have been driven home to Simon de Novers as Gilbert of Hastings, the first bishop of the newly conquered Lisbon, was back in England in 1150 recruiting. See R. A. Fletcher, "Reconquest and Crusade in Spain, c. 1050–1150," *Transactions of the Royal Historical Society* 5th series 37 (1987), 31–47 at 44.

Chapter 3

1. The Bavarian reference is undated; McCulloh, "Jewish Ritual Murder," makes a detailed argument for placing it in the 1140s. Concluding that news about William was circulating internationally within just a few years of his death, McCulloh, therefore, does not observe any sudden transformation in William's status.

2. *Vita*, Prol., 3.

3. *Vita*, II, xiii, 64. Cronne, *Stephen*, 263, is less persuaded of the guilt of the knight, Simon de Novers, than is Thomas of Monmouth. There are clear parallels here to the 1170 murder of Thomas Becket, who was also dragged off and killed.

4. Jews were not allowed burial plots outside the capital before 1177.

5. *Vita*, II, xiv, 66.

6. Riley-Smith, "Costs of Crusading," 240: "The standing of many returning crusaders could have helped to ease any financial burdens they faced."

7. R. Allen Brown, "The Status of the Norman Knight," in *Anglo-Norman Warfare*, ed. Matthew Strickland (Woodbridge, Suffolk: The Boydell Press, 1992), 128–142.

8. See, for example, the acknowledgment of knights Roger of Mowbray and John de Chesney at the end of the civil war. Gilbert de Gant, first earl of Lincoln, also made restitution for excesses committed against possessions of the church of Norwich during Stephen's reign. He had been temporarily excommunicated for his attack on Pontefract priory during the war.

9. For Hubert de Montchesney, see Andrew Wareham, "The Motives and Politics of the Bigod Family, c. 1066–1177," *Anglo-Norman Studies* 17 (1994): 223–242 at 238, at the abbey of St Benet of Holme where the king's nephew became abbot in 1145.

10. J. H. Round, *Geoffrey De Mandeville, a Study of the Anarchy* (London: Longmans, Green and Co., 1892), 221.

11. See most recently the essays in Rees Jones and Watson, *York Massacre of 1190*. The classic treatment is R. B. Dobson, *The Jews of Medieval York and the Massacre of March 1190* (York: Borthwick Papers no. 45, 1974).

12. The practice began with the *saccarium Aaronis* on the death of Aaron of Lincoln in 1187.

13. I. Abrahams and H. P. Stokes, *Starrs and Jewish Charters Preserved in the British Museum with Additions by H. Loewe* (Cambridge: Cambridge University Press, 1930–1932), were among the first to recognize their importance. Additional information from post-Expulsion lists has now been analyzed by Robin Mundill, *England's Jewish Solution, Experiment and Expulsion, 1262–1290* (Cambridge: Cambridge University Press, 1998).

14. It was not recorded out of shame or as a moral example. The monastic author Thomas of Monmouth makes no suggestion that Novers behaved reprehensibly.

15. Jacob of Cambridge, Aaron of Lincoln, and Jurnet of Norwich were among the first in their respective communities to build stone houses. Jews had stone houses in London, York, and Canterbury as well in the twelfth century. For assaults

on individual Jews, see, for example, the early eleventh-century case of the murdered son (known only from the chance survival of a letter in the Cairo Genizah, an archive of discarded documents), whose father settled in the Holy Land when he could not receive legal satisfaction in Normandy, cited in Norman Golb, *The Jews in Medieval Normandy: A Social and Intellectual History* (Cambridge: Cambridge University Press, 1998), 51ff. Even in succeeding centuries more notable for "law and order," exempla and homiletic literature are replete with instances of Jews killed, often on roads. Such literary tales reflected historical fact recorded, for example, in the fines levied on those found guilty of killing a Jew. See *Pipe Roll 2 Henry II*, ed. Hunter (London: Pipe Roll Society, 1844), 15: the fine was the substantial sum of twenty shillings. There were other such attacks during the First and Second Crusades, as detailed in Ephraim of Bonn, "Sefer Zekhirah," 125.

16. *Vita*, II, xiv, 65.

17. The murder of the Jewish banker was not "an incident which stands quite alone," as Jessopp contends in his chapter on the Norwich Jews, *Life and Miracles*, xliii.

18. *Vita*, II, xiii, 64–65. "After some time had passed, when the king visited Norwich, the Jews assembled in front of him and brought forward the case of the murder of the aforesaid Jew."

19. Thomas of Monmouth offers the sole indication that the king was in Norwich between 1140 and 1154: no stop in Norwich is noted in the itinerary of H. A. Cronne and R. H. C. Davis, eds., *Regesta Regum Anglo-Normannorum, 1066–1154*, vol. 3 (Oxford: Clarendon Press, 1968), xxxix. It may well be that Stephen stopped in Norwich on his way to or from Lincoln in September 1149, before heading to Worcester for the siege of 1150. Norwich was the second-largest city of his realm and a bastion of his support during the civil war. Another possibility is that Stephen visited Norwich around 1150, when he came to St. Edmund's abbey at Bury for a trial in the same diocese as Norwich, only a few hours southeast, or when his son married Isabel de Warenne, shortly after the king learned of her father's death.

20. *Vita*, II, x, 70. Chesney was frequently in attendance upon Stephen, but William Turbe rarely was. Both Chesney and Turbe were recorded together with the king in London on one occasion between December 1148 and November 26, 1149 (Cronne and Davis, *Regesta*, 67, no. 183).

21. Lipman, *Norwich*, 38: the community was never likely to have numbered more than 200, of which 60 or fewer were adults.

22. The crown did not become a major borrower from the Jews until the mid-1160s.

23. Robert Stacey, "Jewish Lending and the Medieval English Economy," in *A Commercializing Economy—England 1086 to c. 1300*, ed. Richard H. Britnell and Bruce M. S. Campbell (Manchester: Manchester University Press, 1995), 78–101 at 85, suggests that the Jewish communities of Bungay and Thetford may owe their existence to the rivalry for control of Norwich between Stephen and Earl Hugh Bigod beginning in 1142. The Jews of Norwich were protected by Stephen. But

Bigod was not the sole lord of Thetford: it appears that Earl Warenne's control of some part of Thetford played an unacknowledged and earlier role in Jewish settlement there. (See also the following note.)

24. Excavations of the ringwork ditch at Thetford reveal a timber palisade that may have been erected by Warenne in 1139, when he held the land south of the river. Kevin T. Streit, "The Expansion of the English Jewish Community in the Reign of King Stephen," *Albion* 25, no. 2 (1993), 177–192 at 180 n. 6: "The lordship of Thetford and its Jews, between 1140 and 1156 would seem to have been a double borough, a royal town granted out, evidently to the first and third earls Warenne, and a linked new urban settlement on a manor belonging to the Bigods." Richardson, however, believed that Stephen had given Hugh Bigod control over the Jews in East Anglian towns. A moneyer named David lived at Theftord, where he minted coins.

25. See Tyerman, *England and the Crusades*, 179, for the dependence of crusaders on the resources of their leaders.

26. Kenneth R. Stow, *Alienated Minority: The Jews of Medieval Latin Europe* (Cambridge, MA: Harvard University Press, 1992), 114.

27. This move on the part of King Louis has been described as the first "Tötbrief," the term used in German to describe edicts or exemptions for paying interest or principal on Christian debts to Jews. Eidelberg, *Jews and Crusaders*, 119, comments: "Ephraim's report of Louis VII's cancellation of Crusader debts to the Jews is extreme; in reality, he granted remission from interest and deferred principal payments; never were the debts themselves canceled." He adds (177 n. 59): "Ephraim, however, echoes the reality of the situation, for the Crusaders never repaid their debts." See also Stow, *Alienated Minority*, 121.

28. Ephraim of Bonn, "Sefer Zekhirah," 131.

29. Stow, *Alienated Minority*, 13. Dominique Iogna-Prat, *Order and Exclusion: Cluny and Christendom Face Heresy, Judaism, and Islam (1000–1150)* (Ithaca, NY: Cornell University Press, 2002), Chapter 10, for an extended discussion of Peter the Venerable's attitudes toward Jews and citations of extensive recent bibliography. See now Irven M. Resnick, ed. *Peter the Venerable, against the Inveterate Obduracy of the Jews* (Washington, DC: Catholic University of America Press, 2013).

30. Christopher Brooke, *The Monastic World 1000–1300* (London: Paul Elek, 1974), 95. Iogna-Prat, *Order and Exclusion*, 280, questions Georges Duby's inference that Cluny was indebted to Jews. He argues that Peter may have consciously avoided Jewish creditors, as did his role model Matthew of Albano.

31. Jessopp and James, *Life and Miracles*, 98 n. 1, noted of Novers, that "the chief manor of the family was at Swanton Novers, about six miles from Holt, which Sir Simon held of the Bishop of Norwich." They did not attempt to identify the banker. Swanton Novers, however, appears to have descended to another branch of the family, not to Simon's.

32. Jessopp and James translated the monk's Latin *Deus-adiuvet* as *Eleazar* in their edition of 1896, followed by all subsequent scholars. As the name "Eleazar" could easily have been written in Vulgate Latin by a monk familiar with the Bible, it is probable that Thomas was not familiar with the banker's name. *Eleazar* translates as "my God has helped" in the past tense. *Adiuvet* can only be the present subjunctive, "*may* he help."

H. P. Stokes, *Studies in Anglo-Jewish History* (Edinburgh: Jewish Historical Society of England, 1913), 63–67, has a good discussion of Jewish surnames, specifically acknowledging the use of subjunctive ("for Jews use prayers in this way instead of proper names"). See pp. 68–71 for the tradition of Jewish double-names, the sacred name for religious or home purposes (*shem hakkodesh*) and the secular name (*kinnnui*) for worldy affairs. Stokes's example is instructive: "Another Benedict of Lincoln who was popularly called le Riche had as his synagogue name Elias, while his father Isaac (so-named among his co-religionists) was known to his English debtors as Ursell, so that this Benedict of Lincoln was variously called Benedict le Riche, Benedict the son of Isaac, Elias ben Isaac, and Elias the son of Ursell. Another family—whose dwelling place was at Norwich—illustrates this multiplicity of names. Solomon, the father, changed his name to Mordecai, but he was also recognized among his contemporaries as Deulecresse. One of his sons was called Eliezar in his family, but he was known as Diaia to outsiders." Michael Adler, "The Medieval Jews of Exeter," *Transactions of the Devonshire Association for the Advancement of Science, Literature, and Art* 63 (1931): 221–240 at 224, makes note of a Jew of Exeter named Piers Delesalt (Dieu-le-saut, "may God save"), the French translation of the Hebrew Isaiah, who paid the king ten marks for official care for his bonds in 1181 (citing Pipe Roll 27 Henry II). See also Eleazar ha-Levi, "Jewish Naming Convention in Angevin England" (2005) found at http://heraldry.sca.org/laurel/names/jewish.html.

33. His name could also have been *Deulecresse* or even *Diaia*, the French for Eleazar. Deulecresse (for *Deus eum crescat*), the Latinized form for Gedaliah (or occasionally Solomon), was one of the most popular names for French and Anglo-Norman Jews in this period. Norwich boasted a Diaia son of Deulecresse. In the early thirteenth century Diaia of Rising son of Mosse and (an unrelated) Deulecresse son of Diaia appear in the records of East Anglia.

34. *Vita*, II, xiii, 64, xiv, 66.

35. *Vita*, II, xiv, 64. See translation of Jessopp and James, *Life and Miracles*, 106. "These men came, seized them, threw them from their horses, and dragged them violently away to despoil them. Upon this, the Jew, while attempting to defend himself with the sword which he carried, fell slain by a hostile weapon."

36. *Vita*, II, xii, 62–63. The rabbinical synod of around 1150 specifically legislated on Jewish informers; Louis Finkelstein, *Jewish Self-Government in the Middle Ages* (New York: Philipp Feldheim, 1964), 42.

37. *Vita*, II, xiv, 68. "The Jew of whose death the knight Simon is being accused had, in his lifetime, very many debtors besides Simon: some owed him smaller, some equal, and others with even greater debts."

38. Brown, "Status of the Knight," 138, discusses the heavy costs. He refers to a landowner cited by Mark Bloch who exchanged his ancestral fields and a slave for a horse and sword.

39. *Vita*, I, vi, 18.

40. Finkelstein, *Jewish Self-Government*, 42.

41. Nahon, "Rue de Juifs," 2–4, considers Jewish emigration north.

42. For example, the famous philosopher Abraham ibn Ezra left Spain because of attacks and came to England via France in 1158. The family of Maimonides fled Spain at this time and moved east, eventually settling in Egypt.

43. After Aimery's death at the Battle of Fraga (1134), conflict between his sister, viscountess Ermentrude, and Alphonse-Jourdain, count of Toulouse, resulted in Jews fleeing to other towns in Anjou, Poitou, and Île-de-France. Abraham ibn Daud reported two thousand Jews in Narbonne in 1143; by the time of Benjamin of Tudela's visit in 1165 the Jewish community was significantly reduced.

44. Historians allude to a supposed charter of Henry I that has never been found. Its existence is hypothesized from confirmations and reissues by subsequent rulers. Henry may have granted permission to Jews or only to some Jews for travel and settlement, but this is far from certain.

45. Pipe Roll Henry I: Joseph Jacobs, *The Jews of Angevin England: English History from Contemporary Writers* (London: David Nutt, 1893), 15, translates this name *Deulesult* as *Isaiah*; ha-Levi translates it as *Joshua*.

46. Lipman, *Norwich*, 95, suggested that Jurnet's father may have been *Deodatus*, "Gift of God" (which may translate as Mattathias or Jonathan), but the identification is dubious, as it involves suppositions about letter reversals in word abbreviations in Hebrew. Jurnet's son Isaac was the richest man in early thirteenth-century Norwich, the subject of a famous caricature on the Exchequer rolls. He first appears in the records as a business partner with his parents, just as Jurnet may have partnered with his father when he got his start in business.

47. William Buston, "The Monastic Infirmary, Norwich," *Norfolk Archeology* 28 (1944), 124–132; Ernest A. Kent, "Isaac's Hall or the Music House, Norwich," *Norfolk Archeology* 28 (1945), 31–36.

48. *Vita*, II, ix, 60: A Christian serving girl "pointed out the signs of maryrdom on the doorposts of the house." Compare Thomas's earlier comments in I, v, 17: "And when we were enquiring carefully into the affair, we found the house and in it most definite and clear signs of the affair."

49. *Vita*, II, xiv, 65.

50. *Vita*, II, xiv, 67.

51. *Vita*, II, xiv, 66.

52. Thomas may have been given Bishop's Turbe's notes from the trial.

53. *Vita*, II, xv, 72. The sheriff "presumed to disturb its right... to elect its bishop." The first known papal confirmation for free election is that of the Englishman Adrian IV in 1155, for which see Dodwell, *Charters of the Norwich Cathedral Priory*, no. 278; Harper-Bill, *Norwich Episcopal Acta*, appendix II, Itineraries, 370. Turbe was bishop by August 1147, when he assisted at the consecration of Bishop Hilary of Chichester, with whom he was to attend the Council of Rheims, which convened in March 1148. Christopher Harper-Bill, "Bishop William Turbe and the Diocese of Norwich, 1146–1174," *Battle Conference on Anglo-Norman Studies* 7 (1985), 142–160 at 143, suggests that Turbe's performance at the trial "persuaded Stephen to appoint him, along with the bishops of Chichester and Hereford, to represent the entire English episcopate at the Council of Rheims," but the murder trial must have followed the council rather than preceded it.

54. *Vita*, II, x, 61, the bishop "considered his own reputation" according to Thomas, when he turned down payment from the Jewish leaders.

55. Harper-Bill, *Turbe*, 142.

56. Harper-Bill, *Turbe*, 146–147.

57. How active he was in his later years remains open to debate. Some historians, following David Knowles, presume that he was effectively retired for some years before his death.

58. James Craigie Robertson, ed., *Materials for the History of Thomas Becket, Archbishop of Canterbury* (London: Rolls Society, 1875), vol. 67, 7:50.

59. *Vita*, II, xiii, 654–655.

60. *Vita*, II, xiii, 67.

61. *Vita*, II, xiii, 67.

62. *Vita*, II, xiii, 70.

63. *Vita*, II, xiii, 70.

64. *Vita*, II, xiii, 69.

65. *Vita*, II, xiv, 70.

66. Wareham, "Motives and Politics," 237, mentions the meeting of the archbishop of Canterbury with the bishops of Norwich, London, and Chichester in 1147.

67. The phrase describing William is from the *Anglo-Saxon Chronicle*, ed. Dorothy Whitelock (London, 1961; repr. Westport, CT: Greenwood Press, 1986), ed. Michael Swanton (London: J. M. Dent, 1996), 256, summing up the details laid out in the *Vita* I, v, 16–18.

68. *Vita*, I, vii, 20–21.

69. *Vita*, I, viii, 22–23; II, xv, 72.

70. R. Po-Chia Hsia, *The Myth of Ritual Murder: Jews and Magic in Reformation Germany* (New Haven: Yale University Press, 1989), 107, described *mala fama* with reference to the case in Freiburg. See also the discussion of the legal doctrine of *semel malus, semper malus* ("once evil, always evil") and ritual murder in David S. Areford, *The Viewer and the Printed Image in Late Medieval Europe* (Aldershort, Hampshire: Ashgate, 2010), 192.

71. Uri Z. Shachar, "Inspecting the Pious Body: Christological Morphology and the Ritual-Crucifixion Allegation," *Journal of Medieval History* 41, no. 1 (2015), 21–40.

72. *Vita*, II, xi, 61.

73. *Vita*, II, xi, 62.

74. A convert was most likely to have taken his name from his godfather, as was customary, perhaps a French *Thibaut*. King Louis VII addressed the issue of conversion in 1145, banishing relapsed Jews from the kingdom. The synod of rabbis in Troyes around 1150 also addressed the issue and legislated on it; Ephraim of Bonn mentioned forcible conversion in 1147, so it was not an insignificant issue in France at this time. Few instances of Jewish converts are known from twelfth-century England, however, and there is no documentation for an alleged *domus conversorum*, or "House of Converts," in twelfth-century Bristol. Yet its existence was repeated as recently as 1995 in Joseph Shatzmiller, "Jewish Converts in Medieval Europe, 1200–1500," in *Cross-Cultural Convergences in the Crusader Period*, ed. Sophia Menache, Michael Goodich, and Sylvia Schein (New York: Peter Lang, 1995), 297–318 at 312. There is much evidence to suggest that Jews were streaming north in the mid- to late 1140s.

75. Harper-Bill, *Norwich Episcopal Acta*, 119, no. 151 [ca. 1152–1173]; 120, no. 152 [ca. 1152–1173]; Stoke 55–62 [1152–1173]; 71 [1161–1175]. A *magister* was any clerk qualified to teach after a period of advanced study; at this time it was not a formal designation; see Frank Barlow, *Thomas Becket* (London: Weidenfeld and Nicolson 1987), 20–21.

76. *Vita*, II, ix, 59–60.

77. Jody Enders writes of the portrayal of the "wicked woman" or *mauvaise femme*, in late medieval French drama. See Jody Enders, "Theatre Makes History: Ritual Murder by Proxy in the *Mistere de la Sainte Hostie*," *Speculum* 79 (2004), 991–1016, and Chapter 9 of Jody Enders, *Death by Drama and Other Medieval Urban Legends* (Chicago: University of Chicago Press, 2005) on host desecration.

78. *Vita*, II, xi, 61.

79. Langmuir, *Toward a Definition*, 216.

80. Finkelstein, *Jewish Self-Government*, 42. Compare Robert Chazan, "The Blois Incident of 1171: A Study in Jewish Intercommunal Organization," *Proceedings of the American Academy for Jewish Research* 36 (1968), 13–31 at 28: "It is clear that there was no joint meeting of all the notables enumerated." Nahon, "*Rue de Juifs*," argues that large numbers of Jews attended in person. The map of the 1150 synod prepared for the Nouvelle Gallia Judaica project (accompanying Nahon's essay on p. 321) suggests how striking such a meeting would have been to contemporaries.

81. Gerd Mentgen, "Über den Ursprung der Ritual Mordfabel," *Aschenaz* 4 (1994), 405–416, a revised version of the article [in Hebrew] in *Zion* (1994), 343–349; Elliot Horowitz, "The Rite to Be Reckless: On the Perpetuation and Interpretation of Purim Violence," *Poetics Today* 15, no. 1 (1994), 9–54, and Elliott Horowitz, *Reckless Rites*. See also Roth, "Feast of Purim."

82. Josef Hayim Yerushalmi, *Zakhor: Jewish History and Jewish Memory* (Seattle: University of Washington Press, 1982), 47. The quotation is from Robert Chazan, "The Timebound and the Timeless: Medieval Jewish Narration of Events," *History and Memory* 6 (1994), 5–34 at 7, characterizing Yerushalmi's interpretation.

83. Langmuir, *Toward a Definition*, 225, follows Joseph Jacobs, "St. William of Norwich," *Jewish Quarterly Review* 9 (1897), 748–755, in concluding that Theobald must have been a real person because Thomas would not have known about the *Nasi* of Narbonne.

84. Peter Carter, "The Historical Content of William of Malmesbury's Miracles of the Virgin Mary," in *The Writing of History in the Middle Ages: Essays Presented to Richard William Southern*, ed. R. H. Davis and J. M. Wallace-Hadrill (Oxford: Clarendon Press, 1981), 127–164.

85. Resnick, *Inveterate Obduracy*, 140. See also Iogna-Prat, *Order and Exclusion*, 294.

86. Benjamin of Tudela and Abraham ibn Daud both mention the *Nasi* but do not attach much importance to it. See Sandra Benjamin, *The World of Benjamin of Tudela: A Medieval Mediterranean Travelogue* (Teaneck, NJ: Fairleigh Dickinson University Press; London: Associated University Presses, 1995), 62. Golb, "New Light," notes that R. Todros II ruled around 1130–1150 and died sometime between 1150 and 1160. His son Kalonymos II ruled around 1160–1195.

87. George Anderson, *The Legend of the Wandering Jew* (Providence, RI: Brown University Press, 1965, repr. 1991), and Galit Hasan-Rokem and Alan Dundes, eds., *The Wandering Jew: Essays in the Interpretation of a Christian Legend* (Bloomington: Indiana University Press, 1986).

88. Ruth Mellinkoff, *The Mark of Cain* (Berkeley: University of California Press, 1981), 92.

89. Philippe Buc, "David's Adultery with Bathsheba and the Healing Power of Capetian Kings," *Viator* 24 (1993), 101–120.

90. David J. Malkiel, "Infanticide in Passover Iconography," *Journal of the Warburg and Courtauld Institutes* 56 (1993), 85–99.

91. Moshe Lazar, "The Lamb and the Scapegoat: The Dehumanization of the Jews in Medieval Propaganda Imagery," in *Anti-Semitism in Times of Crisis*, ed. Sander L. Gilman and Steven T. Katz (New York: New York University Press, 1991), 38–101 at 52, citing lines 887–903 of the *Jeu d'Adam*.

92. Ivan G. Marcus, *Rituals of Childhood: Jewish Acculturation in Medieval Europe* (New Haven, CT: Yale University Press, 1996), discusses the ritual and many parallels. The rite is not documented in England, but there was significant cultural overlap between British and continental Jews.

93. For the importance of First Crusade memories, see Yuval, "Vengeance and Damnation." See also Mary Minty, "Kiddush Ha-Shem in German Christian Eyes in the Middle Ages" [in Hebrew], *Zion* 59 (1994), 209–266.

94. *Vita*, II, x, 61.

95. *Vita*, II, xiv, 71.

96. Cronne, *Stephen*, 263.

97. Ibid. Streit, "Expansion," 1185, calls into question Cronne's praise of Stephen's "good sense" for not having been swayed by religious fanaticism.

98. Ephraim of Bonn, "Sefer Zekhirah," 131.

99. *Vita*, II, xiv, 67.

100. *Vita*, II, xiii, 63–64.

101. To judge from the Northampton *Donum* lists (tax payments), *responsa* about *herem* (discussion of Jewish rules concerning a ban on new settlement) and contemporary anecdotes, under Henry II the Jews were rapidly spreading out from a few urban centers and aristocratic settlements.

102. Hyamson, *History of the Jews*, 30.

Chapter 4

1. As correctly noted in Anna Sapir Abulafia, *Christians and Jews in the Twelfth Century Renaissance* (London: Routledge, 1995), 139, there is no historical evidence to support the contention, especially of literary scholars, that a riot ensued. See, for example, Cohen, "The Flow of Blood," 63: "just as happened during the crusades, Jewish blood must be spilled in order to purge the community of alien content." This idea is revised in *Hybridity* at 169, where he adds the phrase "in Thomas's text," acknowledging, 172, "so far as we know, no Jew was killed as a direct result of William's murder." The only example of retribution that Brother Thomas offers is the death of Deulesalt, and that was motivated not by revenge for allegedly killing a boy, but by the knight's inability to pay his debts. See Elisa Narin van Court, "Invisible in Oxford: The 'Public Face' of Medieval Jewish History in Modern England," *Engage* 3 (2006), http://www.engageonline.org.uk/journal/. In her otherwise excellent analysis of English public historiography of medieval Jews, see her assertion that "several Norwich Jews, including one of the leaders of the community, were murdered," as a result of the accusation.

2. The exact means of death was not important: death by crucifixion may have made it easier to persuade people that the victim was killed in *odium fidei*, but it was not necessary to have a crucifixion to make the charge of *odium fidei* stick.

3. Compare, for example, Abingdon: "no doubt because it lacked the whole remains of a single saint to whom it had a unique claim, [Abingdon] never ranked among England's principal centers of pilgrimage and of devotion to the saints," Susan J. Ridyard, "Condigna Veneratio: Post-Conquest Attitudes to the Saints of the Anglo-Saxons," *Anglo-Norman Studies* 9 (1987), 179–206 at 193. Patrick Geary, "Saint Helen of Athyra and the Cathedral of Troyes in the Thirteenth Century," *Journal of Medieval and Renaissance Studies* 7 (1977), 149–168, especially 155ff emphasizes the challenges for a city trying to find a unique claim to a complete holy body. He describes a saint's *Life* written "to order" to fill the requirements of the cathedral chapter in this period, and a cult that successfully built on and combined pre-existing feasts in the diocese—much as the monks of Norwich were to do.

4. For details of the stone throne and its consciously anachronistic placement in the twelfth-century cathedral, see Stephen Heywood, "The Romanesque Building," in *Norwich Cathedral, Church, City and Diocese*, 73–115 at 91. The placement of the bishop's throne behind the apse near the high altar is unique in England. In current publications, Norwich Cathedral does not mention Felix in connection with the throne.

5. See, for example, the documents discussed in Antonia Gransden, "Propaganda in English Medieval Historiography," *Journal of Medieval Studies* 1 (1975), 363–382 at 364. On Bishop Herbert's maneuvering, see most recently Licence, "Herbert Losinga's Trip to Rome."

6. D. H. S Cranage, ed., *Thirteenth-Hundred Anniversary of the Diocese of East Anglia* (Norwich: Jarrold and Sons, 1930), 79.

7. The initial visions about William coincided with the feast of St. Felix, whose stone portrait dominated the cathedral. In the first vision, "a man of venerable appearance, grey with age, dressed in episcopal garb" roused the dreamer with his episcopal staff. The newcomer asked who was making this announcement, and he was told that it was "Herbert, first founder of the church of Norwich" (*Vita*, III, i, 77). One could easily suspect he was dreaming of Felix, whose annual feast was to be celebrated the following day and whose image was easily confused with that of Herbert. Susan Yaxley, *Herbert De Losinga, First Bishop of Norwich* (Dereham, Norfolk: The Larks Press, 1995), a book sold at the cathedral, identifies the sculpture on the cover as that of Herbert, although it is now generally believed to be that of Felix. The effigy was initially removed from the cathedral to the ambulatory, and is now identified as that of Felix, a deliberately anachronizing work of art from the early eleventh century.

8. William's translation into the cathedral in July 1154 coincided with one of the memorial celebrations for Bishop Herbert. Subsequently he was again translated on a day that may also have been associated with Herbert, and Losinga was already entombed in the high altar to which William's relics were moved in 1151.

9. Hayward, "Innocent Martyrdom," especially 83ff.

10. R. W. Southern, "The English Origins of the 'Miracles of the Virgin,'" *Medieval and Renaissance Studies* 4 (1958), 183–200 at 177.

11. Kathy Lavezzo, "Shifting Geographies of Anti-Semitism: Mapping Jew and Christian in Thomas of Monmouth's Life and Miracles of St William of Norwich," in *Mapping Medieval Geographies: Geographical Encounters in the Latin West and Beyond, 300–1600*, ed. K. D. Lilley (Cambridge: Cambridge University Press, 2014), 25–270 rightly emphasizes the "cloistral ideology" and "anxiety about Christian laity" that Brother Thomas demonstrates. Koopmans, *Wonderful to Relate*, 4, emphasizes that in this period of miracle collecting, monks were listening to lay persons recount their miracle stories.

12. Knowles et al., *Heads of Religious Houses*, 119.

13. By the time William's cult peaked in 1154, his mother, a primary source for the passion story, was dead and buried, *Vita*, V, xxi, 142.

14. In *Toward a Definition*, 232, 234, Langmuir famously argued that "the fantasy that Jews ritually murdered Christians by crucifixion was created and contributed to western culture by Thomas of Monmouth... an influential figure in the formation of Western culture."

15. *Vita*, I, prologue, 3–7.

16. Finucane, *Miracles*, 116, is misleading in emphasizing the wide range of social backgrounds of pilgrims who benefited from twelfth-century miracles, from the simple monks "barely distinguishable from their parishioners" to the *nobilissimi* like William de Warenne—at least in reference to the miracles of St. William. The Warenne miracle he mentions two pages earlier is that of the earl's granddaughter—the youthful female offspring of a younger son of the deceased earl—not an adult male aristocrat, as he implies.

17. Antonia Gransden, "The Growth of the Glastonbury Traditions and Legends in the Twelfth Century," *Journal of Ecclesiastical History* 27 (1976), 337–358.

18. Finucane, *Miracles*, Chapter 4, draws attention to the merchants, artisan class, and lower clergy who populate William's miracle stories and notes that slightly more than half were men. Other readers might focus on the striking number of mothers and children, rather than adults; note that the brothers of the cathedral priory were far from the simple lower-class monks Finucane invokes elsewhere and observe that most of the beneficiaries were economically dependent on the cathedral.

19. The relics were at the altar of the Holy Cross before 1300, when the compiler of the *First Register* of the cathedral noted that Bishop Herbert had built "up to the altar of the Holy Cross, now called the altar of St. William." Saunders, *First Register*, 51 (fol. 8). See also Eric Fernie, *An Architectural History of Norwich Cathedral* (Oxford: Clarendon Press, 1993), 15. Since only nine pence was donated at his tomb in 1305, and two pence in 1363, it is likely that the altar of the Holy Cross was dedicated to St. William well in the past, most likely at the time of the flowering of his cult in the mid-twelfth century. The relics were moved once to an altar north of the rood loft at the entrance to the choir (possibly in 1436), and once to a niche in the wall north of the central arch; see Shinners "Veneration of Saints."

20. The conclusion of Finucane, *Miracles*, 119, that William's cult was "strongly supported by the people of Norwich" is without foundation.

21. *Vita*, V, xxi, 213ff.

22. *Vita*, II, viii, 56–58.

23. *Vita*, III, i, 76ff.

24. *Vita*, III, i, 79.

25. For the disputed date of Simon's trial, see the Appendix, "A Note on Chronology." One of the "unknown reasons" (Finucane, *Miracles*, 119; Cohen, *Hybridity*, 142; Rubin, *Life and Passion*, xiv) that Thomas made himself William's champion was perhaps the usefulness to his bishop of such action.

26. *Vita*, III, i, 79.

27. Langmuir pointed out a similar rhetorical freedom that Thomas takes with the overall narrative.

28. *Vita*, III, i, 79.

29. Antonia Gransden, "The Alleged Incorruption of the Body of St. Edmund, King and Martyr," *Antiquaries Journal* 74 (1994), 135–168 at 153ff. I thank the author for supplying me with her copy. This article informs my discussion here.

30. H. E. Butler, ed., *The Chronicle of Jocelin of Brakelond* (London: Thomas Nelson and Sons, 1949), 113ff. Abbot Samson "called the convent together before the High Altar, and briefly set forth what had been done, saying that it was neither right nor possible to summon all to see such things."

31. *Vita*, III, i, 80.

32. *Vita*, III, i, Jessopp and James translation, 120.

33. This may indicate that William or his brother was "one of the boys." Dinn, "Burial Patterns," 248: "From the late fifteenth century onwards, four testators asked to be buried near to where they, or a close friend, had sat in church." Warenne family members were notably buried in the chapter house of Lewes. See also Roberta Gilchrist, *Norwich Cathedral Close: The Evolution of the English Cathedral Landscape* (Woodbridge, Suffolk: Boydell Press, 2005), 109: "the chapter house was the preferred site of burial for monastic superiors from the eleventh up to the thirteenth or fourteenth centuries." Children associated with a monastery were sometimes buried in the chapter house; Thomas suggests the space in Norwich had already been used for this purpose. See Gilchrist, *Norwich Cathedral Close,* 95.

34. *Vita* III, i, 80–81. This miracle—a religious interpretation of the observation that William's sarcophagus stuck out above the place appointed for it—could be a commonplace about the inability of a grave to contain a sainted figure, but the wealth of detail and the emphasis on the role of the *lathomis* (stonemasons), *cemetariis* (plasterers), and *ministri* (workers) suggests an actual event. To judge from later English burial practices, this miracle could equally be a subtle way of reinforcing William's status. Dinn, "Burial Patterns," 250, cites one seventeenth-century writer, who notes that "lesser gentry had a flat horizontal gravestone, the higher gentry effigies 'raised somewhat above the ground', kings, nobles and princes, had 'their Tombes or sepulchres raised aloft above ground, to note the excellence of their state and dignitie'. Thus both the height of the memorial and its form were seen as directly proportional to the deceased's social status."

35. *Vita*, III, i.

36. Prior Elias, following instructions and eager to do no more than necessary, was reluctant to countenance further recognition of William and demanded that a light and carpet that Brother Thomas wanted on the tomb be removed. Neither Brother Thomas nor any subsequent historians have offered an alternative explanation as to why Elias at once "rejoiced" in the possession of the martyr and simultaneously removed signs of his veneration; nor have they suggested why Bishop Turbe was absent from William's installation in the chapter house.

37. *Vita*, III, i, 79.

38. Richard Eales, "The Political Setting of the Becket Translation of 1220," in *Martyrs and Martyrologies*, 127–139 at 130.

39. Ibid., 129.

40. The Bavarian notice of William's death was also Maundy Thursday for that year (xvkl Mai, 1147). Only in 1144 did Good Friday, the day after Maundy Thursday, fall on March 24.

41. The *improperia*, texts apparently derived from the preaching of the second-century Bishop Melito of Sardes, is still a fiercely contested topic, with some scholars arguing that they are aimed at Christians and not Jews. See, for example, Louis Weil, "The Debate about Anti-Semitism in the Good Friday Liturgy with Special Reference to the Reproaches," unpublished paper, *Triduum Workshop*, Graduate Theological Union, Berkeley (2005), manuscript text from the author.

42. Lester Little, "The Jews in Christian Europe," in *Essential Papers on Judaism and Christianity in Conflict*, ed. J. Cohen (New York: New York University Press, 1991), 276–297 at 285.

43. In later years, William's feast day was rescheduled so as not to coincide with Holy Week rituals.

44. "Lady Day," the feast of the Annunciation, was always March 25, while Maundy Thursday was always the Thursday before Easter (Holy Week) and could fall on different dates in March or April.

45. William Chester Jordan, *The French Monarchy and the Jews, from Philip Augustus to the Last Capetians (1179–1328)* (Philadelphia: University of Pennsylvania Press, 1989), 18.

46. *Vita*, III, vi, 84–85: Mary plaits a crown of flowers for William. See also *Vita*, II, iv, 46 (Lewin's vision), and v, 50 (the vision of the young virgin of Mulbarton), where Mary and William appear together in visions.

47. *Vita*, III, viii, 133.

48. *Vita*, IV, viii, 173–174.

49. *Vita*, III, xii, 142–143.

50. *Vita*, V, i, 186. Giulf is an uncommon name.

51. *Vita*, I, 186.

52. *Vita*, V, ii, 188–189.

53. McCulloh, "Early Dissemination," 706 ff.

54. *Vita*, V, ii, 189.

55. Geoffrey of Wells [Gaufridus de Fontibus], "De Infantia Sancti Eadmundi," in *Memorials of St. Edmund's Abbey*, ed. Thomas Arnold (London: Rolls Series, vol. 96, 1890–1896), 1:93–106. See also Hayward, "Geoffrey of Wells."

56. For details of the trial presided over (unusually) by the king's steward, see Cam, "East Anglian Shire-Moot," and Robert Bartlett, *England under the Norman and Angevin Kings, 1075–1225* (Oxford: Oxford University Press, 2000), 152–153.

57. John McCulloh argued that knowledge of William existed independently of Thomas and that William was known in Germany by the late 1140s. Yet William's miracles were negligible. No feast was celebrated, no pilgrims visited,

no liturgy recalled him, no artwork memorialized him, and no *Life* extolled his virtues at the time that McCulloh supposed the cult had spread. This is a telling contrast with a saint like St. Thomas Becket. See Eales, "Becket Translation," 127: "the fame of St. Thomas was diffused through almost every means known to the age: personal networks of family and locality; organizations within the church, especially the Cistercian order; liturgy, letters, lives and miracle collections, sermons, Latin and vernacular poetry, music, painting, sculpture, and stained glass, cult objects ranging from elaborately decorated *chases* to badges and vials of water."

58. The twelfth-century career of Honorius *Augustodunensis* suggests the path that information about William may have taken, for Honorius was a monk, probably of Regensburg, who spent the early part of his career in England. He studied in a monastic environment with strong Anglo-Saxon influence, possibly at Worcester, and relied heavily on the Lives of English saints for his later work. See Valerie Flint, "The Career of Honorius Augustodunensis: Some Fresh Evidence," *Revue Bénédictine* 82 (1972), 63–86. Honorius was also concerned and influenced by the presence of the important contemporary Jewish community of Regensburg and worked in the same environment as the authors of the Bavarian martyrology. See Valerie Flint, "Anti-Jewish Literature and Attitudes in the Twelfth Century," *Journal of Jewish Studies* 37 (1986) no. 1, 39–57, no. 2, 183–205 at 192–93. This Regensburg circle was extremely interested in Jewish-Christian relations and felt a need to respond to the teachings of Jews; in exactly this period it had close connections to English monastic literature, Flint, *Anti-Jewish Literature*, vol. 1, 47; vol. 2, 190. The Jews of Regensburg likewise were widely celebrated for their learning and acutely aware of the religious competition. See, most recently, Ephraim Kanarfogel, "R. Judah he-Hasid and the Rabbinic Scholars of Regensburg: Interactions, Influences, and Implications," *Jewish Quarterly Review* 96, no. 1 (2006), 17–37.

59. McCulloh dismissed the possibility of a personal contact because he concluded that the author "acquired his information about William independently of the source or sources that underlie his other English notices."

60. Thomas mentions a visiting merchant from Cologne (*Vita*, VI, ix, 236). The close relations with imperial Germany are made manifest in the Germanic model utilized for the dramatic and unusual seal of Norwich priory. See T. A. Heslop, "The Medieval Conventual Seals," in *Norwich Cathedral, Church, City and Diocese*, ed. Ian Atherton, et al., 443–450.

61. Judith Grant, "A New *Passio beati Edmundi: Regis [et] martyris*," *Medieval Studies* 40 (1978), 81–95 at 79.

62. Gransden, "Alleged Incorruption," 143. Notation in an obituary list required far less influence than the distribution of actual relics or the establishment of a chapel as in these two cases. A monk from Bury, either Baldwin or Leofstan, for example, deserves credit for the inclusion of the names of Anglo-Saxon monks in a necrology in the cathedral library in Lucca; Gransden, *Alleged Incorruption*, 163 n. 111.

63. *Vita*, VI, i, 146.

64. *Vita*, VI, i, 146.

65. *Vita*, VI, ii, 147. See above for the suggestion that St. William's grandfather and his daughter were present at the translation of St. Edmund of Bury and that the young girl received a cure a few days later.

66. Nilson, *Cathedral Shrines*, offers an excellent comparative discussion. William's shrine shared some, but perhaps not many, of the attributes of the group Nilson discusses.

67. In 1278 the chapel was re-dedicated to the Savior and all saints, and William retained only a modest presence there.

68. Nicholas Vincent, "The Pilgrimages of the Angevin Kings of England, 1154–1272," in *Pilgrimage: The English Experience from Becket to Bunyan*, ed. Colin Morris and Peter Roberts (Cambridge and New York: Cambridge University Press, 2002), 12–45 at 31, makes clear the importance of royal pilgrimages: "In the Angevin realms, saints needed kings almost as much as kings needed saints." Henry I, for example, made a vow that if his ship was rescued during a particularly stormy crossing of the Channel he would make a pilgrimage to St. Edmund. A royal act in favor of Bury issued c. 1132 suggests he made good on his vow, C. Warren Hollister, "Royal Acts of Mutilation: The Case against Henry I," in *Monarchy, Magnates and Institutions in the Anglo-Norman World* (London: Hambledon Press, 1986), 291–301 at 292.

69. McCulloh, "Early Dissemination," 706 ff., demonstrated that books one to six of the *Life* were composed at one time, in a much shorter period than either Jessopp and James or Langmuir believed. Koopmans, *Wonderful to Relate,* 260 n.40, notes that the text was completed in the 1150s even up to book seven, before only the last two chapters were added.

70. The *Peterborough Chronicle* recounted William's martyrdom in or after 1155, giving the date of martyrdom as 1137, Whitelock, *Anglo-Saxon Chronicle*, xvi. See also McCulloh, "Early Dissemination," 712 n. 56, for other estimates of the date. McCullough also notes ("Early Dissemination," 719), that the first continental reference, aside from the Bavarian mention, in the *Mortemer Annals*, was composed in the decade just after 1155.

71. It occurred exactly a week (octave) before April 12, when the translation from cemetery to chapter house took place in 1150, but neither date became a feast day.

72. A number of saints had their heads placed in a reliquary separate from their bodies within the same church, effectively doubling their efficacy. Guibert of Nogent ridiculed this kind of division of relics.

73. Norwich Cathedral (http://www.cathedral.org.uk/) on the timeline under William of Norwich (1145) indicates that the relics were moved in 1154 to the center where the *pulpitum* screen now stands: that is when they were moved to the chapel of the martyrs (now the Jesus chapel), north of the ambulatory. Gilchrist, *Norwich Cathedral Close*, 96, suggests that the move to a position near the *pulpitum* occurred in the fifteenth century, "and is likely to have been the

focus of a series of episcopal and clerical burials that were excavated on this site in 1899."

74. Parts of the saint could have been relocated to different areas of the church in the course of a single ceremony of translation—some relics to the center nave, others to the high altar. Becket, for example, was venerated at three places within Canterbury Cathedral.

75. Fernie, *Architectural History*, 15.

76. Gilchrist, *Norwich Cathedral Close*, 249: "Thomas draws attention to secular men and women visiting the monks' cemetery and chapter house, clearly an unusual circumstance in the 12th century cathedral priory."

77. *Vita*, IV, viii, 112–113.

78. Finucane, *Miracles and Pilgrims*, and more recently Ronald C. Finucane, *The Rescue of the Innocents: Endangered Children in Medieval Miracles* (New York: St. Martin's Press, 1997). See also Ward, *Miracles and the Medieval Mind*.

79. For the most recent work, see Yarrow, *Saints and Their Communities*.

80. In contrast, Norman Scarfe, in "The Bury St. Edmunds Cross: The Work of Master Hugo?" *Proceedings of the Suffolk Institute of Archeology* 33 (1973–1975), 75–85, considers that Jewish conversion was of signal importance to East Anglian monks in the mid-twelfth century. Of the Bury Cross, which he argues was made around 1150, he says "its central purpose seems to be to address a warning to [local Jews] and a passionate appeal to embrace Christianity."

81. *Vita*, II, xi, 61–62.

82. For twelfth-century examples of Jewish conversion (alleged, attempted, or actual) in the presence of Christian relics, see the miracles of St. Frideswide in the *Acta Sanctorum*. See also Christoph Cluse, "Fabula Ineptissima, die Ritualmordlegende um Adam von Bristol nach der Handschrift London, British Library, Harley 957," *Aschkenas* 5 (1995), 293–330. For later examples, Miri Rubin, *Gentile Tales: The Narrative Assault on Late Medieval Jews* (New Haven, CT: Yale University Press, 1999), and for one of the earliest examples, see E. M. Rose, "Gregory of Tours and the Conversion of the Jews of Clermont," in *The World of Gregory of Tours*, ed. Ian Wood and Kathleen Mitchell (Leiden; Boston: E. J. Brill for the Medieval Academy of America, 2002), 307–320.

83. Stanley Spector, "Anti-Semitism and the English Mystery Plays," in *The Drama of the Middle Ages: Comparative and Critical Essays*, ed. G. J. Gianakaris, Clifford Davidson, and John H. Stroupe (New York: AMS Press, 1982), 328.

84. Spector, "Mystery Plays," 332.

85. Langmuir, *Toward a Definition*, 13.

86. Antonia Gransden, "The Composition and Authorship of the *De miraculis Sancti Eadmundi* Attributed to 'Hermann the Archdeacon,'" *Journal of Medieval Latin* 5 (1995), 1–52 at 23ff.

87. *Vita*, III, xvi, 97. Thomas almost always uses the Latin plural to describe his role, so it is not always clear whether he was the only eyewitness.

88. *Vita*, V, viii, 128–129.

89. *Vita*, V, xii, 134.

90. *Vita*, V, xiii, 134.

91. *Vita*, V, xiv, 135.

92. *Vita*, V, xvi, 137.

93. *Vita*, III, xvii, 98.

94. *Vita*, III, xix, 99.

95. *Vita*, III, xxiii, 101–102.

96. *Vita*, III, xxvi, 103.

97. *Vita*, VII, xviii, 188 ff.

98. *Vita*, III, xxxii, 106.

99. *Vita*, V, xvii, 137.

100. *Vita*, VI, ix, 153.

101. *Vita*, III, xxviii, 104.

102. In the same way, Thomas apparently multiplied his alleged source Theobald as well, referring to him in the plural to sound more convincing. Langmuir, *Toward a Definition*, 226.

103. *Vita*, V, xii, 133.

104. *Vita*, VI, ix, 156.

105. *Vita*, V, iv. 125–126. This miracle is sandwiched between the translation of July 1151 (V, i) and the miracles of Lent 1152 (V, x).

106. Dodwell, *Norwich Charters*: Adam *dapifer* attested no. 134, ca. 1150–ca. 1159; to judge from its placement in the *Vita*, the miraculous recovery occurred in late 1151, or early 1152, but Adam's successor, Geoffrey *dapifer*, attested no. 124, 1146–c. 1150, suggesting that Adam died around 1150. See Harper-Bill, *Norwich Episcopal Acta*, xlix, for the supposition about Adam's widow and her remarriage to Geoffrey *dapifer*, son of Peter the Constable.

107. *Vita*, IV, iv, 111.

108. *Vita*, V, v, 126.

109. *Vita*, V, xviii, 138.

110. Lipman, *Norwich*, 79.

111. *Vita*, VI, iv, 148.

112. *Vita*, V xiii, 134.

113. *Vita*, VI, vi, 149ff.

114. Many saints offered something for children's illnesses. See Finucane, *Rescue of the Innocents*, chapter 3.

115. *Vita*, III, xi, 88.

116. *Vita*, II, vi, 51–52.

117. Finucane, *Miracles and Pilgrims*, 87, 167.

118. *Vita*, III, ix, 87, for the cure of the young son of Ralph, Prior Elias's nephew; and III, viii, 86, for the visit of Richard's aunt and uncle and her cure of a bloody flux.

119. *Vita*, III, vi, 84ff.

120. *Vita*, II, iv, 48.

121. *Vita*, III, xi, 88.

122. Jessopp and James, *Life and Miracles*, 135 n, note that she was a benefactor during the pontificate of Pope Eugenius III (1145–1153). One gift, recorded with the approval of her husband and three sons (Walter, Gilbert, and William) for the souls of her mother and father, is dated 1149; Pope Eugenius confirmed them. She made an (undated) gift of twenty shillings a year from her manor of Harpley (30 miles northeast of Norwich, near King's Lynn) and in a grant attested also by Alan, priest of Flockthorpe, she gave the Norwich monks her land in Harpley with all its men and appurtenances, which she had inherited from her ancestors (the date of 1109 in Blomefield, *Topographical History*, is apparently a misprint). Eric Stone, "The Estates of Norwich Cathedral Priory 1100–1300," unpublished Ph.D. thesis (Oxford University, 1956), 72, expresses doubt by noting that the consent of her family "is alleged." Paul A. Fox, "A Study of Kinship and Patronage: The Rise of the House of Bek," *Medieval Prosopography* 24 (2003), 171–193 at 181, notes that the knight's fee her father Walter de Bec received from King William Rufus was subinfeudated to her during the reign of his successor Henry I, presumably as a dowry; William de Warenne was her overlord.

123. Stephen de Cameis is mentioned in the pipe roll of 1131. Like the Clare family (for which see the following chapter), he held land and was involved in the affairs both of Wales and Suffolk. He granted a mill in Flockthorpe to the abbey of Wymondham, reserving the tithe to go to the Church of St. George in Hardingham. In 1111 at Clare in Suffolk, he attested a gift to Cardigan Priory in Wales. Mabel was likely the granddaughter of Walter I de Bec (Walter *Flandrensis*), who had been granted lands by William the Conqueror (her father appears to have been Walter II de Bec as indicated by K. S. B. Keats-Rohan, *Domesday Descendants: A Prosopography of Persons Occurring in English Documents 1066–1166* (Woodbridge: Boydell Press, 2002), 306, not Walter I de Bec as indicated by Fox, "House of Bek," 177). Mabel's son Walter de Umvraville (Anfraville) by a different (presumably earlier) husband and her son William de Chameys attested documents in the time of Henry I. Her grandson Stephen de Cameis, baron of Flockthorpe, attested a Clare charter sometime after 1154.

124. For details of Mabel's grants, see Stone, "Estates of Norwich Cathedral Priory," vol. 1, 72–73.

125. The family tree is summarized in Fox, "House of Bek," 175.

126. *Vita*, III, xxv, 102. Mabel de Bec was not the daughter of Bartholomew Creak as indicated by Susan S. Morrison, *Women Pilgrims in Late Medieval England: Private Piety and Public Performance* (London; New York: Routledge, 2000), 1.

127. For family holdings, see Jessopp and James, *Life and Miracles*, 157, and Farrer, *Knights' Fees*, 428. Bartholomew, the illegitimate son of Ralph II (de Chesney), was known as a cousin of the sheriff's family. For the Creak family's extensive benefactions, see Jessopp and James, *Life and Miracles*, 15 n. 1, and Farrer, *Knights' Fees*, vol. 3, 394. Charter printed in *Norwich Episcopal Acta*, no. 62, 55–56 (1171–January

1174); reconfirmed in no. 167, 131–132 (December 1182–March 1184) and no. 328, 260–262 (1206). Sometime between 1150 and 1154, Bartholomew acknowledged the Chesney family connection by attesting the foundation charter for Sibton Abbey, established by his cousin William de Chesney in memory of his brother Sheriff John. See R. Allen Brown, "Early Charters of Sibton Abbey, Suffolk," in *A Medieval Miscellany in Honour of Doris Mary Stenton* (London: Pipe Roll Society, 1962), 65–76. Bartholomew's son held three fees from the honor of Eye in Suffolk (which King Stephen held as count of Blois, and which went to his son), and he endowed Leiston Abbey, Brown, *Sibton Charters*, I:8. According to Keats-Rohan, *Domesday Descendants*, 415, "The Bartholomeus of Creake who occurs in a charter of the early 1130s was probably the father of a second Bartholomeus who was dead in 1188."

128. *Vita*, V, xvi, 136.

129. West, *St. Benet of Holme,* vol. 2, 63 (no. 105).

130. *Vita*, VI, xxi, 171ff.

131. He gave land at Barton Turf and the advowsons of St. Peter's, Hoveton (Brown, *Sibton Charters*, vol. 4). Albert's father died when the boy was young, and he was raised by a guardian.

132. Albert Gressley (d. 1181) held land in Lancashire and Lincolnshire, as well as in Norfolk.

133. Ronald C. Finucane, "The Use and Abuse of Medieval Miracles," *History* 60 (1975), 1–10 at 7 n. 41.

134. *Vita*, IV, xii 119; IV, viii, 113.

135. *Vita*, III, xxii, 100–101; IV, xiii, 119–120.

136. Gransden, *"De miraculis S. Eadmundi,"* 23: "Hermann refers to information on the 'great tabula'; this would have been a board or stone tablet in the church. (It was not unusual for a church to have a tabula on which was recorded the life of its patron saint and its early history)." In later cases of purported ritual murder or host desecration, the contents of a tabula were on occasion circulated in a printed broadside with woodcuts and poetry.

137. *Vita*, I, prol., 6. "let the diligent reader pay careful attention, lest both our hard work and his efforts be wasted."

138. *Vita*, I, prol., 6ff.

139. *Vita*, I, prol., 4.

140. Shinners, "Saints at Norwich," 140.

141. *Vita*, I, prol., 6.

142. *Vita*, IV, xiii, 120.

143. Gransden, *"De miraculis S. Eadmundi,"* 18, 33. The Norwich monks would have known of the various versions of Goscelin's work because Goscelin had been employed by Herbert Losinga to write the *Miracula* and the *Vita* of St. Ives while he was abbot of Ramsey, before Losinga's election as bishop of Norwich.

144. Some bloodstained clothing and a piece of the cross appear on a list of relics from Reading dating to around 1200, I. G. Thomas, "The Cult of Saints' Relics in Medieval England," unpublished Ph.D. thesis (University of London, 1974),

appendix. A priest at Haveringland claimed to have fetters from a miracle that St. William performed as a child (*Vita*, I, ii, 11), Uncle Godwin showed the alleged instrument of William's murder, the teazle gag (*Vita*, V, v, 126), and Thomas kept some tooth relics for himself, as well as saving a shoe (*Vita*, III, i, 80, IV, viii, 113, ix, 114). Based on an old transcription of a fragmentary relic list, Julian Luxford of the University of St. Andrews has suggested that the secular canons of Wimborne Minster in Dorset may have had a shoe of St. William among their relics, Julian Luxford, "St William of Norwich in Late Medieval Art," paper given at *Youth, Violence and Cult* conference, based at Queen Mary College, University of London, January 2010.

145. *Vita*, III, xxxi, 105.

146. Roth, *Ritual Murder Libel and the Jew*, 15, mentions "a wave of religious frenzy swept the city" in consequence of William's death, an idea reiterated by, among others, R. H. C. Davis, *King Stephen, 1135–1154* (London: Longman, 1980), 88, who adds, "Neither the sheriff nor the bishop seem to have believed it, but they were powerlesss in face of the popular frenzy."

147. Finucane, *Miracles and Pilgrim*; Ward, *Miracles and the Medieval Mind*; Friedrich Lotter, "Innocens virgo et martyr: Thomas von Monmouth und die Verbreitung der Ritualmordlegende im Hochmittelalter," in *Die Legende vom Ritualmord: Zur Geschichte der Blutbeschuldigung gegen Juden*, ed. R. Erb (Berlin: Metropol, 1993), 25–72.

Part 2

1. Anderson, *Saint at the Stake*, entitles her concluding chapter "The Need for a Saint." She is followed by Lipman, *Norwich* and Hillaby, "Accusation," who notes, "the Benedictine monks of Norwich and Gloucester... were earnestly seeking a patron" (94), pointing out that St. Peter's failed to establish a shrine on three previous occasions (82). Yet he adds that Harold performed no miracles and was not referred to as a saint (83).

Chapter 5

1. *Historia et Cartularium Monasterii Sancti Petri Gloucestriae*, ed. William Henry Hart (London: Rolls Series, 1863–1867), vol. 1, 20–21.

2. Joe Hillaby, "The Ritual-Child-Murder Accusation: Its Dissemination and Harold of Gloucester," *Jewish Historical Studies* 34 (1997), 69–110 at 74–75, concludes that the description of the alleged martyrdom must have been drawn from a contemporary Life of Harold. There is no evidence, however, that such a text existed.

3. The background information on Gloucester offered here follows the Victoria History of the County of Gloucester, ed. William Page (London: A Constable and Co., 1907).

4. The saying "as sure as God's in Gloucester" reflects the popular view. Oliver Cromwell is reported to have said the city had "more churches than godliness."

5. The first Richard fitzGilbert, the founder of the family, held ninety-five lordships in Suffolk alone; his descendant Richard fitzGilbert de Clare used the title earl of Striguil (Chepstow), the castle that dominated at the confluence of the Wye and Severn rivers, but he also had ties to Suffolk. Their family seat was Castle Clare in Suffolk, although they made their reputation as the lords of South Wales. The main Clare interests centered on the estates in Suffolk (the *honour* of Clare) and switched over from eastern England to the west only when the family increased its holdings there in the thirteenth century (with a grant of the *honour* of Gloucester), thereby doubling their estates. See Jennifer C. Ward, "Fashions in Monastic Endowment: The Foundations of the Clare Family, 1066–1314," *Journal of Ecclesiastical History* 32 (1981), 427–451 at 447. As noted in the previous chapter, Anglo-Norman vassals of the Clare family, such as Stephen de Cameis, the husband of Mabel de Bec, were active both in Wales and in East Anglia.

6. Scholars rely on the possible but highly implausible series of links first put forward by M. R. James at the suggestion of Augustus Jessopp: that a monk at Eye in Suffolk (in 1138) learned about the accusation in Norwich and took the story with him when he went as abbot to Pershore (before about 1170), a story he then passed on to the nearby monastery at Gloucester (Jessopp and James, *Life and Miracles*, lxxvi). Hillaby, "Accusation," 99, likewise emphasizes monastic connections. Yet the accusation was not raised at any other time or place during the two intervening decades. As discussed below, the information and influence most likely went from Gloucester to Pershore after 1168, and not in the opposite direction prior to that date.

7. The Gloucester monks had owned the most important church, St. Peter Mancroft, in the center of the city since the Conquest. See W. Hudson, "The Parish Churches and Religious Houses of Norwich," in *Memorials of Old Norfolk*, ed. H. J. D. Astley (London: Bemrose, 1908), 48–59 at 51. Just before the beginning of the twelfth century, Roger Bigod, ancestor of the earls of Norfolk, gave a market in Norwich to St. Peter's during the time of Gloucester's rapid expansion under Abbot Serlo (1072–1104), noted in David Bates, "The Building of a Great Church: The Abbey of St Peter's, Gloucester and Its Early Norman Benefactors," *Transactions. Bristol and Gloucestershire Archeological Society* 102 (1984), 130–131: Bates makes no mention of St. Peter's, Mancroft. David Welander, *The History, Art and Architecture of Gloucester Cathedral* (Far Thrupp, Gloucestershire: Alan Sutton, 1991), 21, follows Bates. In the 1160s, the Church of St. Augustine, Norwich, was given to the Augustinian priory at Llanthony, on the outskirts of Gloucester, Harper-Bill, *Norwich Episcopal Acta*, 95, no. 114.

The Gloucester possessions in East Anglia were sufficiently extensive, important, and well known for the future Henry II, supported by the archbishop of Canterbury, to warn Bishop Turbe of urgent threats to the monks' property in the wake of the civil war. See Avrom Saltman, *Theobald, Archbishop of Canterbury* (London: University of London, Athlone Press, 1956), no. 120, 2, and Harper-Bill,

"Bishop Turbe," 149. The presence at Norwich Cathedral Priory of a monk from Monmouth, another town near the Welsh border, also suggests that there were communications between eastern England and the English-Welsh border towns. Although Jessopp and James, *Life and Miracles*, xi, tentatively attribute Thomas's presence at Norwich to Geoffrey of Monmouth's trip to England, the connections between the elite of Monmouth and East Anglia predate Geoffrey's visit. The strong Welsh literary influence noted in Thomas's *Life* must have been presumed to appeal to the Norwich audience, Hillaby, "Accusation," 71.

8. Emma Cownie, *Religious Patronage in Anglo-Norman England, 1066–1135* (Woodbridge, Suffolk: Boydell & Brewer, 1998), 56ff.

9. Adrian Morey and C. N. L. Brooke, eds., *The Letters and Charters of Gilbert Foliot, Abbot of Gloucester (1139–48), Bishop of Hereford (1148–63) and London (1163–87)* (Cambridge: Cambridge University Press, 1967), 54, no. 20 (ca. 1142–1148). William de Chesney, Sheriff of Norfolk and Suffolk, the son of Robert fitzWalter and Sybil de Chesney (d. 1174), should be distinguished from his relative, William de Chesney of Oxfordshire, son of Roger de Chesney and Alice de Langetot (d. shortly after 1169). The sheriff may have been the great nephew of the Oxford William de Chesney. Both men named William de Chesney were strong and reliable supporters of the king and benefited accordingly. For the prolific and complicated Chesney family, see L. F. Salzman, "Sussex Domesday Tenants IV. The Family of Chesney or Cheyney," *Sussex Archeology* 65 (1924), 20–53, which corrects J. H. Round, "The Origin of the Stewarts and Their Chesney Connection," *The Genealogist* 18 (1901), 1–16, and J. H. Round, "The Early Sheriffs of Norfolk," *English Historical Review* 35 (1920), 481–496. See, more recently, Keats-Rohan, *Domesday Descendants*.

10. Green, "Financing Stephen's War," 99.

11. Austin Lane Poole, *From Domesday Book to Magna Carta 1087–1216* (Oxford: Clarendon Press, 1954), 151.

12. Robert B. Patterson, ed., *The Original Acta of St. Peter's Abbey. Gloucester, c. 1122–1263* (Gloucestershire: Bristol and Gloucestershire Archeological Society, 1998), 31.

13. Welander, *Gloucester Cathedral*. Norwich Cathedral, which had been built at almost exactly the same time, was better planned.

14. The candlesticks were commissioned by Abbot Peter (d. 1113) at the beginning of the century, and one was given by a layman to the church at Le Mans in the late twelfth century. Hart, *Historia*, xxiv, believed that it must have left the cathedral before the fire of 1122. It is more likely that the candlestick was sold later in the century, rather than within a decade of its creation. The gift to Le Mans of the surviving candlestick, now a highlight of the medieval collection in the Victoria and Albert Museum, is noted in an inscription on the drip pan; the earlier inscription on the stem notes the gift of "Abbot Peter and his gentle flock."

15. The manuscript, an antiphonal with other liturgical texts (Oxford, Jesus College, MS 10), contains a calendar that was probably used at St. Peter's in the early twelfth century and possibly later. Harold's name was not included when

additions to the calendar were apparently made in the 1170s and about 1200. Welander, *Gloucester Cathedral*, 88; Hillaby, "Accusation," 85.

16. Page, *History of the County of Gloucester*, vol. 2, 56.

17. Robert B. Patterson, "Robert Fitz Harding of Bristol: Profile of an Early Angevin Burgess-Born Patrician and His Family's Urban Involvement," *Haskins Society Journal* 1 (1989), 109–122 at 116 and 120.

18. Patterson, *Acta of St. Peter's*, xxiii. Among the requirements of a tenant-in-chief was the need to pay *scutage*, a payment, usually in cash, by a vassal to an overlord in place of providing knights. It is not certain that Gloucester was indeed obligated to pay *scutage*. Patterson, *Acta of St. Peter's*, xxiii, suggests it was obligated; D. Knowles, "The Growth of Monastic Exemption," *Downside Review* 50 (1932), 201–231, 396–436, implies that it was a specific liberty for Gloucester not to supply knights. Keefe, *Feudal Assessments*, does not mention Gloucester.

19. Cecil Roth, *A History of the Jews in England* (Oxford: Clarendon Press, 1949), 12. The *tallage* was usually levied on towns and demesne lands of the crown. The 1159 *tallage* on Jews appears to have been the first of its kind, but one that was frequently to be repeated.

20. A mark at this time was equal to two-thirds of a pound of silver, so the tallage would have totaled 3,333 pounds of silver—a substantial amount. For the 5,000-mark *tallage* on the Jews, see Gervase of Canterbury, *Opera Historica*, ed. Stubbs, 1:205. For discussion of this obscure passage, see Roth, *History of the Jews*, 12, and Albert M. Hyamson, *A History of the Jews in England* (London: Jewish Historical Society, 1908), 29. The impact of this considerable financial pressure is indicated in the pipe rolls by the case of Sampson fitzSamuel, who disappeared to France, leaving obligations to the crown (1167), Lipman, *Norwich*, 95 n. 1.

21. Richard (fitzGilbert) de Clare (ca. 1130–1176) was the son of Gilbert fitzGilbert, first earl of Pembroke, who succeeded to his father's estates in southern Wales in 1148/1149. "Strongbow" is a later appellation: he was not actually called Strongbow during his lifetime, nor was he in possession of the earldom of Pembroke before the conquest of Ireland. He used the title "earl of Striguil" (Chepstow in Monmouthshire).

22. The king of Leinster had received permission from Henry II to come through England to raise help after he was banished and his kingdom was invaded by his old enemies, O'Connor and O'Rourke.

23. William of Newburgh, *Historia Rerum Anglicarum*, ed. Howlett (London: Rolls Series vol. 82, 1884–89), 167–168.

24. A. B. Scott and F. X. Martin, *Expugnatio Hibernica, The Conquest of Ireland by Giraldus Cambrensis* [Gerald of Wales], *Irish Medieval Texts* (Dublin: Irish Royal Academy, 1978), 54–55: "vir quidem plus nominis hactenus habens quam ominis, plus genii quam ingenii, plus successionis quam possessionis."

25. W. L. Warren, *Henry II* (London: Eye Metheun, 1973), 193.

26. Robin Frame, *Ireland and Britain, 1170–1450* (London: Hambledon Press, 1998), 223; Scott and Martin, *Expugnation Hibernica*, 30–33: "vir quoque fugitivus

a facie fortunae, inermis et inops"; Lynn H. Nelson, *The Normans in South Wales, 1070–1171* (Austin: University of Texas Press, 1966), 141.

27. One scholar points to "the advantage of military techniques that baffled or terrified his Irish opponents—the continental device of motte-and-bailey fort, and the combination, learned in the Welsh March, of skirmishing archers, disciplined footmen, and mounted knights," Warren, *Henry II*, 193. Such skills, we are told, were just enough to swing the balance. But "superior weapons and defensive armor, more powerful horses and greater discipline" were utilized in an essentially Irish mode of warfare. Frame, *Ireland and Britain*, 223. Richard Roche, *The Norman Invasion of Ireland* (Dublin: Anvil Books, 1995), in his chapter on preparations, never mentions money but suggests that promises of land were sufficient to induce the soldiers to join. Edmund Curtis, *A History of Medieval Ireland from 1086 to 1513* (New York: Barnes and Noble, 1968), 46, concludes, "It would seem that his own king ironically encouraged him to repair his ruined fortunes in Ireland," although Henry recalled the expedition even before they embarked.

28. See Tyerman, "Paid Crusaders," for the importance of military stipends.

29. S. D. B. Brown, "The Servant and His Master: Military Service and Monetary Reward in the Eleventh and Twelfth Centuries," *History* 74 (1989), 20–38 at 35.

30. Judith Green, *The Aristocracy of Norman England* (Cambridge: Cambridge University Press, 1997), 145.

31. Lipman, *Jews of Norwich*, 98.

32. By the 1160s the Clares had endured decades of gradual failure, not likely to bolster confidence in their eventual success. Ceredigion was lost in 1136, Camarthen and Llanstephen in 1146, Tenby in 1153, Ystard Tywy and a large part of Dyfed by 1166: "Clare fortunes in south-west Wales were at low ebb," Nelson, *Normans in South Wales*, 13.

33. Hyamson, *History of the Jews*, 30, following Jacobs, *Jews of Angevin England*, 47. Cecil Roth disagreed, *Jews of England*, 14 n. 3.

34. Adler, *Jews of Medieval England*, 89, calls Jacobs's theory "very doubtful"; Roth concurs, see previous note. Most histories of Richard fitzGilbert's venture do not discuss financing and do not mention the Jewish loans that are documented. For examples of omissions, see Poole, *From Domesday Book*; Warren, *Henry II*; Frank Barlow, *The Feudal Kingdom of England, 1042–1216*, 3rd ed. (London: Longman, 1972), 333; Richard English, *History of Ireland* (Dublin: Gill and Macmillan, 1991), 38; Desmond McGuire, *History of Ireland* (London: Hamlyn [Bison], 1987), 26–28; Nelson, *Normans in South Wales*; Michael Dolley, *Anglo-Norman Ireland, c. 1100–1318* (Dublin: 1972). A. J. Otway-Ruthven, *A History of Medieval Ireland* (London: Ernest Benn Ltd., 2nd ed., 1980) also does not suggest how Richard fitzGilbert financed his venture. Marie-Thérèse Flanagan, "Strongbow, Henry II and Anglo-Norman Intervention in Ireland," in *War and Government in the Middle Ages*, ed. J. Gillingham and J. C. Holt (Cambridge: D. S. Brewer, 1984), 62–77 at 65, cites the known borrowings from Jews but relegates them to a footnote without

discussion (in contrast to her intriguing analysis of the apparent financing from Richard FitzHarding, the Bristol merchant who died in 1170). See Colin Richmond, "Englishness and Medieval Anglo-Jewry," 42–59, for a discussion of such omissions. Histories of Gloucester, in contrast to those of Ireland, mention the recorded debts.

35. Anthony Wood, *History and Antiquities of Oxford* (Oxford: J. Gutch, 1792), 1:148. Hyamson, *History of the Jews,* 16 n. 2 discusses the competing threats.

36. Roger of Wendover in Matthew Paris, "Chronica Majora," ed. Luard, 2:528.

37. Streit, "Expansion," 188, considers the Jewish communities of Cambridge, Winchester and Lincoln "old"; Norwich, Northampton, and Oxford "new"; and Gloucester and Worcester "extremely recent." Gloucestershire was territory firmly devoted to Empress Matilda. Both castellan and earl fought on her side, and in such areas no Jewish settlement occurred until the war was over. The Jewish community of Gloucester first appears in the account rolls at the beginning of the reign of Henry II (1154) and may be tied to the mint there. At the time of Harold's death, therefore, Jews had lived in Gloucester for little more than a decade at most; the years just before 1168 may have seen a sudden increase. These Jews were not merely newcomers, they were "foreigners" as well, having emigrated directly from the German Empire (not by way of France). The influx of Jews from Germany to England in the 1160s prompted a strong response from Frederick Barbarossa, as pointed out by Stacey, "Jewish Lending," 81.

38. Flanagan, "Strongbow": "FitzHarding [of Bristol] had been an astute money-lender during Stephen's reign with a keen eye for impoverished landowners. . . ." (65); it is "likely that Tickenham was a portion of the lordship of Striguil which had been mortgaged or sold by Strongbow to Robert fitzHarding" (66); it then passed to fitzHarding's son Nicholas.

39. *Pipe Roll 16 Henry 2* (London: Pipe Roll Society, 1892), 78.

40. For the activities of Aaron of Lincoln, see the well-annotated *Jewish Encyclopedia,* s.v. "Aaron of Lincoln," which mentions neither St. Peter's nor Richard fitzGilbert.

41. The earl owed 80 marks mortgaged on Weston. Flanagan, n. 18: "The debt is listed under Gloucestershire, a county under which Strigoil was occasionally entered on the pipe rolls, but "Weston" must refer to Strongbow's manor in Hertfordshire. The debt was re-entered each year until 1202, when William Marshall, who had married Strongbow's daughter and heir in 1189, finally secured a pardon for it from King John."

42. Flanagan, "Anglo-Norman Intervention," 64 n. 8, 66. Richard fitzGilbert inherited the earldom of Pembroke, but Henry II refused to recognize his title. After 1153 Richard usually attested as count (*comes*), but in official sources he is merely acknowledged as Richard fitzGilbert, or at best Richard, son of earl Gilbert.

43. Flanagan, "Anglo-Norman Intervention," 66, suggests that "possibly Strongbow had gone to the king to request permission to go to Ireland and Henry had delayed his departure deliberately by dispatching him on the embassy to

Germany." Other historians do not venture an explanation for Henry's selection of Richard fitzGilbert for the marriage embassy.

44. Goddard Henry Orpen, *Ireland under the Normans*, 4 vols. (Oxford: Clarendon Press, 1911–1920), vol. 1, 93 n1.

45. Marjorie Chibnall, ed., *The Ecclesiastical History of Orderic Vitalis*, 6 vols. (Oxford: Clarendon Press, 1969), vol. 6, 168.

46. Ralph de Diceto, *Opera Historica*, ed. W. Stubbs (London: Rolls Series, 1879), 1:330. See also Karl Jordan, *Henry the Lion, A Biography*, trans. P. S. Falla (Oxford: Clarendon Press, 1986), 147.

47. Farrer, *Knights' Fees*, 317.

48. Round, "Early Sheriffs," 488.

49. Brown, *Sibton Charters*, 1:15.

50. See note 41 above.

51. Walter de Clare (d. 1149) is sometimes described as the uncle, rather than the brother, of Gilbert fitzGilbert (d. 1148) and thus would be Strongbow's great-uncle, rather than his uncle.

52. That same year marked the first recorded extortion of Jews in London, when they were forced to pay 2,000 marks for killing a sick man, possibly a patient. See Joseph Hunter, ed., *Pipe Roll 31 Henry 1* (London: Public Records Commission, 1833), 149; Green, "Stephen's War," 105, terms the fine "clearly punitive." See also Roth, *History of the Jews*, 8, who speculates that this may have been an early example of the ritual murder accusation.

53. Roth, *History of the Jews*, 278. This Richard fitzGilbert (d. 1262 and buried at Tewkesbury) was the sixth earl of Hertford and fifth earl of Gloucester, but it is not clear that he accompanied Louis IX on the Sixth Crusade. He did go on pilgrimage to Pontigny the previous year.

54. Aside from the records of St. Peter's itself, the only mention of the Gloucester accusation in twelfth-century English chronicles occurs in the *Chronicle of Melrose* (Mailros). See Hillaby, "Accusation," 83.

55. Jacob Freedman, *Polychrome Historical Haggadah for Passover* (Springfield, MA: Jacob Freedman Liturgy Research Foundation, 1974) reproduces some fifteenth-century miniatures of the ritual, 79ff.

56. *Vita*, II, ix, 90–91.

57. Goodich, *Violence and Miracle*, 97ff.

58. Finucane, *Rescue of Innocents*, 103ff.

59. Joseph Jacobs, "Little St. Hugh of Lincoln, Boy and Martyr: Researches in History, Archaeology and Legend," *Transactions of the Jewish Historical Society of England* 1 (1894), 89–135 reprinted in Dundes, *Blood Libel Legend*, 41–71, and Gavin Langmuir, "The Knight's Tale of Young Hugh of Lincoln," *Speculum* 47 (1972), 459–482 reprinted in Langmuir, *Toward a Definition*, 237–262.

60. The theme of a child drowned in a well is also associated with the idea that Jews were prepared to throw their victims into a privy or outhouse. Thomas of Monmouth suggests that the Jews of Norwich first considered throwing William into a privy when

they discussed disposing of his body. The association of Jews, privies, and excrement was a popular theme in the thirteenth century. See Alexandra Cuffel, *Gendering Disgust*, and Anthony Bale, *The Jew in the Medieval Book: English Antisemitisms, 1350–1500* (Cambridge: Cambridge University Press, 2007), 23–55 on the Jew of Tewksbury who fell in the latrine. See Yuval, *Two Nations*, 174–184, for a discussion of the symbolism of water in the context of Jewish and Christian polemics in this period.

61. James Hooper, "Curious Church Dedications in Norfolk; and Some Rood Screen Figures," in *Memorials of Old Norfolk*, ed. Hugh J. D. Astley (Norwich: Bemrose and Sons, 1909) 253–273 at 271. W. T. Bensly, "St. Leonard's Priory, Norwich," *Norfolk Archeology* 12 (1895), 190–227 at 192, states that chapel of St. William-in-the-Wood on Mousehold Heath had been St. Catherine's chapel before it was re-dedicated to St. William.

62. Orpen, *Ireland under the Normans*, 1: 93, explains the two-year delay of Richard's departure by his need to wait for the king's reluctant approval.

63. Hyamson, *Jews in England*, 30.

64. Among the most recent work, see Robin Frame, *Ireland and Britain*.

65. The celebration of the Feast of Mary's Conception began at St. Peter's under Abbot William Godemon (1113–1131); see Welander, *Gloucester Cathedral*, 60.

66. Carter, "Historical Content," 137; Southern, "English Origins," 182.

67. A monk of Pershore learned about William of Norwich, possibly by way of Gloucester; *Vita*, VII, xviii, 284. Malmesbury was in close proximity to Gloucester and under her influence. One of the stories in William of Malmesbury's Marian collection was used to promote the Feast of the Conception; Gloucester and Bury were two of the earliest houses that adopted the feast; Carter, "Malmesbury's Miracles," 139.

68. Carleton Brown, "The Prioress's Tale," in *Sources and Analogues of Chaucer's Canterbury Tales*, ed. W. F. Bryan and Germaine Dempster (Chicago: The University of Chicago Press, 1941), 447–485, at 453. This is the earliest of the "C" versions of Chaucer's Prioress's Tale.

69. See, for example, the work of Kati Ihnat, "Mary and the Jews in Anglo-Norman Monastic Culture," unpublished Ph.D. Dissertation (Queen Mary, University of London, 2011). See also Adrienne Williams Boyarin, *Miracles of the Virgin in Medieval England: Law and Jewishness in Marian Legends* (Woodbridge, Suffolk: Boydell and Brewer, 2010) and the work of Denise Despres, such as "Immaculate Flesh and the Social Body: Mary and the Jews," *Jewish History* 12, no. 1 (1998), 47–69, for a later period.

70. In 1275, for example, when the Jews were expelled from Gloucester, they were deported to Bristol. During that year there were also riots at Bristol, and the synagogue was burned. F. Neale, *Report on Planned Archeological Excavations of St. Peter's/Bristol Jewry* (Bristol: Bristol Record Office, 1975). See Richardson, *English Jewry*, 127, for men owning property in both places and identified alternately with one or the other.

71. Adler's classic work "The Jews of Medieval Bristol," in Adler, *Jews of England*, 175–254, does not address the striking differences between Bristol and other contemporary Jewish communities.

72. Lipman, *Norwich*, 9.

73. *Vita*, II, xiii, 63–64.

74. Because of a mistranslation from the Latin, it was long assumed that Bristol had an early house of converts. Note the correction in the final (1964) edition of Roth, *History of the Jews*, 43 n. 2, based on Richardson, *English Jewry*, 31–32, and the explanation of the confusion in Joe Hillaby and Richard Sermon, "Jacob's Well, Bristol: Mikveh or Bet Tohorah?" *Transactions of the Bristol and Gloucestershire Archaeological Society* 122 (2005), 127–151 at 130. Nonetheless, the idea still arises, for example, in R. R. Emanuel and M. W. Ponsford, "Jacob's Well, Bristol: Britain's Only Known Medieval Jewish Ritual Bath (Mikveh)," *Transactions of the Bristol and Gloucestershire Archeological Society* 112 (1994), 73–86 at 79; and Judith Samuel, *Jews in Bristol: The History of the Jewish Community in Bristol from the Middle Ages to the Present Day* (Bristol: Redcliffe, 1997), 21. The myth of the domus lives on: in 1975 archaeologists proposed a plan to dig for it on the site of Chequer/Church Lane and Narrow Wine Street, where local tradition placed it. See F. Neale, *Report on Planned Archeological Excavations of St. Peter's/Bristol Jewry* (Bristol: Bristol Record Office, 1975).

75. Hillaby and Sermon, "Jacob's Well, Bristol," 145, suggest a date between 1218 and 1222 for the grant of the well. After its recent (re)discovery it was declared a protected Scheduled Ancient Monument.

76. The *Annals of Innisfallen* notes that five Jews (probably merchants) came with gifts for the king of Munster and then were sent back again over the sea in 1079. There is no further mention of Jews until "Joseph the doctor" appears in 1171, *Calendar of Documents Relating to Ireland Preserved in Her Majesty's Public Record Office* (London: Longman, 1875–1886), 5.

77. Moses of Bristol could trace his ancestry back many generations to the great mystic and poet Rabbi Simeon "the Great" of Mainz (ca. 1000). His grandfather may have been Simeon of Trier, who was killed by crusaders near Cologne on his way back from England during the Second Crusade.

78. Cecil Roth, *The Jews of Medieval Oxford* (Oxford: Clarendon Press for the Oxford Historical Society, 1951), 8.

79. Robert Stacey, "'Adam of Bristol'," concludes that the text is an early fourteenth-century copy of a tale that was composed in the mid-thirteenth century before the Jews moved from the western side of Bristol near the city walls to the opposite side, close to the castle.

80. See Harvey J. Hames, "The Limits of Conversion: Ritual Murder and the Virgin Mary in the Account of Adam of Bristol," *Journal of Medieval History* 33 (2007), 43–59, and Christoph Cluse, "*Fabula Ineptissima*: Die Ritualmordlegende um Adam von Bristol nach der Handschrift London, British Library, Harley 957," *Aschkenas* 5 (1995), 293–330. See also Robert Stacey, "From Ritual Crucifixion to Host Desecration: Jews and the Body of Christ," *Jewish History* 12 (1998), 11–28.

81. Stacey, "Adam of Brisol," 8. The manuscript is now in the British Library, Harley 957, ff. 19–27v. The colored illustration is f.22.

Chapter 6

1. It is a commonplace that the ritual murder accusation had spread widely by this time; see, for example, Chazan, "The Blois Incident," 275, and Robert Chazan, *Church, State and Jew in the Middle Ages* (New York: Behrman House, 1980), 114. Before 1170 there had been only two such accusations: in Norwich and Gloucester.

2. Roth, *History of the Jews*, 8. The case for a flourishing Jewish communal life, especially in Angevin lands, is made even stronger in light of recent work on the Jewry of Rouen, for which, see Golb, *Jews in Medieval Normandy*. There is no mention of Jews in Christopher Harper-Bill and Nicholas Vincent, eds., *Henry II: New Interpretations* (Woodbridge and Rochester: Boydell and Brewer, 2007).

3. Robert Chazan explores the material and spiritual challenges, successes and failures in two chapters of *The Jews of Western Christendom, 1000–1500* (Cambridge: Cambridge University Press, 2006), 209–283. The essays in Signer and Van Engen, *Jews and Christians in Twelfth-Century Europe* explore various aspects of this interaction. See especially the essay by Ivan Marcus, "The Dynamics of Jewish Renaissance and Renewal in the Twelfth Century," 27–45. The twelfth century was a period of "dazzling achievement" for northern European Jews according to David Berger, "Mission to the Jews and Jewish-Christian Contacts in the Polemical Literature of the High Middle Ages," *American Historical Review* 91 (1986), 576–591.

4. Jonathan M. Elukin, *Living Together, Living Apart: Rethinking Jewish-Christian Relations in the Middle Ages* (Princeton, NJ: Princeton University Press, 2007), emphasizes peaceful coexistence over continuous persecution and unremitting hostility.

5. B. Blumenkranz, "Les juifs à Blois au Moyen Age: À propos de la demographie historique des juifs," in *Mélanges offerts à E. R. Labande* (Poitiers: Centre d'études supérieurs de civilization médiévale, 1974), 33–38.

6. The burned stone is still visible in parts of the building work. See Barbara Dodwell, "Herbert De Losinga and the Foundation," in *Norwich Cathedral, Church, City and Diocese*, 36–43 at 42, and Stephen Heywood, "The Romanesque Building," 74.

7. The quotation is from the *First Register*, of the priory, fol. 14d, composed in the early thirteenth century (printed in Saunders, *First Register*, 76–77). Harper-Bill, "Bishop Turbe," 151. Both Christopher Harper-Bill, the leading historian on Bishop Turbe, and Eric Fernie, the expert on Norwich Cathedral, date the fire to 1171, but their source is the *First Register*, which does not cite a date. The hypothesis developed below accords with a date of about 1169/1170.

8. *Vita*, II. i, 39–42, where all the rest of the quotations in this paragraph are found.

9. A twelfth-century expedition from Durham carried the relics of St. Cuthbert to the Scottish capital of Perth; Reginald of Durham cited in Thomas, "Saints' Relics."

At about the same time, Abbot Walter of Evesham sent the relics of St. Egwin on tour to raise money to rebuild the abbey church. He also "planned to send the relics of St. Odulf to Winchcombe in the hope of raising money for the new church; the saint being reluctant to leave his church however, the shrine became immovably heavy"; Dominic of Evesham's *Life of St. Egwin* and his *Life of St. Odulf*, quoted in Ridyard, "*Condigna Veneratio*," 204. In the 1180s two monks of Canterbury, traveling in the retinue of Archbishop Baldwin, brought some of St. Thomas Becket's relics to Saint-Benigne in Dijon; see H. E. J. Cowdrey, "An Early Record at Dijon of the Export of Becket's Relics," in *Popes, Monks and Crusaders* (London: Hambledon Press, 1985), 251–253, for the kind of brief and modest tour, otherwise unrecorded, that Turbe may have made. Geoffrey, prior of Canterbury (1191–1206), brought some of Becket's relics to Rouen and then lost some at Amiens and Eu, where he miraculously discovered them on the altar; they also appeared at Pontigny, where they performed miracles as well; Robertson, *Materials for Becket*, 268, 287.

10. Pierre Heliot and Marie-Laure Chastang, "Questes et voyages de reliques au profit des églises françaises du Moyen Age," *Revue d'Histoire Écclesiastique* 59 (1964), 789–822, and 60 (1965), 5–32, offer an excellent overview of such tours; they cite forty-two "itinerant quests" in the Middle Ages for the benefit of ecclesiastical institutions and an additional forty that specifically included the carrying and display of relics.

11. One of the most detailed surviving accounts concerns a successful relic tour that French clerics made to raise funds in England early in the twelfth century, a year after they traveled through France. The funds raised from this tour enabled the church of Laon to be restored and rededicated. J. S. P. Tatlock, "The English Journey of the Laon Canons," *Speculum* 8 (1933), 454–465. Setting the pattern, the bishop of Laon made a couple of trips to England to raise funds, and, after his murder upon his return home, the cathedral canons embarked on their own tour. The canons appear to have journeyed where they might have expected to receive hospitality or greet friends, perhaps former students of their famous abbot, Anselm of Laon. See Yarrow, *Saints and Their Communities*, 63–99.

12. After a fire at his church in 1174, the abbot of St. Evurtius in Orléans sent his canons to Tours with relics to preach and collect gifts. Two monks of St. Eparchus in Angoulême received letters of protection and a recommendation from King John when their church burned to the ground and their abbot sent them to preach and raise funds in England. C. R. Cheney, "Church-Building in the Middle Ages," in *Medieval Texts and Studies* (Oxford: Clarendon Press, 1973), 356.

13. Eliot and Chastang, "Questes et voyages," 809.

14. Pierre Kunstmann, *Miracles de Notre-Dame de Chartres* (Ottawa: Éditions de l'Université d'Ottawa, 1973).

15. Christopher Harper-Bill, "Church and Society in Twelfth-Century Suffolk," *Proceedings of the Suffolk Institute of Archeology* 35 (1983), 203–211 at 205.

16. The locations of the "copycat" accusations would be compatible with an itinerary for Turbe comparable to that of the Benedictine monks of Corbeny, who took

a fundraising tour earlier in the twelfth century to Chalons, Épernay, Soissons, Noyon, and Peronne under the auspices of the monks of Saint-Rémi and with the permission of the archbishop of Rheims. See Heliot and Chastang, "Questes et voyages," 811.

17. M. R. James (Jessopp and James, *Life and Miracles*, lxxvi) originally suggested that accounts of St. William were passed on by Eborard of Calne, bishop of Norwich (1121–1145), but this is implausible. A native of England, Bishop Eborard never went to France before his retirement to the Burgundian abbey of Fontenay. Although Eborard had left Norwich by 1145 and died by 1147, the accusation appeared in France only in 1170.

18. Harper-Bill, *Norwich Episcopal Acta*, Appendix: Itineraries of Bishops.

19. *Vita*, I, Prologue, I, 3.

20. David Knowles, *The Episcopal Colleagues of Archbishop Thomas Becket* (Cambridge: Cambridge University Press, 1951), 33, intimates that Bishop Turbe was incapacitated.

21. Thomas Becket had been King Henry's most trusted advisor and chancellor, but once consecrated as archbishop of Canterbury he vigorously defended the privileges of the church against those of the crown. After much conflict, Thomas fled to France (financing his sudden departure with a loan from a Jew of London), while the dispute dragged on for years.

22. Alan of Tewkesbury, writing of the Council of Northampton in 1164, when Becket was condemned for defying the king, states that "it was said that if Becket did not submit, [the bishops of] Salisbury and Norwich would immediately be dragged off to execution, and they begged him to yield for their sake." Gervase of Canterbury says that Turbe absented himself from the council because he had heard what the king intended against Becket, Harper-Bill, "Bishop Turbe," 145. Robertson, *Materials for Becket*, ii, 331; i, 16.

23. According to Harper-Bill, "Turbe," 144, Henry excommunicated the earl, a powerful tenant-in-chief of the king, in response to an appeal from the Augustinian canons of Pentney when he settled their long-running dispute over land ownership. For details of the case, see Raymonde Foreville, *L'église et la royauté en Angleterre sous Henri II Plantagenet (1154–1189)* (Paris: Bloud et Gay, 1943), 206–207; Robertson, *Materials for Becket*, vii, 543–557; Morey and Brooke, *Letters of Gilbert Foliot*, VII, nos. 159, 160.

24. To escape the king's wrath, Becket had fled to France (in exile 1164–1170), as had one of Becket's chief opponents, Gilbert Foliot, the former abbot of St. Peter's, now the bishop of London (in exile 1170–1172).

25. Douglas and Greenaway, *English Historical Documents*, 803, no. 145; Anne Heslin, "The Coronation of the Young King," *Studies in Church History* 2 (1965), 165–178. Young Henry predeceased his father, so never ruled in his own right.

26. Only three bishops missed the coronation, one of whom was ill.

27. Heliot and Chastang, "Questes et voyages," 814.

28. Yarrow, *Saints and Their Communities*, 78ff, who points out that not all relic tours were successful, such as those of the monks who toured the relics of St. Eusebius around England.

29. *De pigneribus* 1, 97. A fresh translation of Book I of Guibert's work may be found in Thomas Head, *Medieval Hagiography: An Anthology* (New York: Garland, 2000), 399–428, with notes and introduction. For the English quotations that follow I have relied on translations by Jay Rubenstein, *Guibert, Portrait of a Medieval Mind*, 125 and Coulton, *Life in the Middle Ages*. For Guibert's critique, see also Morris, "A Critique of Popular Religion."

30. Thomas of Monmouth mentions the shoe in *Vita*, IV, viii, 113, and the teeth which he had squirreled away, *Vita*, IV, ix, 114. D. Bethell, "The Making of a Twelfth Century Relic Collection, in *Popular Belief and Practice*, ed. Cuming and Baker, 61–72 at 68, described Reading Abbey (Berkshire) as "very up-to-date in its collecting" because according to its cartulary it had relics of both William of Norwich (d. 1144) and Robert of Bury (d. 1181) before the end of the twelfth century. Julian Luxford, "St William of Norwich in Late Medieval Art," paper given at the conference on "Youth Violence and Cult" at Queen Mary College, University of London, on January 29, 2010, suggested that William of Norwich is mentioned in a late copy of a fragmentary relic list of Wimborne Minster, Dorset. See also Rubin, *Life and Passion*, 234–235 n.

31. For some details of the continental references, see Langmuir, *Toward a Definition*, 284ff. The name Janville is written in medieval Hebrew without vowels and could equally well read "Joinville," where there was a large and eminent Jewish community. Because the case was appealed to the king of France, however, it must be Janville [Yenville] in Eure-et-Loire and not Janville in Angevin Calvados, nor Joinville in the Haute-Marne, which was under the authority of the count of Champagne. See Henri Gross, *Gallia Judaica* (Paris: Librairie Léopold Cerf, 1897). Nothing else is known of the Jewish community of Janville. Some writers suggest that Joigny was meant.

32. The case in Loches was different, for it involved a frustrated suitor turning on the parent of his intended and threatening to turn him over to Christian authorities; see Yuval, *Two Nations*, 183–184.

33. On patterns of repeated violence, see David Nirenberg, *Communities of Violence: Persecution of Minorities in the Middle Ages* (Princeton, NJ: Princeton University Press, 1996).

34. The Blois case is not mentioned in most of the standard French histories, such as those by Hallam and Dunbabin, nor in Yves Sassier, *Louis VII* (Paris: Fayard, 1991). Thibaut V of Blois has never been the subject of much scholarly interest. Bernard Blumenkranz, "Les Juifs à Blois," is one of the few French authors who deals with the burnings; Jean-Paul Sauvage, "Le massacre des Juifs à Blois en 1171," *Mémoires de la Societé des Sciences et Lettres du Loire-et-Cher* 49 (1994), 5–22, summarizes the secondary works in English.

35. See the evocative treatment in Simon Schama, *The Story of the Jews: Finding the Words, 1000 bce–1492 ce* (London: Bodley Head. 2013), 292ff. For S. D. Gotein's 1927 theatrical treatment *Polcellina* and subsequent historiography, see Elliott Horowitz, "Dangerous Liaisons: Twentieth-Century Scholars and Medieval Relations between Jews and Christians," *Jewish Review of Books* 5, no. 1 (2014), 44–47.

36. The accusations and the burnings are recorded both in Latin (briefly) and in Hebrew, most notably in a number of liturgical commemorations for the burned Jews (poems and memorial lists), and in letters from the Jewish communities in Paris, Troyes, and Orléans to their co-religionists. Many of the texts alluding to the Blois burnings were first published in Adolf Neubauer and Morris Stern, *Hebräische Berichte über die Judenverfolgung während der Kreuzzüge* (Berlin: L. Simon, 1892; repr. New York: Olms, 1997), and A. M. Habermann, *The Persecutions of France and Germany* [Hebrew] (Jerusalem: Tarshish, 1945; repr. Ofir, 1971), 142–144. They are discussed, with an additional poem, in Shalom Spiegel, "*In Monte Dominus Videbitur*: The Martyrs of Blois and the Early Accusations of Ritual Murder" [Hebrew], in *The Mordecai M. Kaplan Jubilee Volume* (New York: Jewish Theological Seminary of America, 1953), Hebrew section, 267–287. Some of the letters and the later account by Ephraim of Bonn are translated into English in Jacob Marcus, *The Jew in the Medieval World: A Source Book, 315–1791* (Cincinnati, 1938; repr. Hebrew Union College Press, 1999), 127–130, and widely available online. Other translations of the letters appear in Chazan, *Church, State and Jew,* 114–117, 300–304, and in appendix 2 of Kenneth Stow, *Jewish Dogs: An Image and Its Interpreters: Continuity in the Catholic-Jewish Encounter* (Stanford, CA: Stanford University Press, 2006), who emphasizes (99, 111) that the letters were probably copied and heavily reworked in France, in Speyer, and in Treviso, where they survive in a unique manuscript from 1453. Susan L. Einbinder, *Beautiful Death: Jewish Poetry and Martyrdom in Medieval France* (Princeton, NJ: Princeton University Press, 2002), 65 n.2, has a full discussion of the extant sources and identifies additional memorial poems that refer to the burnings. Lists of the victims are published in Siegmund Salfeld, *Das Martyrologium des Nürnberger Memorbuches* (Berlin: L. Simion, 1898). For a linguistic analysis of the letters, see Kirsten Anne Fudeman, *Vernacular Voices: Language and Identity in Medieval French Jewish Communities* (Philadelphia: University of Pennsylvania Press, 2010), Chapter 2, 60–88.

37. In the early twelfth century the counties of Blois and Champagne were politically and economically powerful and of great strategic importance. Thibaut IV established the great round of Champagne fairs, and in so doing drew off business not only from surrounding areas, but also from Paris. See Elizabeth M. Hallam, *Capetian France, 987–1328* (London: Longman, 1980), 49.

38. Thibaut "the Great" (d. 1152) was Thibaut IV of Blois and Chartres, but Thibaut II of Champagne and Brie, which he had inherited from an uncle in 1125. His son, the subject of this chapter, was Thibaut V of Blois and Chartres (d. 1191 on the Third Crusade). Thibaut IV's brother Stephen of Blois became king of England (d. 1154); his grandson, the younger son of Henri I, was Thibaut III of Champagne (d. 1201 preparing for the Fourth Crusade).

39. Artists and writers, *jongleurs, troubadours,* and *trouvères* enjoyed the patronage of the court of Champagne, most notably Chrétien de Troyes, the author of Arthurian romances, Andreas Capellanus, the author of *De Amore* ("The Art of Courtly Love"), Nicholas of Clairvaux, and Gautier d'Arras. Henri's tastes were serious and traditional; Marie's were *avant-garde,* according to John F. Benton, "The Court of Champagne as a Literary Center," *Speculum* 36 (1961), 551–591. Countess Marie's responsibility for the cultural flowering attributed to her patronage is now open to question. See Karen M. Broadhurst, "Henry II of England and Eleanor of Aquitaine: Patrons of Literature in French?" *Viator* 27 (1996), 53–84. Marie has been credited not only with the flowering of Troyes, but with that of Poitiers as well. The statement of Amy Kelly, *Eleanor of Aquitaine and the Four Kings* (Cambridge, MA: Harvard University Press, 1974), 160, that Marie was *"maitresse d'école* for the royal academy in Poitiers" is not supported by the evidence, for which see Edmond-René Labande, "Les filles d'Alienor d'Aquitaine: étude comparative," *Cahiers de civilizations* (1986), 101–112 at 103.

40. For the sake of clarity and consistency, I use "Thibaut" and "Alix" here for the count and countess of Blois, and Alice for his sister, the queen of France by her marriage to Louis VII. Stow, *Jewish Dogs,* 99, confusingly refers to Thibaut V as "Theobald of Champagne," which is the usual designation for his father (Thibaut IV of Blois, II of Champagne), his nephew (Thibaut III of Champagne), and his great-nephew (Thibaut IV of Champagne, *le chansonnier*), but not the designation for Thibaut V of Blois, since he never lived in or ruled Champagne.

His wife, Alix, the countess of Blois, is also identified by historians as Aliz de France or Aliz Capet. Michel Bur, *La formation du comté de Champagne v. 950–v.1150, Mémoires des Annales de l'Est* (Nancy: l'Université de Nancy, 1977), 54, calls her "Eleanore;" Labande calls her "Aelis." This Alix (or Alice) of Blois also should not be confused with the sister of her husband, Adèle (or Alice) of Champagne, also known as Adèle of France after her marriage to the French king, and mother of the future Philip II. Nor should the countess of Blois be confused with another Aliz de France, her half-sister, the daughter of Louis VII and Constance of Castille, his third wife, who was affianced to Richard the Lionheart. See, for example, John T. Appleby, *Henry II: The Vanquished King* (London: G. Bell & Sons, 1962), who has one index entry covering both women; and John Baldwin, *The Government of Philip Augustus* (Berkeley: University of California Press, 1986), who inexplicably has separate entries in the index for Alix, the daughter of Eleanor and Louis, and Alix the countess of Blois (in addition to Alix, the daughter of Constance and Louis). Alix of Blois's sister, the countess Marie de Champagne, also known as Marie de France, should not be confused with the poet Marie de France who lived in England, nor with the countess's daughter, also called Marie de Champagne, who married Baldwin of Constantinople. I use Adela of Blois to refer to Thibaut V's grandmother, the daughter of William the Conqueror who became countess of Blois by marriage.

41. Theodore Evergates, "Blois" in *Medieval France: An Encyclopedia* (New York: Garland, 1998) is the exception: Champagne "became a major principality, while the counties of Blois-Chartres, shorn of their accretions, receded to second-tier

standing." Emily Taitz, *The Jews of Medieval France: The Community of Champagne* (Westport, CT: Greenwood Press, 1994), 2, operates on the assumption that the situation for Jews throughout present-day France was essentially the same and that Champagne can be used as a paradigm for other communities in France. Baldwin, *Philip Augustus*, 9, notes that the eastern lands of the counts were poorer and more sparsely populated, but strategically located.

42. R. W. Southern, "The School of Paris and the School of Chartres," in Robert L. Benson and Giles Constable, eds., *Renaissance and Renewal* (Oxford: Clarendon Press, 1982), 113–137 at 120–121, and Edouard Jeauneau, *Rethinking the School of Chartres* (Toronto: University of Toronto Press, 2009).

43. Not much is recorded about Blois during the twelfth century, either the fortress and walled town (the *ville*, residents of which are called *Blésois*), the countryside immediately surrounding it (the *faubourgs* and *banlieu*), or the small county (*pays*) to which it gave its name (whose residents are called *Blaisois*). The county was eventually sold to the royal family of France at the end of the thirteenth century. Only under the Renaissance king François I did Blois achieve importance.

44. It is described as "administratively backward" in *Medieval France: An Encyclopedia*, s.v. "Blois."

45. The architectural changes during the course of the construction of the church of St. Nicolas indicate that the Blois builders closely followed the progress of architectural developments in Paris and that they anticipated the flying buttresses of Notre Dame before 1170, but the grand plans were interrupted. Saint-Lomer was one of the earliest French churches to plan to incorporate flying buttresses, before the nave of the Cathedral of Notre-Dame of Paris, John James, "Evidence for Flying Buttresses before 1180," *Journal of the Society of Architectural Historians* 51 (1992), 261–287.

46. To date the couple can be identified only with partial patronage of two works, *Eracle* and *Ille* by Gautier d'Arras, and probably, but not definitively, with the patronage of the verse romance *Partonopeus of Blois*. The first composition that Thibaut commissioned was finished for someone else. Gautier d'Arras began the romance *Éracle*, a mythical life of the Byzantine emperor Heraclius, for Thibaut V and then continued it for Marie de Champagne. Composed sometime between 1164 and 1191, it was finished for Baudouin (Baldwin) of Hainaut. Frederick A. G. Cowper, "The New Manuscript of 'Ille et Galeron,'" *Modern Philology* 18 (1921), 601–608, finds it improbable that Gautier broke with Thibaut and Marie while working on *Éracle*, but then returned to Thibaut to finish the romance *Ille*. If Thibaut had been pressed for funds, however, and then came into a fortune, it would explain why he could not finish one commission (prior to 1171) and then could complete another work by the same author a decade or more later. For the text of Partonopeus, see Joseph Gildea, *Partonopeu de Blois,* 2 vols. (Philadelphia: Villanova University Press, 1967–1970), 2:2. A more recent edition with a full bibliography and reproduction of all the early manuscripts can be found online at Penny Eley and Penny Simons, eds., *Partonopeus de Blois: An Electronic Edition* (Sheffield: HriOnline,

2005), http://www.hrionline.ac.uk/partonopeus/ and the first monograph on it, Penney Eley, *Partonopeus de Blois: Romance in the Making* (Woodbridge, Suffolk: Boydell and Brewer, 2011), who notes, 205, that the language of the poem alludes to financial favors the countess can award or withhold.

The composition of *Partonopeus* likely dates from the late 1180s, and the long and convoluted Byzantine romance perfectly reflected contemporary tastes. *Partonopeus* was soon translated into German, Norse, Dutch, Danish, Spanish, Catalan, English, and Italian. There are close affinities with the Arthurian stories of Chretien de Troyes, for which see Peter S. Noble, '*Partonopeu de Blois* and Chrétien de Troyes,' in Rupert T. Pickens, ed., *Studies in Honor of Hans-Erich Keller: Medieval French and Occitan Literature and Romance Linguistics* (Kalamazoo: Medieval Institute Publications, Western Michigan University, 1993), 195–211.

Much has been written on the lavish patronage of the House of Blois-Champagne. For a sense of the excellent taste and lavish purchases and commissions of Thibaut V's uncle Henry (d. 1171), see most recently Jeffrey West, "A Taste for the Antique? Henry of Blois and the Arts," *Anglo-Norman Studies* 30 (2008), 213–230.

47. Adela of Blois made generous donations to the monks of Saint-Lomer and arranged for a weekly sung mass and an annual celebration worthy of an abbot on the anniversary of her death. For the context of Adela's connections to Saint-Lomer, see Kimberly LoPrete, "Adela of Blois and Ivo of Chartres: Piety, Politics and the Peace in the Diocese of Chartres," *Anglo-Norman Studies* 14 (1991), 131–152. Her two sons confirmed her grant, and Count Thibaut IV laid the foundation for the abbey church of Saint-Lomer (known as the Church of Saint-Nicholas) in 1138, after a fire of 1114. Bibliothèque Nationale de France, MS lat. 7297, fol. 102v, cited by F. Lesueur, *Les églises de Loir-et-Cher* (Paris: Editions A. et J. Picard, 1969), 55. Count Thibaut V likewise confirmed his grandmother's grants in 1169 and made further donations to the monks for the soul of his father, LoPrete, *Adela of Blois* (Dublin: Four Courts Press, 2007), 477. There were three distinct building campaigns in the twelfth and early thirteenth centuries, for a discussion of which see F. Lesueur, "L'église et l'abbaye bénédictine de St.-Lomer de Blois," *Memoires de la Société des Sciences et Lettres de Loir-et-Cher* 25 (1924), 59–155. The first phase was finished before 1186, the second phase, which comprised the choir, transept, and the first row of columns in the nave, was started at the end of the twelfth century. The third phase, of the early thirteenth century, completed the medieval church.

48. The epic *Partonopeu of Blois* remained influential but did not bear the name of its patrons. The enchantingly light vaults of the abbey church of Saint-Lomer were believed to have been created by fairies; the lantern at the top of the nave was strikingly innovative, described by visitors as late as the eighteenth century as "a minor wonder of the world," but now is scarcely known. See *St. Nicolas, Abbey of Saint Laumer, Blois*, n.p., n.d., brochure available at the church, 2008.

49. By the middle of the twelfth century, one no longer hears of leaders comparable to the educated abbot Maurice of Saint-Lomer or the noted poet and diplomat

Peter of Blois (ca. 1135–ca. 1203), who moved on to Paris and Bologna and made his career in England.

50. In the song *Ja nus hons pris*, Richard concludes his complaint about the slowness in collecting the ransom (which was eventually to equal almost three times the annual income of the English state) with the declaration to Marie, "Sister countess, may He to whom I appeal, and through whom I am made prisoner, save you and your sovereign worth, I do not speak of Chartres' dame, the mother of Louis" ("Contesse suer, vostre pris soverain Vos saut et gart cil a cui je m'en clain—Et por cui je sui pris. Je ne di mie a cele de Chartain—La mere Loës"). These lines are considered obscure and are therefore often left out of modern translations, but they make clear Richard's disdain for the countess, most likely at the instigation of their mother Eleanor of Aquitaine, who regularly sent her favorite son lists of the donors who had contributed to his ransom. Alix, the mother of Louis, count of Blois, was also the called the countess of Chartres (just as her sister Marie, the countess of Champagne, was sometimes called countess of Brie for poetic reasons).

51. Thomas N. Bisson, *Conservation of Coinage, Monetary Exploitation and Its Restraint in France, Catalonia, and Aragon (c. a.d. 1000–c. 1225)* (Oxford: Clarendon Press, 1979), 230ff.

52. This inscription at Pont Saint-Fiacre was destroyed before the Revolution, most likely around 1716. The Latin is recorded in Bernier, *Histoire de Blois* (Paris: Chez François Muguet, 1682), 301, who reproduced a drawing of it. The exact meaning of some of the rights it mentions is still unclear. The publicly inscribed promise did not stop the rulers of Blois from manipulating the coins and pressuring the minters. In the next generation, the countess of Blois, the widow of Alix and Thibaut's son Louis, in 1211 once again promised to restore the many taxes she had claimed and to return the boutiques and stalls she had seized unjustly from the moneychangers.

53. This is one of the first uses of the term *cornagium* and suggests that the Blois rulers were in the forefront of monetizing the privileges they claimed.

54. Taitz, *Jews of Medieval France*.

55. Blumenkranz, *Les juifs à Blois*, 37, estimates there may have been a community of between 105 and 140 in 1170. Scholars either cite that number or rely on Ephraim of Bonn, who mentioned four *minyanim* (congregations of ten adult men), so that the adult population of Blois is also calculated at forty, of which thirty-two or thirty-three were burned. See, for example, Susan L. Einbinder, "The Jewish Martyrs of Blois," in *Medieval Hagiography*, ed. Head, 537–561 at 555 n.13.

56. Communal leaders from Blois and Chartres are not recorded at the mid-century rabbinical synods held at Troyes. A number of the martyrs of Blois are identified in the memorial poetry as scholars, but their writings have not survived, and they are not cited by later scholars. There is no evidence, for example, that the scholar Samuel ben Meir ("Rashbam"), Rashi's grandson, died at Blois, as suggested by the *Jewish Encyclopedia*. Jewish cultural and intellectual

leadership came from the famous academies (*yeshivot*) in Champagne and the Rhineland, not the Jewish communities of Blois, Le Mans, and Tours, which were among the oldest in western Europe. The tendency to lump together the Jews of French lands (*Tzarfat*) without differentiation is manifest in Taitz, *Jews of Medieval France*, whose interpretation is evident from her subtitle "The County of Champagne." Jordan, *French Monarchy*, 5, is more judicious: "The Jewish population of France was concentrated largely to the east and south, far distant from the limits of the royal domain, in areas that few if any contemporary northerners would have called France."

57. A "captio" could refer to the seizure of Jewish debts, or the seizure and sudden mass imprisonment of Jews themselves, which would then obligate them to pay a penalty for their freedom.

58. Ephraim of Bonn in Marcus, *Jew in the Medieval World*, 128.

59. This cleric is described as a priest (Marcus), an Augustinian canon (Chazan, Einbinder), or a friar. Stow, *Dogs*, 103, says he was a "clergyman (of indeterminate, probably low, rank) from the Gastinais, or Gatinais, near Orléans and Blois." In 1215 the Fourth Lateran Council forbade priestly cooperation in trials by fire or water.

60. For the importance of the ordeal, see Robert Bartlett, *Trial by Fire and Water: The Medieval Judicial Ordeal* (Oxford: Oxford University Press, 1986), and Hyams, "Trial by Ordeal." Jews had traditionally been exempt from the ordeal, as in the Norwich case. The proof of veracity in the water ordeal was that the person undergoing it sank; in Blois, however, he floated but was judged truthful nonetheless. Since the determination of "sinking" or "floating" was a judgment of the community, it might appear that the community sided with the Jews of Blois in this case, and the count overrode the wishes of those present.

61. Einbinder, *Beautiful Death*, explains that the confusion over the outcome over the ordeal reflects the Jewish author's ignorance of how it worked. Cf. Stow, *Dogs*, 102–103.

62. Chazan, "Blois Incident."

63. Well into the second half of the seventeenth century, throughout Poland the Blois martyrs were recalled by Jews who undertook this annual fast. The date thus remained important in the communal memory for centuries, long after details of the events of Blois were forgotten.

64. Susan Einbinder, *Beautiful Death*, discusses their literary qualities; Fudeman analyzes the language of the prose letters.

65. Ephraim of Bonn in Marcus, *Jew in the Medieval World*, 143.

66. Susan L. Einbinder, "Pulcellina of Blois: Romantic Myths and Narrative Conventions," *Jewish History* 12, no. 1 (1998), 29–46, proposed the moneylender scenario and describes the relationship in *Beautiful Death*, 47. Shmuel Shepkaru, *Jewish Martyrs in the Pagan and Christian World* (Cambridge: Cambridge University Press, 2005), 225, refers to a "torrid affair."

67. Einbinder, "Pulcellina of Blois"; see also Einbinder, "Jewish Martyrs of Blois."

68. For some English examples of female Jewish moneylenders in the thirteenth century, see Reva Berman Brown and Sean McCartney, "The Business Activities of Jewish Women Entrepreneurs in Medieval England," *Management Decision* 39, no. 9 (2001), 699–709.

69. Assuming that Pulcellina was Thibaut's lover and not merely his creditor, their relationship would have been notorious. Intercourse between Christians and Jews was scandalous. The documented concern of the Church on such relationships dated back to the Council of Elvira in the early fourth century. "The taboos on sexual relations between Christians and Jews were strongly reinforced by secular laws that authorized harsh penalties for anyone audacious enough to violate the ban. The sanctions ranged from fines to confiscation of property and castration to death by burning," James A. Brundage, "Intermarriage Between Christians and Jews in Medieval Canon Law," *Jewish History* 3 (1988), 30. "Some authorities equated sexual relations between a Christian and a Jew with sodomy or bestiality," Trachtenberg, *Devil and the Jews*, 187. Sodomites were subject to burning since 1120, following the laws of Justinian.

70. Ephraim of Bonn in Marcus, *Jew in the Medieval World*, 143.

71. Thibaut V held his land from his brother the count of Champagne, who in turn held his land from the king; Thibaut's leading vassals would not have looked forward to being ruled either from Troyes or Paris. Over the next century, Blois, Chartres, Sancerre, and finally Champagne fell into the hands of the Capetian kings, either through marriage and inheritance or through the failure to produce a male heir.

72. The quotation is from the Paris letter in Chazan, *Church, State and Jew*, 115; cf. Stow, *Dogs*, 199. Philip, the son of Louis VII's third wife Adèle, Thibaut V's sister, was born in 1165 and called "godgiven" (*dieudonné*).

73. Alix and Thibaut's son Louis, daughter Marguerite, and younger siblings are documented in a donation charter of their parents dated 1183. The charter of 1183 is printed in Basile Fleureau, "De la maladerie Saint-Lazare d'Estampes," *Les antiquitez de la ville et du duché d'Estampes* (1668) (Paris: Coignard, 1683), ii.21: 451–462. On the basis of the date of her marriage, it is assumed that Marguerite was born in 1170 and Louis around 1172, although their birth years are uncertain. The charter indicates, therefore, that there was no male heir when the Blois burnings occurred in 1171. A better-known donation charter of 1883 is printed in A. de Belfort, *Archives de la maison-dieu de Châteaudun* (Paris: Société française de numismatique et d'archéologie, 1881), no. 25, 20, which indicates that Louis was not the oldest son. This charter lists the children Thibaut (*Theobaldus*), Louis (*Ludovicus*), Marguerite, and younger siblings. A grant dated 1189/1190?, no. 32, 24 mentions only Louis and the younger siblings. See also L. Merlet and L. Jarry, eds, *Cartulaire de l'abbaye de la Madeleine de Châteaudun* (Châteaudun: Pouillier, 1896), no. 36, 41, for another grant of 1190 mentioning the same children. It is generally assumed, therefore, that there was an eldest son, Thibaut, who must have been born before 1170. Since only Louis and the younger

offspring are mentioned in the charters of 1190, scholars assume that Thibaut died in the interim, most likely before the dedication of the church at Blois in 1186. Nothing else is known of the younger Thibaut, and he may have been sickly, or he may be simply a slip of the editor's pen, mistakenly recopying his father's name. Other charters mention younger sons Jacques (*Jacobus*) or Henri (*Henricus*), who may also have died in infancy.

74. There is no evidence of "inflammatory preaching" for which see Chazan, *Church, State and Jew*, 301.

75. Bisson, *Coinage*, 129: "The concession was advisedly addressed to men of the *patria*, by which, however, something less than the whole county was probably intended," possibly those within the jurisdiction of the *banlieu*.

76. These would include men who appear in Thibaut's charters with such names and titles as Lambert the chamberlain (*cubicularius*), Fulco the chamberlain (*cammerarius*), Gilbert the shoemaker (*cordubanarius*), Nicholas de Belvaco, the notary (*notarius*), Humfrey the cook (*coquus*), Huldric the chancellor (*cancellarius*), Espechardus the provost (*praepositus Blesensis*), Reginald the chaplain, (*capellanus*), Herbert, and later Reginald Crispin the marshall (*marescallus*). Most noteworthy among these is Reginald of Milly (*de Milliaco*), who attested to documents both for Thibaut V, the count of Blois, and his brother Henri, the count of Champagne, after he was officially manumitted. Robert's son became a noble and the count of Blois's chamberlain.

77. For the role of the nutricius and the magister in the education of elite children, see Kathryn Dutton, "'Ad erudiendum tradidit': The Upbringing of Angevin Comital Children," *Anglo-Norman Studies* 32 (2010), 24–39.

78. Alix's guardian from infancy must have been the most important person in her life, for she moved to Blois to be raised in the county of her future spouse on her engagement at the age of two. There is no direct evidence that once she moved to Blois, Alix ever saw her mother, Eleanor of Aquitaine, again. Einbinder, *Beautiful Death*, 47, suggests that the governess accompanied Alix from royal France. It is more likely that Alix's guardian was a lady of the local Blois aristocracy who raised and instructed her once she arrived in her husband's lands. Louis and Eleanor took great pains over the guardians chosen for their daughters, and they were all well educated. Alix's sister Marie was raised by the abbess of Avenay, the influential Alice of Mareuil; Louis's younger daughter by Constance of Castile, Marguerite, was raised by Robert of Newburgh, "a man of unimpeachable character and piety," for which see Regine Pernoud, *Eleanor of Aquitaine*, trans. Peter Wiles (London: Collins, 1967), 123–124. Queen Eleanor's younger daughters were raised at the abbey of Fontevrault.

79. Einbinder, "Pulcellina of Blois," 35.

80. Wary of local pressures to accommodate aristocratic women in the late twelfth century, ecclesiastical authorities forbade convents from expanding to accept more women than they could support. Heloise's convent of the Paraclete in Champagne faced financial hardship, for example, as did Marie's convent at Avenay. These two were in a county far more prosperous than Blois-Chartres and

endowed by wealthy and famous patrons. Alix's home likely faced similar financial hardship at a time when, unlike Marie and Heloise, neither she nor her husband was able to help.

81. The Orléans letter, in Chazan, *Church, State and Jew*, 303–304; cf. Ephraim of Bonn in Marcus, *Jew in the Medieval World*, 143–144.

82. The letter of Nathan ben Meshullam in Chazan, *Church, State and Jew*, 117. For the second letter from Paris concerning Thibaut's brothers, cf. Stow, *Dogs*, 202.

83. Ephraim of Bonn in Marcus, *Jew in the Medieval World*, 129. Einbinder, "Jewish Martyrs of Blois," 541, remarks that "the Jews made an absurdly low offer." The Orléans letter says the Jewish negotiators offered 100 pounds from the imprisoned Jews, and an additional 180 pounds on their own behalf.

84. *Vita*, I, viii, 22, promising the sheriff 100 marks, II, x, 60, offering ten marks to William's brother Robert and II, x, 61 offering the bishop "a great deal of money." Brother Thomas adds, II, xiv, 70, that "if we are to believe common rumour, by giving money to very corrupt royal advisors, they met the king himself and—as they say—having given him a large sum of money, just managed to extort a pardon from him."

85. Even though Jews raised the 23,000 silver marks to free him, Meir of Rothenburg remained imprisoned for seven years because he would not allow it to be paid. Seven years after his death in 1293, his body was ransomed by an admirer, who was buried near him. See also Einbinder, *Beautiful Death*, 71ff.

86. The Troyes letter says even though Count Henri did not believe the charge, "we gave money to quash the accusation." The letter of Nathan b. Rabbi Meshullam says yesterday I paid the bishop of Sens "a bribe of 120 pounds with a promise of 100 pounds for the count, for which I had already given guarantees," see Chazan, *Church State and Jew*, 117.

87. Stow, *Dogs*, 111, argues that "[p]olitical reality, moreover, dictated that Louis VII ally himself with Theobald, who was also his son-in-law, . . . not defame him." On the contrary, the twelfth-century Capetian kings were often at odds with their leading vassals, with whom they were also simultaneously negotiating marriage treaties. Indeed, it has been suggested that it was opposition to the king that brought the house of Blois-Champagne together, most notably in the spring of 1181, for which see Chapter 8.

88. The seneschal was nominally head of the royal household and head of the army, but the position was not filled when Thibaut died.

89. He surrendered both to become archbishop of Rheims in 1176. John R. Williams, "William of the White Hands and Men of Letters," in *Anniversary Essays in Mediaeval History by Students of Charles Homer Haskins*, ed. Charles Taylor (Boston: Houghton Mifflin Co., 1929), 365–388 at 366.

90. In the end Count Étienne did not marry Sibylla (it is not known what happened), and he returned to France. He headed back to the Holy Land with his brother Thibaut V and his nephew Hugh III of Burgundy on the Third Crusade. The three crusaders died there within months of each other in 1191.

91. In charters from the time of the burnings, Thibaut styles himself "by the grace of God count of Blois and royal seneschal." A. de Belfort, *Maison-Dieu de Châteaudun* 10 (1164), repr. in Joseph Thillier and Eugene Jarry, eds., *Cartulaire de Sainte-Croix D'orléans (814–1300)* (Paris: Picard, 1906), no. 58, 10–112, and no. 22 (1173), 17. Daniel Power, *The Norman Frontier in the Twelfth and Early Thirteenth Centuries* (Cambridge: Cambridge University Press, 2004), 217, notes that the attribution of their title to divine favor was a common way for counts (*comites*) to raise their status. Among those who employed this tactic he lists the counts of Meulan, Clermont, Soissons, Mortain, Evreux, Eu, Aumale, Warenne, Dreux, Ponthieu, Perche, and the earls of Richmond. The count of Blois should be included in this group. But Thibaut soon abandoned his claim to his position by "the grace of God."

92. Dunbabin, *France in the Making*, 378.

93. Dunbabin, *France in the Making*, 374.

94. The *Grandes chroniques de France*, the illuminated vernacular history of the French kings that represents the royal ideology, depicts many burnings, including ones where Louis IX, Saint Louis, is calmly present, presiding over the fire. Copies of this luxury manuscript demonstrated how killing should be done, not secretly and with blood, as allegedly the Jews had done, but proudly, publicly, and unhurriedly.

95. Unlike his cousin King Louis and his brother Henri of Champagne, Thibaut V had not gone on the Second Crusade; instead he remained at home with his aging father. His failure to participate in the enterprise must still have rankled in the 1160s, by which time bitter memories of the crusade had faded, and King Louis was heralded for his piety and moral suasion.

96. For a sense of the obligation the descendants of twelfth-century crusaders felt, see Nicholas Paul, *To Follow in Their Footsteps: The Crusades and Family Memory in the High Middle Ages* (Ithaca, NY: Cornell University Press, 2013). For the celebration of crusading heritage in other twelfth-century families, see Chapter 2 above; and Marcus Bull, "The Capetian Monarchy and the Early Crusade Movement: Hugh of Vermandois and Louis VII," *Nottingham Mediaeval Studies* 40 (1996), 25–46. The importance of the family crusading tradition in the House of Blois is reflected in their history: Thibaut V would die on the Third Crusade in 1191, along with his brother Étienne, count of Sancerre, their nephew Hugh III of Burgundy, and Raoul of Clermont, the father-in-law of Thibaut's son. Thibaut V's son and heir, Louis, one of the organizers of the Fourth Crusade, died of disease at Adrianople, and his younger brother, Philippe (d. 1202), is said to have died on crusade as well. Louis's son Thibaut VI fought on the Albigensian Crusade and fought Muslims on the Iberian Peninsula. The brother of Thibaut V of Blois, Henri I of Champagne, had fought on the Second Crusade and died shortly after returning from a later expedition to the Holy Land. His son Henri II of Champagne joined the Third Crusade and remained in the Holy Land on his marriage to Isabella, queen of Jerusalem. His brother and heir, Thibaut (III of Champagne) had been elected to lead the Fourth Crusade when he died in 1201, and his son and heir, Thibaut IV

of Champagne "the troubador," led the Barons' Crusade of 1239. For recent scholarship focusing on a slightly later period, see the special issue of the *Journal of
Medieval History* 40.3 (2014) on Crusades and Memory.

97. Alexander's presentation to Louis was one of the earliest recorded gifts of
the golden rose that later became a tradition through which popes recognized especially pious sovereigns.

98. Michael D. Barbezat, "The Fires of Hell and the Burning of Heretics in the
Accounts of the Executions at Orleans in 1022," *Journal of Medieval History* 40, no. 4
(2014), 399–420 emphasizes the novelty and importance of the execution by fire
"for those who failed to take their place within a united Christian society." What he
writes about the authorities handing the eleventh-century victims to their destiny
in the fires of hell is applicable to the twelfth-century Blois victims as well.

99. Eleven of the twelve dioceses of Rheims sent bishops, along with the archbishop and three of the eight dioceses of Sens. See Michael Lower, "The Burning
at Mont-Aimé: Thibaut of Champagne's Preparations for the Barons' Crusade of
1239," *Journal of Medieval History* 29 (2003), 95–108.

100. Alberic de Trois-Fontaines, quoted in Lower, "The Burning," 104.

101. Theodore Evergates, ed. *Feudal Society in Medieval France, Documents from
the County of Champagne* (Philadelphia: University of Pennsylvania Press, 1993),
no. 100, 130.

102. Chazan, for example, in his useful sourcebook *Church, State and Jew*, places
the source documents under the headings "governmental protection" and "governmental attacks," thereby emphasizing the political aspects of the events.

103. Chazan, "Blois Incident," argues that the coordinated efforts of various
Jewish communities under the leadership of Rabbi Jacob Tam were strikingly new.

104. R. I. Moore, who has linked the persecution of heretics, lepers, and Jews,
misses this important connection between heretics and Jews when he mistakenly
says that the count of Blois hanged the Jews in 1171 (*Persecuting Society*, 35).

105. Paula Fredriksen, "*Excaecati occulta iustitia Dei*: Augustine on Jews
and Judaism," *Journal of Early Christian Studies* 3 (1995), 299–324, and Paula
Fredriksen, *Augustine and the Jews: A Christian Defense of Jews and Judaism* (New
York: Doubleday, 2008).

106. Thomas Head, "Saints, Heretics, and Fire: Finding Meaning Through the
Ordeal," in Barbara Rosenwein and Sharon Farmer, eds., *Monks and Nuns, Saints
and Outcasts: Religious Expression and Social Meaning in the Middle Ages* (Ithaca,
NY: Cornell University Press, 2000), 220–238 at 235, makes the connection
between the two ritual uses of fire, and informs my understanding of these events.

107. The names and brief details of the victims are recorded in two books of
remembrance (*Memorbucher*) compiled by the Jewish community.

108. See, for example, the characterization of Peter the Venerable in Iogna-Prat,
Order and Exclusion, 279. See more generally Jeremy Cohen, *Christ Killers: The
Jews and the Passion from the Bible to the Big Screen* (New York: Oxford University

Press, 2007), especially 202ff for the artistic representation of late medieval ritual murder as a contemporary crucifixion.

109. The Tosafist acceptance and even celebration of martyrdom, *Kiddush ha-Shem*, stands in contrast to that of other commentators. Maimonides, for example, considered martyrdom suicide. The issue of Jewish martyrdom in this period, once taken for granted, is now subject to renewed scrutiny. See, for example, Mary Minty, "Kiddush Ha-Shem" and Simha Goldin, "The Socialization for Kiddush Ha-Shem among Medieval Jews," *Journal of Medieval History* 23 (1997), 117–138. For the development of the theme of the "fireproof martyr," see Einbinder, *Beautiful Death*, Chapter 2.

110. The *Ordo* derives from a sermon believed to have been composed by Augustine's student Quodvultdeus, a fifth-century bishop of Carthage: *Sermo contra judaeos, paganos et arianos de Symbolo, Patrologia Latina* 42:1117; E. N. Stone, *A Translation of Chapters xi–xvi of the Pseudo-Augustinian Sermon Against Jews, Pagans, and Arians, Concerning the Creed; Also of the Ordo Prophetarum of St. Martial of Limoges* (Seattle: University of Washington Press, 1928).

111. Dunbar H. Ogden, *The Staging of Drama in the Medieval Church* (Newark: University of Delaware Press, 2003), 111. The scene is documented by the fourteenth century in Rouen.

112. Resnick, *Peter the Venerable, Obduracy*, 49ff; Iogna-Prat, *Order and Exclusion*, 285, and the works cited there.

113. Regula Meyer Evitt, "Undoing the Dramatic History of the Riga Ludus Prophetarum," *Comparative Drama* 25 (1990/91), 242–256 at 250, argues that on this occasion the conversion of the Jews became a metaphor for the conversion of the heathens.

114. This comedic trope became a prime element in the Feast of Fools (*festum asinorum*), staged in France on January 1, the date of the Feast of the Circumcision, which was especially popular in twelfth-century France, where bishops inveighed against the lords of misrule. For the clerical attempt to rein in the excesses of the twelfth-century Feast of Fools celebrated by the subdeacons, see Margot Fassler, "The Feast of Fools and Danielis Ludus: Popular Tradition in a Medieval Cathedral Play," in *Plainsong in the Age of Polyphony*, ed. Thomas Forrest Kelly (Cambridge: Cambridge University Press, 1992), 65–99, especially 73ff, where she points out that Richard of Saint-Victor was already complaining by mid-century of the traditional New Year's celebrations in Paris. For the later history, see now Max Harris, *Sacred Folly: A New History of the Feast of Fools* (Ithaca, NY: Cornell University Press, 2011).

115. The story of the Jewish Boy of Bourges has received extensive treatment. Among the forty medieval versions of the story that survive are those preserved in Greek, Latin, Old French, German, Spanish, Arabic, and Ethiopian. See Lazar, "Lamb and the Scapegoat," 57. For a recent bibliography and discography of recordings of the poem, see *The Oxford Cantigas de Santa Maria Database: Jew of Bourges* (http://csm.mml.ox.ac.uk) with a long list of manuscripts in which the story and image appear. For dissemination, see J. C. Jennings, "The Origins of the 'Elements

Series' of the Miracles of the Virgin," *Medieval and Renaissance Studies* 6 (1968), 84–93. See also Rubin, *Gentile Tales*, Chapter 2, which discusses the spread of the story and its importance as a prelude to the host desecration accusation of the thirteenth century. Joan Young Gregg, *Devils, Women, and Jews: Reflections of the Other in Medieval Sermon Stories* (Albany: State University of New York Press, 1997), confusingly explains that the Jew of Bourges is a variant of Chaucer's Prioress's Tale. William F. MacLehose, *"A Tender Age": Cultural Anxieties over the Child in the Twelfth and Thirteenth Centuries* (New York: Columbia University Press, 2006), 139ff briefly discusses the two tales and places them in the context of medieval attitudes toward children.

116. The story of the Jewish Boy of Bourges was included in the Miracles of Gregory of Tours in sixth-century France and was widely circulated throughout Europe. In Gregory's version the comparison with the boys of the Book of Daniel is made explicit: "But that mercy, which of old sprinkled with a dewy cloud the three Hebrew children in the furnace of Babylon, was not wanting on this occasion. For the same mercy did not suffer this boy to be consumed. . . ." Although the earliest surviving vernacular text dates from the second half of the twelfth century, the story was well known outside monastic circles much earlier. Bishop Herbert of Losinga of Norwich included it as an anecdote (*exemplum*) in his sermon on Christmas; it was often reproduced in art and was included in the earliest collections of Latin Marian miracles that began to circulate in the twelfth century. See Heinz Schreckenberg, *The Jews in Christian Art: An Illustrated History* (New York: Continuum, 1996), 255ff.

117. Yuval, *Two Nations in Your Womb*, Chapter 4, discusses the Blois burnings, and at 195, the context of mockery of Mary as a Jewish response to the growth of her cult in the twelfth century in northern France.

118. Goulbourn and Symonds, *Losinga*, 30–33; Losinga's sources are discussed in the Appendix, 433–437.

119. Objecting to Rubin's persuasive argument that the story of the Jewish Boy is closely related to fantasies of ritual murder and host desecration, Peter Schäfer, *Mirror of His Beauty: Feminine Images of God from the Bible to the Early Kabbalah* (Princeton NJ: Princeton University Press, 2002), 206, does "not believe that the stereotype of the Jewish threat plays a prominent role" in the fantasies the story invoked.

120. For the scriptural analogue, see Charles W. Jones, *The Saint Nicholas Liturgy and Its Literary Relationships (Ninth to Twelfth Centuries)* (Berkeley: University of California Press, 1963), 110.

121. An alternative version, in which the innkeeper planned to pickle them in a barrel or pickling tub, is a late variation.

122. Depictions of the story appear in the windows of York Minster and Rouen Cathedral. The two earliest depictions of the *Tres Clerici* occur on the baptismal fonts of Winchester and Zedelghe. See Otto Albrecht, *Four Plays of St. Nicholas from the Twelfth-Century Fleury Playbook. Text and Commentary* (Philadelphia: University

of Pennsylvania Press, 1935), 41. Although the three young men are sometimes assumed to be sailors, in medieval art they are represented as tonsured clerks.

123. One wonders whether the condemned Yehiel b. David ha-Cohen was the younger brother of Baruch b. David ha-Cohen, the representative who negotiated on behalf of the Blois survivors. It is curious that the authorities focused their punishment on the younger man and not on the elder leader of the community.

124. For the cult of St. Nicholas in the region, see Clyde W. Brockett, "Persona in Cantilena: St. Nicholas in Music in Medieval Drama," in *The Saint Play in Medieval Europe*, ed. Clifford Davidson (Kalamazoo: Medieval Institute Publications EDAM, 1986), 11–30 at 23ff.

125. The playbook text is pages 176–243 of the miscellany MS 201 of the Municipal Library of Orléans. The manuscript was discovered at the Benedictine monastery of Saint-Benoît-sur-Loire, Fleury, in the vicinity of Orléans, a city less than thirty miles from Blois, and is often called the Fleury Playbook, but the attribution is still fiercely debated. See Wyndham Thomas, "The Cultural Context of the Fleury Playbook: Liturgy and Drama in a Corner of Twelfth Century France," *Proceedings of the Bath Royal Literary and Scientific Institution* 9 (2005). Fleury has been favored because of its well-known intellectual prominence, but there is no positive evidence that the plays were ever performed there, and the musical notes (*neums*) are not characteristic of the monastery. See Ogden, *Staging of Drama*, 84.

126. Fleury, Angers, and Blois are among the locations proposed for the composition of the Playbook. V. A. Kolve, "Ganymede/Son of Getron: Medieval Monasticism and the Drama of Same-Sex Desire," *Speculum* 73 (1998), 1014–1067 at 1029 n. 40, opts for Fleury, following Fletcher Collins, Jr., "The Home of the Fleury Playbook," in *The Fleury Playbook: Essays and Studies*, ed. C. Clifford Flanigan, Thomas P. Campbell, and Clifford Davidson (Kalamazoo: Medieval Institute Publications, 1985), 26–34. They are not persuaded by Corbin's claims for Blois, Solange Corbin, "Le Manuscrit 201 d'Orléans: Drames liturgiques dits de Fleury," *Romania* 74 (1953), 1–43. Lee Patterson, "'The Living Witnesses of Our Redemption': Martyrdom and Imitation in Chaucer's Prioress's Tale," *Journal of Medieval and Early Modern Studies* 31 (2001), 507–560 at 531, considers Blois but argues for the cathedral school of Orléans as the place of composition. Susan Boynton, "Performative Exegesis in the Fleury Interfectio Puerorum," *Viator* 29 (1998), 39–64 at n. 6, discusses attribution without specifying a precise place of origin in central or northern France, as does Theresa Tinkle, "Jews in the Fleury Playbook," *Comparative Drama* 38 (2004), 1–38 at n. 8.

127. Corbin, "Le Manuscrit 201 d'Orléans."

128. Grace Frank, *The Medieval French Drama* (Oxford: Clarendon Press, 1954), 44, characterized Saint-Lomer as "relatively obscure."

129. Fassler, "Feast of Fools," 95.

130. By way of contrast, Einbinder argues that the memorialization of the Blois burnings in Jewish literature was intended for an elite audience of scholars.

131. The image had a role in the play, originally as a static backdrop (perhaps a church wall), and later as a sculpted figure that comes to life (represented by an actor). See Brockett, "Persona in Cantilena," 18ff. Of all the St. Nicholas plays, *Iconia* has received much scholarly attention, especially in the context of Christian-Jewish relations.

132. C. Samaran, "Fragments de manuscrits Latins et Français du Moyen Age," *Romania* 51 (1925), 161–202 at 192.

133. The Orléans letter, in Chazan, *Church, State and Jew*, 304.

134. The Troyes letter notes that Nathan ben Meshullam offered a bribe of 220 pounds to the count for the right to bury the Jewish dead.

135. Kolve, "Ganymede/Son of Getron," 1065, alluding to the work of Steven Kruger, who writes of the stigmatizing of homosexuals, or those expressing same-sex desire, in the person of the exotic ruler.

136. See Frank, *Medieval French Drama*, 50, and Kolve, "Ganymede/Son of Getron," 1059.

137. Lesueur, "Saint-Lomer," 65.

138. Lesueur, "Saint-Lomer," 65, notes the inclusion of *Ludovicus, filius noster* in the account of the dedication.

139. Marcus, *Rituals of Childhood*, identified and described the rite discussed in this paragraph.

140. Marcus, *Rituals of Childhood*, 84.

141. St. Nicholas's feast was traditionally celebrated on December 6, but once Normans carried off the famous relics to Bari in 1087, many Norman communities celebrated the translation on May 9, a feast promulgated by Pope Urban II that superseded the December observance. See Jones, *Saint Nicholas Liturgy*, 5.

142. Corbin, "Le Manuscrit 201 d'Orléans," 33.

143. Some scholars, such as Einbinder, have assumed this to be a reference to Maundy Thursday of Easter week, which is unlikely. See also Yuval, *Two Nations*, 191, and following note.

144. Yuval, *Two Nations*, 191, assumes that the accusation (which he calls "the act") occurred on the eve of Easter and that the sentence was carried out later: "During these two months a trial was conducted against the Jews of Blois and the prosecution clearly did all it could to prove the accusation made against the Jews." He is probably correct about tying the charge to Easter, but as I argue in this chapter, it is doubtful that there was a formal courtroom trial or that the prosecution went to much effort: the ordeal was sufficient proof, and its outcome was not in doubt.

145. A crusade had been planned as part of the reconciliation between Henry II and his archbishop, Thomas Becket, but failed to materialize after Becket's murder in the preceding December. Nonetheless, some of those involved proceeded with their plans: Henry the Lion, duke of Savoy, the new husband of Henry II's daughter Matilda, went to Constantinople and Jerusalem with a large retinue, said to number more than a thousand.

146. Robert Potter, "The *Auto da Fé* as Medieval Drama," in *Festive Drama*, ed. Meg Twycross (Cambridge: D. S. Brewer, 1996), 110–118.

147. Bisson, *Coinage,* 129, discussing the privilege of 1196 as modeled on a conjectured ceremony for the earlier privilege.

148. To judge from the men regularly attending the count and countess of Champagne, about one-third of the court was composed of clerics, mostly canons; a courtly audience would have included a large percentage of people who shared attitudes and tastes learned in the monastery and cathedral schools. See Benton, "Court of Champagne." 590.

149. This is what Stow, *Dogs,* 100, calls "inversion," or "the ironic contrapositive" of the literal meaning of the surviving texts.

150. Hariulf of Saint-Riquier, *Chronique,* 4.22, 228, quoted in Head, "Saints Heretics and Fire," 227ff.

151. Einbinder, *Beautiful Death,* Chapter 2.

152. Jacob Katz, *Exclusiveness and Tolerance: Studies in Jewish-Gentile Relations in Medieval and Modern Times* (New York: Behrman House/Oxford University Press, 1961), 92.

153. The *Alenu,* composed in the third century, was originally recited annually at the New Year (Rosh Hashanah), but later was added to the liturgy of the Day of Atonement (Yom Kippur) as well. Yisrael Ta-Shma, "The Source and Place of the Prayer *Alenu le-shabeah*" [Hebrew], in *The Frank Talmadge Memorial Volume,* 2 vols., ed. Barry Walfish (Haifa: Haifa University Press, 1993), 1:90, concludes that the *Alenu* and related prayers exist as an extremely abridged—almost symbolic—version of an antique and much longer daily Torah study (*ma-amadot*), which can be traced from the twelfth century. The change is popularly attributed to the events in Blois. However, Stefan C. Reif, *Judaism and Hebrew Prayer: New Perspectives on Jewish Liturgical History* (Cambridge: Cambridge University Press, 1995), 209, notes that "the more general usage [of the *Alenu*] seems to have predated the massacre." Ismar Elbogen, *Jewish Liturgy: A Comprehensive History* (Philadelphia: Jewish Publication Society, 1993), 71ff, traces the change in the daily liturgy in manuscripts from ca. 1300.

154. See the Orléans letter, in Chazan, *Church, State and Jew,* 302.

155. The Vulgate refers to the youth as men (*viri*), but they are often portrayed as children, and the text used in the Divine Office is called the *Canticum Trium Puerorum.*

156. H. Wagenarr-Nolthenius, "Der *Planctus Iudei* und der Gesang jüdischer Märtyrer in Blois anno 1171," in *Mélanges offerts à René Crozet* (Poitiers, 1966), 262. The quoted phrases are from Brockett, "Persona in Cantilena," 12.

157. Ogden, *Staging of Drama,* 182, quoting Smolden.

158. Chazan, "Blois Incident," 19.

159. See Yerushalmi, *Zakhor,* 48–50, and Jacob J. Schacter, "Remembering the Temple Commemoration and Catastrophe in Ashkenazi Culture," in *The Temple of Jerusalem: From Moses to the Messiah: In Honor of Professor Louis H. Feldman,* ed. Steven Fine and Louis H. Feldman (Leiden, Boston: Brill, 2011), 275–302, for the commemoration of the fast of 20 Sivan, which does not seem to have been continuous.

Chapter 7

1. Rubin, *Life and Passion*, lii–lvii traces the provenance of the manuscript.

2. There is no evidence that there were ever more than three manuscripts: an original at Norwich and possibly copies at Sibton and Bury. Late medieval and early modern authors read about St. William while they were in Norwich and quoted from the text that remained in the cathedral priory. M. R. James, *On the Abbey of St. Edmund at Bury,* Cambridge Antiquarian Society, Octavo Publications no. 28 (Cambridge 1895), lxi.; Langmuir, *Toward a Definition,* 286–287. The Norwich volume has not been located since the mid-eighteenth century.

3. It does not appear in the twelfth-century Bury library catalogue, but at least thirty-five other books survive that were written at Bury in the twelfth century and are not mentioned in the abbey's medieval catalogue. R. M. Thomson, "The Library of Bury St Edmunds Abbey in the Eleventh and Twelfth Centuries," *Speculum* 47 (1972), 617–645 at 618. William does not appear in any twelfth-century English calendars outside the priory, and Wulfric and Godric were not important in Norwich, raising the possibility that the surviving volume comes from Bury. Jessopp and James, *Life and Miracles,* l. See also Thomson, "The Library of Bury St Edmunds Abbey," 622 n. 23.

4. Antonia Gransden, "Legends and Traditions Concerning the Abbey of Bury St. Edmunds," *English Historical Review* 100 (1985), 1–24, especially 12–13. Here and in much of her earlier work Gransden traces the many attempts of Bury to assert its independence from the bishop of East Anglia, beginning in the late eleventh century. See more recently the essays in Gransden, ed., *Bury St. Edmunds: Medieval Art, Architecture, Archeology and Economy, Conference Transactions* vol. 20 (Leeds: British Archeological Association, 1998).

The Bury monks tried to demonstrate that the East Anglia bishops had no role in Edmund's cult. In promoting William, the Norwich monks may have identified a son of Bury who had now blessed the city with his holy presence.

5. Under English pope Adrian IV in 1155, Norwich had managed to receive papal confirmation to bring the cure of souls at the churches Bury owned under the spiritual authority of the bishop, Christopher Harper-Bill, "The Medieval Church and the Wider World," in *Norwich Cathedral: Church, City and Diocese,* 281–313 at 286.

6. Bale, *Jew in the Medieval Book,* 109.

7. Butler, *Chronicle,* 16: "Eodem tempore fuit sanctus puer Robertus martirizatus, et in ecclesia nostra sepultus, et fiebant prodigia et signa multa in plebe, sicut alibi scripsimus."

8. For the most recent English translation, see Jocelin of Brakelond, *Chronicle of the Abbey of Bury St. Edmunds,* trans. D. Greenway and J. Sayers (Oxford: Oxford University Press, 1989). For an edition of the Latin with an English translation see Butler, *Chronicle.*

9. Bale, *Jew in the Medieval Book,* is an exception.

10. R. Po-Chia Hsia, *The Myth of Ritual Murder: Jews and Magic in Reformation Germany* (New Haven, CT: Yale University Press, 1989), 4, 12.

11. For developments in the later Middle Ages, see Bale, *Feeling Persecuted* and Anthony Bale, "'House Devil, Town Saint': Anti-Semitism and Hagiography in Medieval Suffolk," in *Chaucer and the Jews,* ed. Sheila Delany (New York: Routledge, 2002), 185–209.

12. The work on Bury and the cult of St. Edmund in the Middle Ages is vast. See in particular the works by Antonia Gransden, especially "Legends and Traditions," and Barbara Abou-El-Haj, "Bury St. Edmunds Abbey Between 1070 and 1124: A History of Property, Privilege, and Monastic Art Production," *Art History* 6 (1983), 1–29.

13. Bishop Augustine (Eystein) of Trondhjem, Norway, was resident in Bury from August 1181 until February 1182. See Butler, *Chronicle,* 15. He took the cult back to Norway: Judith Grant, "A New *Passio Beati Edmundi,*" 88.

14. Nicholas Vincent, "Warin and Henry Fitz Gerald, the King's Chamberlains: The Origins of the Fitzgeralds Revisited," *Anglo-Norman Studies* 21 (1998), 233–260 at 236.

15. In 1203 King John borrowed the jewels his mother had previously donated.

16. John Gillingham, *Richard the Lionheart* (London: Weidenfeld & Nicolson, 1989), 38 and Vincent, "Pilgrimages of the Angevin Kings," 25, citing Howden, *Chronica,* 3:107–108.

17. In subsequent cases it appears that authorities wasted no time: orders of expulsion followed immediately upon accusations of murder (or alleged Jewish desecration of the host), which served as their immediate justification in Paris, Pulkau, Vienna, Trnava, Regensburg, and various towns in Spain.

18. Daniel Gerard, "Jocelin of Brakelond and the Power of Abbot Samson," *Journal of Medieval History* 40, no. 1 (2014), 1–23 at 23 concludes that the head of the abbey who promoted the ritual murder accusation was "a strategist who schemed, manipulated, terrified, bribed and lied his way through a shifting and largely hostile political environment."

19. The unique copy of Lydgate's poem "To St. Robert of Bury," is in Oxford, Bodleian Library, MS Laud 683. It is printed in H. Coppinger Hill, "S. Robert." and in the appendix to Bale, *Jew in the Medieval Book.* The picture appears in an English Life of Christ and the Virgin (ca. 1190–1200), supplemented by late fifteenth-century pictures and prayers, assembled in a single devotional codex by a private owner in East Anglia not earlier than 1479, and now Los Angeles, J. Paul Getty Museum MS 101, "Illustrated Vita Christi, with devotional supplements." The interpolated devotion to Robert of Bury is found on folios 43 and 44. The manuscript is fully described with extensive color photographs in the Sotheby's sale catalogue, *Western and Oriental Manuscripts,* December 7, 2007 (London: Sotheby's, 2007), lot 45, pp. 67–87.

20. "To St. Robert of Bury," from which all quotations here are taken.

21. "Was it nat roughte [pity] to se thi veynes bleede?" (line 18) . . . "al sangweyn was thy weede [garment]" (line 20). This could imply that his blood was collected, as in later allegations against Jews from the thirteenth century.

22. There is no suggestion here that the nursemaid was a Christian working in a Jewish household, although Christian employment in Jewish homes was a habitual cause of concern to both Jews and Christians.

23. "Meritis Sancti Roberti hic in euum misereatur mei." Copinger Hill, "S. Robert," 100: "St Edmund's soul was occasionally represented carried in a sheet in the same manner." Bale has suggested that the donor is Robert Themilthorpe (d. 1505) or a member of his wealthy family. Christopher de Hamel writing in the Sotheby's catalogue suggested the manuscript was put together by Robert Leake (d. 1517), a hermit of Blythborough, Suffolk.

24. Other manuscripts of the period, such as the *Sherborne Missal*, London, British Library, Add. MS 74236, use a similar rebus to represent the name "Robert." I thank Michelle Brown, former Keeper of Manuscripts at the British Library, for drawing my attention to this; see Janet Backhouse, *The Sherborne Missal* (London: British Library, 1999).

25. The domain consisted of the "eight and a half hundreds" that constitute the "Liberty" of Bury St. Edmunds. R. H. C. Davis, "The Monks of St. Edmund, 1021–1148," *History*, n.s. 40 (1955), 227–239. The contents of the original charter are known only from later copies. The manuscript is wide, rather than the typical long and narrow shape. Copinger Hill, "S. Robert," 101, notes a similar picture of a charter of the same unusual shape on painted glass which portrays St. Edward the Confessor granting a charter to the priory of Great Malvern in Worcestershire.

26. Lilian J. Redstone, "The Liberty of St. Edmund," *Proceedings of the Suffolk Institute of Archeology and History* 15 (1913), 200–211.

27. Greenway and Sayers, *Chronicle*, xvi.

28. Cam, "East Anglian Shire-Moot."

29. Mary D. Lobel, "The Gaol of Bury St. Edmund's," *Suffolk Institute of Archeology and Natural History* 21, no. 3 (1933), 203–207.

30. Greenway and Sayers, *Chronicle*, 37, questioning the charter no. 105, dated around 1180 in Douglas, *Feudal Documents*.

31. The earliest charters do not survive but are known from the later confirmations.

32. Greenway and Sayers, *Chronicle*, x.

33. Redstone, "Liberty," 204.

34. As far back as the eleventh century, St. Edmund demonstrated his power when threatened by King Sweyn. In 1153 the monks took spiritual and practical revenge on the king's son, who was despoiling their resources, attributing his sudden death to the ire of St Edmund. The sacrist hung criminals found guilty. Abou-El-Haj, "Bury St. Edmunds Abbey"; Callahan, "Saintly Retribution," 109–117; Greenway and Sayers, *Chronicle*, 137.

35. Greenway and Sayers, *Chronicle*, 80; Butler, *Chronicle*, 7.

36. Butler, *Chronicle*, 10.

37. Butler, *Chronicle*, 7.

38. Hillaby, "Accusation," 88–89, argues that "here we have the motives that lay behind the Bury ritual murder accusation": "not merely to bring in funds for

Samson's building programme" but to provide Samson "with just the weapon needed in the contest over the election for the vacant abbey." Some scholars write that he "paid off his debts," but Jocelin reports that the new abbot renegotiated some of them first. In the wake of the accusation and the expulsion, he almost certainly was relieved of the abbey's many debts to Jews without having to pay the full amount owed, if he had to pay at all. Butler, *Chronicle*, 30: "For all these bonds he had come to terms within a year of his election, and within twelve years he had paid them all."

39. While the acts of the council included little that was new—church councils had been making such pronouncements on the dangers of social intercourse with the Jews since the fourth century—this was the first time that restrictions against Jewish-Christian interactions were given such prominence. For a thorough discussion of Jews and later canonical legislation, see J. A. Watt, "The English Episcopate, the State and the Jews: The Evidence of the Thirteenth Century Conciliar Decrees," in P. R. Coss and S. D. Lloyd, eds, *Thirteenth Century England*, 2 (Woodbridge, Suffolk: Boydell & Brewer, 1988), 137–147.

40. Douglas and Greenaway, *English Historical Documents*, 449–451, assize of arms no. 7: "Item, Let no Jew keep in his possession a hauberk or an 'aubergel,' but let him sell them or give them away or otherwise dispose of them that they may remain in the king's service. No. 12: Item. . . And the king commands that none shall be accepted for the oath of arms except a free man."

41. Stephen P. Halbrook, "Nazi Firearms Law and the Disarming of the German Jews," *Arizona Journal of International and Comparative Law* 17, no. 3 (2000), 483–535.

42. Roth, *History of the Jews*, 14 n.1.

43. Stow, *Alienated Minority*, 115, 116. See also Benjamin Z. Kedar, "Crusade Historians and the Massacres of 1096," *Jewish History* 12, no. 2 (1998), 11–32.

44. For the latest scholarship on the events in York in 1190, see Rees Jones and Watson, *York Massacre of 1190*.

45. For an overview, see Martin Allen, "Henry II and the English Coinage," in *Henry II: New Interpretations*, ed. Harper-Bill and Vincent, 257–277, and Derek F. Allen, *A Catalogue of English Coins in the British Museum, the Cross-and-Crosslets ("Tealby") Type of Henry II* (London: Trustees of the British Museum, 1951), Chapter 11: Finance and Administration of the Coinage, lxxiv–cxiv.

46. Nightingale, "London Moneyers and English Mints," 49.

47. Robin J. Eaglen, "The Mint at Bury St Edmunds," in Grandsen, *Bury St Edmunds*, 111–121.

48. Robin J. Eaglen, *The Abbey and Mint of Bury St. Edmunds to 1279* (London: Spink, for the British Numismatic Society, 2006), 71.

49. The quotation is from Eaglen, "Mint," 116. Eaglen notes the remarkable survival of the Bury mint through the centuries, 111, 113, and 114. Countering the notion that the end of minting was brought about by Abbot Samson's preoccupation with building

works, he suggests, 132, that without the ability to exchange money it was no longer profitable for the abbey to mint only the abbot's own silver and not that of others.

50. Brand, *English Coinage*, 22, who notes, 26, that Norwich did not have a moneyer for a decade after 1170.

51. N. J. Mayhew, "From Regional to Central Minting, 1158–1464," in *A New History of the Royal Mint*, ed. C. E. Challis (Cambridge: Cambridge University Press, 1992), 83–178 at 87. See also 91, for a discussion of the arbitrary treatment of moneyers in Henry II's reign, which climaxed with the purge of 1180.

52. Martin Allen, "Documentary Evidence of the Output, Profits and Expenditure of the Bury St Edmunds Mint," *British Numismatic Journal* 69 (1999), 210–213.

53. Allen, "Documentary Evidence."

54. Antonia Gransden, "John de Northwold, Abbot of Bury St. Edmunds (1279–1301) and His Defence of Its Liberties," *Thirteenth Century England* (Woodbridge, Suffolk: Boydell Press, 1991), 91–112 at 91.

55. Daniel M. Friedenberg, *Jewish Minters and Medalists* (Philadelphia: Jewish Publication Society of America, 1976), 27.

56. Cecil Roth (*History of the Jews*, 12 n. 5), identified as possible Jewish moneyers Isaac of York and David of Thetford, while numismatists unfamiliar with Roth's classic study have identified three more Jewish moneyers from surviving coin hoards of Henry II, Daniel, Joseph, and Sansun; see Allen, *A Catalogue of English Coins*, cvii. Another man appearing in sources from the Anarchy, Sansun of Southampton, might be a Jewish moneyer. See George C. Boon, *Coins of the Anarchy, 1135–54* (Cardiff: National Museum of Wales, 1988), no. 32, although there was no Jewish community in Southampton. Men with the Jewish names Saul of Gloucester and Solomon of Canterbury were also making coins under Henry II. Friedenberg, *Jewish Minters*, 9, discusses the coins and documentation and is suitably cautious in concluding that "the evidence is too spotty to allow definite conclusions."

57. Allen, *Catalogue of English Coins*, cvii, notes the names of moneyers David and Solomon.

58. Adler, *Jews of Medieval England*, 65.

59. The term for die-master was *aurifaber* (goldsmith), but the term could refer to other trades as well. Lipman, *Jews of Medieval Norwich*, 94, mentions Richard de Elingham, *aurifaber*. In the first year of his reign, King John called "Leo the Jew our goldsmith" and "took him into our hand, custody and protection," ibid., 206–207.

60. The Jews associated with Norwich and those of St. Augustine's, Canterbury, may initially have been connected to the mints established there, as both places had ecclesiastical privileges early in the reign of Henry II when Jews moved out beyond London.

61. The importance of Thetford may be due to the fact that, like Norwich, it had a mint (see Roth, *History of the Jews*, 8; but Roth did not consider that a diminution in the Jewish communities could follow a decline in the mint). Bristol, Thetford, and Bury did not mint coins for at least two decades after 1180 (the "Short-Cross"

coinage), although all three had been very active in earlier minting (the "Tealby" or "Cross-and-Crosslets" coinage).

62. Stacey, "Jewish Lending," 85.

63. Anthony Wood, *History and Antiquities of the University of Oxford*, 2 vols. (Oxford: John Gutch, 1792), 1:148. Jewish historians are at a loss to explain the meaning of the term "exchange" in this context, while numismatists do not know the reference at all and English historians ignore it. Jacobs, *Jews of Angevin England*, 18, and Cecil Roth, *Jews of Medieval Oxford*, 2, are baffled by the term. Allen, *Catalogue of English Coins*, cliv: "In 5 Hen II (1158–59) the sheriff accounts for 12 pounds for the Change (or Exchange) of Money (*de Cangio Monete*). This is the only contemporary use of the word *Camium* or *Cambium* in connexion with the mint before 1180 when it was universally used to describe the new exchange; it is not clear what it refers to in this context... it is presumably to be associated in some way with the termination of the old or the commencement of the new coinage." Jim Bradbury, *Stephen and Matilda: The Civil War of 1139–53* (Stroud, Gloucestershire: Sutton, 1996), for example, does not mention Jews at all in this detailed study.

64. Friedenberg, *Jewish Minters*, 9.

65. Mayhew, *Regional to Central Minting*, 88.

66. Martin Allen, "Ecclesiastical Mints in Thirteenth-Century England," in *Thirteenth Century England*, ed. M. Prestwich, R. Britnell and R. Frame (Woodbridge, Suffolk, Boydell and Brewer, 2001), 113–122.

67. Robert C. Stacey, "Crusades, Martyrdoms and the Jews of Norman England, 1096–1190," in *Juden und Christen zur Zeit der Kreuzzüge*, ed. A. Haverkamp (Sigmaringen: Jan Thorbecke Verlag, 1999), 233–251 at 249ff, offers a good analysis of Richard's ambivalent role toward the Jews of his kingdom. Earlier works tend to argue that Richard should have done more to prevent the massacre at York (and Norwich, Bury, etc.). Some exculpate the king because of his absence from the country by the time the massacres occurred. The massacres are widely discussed in survey histories and biographies of Richard I. Some believe they are easily forgotten: in 2008 a campaign was organized, opposing a proposed shopping mall in York next to the site of the massacre out of concern that it would obliterate the memory of the murdered Jews, who are memorialized in a plaque on the site. Rees Jones and Watson, *York Massacre of 1190*; Dobson, *Jews of Medieval York*; and R. B. Dobson, *Clifford's Tower and the Jews of Medieval York* (London: English Heritage, 1995).

68. Butler, *Chronicle*, 46.

69. The dramatic depiction of William's alleged crucifixion has been reproduced in books by Jessop and James, Jewson, Anderson, Scarfe, and Shapiro, to name just a few. The splayed depiction of St. William on the rood screen is still visible in the Loddon church in Suffolk. For the provenance of the Loddon painting, see Bradbury, "Norfolk Saint," and Luxford, "Iconography."

70. Gabrielle M. Spiegel and Paul Freedman, "Medievalisms Old and New: The Rediscovery of Alterity in North American Medieval Studies," *American Historical Review* 103, no. 3 (1998), 677–704.

Chapter 8

1. Rigord, "Gesta Philippi," 1:15 (English quotation based on the translation of Paul Hyams).

2. Alix and Philip shared a father in Louis VII of France. Alix was the daughter of Louis's first wife, Eleanor of Aquitaine; Philip was the son of his third wife, Adèle of Champagne, who was Thibaut V's younger sister. Alix and Richard Lionheart of England shared a mother in Eleanor of Aquitaine. It is not clear who else would have been raised with Philip. No accusations of ritual murder are documented after Blois and before Philip's decision to expel the Jews once he ascended the throne.

3. The funeral oration was composed in the late fifteenth century by the royal diplomat and writer Robert Gauguin. The text was retrieved by the Bollandists for the *Acta Sanctorum* from a printed book (as yet unidentified) by the prolific French Jesuit Gabriel Gossart, librarian and professor of rhetoric; *Acta Sanctorum* (Antwerp, 1668), 3:591–594.

4. Pontoise, the ancient capital of the French Vexin, is about 17 miles from the center of Paris—the new town (conurbation) of Cergy-Pontoise is on the N14 highway from Paris to Rouen.

5. Rigord, "Gesta Philippi," 1:15. Other than this mention, there is no other indication that Richard performed miracles at this time, and even Rigord reports the information as hearsay, rather than personal knowledge.

6. The introduction to the *Life* by the scrupulously diligent seventeenth-century Jesuit hagiographers notes that the boy was killed in Pontoise and that the body was buried in the cemetery and then moved into the church (*ceterum e coemetario in templum translatum fuisse corpus sanctum*), attributing the information to the chronicler Rigord. But Rigord merely says that the body rests in the church, not that it was ceremoniously translated there from the cemetery. The introduction also notes that Richard was killed at Pontoise (*occisus Pontisarae*) but that, too, is not clear from Rigord's text. The early modern editors also offer a hint of doubt about the information in a construction that is awkward and unclear: they include the citation from Rigord and continue "unless someone should think that the significance of this passage should be extended" and admit they have no more information (*nisi ampliandum aliquis putet huius locutionis signficiationem: de qua cum viterius nihil certi habeamus*).

7. E. M. Rose, "Royal Power and Ritual Murder: Notes on the Expulsion of the Jews from the Royal Domain of France, 1182," in *Center and Periphery: Studies on Power in the Medieval World in Honor of William Chester Jordan*, ed. K. L. Jansen, G. Geltner, and A. E. Lester (Leiden: Brill, 2013), 51–63.

8. Matthew 2:16–18 and repeated in the apocryphal Infancy Gospel of James, *Protoevangelium* 22. To judge from the work of Honorius *Augustudunenis*, apocryphal versions of the story also circulated in the twelfth century.

9. Macrobius (*Saturnalia* 2.4.11) famously said it was better to be Herod's pig [*ous*] than his son [*houios*], a play on the words in Greek that Abelard included in his Latin hymn for the feast of the Holy Innocents and that was repeated in Jacopo da Voragine's *Golden Legend* of the thirteenth century. The source of the story is likely to have been a conflation of two historic events: the documented killing of Herod's adult sons and the order Herod gave on his deathbed to have a large number of Jewish leaders killed and buried with him in order that he might be mourned along with them. This violent order of mass murder made during Herod's lifetime was countermanded so that the killings never took place, but some memory of the order survived, for which see Vasily Rudich, *Religious Violence in the Roman Empire, Religious Dissent in the Roman Empire* (London: Routledge, vol. 3, 2015), 100–101. The discovery of Herod's mausoleum in 2007 revealed two stone sarcophagi, which may have been the coffins of his two sons.

10. The Holy Innocents were identified with the 144,000 virgin martyrs "sealed" according to the Book of Revelation 7, a text that was read during the feast of the Innocents at Sext and repeated in Revelation 14. The exact number was given as 144,000 in Jacopo da Voragine's immensely influential *Golden Legend* of the mid-thirteenth century. See Mary Martin McLaughlin, "Survivors and Surrogates: Children and Parents from the Ninth through Thirteenth Centuries," in *The History of Childhood*, ed. Lloyd de Mause (New York: Psychohistory Press, 1974), 101–181.

11. Included in the liturgy from the fifth century, the massacre was occasionally represented in art, and some relics of the Innocents were distributed at that time. Notker Balbulus, Fulgentius, Bede, and Prudentius composed sermons and poetry upon which the twelfth-century liturgists drew. See, for example, Martin R. Dudley, "Natalis Innocentum: The Holy Innocents in Liturgy and Drama," in *The Church and Childhood*, ed. D. Wood, Studies in Church History 31 (Oxford: Blackwell, 1994), 233–242.

12. Philippe Ariès, *Centuries of Childhood: A Social History of Family Life* (New York: Knopf, 1962), famously argued that "there was no concept of childhood in the Middle Ages." Among the many critiques of aspects of Aries's work, see McLaughlin, "Survivors and Surrogates"; Harry Hendrick, "Children and Childhood," *Refresh*, 15 (1992), 1–4; Shulamit Shahar, *Childhood in the Middle Ages* (London: Routledge, 1990); Daniele Alexandre-Bidon and Didier Lett, *Children in the Middle Ages: Fifth-Fifteenth Centuries* (Notre Dame, IN: University of Notre Dame Press, 1999), and the introduction to reprints of Ariès's work.

13. Heather Blurton, "William of Norwich Between History and Liturgy," conference paper delivered at *Putting England in Its Place: Cultural Production and Cultural Relations in the High Middle Ages*, Fordham University Medieval Studies Conference, March 9–10, 2013. I thank the author for providing me with a copy of her paper.

14. Patricia Healy Wasyliw, *Martyrdom, Murder and Magic: Child Saints and Their Cults in Medieval Europe* (New York: Peter Lang, 2005), 33.

15. Wasyliw, *Martyrdom, Murder and Magic*, 48.

16. Kathleen Nolan, "Ploratus Et Ululatus: The Mothers in the Massacre of the Innocents at Chartres Cathedral," *Studies in Iconography* 17 (1996), 95–141 at 102, citing the "Life of St. Richtrude" in *Sainted Women of the Dark Ages*, ed. and trans. Joann McNamara and John Halbord (Durham, NC: Duke University Press, 1992), 210.

17. Wasilyw, *Martyrdom, Murder and Magic*, 47.

18. See Sini Kangas, "The Slaughter of the Innocents (Matthew 2. 16–18) and the Depiction of Children in the Twelfth-Century Sources of the Crusades," in *The Uses of the Bible in Crusading Sources*, ed. Elizabeth Lapina and Nicholas Morton (Leiden: Brill, 2015 forthcoming). I thank the author for sending me a copy of her paper in advance of publication. See also Sophie Oosterwijk, "'Long Lullynge Haue I Lorn!': The Massacre of the Innocents in Word and Image," *Medieval English Theatre* 25 (2003), 3–53.

19. Nolan, "Mothers," 109.

20. The crowned heads of England, France, Germany, and Spain all demonstrated a marked interest in the cult. Louis IX of France would not work on such a day; Richard II of England gave relics of the Holy Innocents to York Minster; Edward IV postponed his coronation so that it would not occur on *Childermass*, the English term for the feast of the Holy Innocents. Earlier, King John of England had gone hunting on Holy Innocents' Day and in guilt afterward provided food for 350 paupers. The Spanish royal tombs of Castille and Navarre featured influential sculptures of the Holy Innocents.

21. Lebeuf, *Histoire*, 78, citing Jean Mabillon, *Annales Ordinis S. Benedicti Occidentalium Monachorum Patriarchae* (1739), 6:700, referring to a tract by the twelfth-century bishop Stephen of Paris. The Church of the Innocents is first documented by name about 1150. It is possible that Louis returned from the Second Crusade with some relics of the Innocents with which to endow the church.

22. Before the twelfth century, only one pope took the name Innocent, but Innocent II (pope 1130–1143), Innocent III (pope 1198–1216), and Innocent IV (pope 1243–1254) followed in quick succession, which may in part reflect the popularity of the *Innocenti*. I thank Herb Kessler of John Hopkins University for raising this possibility in discussion. Pope Innocent I (d. 417) had a fairly low profile; it is unlikely, therefore, that the popes of the twelfth century intended to recall him by their choice of papal name. For the campaign of vilification orchestrated against Anacletus, in which Bernard was an active participant, see Stroll, *Jewish Pope* and the letters of Arnulf of Lisieux discussed in Chapter 2.

23. Irven M. Resnick, "Race, Anti-Jewish Polemic, Arnulf of Séez, and to the Contested Papal Election of Anaclet II (A.D. 1130)," in *Jews in Medieval Christendom: Slay Them Not*, ed. Kristine T. Utterback and Merrall L. Price (Leiden: Brill, 2013), 45–70.

24. William F. MacLehose, *"A Tender Age": Cultural Anxieties over the Child in the Twelfth and Thirteenth Centuries* (New York: Columbia University Press, 2007), 73–74.

25. Bernard explained "truly they are martyrs . . . if you search for the meritorious actions for which these infants were crowned by the hand of God, search also for the crimes for which they were cruelly massacred by Herod," cited by Wasilyw, *Martyrdom, Murder and Magic*, 48.

26. See Neil J. Roy, "The Feast of the Holy Innocents and Its Orations in the Missale Romanum of 1970," *Antiphon* 8 no. 1 (2003), 28–33.

27. For the "invention of the dramatist," see Karl Young, *Ordo Rachelis* (Madison: University of Wisconsin, 1919), 36.

28. Boynton "Performative Exegesis," 45. See also Mayke de Jong, *In Samuel's Image: Child Oblation in the Early Medieval West* (Leiden: Brill, 1996).

29. Orderic Vitalis, *Ecclesiastical History*, ed. Marjorie Chibnall (Oxford: Oxford University Press, 1968), 6:522.

30. Denise L. Despres, "Adolescence and Sanctity: *The Life and Passion of Saint William of Norwich*," *Journal of Religion* 90 (2010), 33–62.

31. See, for example, Michael Milway, "Boy Bishops in Early Modern Europe: Ritual, Myth, and Reality," in *The Dramatic Tradition of the Middle Ages*, ed. Clifford Davidson (New York: AMS Press, 2005), 87–97; Edward Rimbault, "Two Sermons Preached by the Boy Bishop," *Camden Miscellany* 14 n.s. (1875), 1–34; and Shulamith Shahar, "The Boy Bishop's Feast: A Case-Study in Church Attitudes Towards Children in the High and Late Middle Ages," in *The Church and Childhood*, ed. Diana Wood (Oxford: Published for the Ecclesiastical History Society by Blackwell Publishers, 1994), 243–260.

32. Marie Padgett Hamilton, "Echoes of Childermas in the Tale of the Prioress," *Modern Language Review* 34, no. 1 (1939), 1–8 at 8, makes the persuasive argument that "Chaucer probably heard the Prioress' tale at an Innocents mass, *ex ore infantium*," but few have taken up her suggestion.

33. See E. M. Rose, "Hugh of Lincoln, Ritual Murder, Henry III and the Crown of Sicily," paper delivered at the Harvard Medieval Seminar, October 3, 2011 for the context.

34. *Vita* II, viii, 58.

35. Bale, *Jew in the Medieval Book*, 118 argues that the patron who caused his portrait to be placed next to an invocation to Robert was a major contributor to the guild of Holy Innocents, and that his family church was dedicated to them.

36. E. Vacandard, *Dictionnaire d'histoire et de geographie ecclesiastique* (Paris: Letouzey et Ane, 1912–), Vol 2: cols. 1700–01 (Paris, 1914), translated into English by Paul Halsall in the *Medieval Sourcebook*, "Anderl von Rinn," www.fordham.edu/halsall/source/rinnenc.html.

37. In addition to kidnapping and torturing children, the Jews of Paris were accused of desecrating liturgical objects they held in pawn and lending money at exorbitant interest.

38. Jews were allowed to return in 1198. In the late thirteenth century, Jews expelled from Anjou, Maine, Gascony, and Nevers were welcomed in Paris by Philip IV but then were expelled from France in 1306. They were readmitted in 1315 by Louis X and expelled by Charles IV in 1321. Some gradually moved back and were finally expelled by Charles VI in 1394. At the beginning of the seventeenth century, when Jews once again returned to France, an edict of 1615 forbade Christians to converse with them on penalty of death.

39. Stow, *Jewish Dogs*, 93.

40. See Rose, "Royal Power and Ritual Murder."

41. As Rigord notes: "in the first year of the reign of Phillip Augustus and the fifteenth of his age, there arose rivalries, or enmities, among the princes of the realm. Certain of his princes, at the instigation of the Devil, enemy to ecclesiastical peace, dared to conspire against their lord Phillip Augustus. They assembled an army and began to waste the king's lands." Rigord, "Gesta Philippi Augusti," in H.-Francois Delaborde, *Oeuvres de Rigord et de Guillaume le Breton*, 2 vols. (Paris: Librairie Renouard, 1885), 1:1–167 at 18. I have not seen the new edition of Rigord, *Histoire de Philippe Auguste*, ed. and tr. E. Carpentier, G. Pon, and Y. Chauvin (Paris: CNRS, 2006).

42. Rather than commencing, as often assumed, while Louis VII was failing but still held the reins of power, the attacks on Jews of the royal domain seem to have occurred within a short span of time in the spring of 1181, only after Louis's death in September 1180. Rigord appears to exaggerate when he says the attack on the Jews occurred a few days after Philip's coronation, whether he refers to Philip's coronation in 1179 while his father was alive, or to the royal consecration with his new wife in May 1180. William Chester Jordan, *The French Monarchy and the Jews, from Philip Augustus to the Last Capetians (1179–1328)* (Philadelphia: University of Pennsylvania Press, 1989), 30, notes that the Sabbath raid of *16 Kal Feb* reported by Rigord was a Thursday in 1180 but was a Saturday in 1181. In this seizure (*captio*) the young king demanded 15,000 silver marks to let the captives go free; Ralph de Diceto, *Opera Historica*, ed. William Stubbs (London: Rolls Series, 1879, Kraus reprint 1965), 1:276.

The martyrdom of Richard of Pontoise was apparently first celebrated the same spring (or even later). Conflicting dates, usually in March, have been put forward for the celebration of Richard's death, discovery, or feast; they include March 25 and March 30. The *Jewish Encyclopedia*, "Blood Libel," suggests March: "immediately after [Philip's] coronation on March 14, 1181, he ordered the Jews arrested." The source for the date of March 14 is not known (a date which seems to be mentioned nowhere else). The fourteenth of March was celebrated as the feast day of Pope Innocent, whose relics were preserved at the church in Paris where Richard was interred (named for Pope Innocent and the Holy Innocents). It is possible that the new king recognized Richard of Pontoise at that church on the feast day, at which time he committed to a rebuilding project. Richard's death (subsequently described as occurring in January) may have been perceived as the justification for the unprecedented seizure, a suitable forfeit for the Jews' great offense. Exactly one year later, having consulted Bernard, a hermit of Vincennes, Philip announced that the Jews must give up moneylending, surrender the debts owed them, and leave the kingdom by the feast of St. John the Baptist (June 24), Midsummer's Day, 1182. The decision was published by April, but some modern secondary sources indicate that it was made on March 14. The Jews were given three months (from April) to settle their affairs.

43. Baldwin, *Government of Philip Augustus*, 378–379, points out how purposefully Rigord rearranges chronology when writing of Philip's birth. Rigord seems to have done much the same thing in his references to Philip's actions toward the Jews of his kingdom.

44. This Pierre Bernard de Boschiac (or de Bré or Coudray) is repeatedly mentioned by Rigord and appears in French records through 1195. The Grandmont order, which was founded by Stephen Muret, flourished in the late twelfth century with benefactions from Henry II. Bernard attempted to work out a settlement between Henry and Thomas Becket and later became an important advisor to Philip II and is found working closely with the bishop of Paris. King Louis VII first established the monks at Vincennes, just over four miles from the center of Paris, where Philip Augustus built a royal manor and constructed substantial walls around it. He paid for it with money taken from the Jews he expelled. *Mémoires de la Société des Antiquaires de l'Ouest, Année 1850* (1852), 172, notes Bernard's "illustrious family," which is alluded to in the epitaph on his tomb in the Limousin, (mis)dated about 1172. The date of his death is not recorded.

45. For Philip's "deliberate attempt to use Jewish policy as an assertion of identity in concert with other assertions of superiority at the commencement of his reign," and for similar actions of two thirteenth-century French successors, see William Chester Jordan, "Princely Identity and the Jews in Medieval France," in Jeremy Cohen, ed., *From Witness to Witchcraft: Jews and Judaism in Medieval Christian Thought*, Wolfenbütteler Mittelalter-Studien 11 (Wiesbaden: Harrassowitz, 1996), 257–273, repr. in Jordan's collected essays, *Ideology and Royal Power in Medieval France* (Aldershot, UK: Ashgate Publishing, 2001).

46. For the importance of royal visits to pilgrimage shrines in this period, see Vincent, "Pilgrimages of the Angevin Kings," 30–31.

47. Pope Innocent I died on March 12, 417. From the thirteenth century onward, his feast was often dated to July 28 but is now celebrated on March 12. Nevertheless, in Paris the medieval feast of Pope Innocent was celebrated on March 14, as repeatedly attested by the calendar entries in Books of Hours: almost half of the calendars identified as "use of Paris" list Innocent for March 14. This date, March 14, is also a day firmly (but inexplicably) associated with the expulsion of the Jews from France.

48. Throughout the Middle Ages and beyond, the name of the church was alternatively referred to, even in the same documents, with both the singular and plural.

49. Jim Bradbury, *Philip Augustus, King of France, 1180–1223* (London: Longman, 1998), 239–240.

50. The gates there may hint at some kind of early ghetto, since in later years the residents were eager to have them pulled down.

51. For centuries this wholesale marketplace remained "the belly of Paris" until it was demolished and replaced with a shopping precinct in the late twentieth century.

52. For the notion that "Philip's cleaning up of Paris also contained a puritanical element," see Bradbury, *Philip Augustus,* 167.

53. Marianne Jaeglé, *Histoire de Paris et des parisiens* (Paris: Compagnie 12, 2005), 5–6, says that these stones were about six centimeters wide and eighteen centimeters long; A. Galignani and W. Galignani, *The History of Paris, from the Earliest Period to the Present Day,* 3 vols. (Paris: A. and W. Galignani, 1825), 70–71, gives the dimensions of the paving stones (*dalles, carreau,* or *quadratos lapide*s) as three and one-half feet square and six inches thick.

54. Danielle Chadych and Dominique Leborgne, *Atlas de Paris: Évolution d'un Paysage Urbain* (Paris: Parigramme, 2007), 30, 54.

55. Jacques Boussard, *De la fin du siège de 885–886 à la mort de Philippe Auguste,* 2nd ed. (Paris: Association pour la publication d'une histoire de Paris, Hachette, 1997), 318.

56. Rigord, "Gesta Philippi," 1:105. For the extant portions of Philip's wall, see François Benveniste, *Balade autour de la muraille de Philippe Auguste* (Saint-Cyr-sur-Loire: Sutton, 2004).

57. Erecting the new walls "appears to have been not so much a decision to protect a city which had grown vastly beyond its walls as an attempt to encourage future growth," Bradbury, *Philip Augustus,* 70.

58. Bradbury, *Philip Augustus,* 68. As previously noted, in the late eleventh century, Paris and Chartres were comparable in size.

59. Jacques Hillairet, *Évocation du Vieux Paris* (Paris: Les Éditions de Minuit, 1952), 244. The fountain on the exterior of the church was located at the crossroads of Saint-Denis and Rue aux Fers. Naomi Miller, "The Form and Meaning of the Fontaine des Innocents," *Art Bulletin* 50 (1968), 270–277, discusses the Renaissance monument that replaced the medieval fountain on the same site. The early modern fountain survives, but was subsequently moved to a different location.

60. Jacques-Antoine Dulaure, *Histoire physique, civile et morale de Paris: Depuis les premiers temps historiques jusqu'à nos jours* (Paris: Guillaume, 1823), 2:292.

61. Illustrations of this unusual tower from the fifteenth and sixteenth centuries appear in the background of various works of art. One appears in a fifteenth-century Book of Hours (reproduced by Lombard-Jourdan in black and white from an 1882 photogravure; now in a private collection). A second one appears in the historiated initial *D* in the *Missal* of Jacques Juvénal des Ursins (d. 1457), published in the mid-nineteenth century before the manuscript was burned in 1871; a third picture is in the background of an anonymous painting of about 1565 from the Museé Carnevalet; Anne Lombard-Jourdan, *Paris, genèse de la ville: La rive droite de la*

Seine des origines à 1223 (Paris: CNRS, 1976). The Carnevalet picture is reproduced in color in Chadych and Leborgne, *Atlas de Paris*, 59. See also http://www.carnavalet.paris.fr/fr/collections/le-cimetiere-et-l-eglise-des-saints-innocents. Falling apart by the late eighteenth century, the slim tower was finally torn down when the cemetery was moved just before the Revolution.

62. Among various possibilities, it has been suggested that the tower served as a lantern for those keeping a vigil for the dead or that it was a lighthouse for those lost in the nearby woods. Anne Lombard-Jourdan, *Aux origines de Paris. La genèse de la rive droite jusqu'en 1223* (Paris: Editions du CNRS, 1985), 55, prefers "silence to vain conjecture." No one has heretofore suggested that it might have been dedicated to Richard of Pontoise, but scholars have proposed no other site for the tomb. It has been suggested that the little tower of *les Innocents* was modeled on structures erected by Waleran de Beaumont, count of Meulan, first earl of Worcester (1104–1166), who took the initiative to build comparable octagonal bell towers around the Vexin and the Pincerais beginning in 1155; Lombard-Jourdan, *Aux origines de Paris*, 57, citing P. Coquelle, "Les clochers romans du Vexin français et du Pincerais," *Memoires de la Societé historique et archéologique de Pontoise et du Vexin*, 25, (1903), 47–65. For the central situation of the tower, see Jean Lebeuf, *Histoire de la ville et de tout le diocèse de Paris* (Paris: Féchoz et Letouzey, 1883), 51.

63. Compare, for example, the bell tower of the Church of St. Nicholas in Pisa of c. 1170 made by the architect Diotisalvi, the builder of the Leaning Tower of Pisa.

64. In Gloucestershire, Somersetshire, Staffordshire, and elsewhere in England, a half-muffled warning bell commemorated the biblical Slaughter of the Innocents. In Worcestershire a half-muffled peal was rung to recall the slaughter and then a peal of joy was rung to celebrate Christ's escape. See Mackenzie E. C. Walcott, *Sacred Archæology: A Popular Dictionary of Ecclesiastical Art and Institutions, from Primitive to Modern Times* (London: L. Reeve, 1868), 313.

65. The tocsin that rang out in some towns in Spain and served as a catalyst for clerical attacks on the Jewish quarter in the fourteenth century may have had a similar origin; for Spanish attacks, see Nirenberg, *Communities of Violence*.

66. An early-fifteenth century arch at *Les Innocents* was supposedly engraved with such "hieroglyphics" taken from an ancient Jewish book of wisdom by a Christian donor who came from Pontoise, and may have recalled earlier decoration of the site.

67. Reference to the version mentioning friendship is found in Ulysse Robert, *Signes d'infamie au Moyen âge: Juifs, Sarrasins, Hérétiques, Lépreux, Cagots et Filles Publiques* (Paris: H. Champion, 1889), 91, but is not repeated in the edition of 1891. The thief version is quoted in R. Anchel, "The Early History of the Jewish Quarters in Paris," *Jewish Social Studies* 2 (1940), 45–60 at 55, citing Charles-Jean-François Hénault, *Nouvel abrégé chronologique de l'histoire de France: Contenant les événemens de notre histoire depuis Clovis jusqu'à Louis XIV* (Paris, 1768), 1:351–353, an

edition I have not seen. The reference does not appear in some other editions of this popular work.

68. Rigord, *Œuvres*, 28.

69. Some of the streets once occupied by Jews in the twelfth century remained in the possession of those who dealt in second-hand clothes. In the early sixteenth century they petitioned the king to pull down the old gates, and they and their neighbors paid generously for permission to do so. Once they became "churchwardens," the old-clothes dealers also petitioned to efface the "hieroglyphics," which suggests that the inscriptions were offensive allusions to the Jewish heritage of their neighborhood. In the mid-seventeenth century, an angry mob assassinated a citizen who shouted at the clothes dealers, "here comes the synagogue"; Anchel, "Jewish Quarters in Paris," 54, 56.

70. Despite heated objections by those who invoked Richard of Pontoise in an effort to save the church, the presence of Richard's relics did not dissuade the urban improvers who led the move to close the cemetery and tear down the church when the cemetery was relocated just before the Revolution.

71. See, for example, F. Berier, "L'humaniste, le prêtre et l'enfant mort: Le sermon 'De Sanctis Innocentibus' de Nicolas de Clamanges," in *L'enfant au Moyen Âge: Literature et civilization* (Communications du quatrième colloque du CUERMA), Sénéfiance 9 (Aix en Provence: CUERMA, 1980), 123–140.

72. Although the authors of the *Acta Sanctorum* (in the introduction to Gaguin's *Vita* of Richard) suggest that the remains of Richard's relics were encased in a silver head-shaped reliquary ("argenteo capiti inclusa") after most of Richard's relics had been carried off by the English during the Hundred Years War, no further details are offered, in marked contrast to the elaborate details given regarding the fifteenth-century silver and crystal reliquary of the Holy Innocents, which suggests that the head reliquary was already missing by the fifteenth century. Many body-part reliquaries, especially Romanesque head reliquaries (of silver over a wood base), date from the twelfth century.

73. King Edward "clearly wanted the new shrine [of little St Hugh] to be associated with the Crown; not only was he the sole monarch recorded as giving alms at the shrine, but it appears that he may have provided expertise from the royal workshops to create this monument ... to reinforce the connection between the Saint and the Crown, the royal arms were prominently displayed. . . . Furthermore, because the shrine was at least partly the product of a temporary political situation, it is not surprising that interest in it declined once the political geography had changed." David Stocker, "The Shrine of Little Saint Hugh," in T. A. Heslop and V. A. Sekules, eds., *Medieval Art and Architecture at Lincoln Cathedral* (Oxford: British Archeological Association, 1986), 109–117 at 115. In marked contrast to the architectural analysis of the shrine of St. Hugh at Lincoln quoted here, detailed architectural and archaeological studies of Philip's church of *les Innocents* (and its fifteenth-century alterations) fail to mention St. Richard or the Jews of Paris: see, for example, Hélène Couzy, "L'Église des Saints Innocents À Paris," *Bulletin*

monumental (1972), 279–302 and Michel Fleury, "Les Fouilles récentes du Square des Innocents," *Les Dossiers de d'archéologie* 7 (1974), 64–76.

74. The Jews were expelled from England in 1290, and the shrine dedicated to Little Hugh was most likely designed in the years between 1290 and 1295, when all three of its craftsmen were working on the same projects, Stocker, "Shrine of Little St Hugh," 113.

75. Jordan, *French Monarchy,* 5.

76. For a detailed analysis of the bishop's rights as a feudal lord in Paris at this time, see Achille Luchaire, *Social France at the Time of Philip Augustus,* trans. Edward B. Krehbiel (New York: H. Holt, 1912), 143ff. See Jaeglé, *Histoire de Paris,* 28, on the king's struggle, even in the capital, for recognition of his rights. The terms of the agreement spelled out in the 1222 charter of Meulan held until 1674.

77. *Gesta Philipi* in *Oeuvres Rigord,* 1:30ff. Roger Berg, *Histoire des juifs à Paris: de Chilpéric à Jacques Chirac* (Paris: Editions du Cerf, 1997), 34, incorrectly records the number as 42.

78. Roblin, *Juifs de Paris,* 12.

79. Anchel, "Jewish Quarters in Paris,"50.

80. Boussard, *Nouvelle histoire de Paris,* 149, 301, argues that the low price demonstrates that the market was in full decline. Alternatively, it could represent a favorable price for a devoted servant who continues to appear in the records.

81. Stow, *Jewish Dogs,* 75, in his chapter titled "Avarice and the Martyr," draws primary attention to Jews' roles as moneylenders in the reworking of Richard's cult and maintains that it was concern about the great oppression of Jewish lending that persuaded Philip to expel the Jews.

82. Rigord, "Gesta Philippi," 24.

83. Roblin, *Juifs de Paris,* 13; Gérard Nahon, "La communauté juive de Paris au XIIIe siècle: Problèmes topographiques, démographiques et institutionnels," in *Études sur l'histoire de Paris et de L'Île-de-France,* Comité des travaux historiques et scientifiques (Paris: Bibliothèque Nationale, 1978), 143–156 at 144.

84. Simon Simonsohn, *The Apostolic See and the Jews: History* (Toronto: Pontifical Institute of Medieval Studies, 1991), 46ff; also Chazan, *Medieval Jewry,* 63ff.

85. Albéric Clement is usually considered the first marshal of France, appointed by Philip Augustus in 1185. Matthew of Bourges, the marshal (*Matheus de Buturis mariscallus noster*), is otherwise unknown.

86. Stow, *Jewish Dogs,* in his chapter on Richard of Pontoise, concentrates on the narrative structure that the *Acta Sanctorum* utilizes to contextualize the charges.

87. Baldwin, *Government of Philip Augustus,* 52, notes that the despoliation of the Jews "produced an enormous windfall for the king's finances." Bradbury, *Philip Augustus,* 53, rightly maintains that the profit from the expulsion "was no windfall, no unexpected accident, but rather the result of determined policy."

88. Jordan, *French Monarchy,* 31, calculates that the raid alone was worth more than the annual predictable royal revenue.

89. Simonsohn, *Apostolic See and the Jews: History,* 46.

90. Jaeglé, *Histoire de Paris*, mentions that Jews were heavily taxed but not that they were expelled from the kingdom and their houses seized. No mentions of Jews are made in Robert-Henri Bautier, "Paris au temps d'Abélard" in *Abélard en son temps*, ed. J. Jolivet (Paris: Belles Lettres, 1981), 21–78; and Chadych and Leborgne, *Atlas de Paris*. Those who make some mention of Jewish habitation do not do so in the context of *les Champeaux*, most notably Lombard-Jourdan, *Paris, genèse de la ville*; Michel Mollat, *Histoire de l'Ile-de-France et de Paris* ([Toulouse]: Privat, 1991); and Jean-Robert Pitte, *Paris, histoire d'une ville* (Paris: Hachette, 1993).

91. Easter fell on March 28, 1182, and the royal decree was made in April.

Conclusion

1. See Hsia, *Ritual Murder*, 4, and John H. Arnold, *Belief and Unbelief in Medieval Europe* (London: Hodder Arnold, 2005), 103. Donald Weinstein and Rudolph Bell, *Saints and Society: The Two Worlds of Western Christendom, 1000–1700* (Chicago and London: University of Chicago Press, 1982), 160: "The child martyrs of the Middle Ages were little more than names, their lives in hagiography beginning only with the stories of their murder by wicked Jews who wanted their blood. Next to nothing is known of them, therefore, nor is knowledge of their lives relevant here." An exception is Robert Bartlett, *Why Can the Dead Do Such Great Things?: Saints and Worshippers from the Martyrs to the Reformation* (Princeton: Princeton University Press, 2013), 179–80.

2. Anna Abulafia has identified a similar mechanism at work in the notion that Jews were tolerated for their service, and when they no longer provided service in this period, they were expendable. Anna Sapir Abulafia, *Christian Jewish Relations 1000–1300: Jews in the Service of Medieval Christendom* (London: Routledge, 2011).

Appendices

1. This is the argument of Langmuir, *History, Religion and Antisemitism*, challenged by Robert Stacey, "History, Religion and Antisemitism: A Response to Gavin Langmuir," *Religious Studies Review* 20, no. 2 (1994), 95–101 at 100.

2. See, for example, Peter Schäfer, *Judeophobia: Attitudes toward the Jews in the Ancient World* (Cambridge, MA: Harvard University Press, 1998) and David Nirenberg, *Anti-Judaism: The Western Tradition* (New York: W. W. Norton, 2013). James Parkes, *Antisemitism* (London: Vallentine, Mitchell, 1963), Edward H. Flannery, *The Anguish of the Jews: Twenty-Three Centuries of Antisemitism* (New York: Paulist Press, 2004), and Leon Poliakov, *The History of Anti-Semitism*, 2 vols. (London: Elek, 1974) are early classics on the topic.

3. Gavin Langmuir differentiated between the two in his influential works. See Langmuir, *Toward a Definition*, 236, for the crucifixion accusation and 268ff for the accusation of ritual cannibalization first made at Fulda in 1235. In this usage he is followed by Robert Stacey, "From Ritual Crucifixion to Host Desecration: Jews and

the Body of Christ," *Jewish History* 12, no. 1 (1998), 11–28 at 23, and Norman Roth, *Medieval Jewish Civilization: An Encyclopedia* (London: Routledge, 2003), s.v. "Ritual Murder." Darren O'Brien, *The Pinnacle of Hatred: the Blood Libel and the Jews* (Jerusalem: Magnes Press, 2011), adopts the distinction in his database, which classifies accusations as "blood libel," "mutilation murder," "crucifixion murder," or "plain murder." Others, however, are not persuaded by such distinctions. See, for example, David Berger, *From Crusades to Blood Libels to Expulsions: Some New Approaches to Medieval Antisemitism* (New York: Touro College Graduate School of Jewish Studies, 1997), and Israel Yuval, "'They Tell Lies: You Ate the Man': Jewish Reactions to Ritual Murder Accusations," in *Religious Violence Between Christians and Jews: Medieval Roots, Modern Perspectives*, ed. Anna Sapir Abulafia (New York: Palgrave, 2002), 86–106 at 90.

4. The *Encyclopedia Judaica* and *Jewish Encyclopedia* likewise treat the terms as similar or overlapping. In a paper delivered at the annual conference, Association for Jewish Studies, Washington, DC, December 21, 2008, "Distinctions without Much Difference? Ritual Murder, Blood Libel and the Need to Classify," I have argued that the notion that the "ritual murder" and the "blood libel" accusations are distinct is a product of European scholars who wrote in the shadow of the Holocaust, and who were eager to identify differences between Continental (especially German) and English attitudes toward Jews.

5. See most recently Raphael Langham, "William of Norwich," paper presented to *The Jewish Historical Society of England* (2005) and posted online in 2008 at http://www.jhse.org/node/44.

Bibliography of Printed Sources

A. Primary Sources

Abrahams, I., and H. P. Stokes, eds., with additions by H. Loewe. *Starrs and Jewish Charters Preserved in the British Museum.* 3 vols. Cambridge: Cambridge University Press for the Jewish Historical Society of England, 1930–1932.

Acta Sanctorum, 3rd ed. 62 vols. Brussels and Paris, 1863–1925.

Arnold, Thomas, ed. *Memorials of St. Edmund's Abbey.* 3 vols. Rolls Series 96. London: HMSO, 1890–1896; repr. Wiesbaden: Kraus, 1965.

Belfort, Auguste de, ed. *Archives de la maison-dieu de Châteaudun.* Paris: Société française de numismatique et d'archéologie, 1881.

Blomefield, Francis. *The History of the City and County of Norwich.* Norwich, 1745.

Blomefield, Francis, and Charles Parkin. *An Essay Towards a Topographical History of the County of Norfolk.* 5 vols. Fersfield, 1739–1775.

Brown, Philippa, ed. *Sibton Abbey Cartularies and Charters.* 4 vols. Suffolk Charters 7–10. Woodbridge, Suffolk: Boydell Press for the Suffolk Records Society, 1985–1988.

Cheney, C. R., and Bridgett E. A. Jones, eds. *Canterbury, 1162–1190.* English Episcopal Acta 2. London: British Academy, 1986.

Cronne, H. A., R. H. C. Davis, and H. W. C. Davis, eds. *Regesta Regum Anglo-Normannorum, 1066–1154*, Vol. 3: *Regesta Regis Stephani ac Mathildis Imperatricis ac Gaufridi et Henrici Ducum Normannorum, 1135–1154.* Oxford: Clarendon Press, 1968.

David, Charles Wendell, and Jonathan Phillips, eds. *De Expugnatione Lyxbonensi.* New York: Columbia University Press, 2001.

Diceto, Ralph de. *Opera Historica.* Edited by William Stubbs. 2 vols. Rolls Series 68. London: Longman, 1879; repr. Wiesbaden: Kraus, 1965.

Dodwell, Barbara, ed. *The Charters of the Norwich Cathedral Priory*, part 1. Rolls Series, n.s. 40. London: Pipe Roll Society, 1974.

———. *The Charters of the Norwich Cathedral Priory*, part 2. Rolls Series, n.s. 46. London: J. W. Ruddock and Sons, 1985.

———. "Some Charters Relating to the Honour of Bacton." In *A Medieval Miscellany for Doris Mary Stenton*, edited by Patricia M. Barnes and C. F. Slade. London: Pipe Roll Society, 1962.

Douglas, David C., ed. *Feudal Documents from the Abbey of Bury St. Edmunds.* Records of the Social and Economic History of England and Wales 8. London: British Academy, 1932; repr. Munich: Kraus, 1981.

Douglas, David C., and George W. Greenaway, eds. *English Historical Documents,* Vol. 2: *Antiquity to Early Medieval, 1042–1189.* London: Routledge, 1996.

Eidelberg, Shlomo, ed. and trans. *The Jews and the Crusaders: The Hebrew Chronicles of the First and Second Crusades.* Madison: University of Wisconsin Press, 1977.

Eley, Penny, and Penny Simons, eds. *Partonopeus de Blois: An Electronic Edition.* Sheffield: HriOnline, 2005, www.hrionline.ac.uk/partonopeus.

Ephraim of Bonn. "*Sefer Zekhirah*, or the Book of Remembrance, of Rabbi Ephraim of Bonn." In *The Jews and the Crusaders: The Hebrew Chronicles of the First and Second Crusades*, edited and translated by Shlomo Eidelberg, 121–133. Madison: University of Wisconsin Press, 1977.

Evergates, Theodore, ed. *Feudal Society in Medieval France: Documents from the County of Champagne.* Philadelphia: University of Pennsylvania Press, 1993.

Farrer, William. *Honours and Knights' Fees.* 3 vols. London: Spottiswoode, Balantyne and Co., 1923–1925.

Fleureau, Basile. "De la maladerie Saint-Lazare. In *Les antiquitez de la ville et du duché d'Estampes, avec l'histoire de l'Abbaye de Morigny, et plusieurs remarques considérables qui regardent l'histoire générale de France* (1668), 2.21: 451–462. Paris: Coignard, 1683.

Foliot, Gilbert. *The Letters and Charters of Gilbert Foliot, Abbot of Gloucester (1139–48), Bishop of Hereford (1148–63) and London (1163–87).* Edited by Adrian Morey and C. N. L. Brooke. Cambridge Studies in Medieval Life and Thought, n.s. 11. Cambridge: Cambridge University Press, 1967.

Geoffrey of Wells [Gaufridus de Fontibus]. *De infantia sancti Eadmundi.* In *Memorials of St. Edmund's Abbey*, edited by Thomas Arnold, 1:93–106. Rolls Series 96, London: HMSO, 1890–1896.

Gerald of Wales [Giraldus Cambrensis]. *Expugnatio Hibernica: The Conquest of Ireland by Giraldus Cambrensis.* Edited by A. B. Scott and F. X. Martin. Dublin: Irish Royal Academy, 1978.

Gervase of Canterbury. *The Historical Works of Gervase of Canterbury, 1: The Chronicle of the Reigns of Stephen, Henri II and Richard I.* Edited by William Stubbs. Rolls Series 79. London: Longman, 1879; repr. Wiesbaden: Kraus, 1965.

Gesta Stephani. Edited by K. R. Potter and R. H. C. Davis. Oxford: Clarendon Press, 1976.

Gildea, Joseph, ed. and trans. *Partonopeu de Blois: A French Romance of the Twelfth Century.* 2 vols. Philadelphia: Villanova University Press, 1967–1970.

Guibert of Nogent. *De sanctis et eorum pigneribus* [*Patrologia Latina* 156 (1853): cols. 607–680]. Edited by R. B. C. Huygens. Corpus Christianorum, Continuatio Mediaevalis, 127. Turnhout: Brepols, 1993.

Habermann, A. M. *The Persecutions of France and Germany.* [Hebrew] Jerusalem: Tarshish, 1945; repr. Ofir, 1971.

Hall, Hubert, ed. *The Red Book of the Exchequer.* 3 vols. Rolls Series 99 (1–3). London: HMSO, 1896; repr. Wiesbaden: Kraus, 1965.

Harper-Bill, Christopher, ed. *English Episcopal Acta 6: Norwich, 1070–1214.* London: Oxford University Press for the British Academy, 1990.

Hart, William Henry, ed. *Historia et cartularium monasterii Sancti Petri Gloucestriae.* 3 vols. Rolls Series 33. London: Longman, 1863–1867; repr. Wiesbaden: Kraus, 1965.

Head, Thomas, ed. *Medieval Hagiography: An Anthology.* New York: Garland, 2000.

Hénault, Charles-Jean-François. *Nouvel abrégé chronologique de l'histoire de France: Contenant les événemens de notre histoire depuis Clovis jusqu'à Louis XIV.* 3rd ed. Paris, 1768.

Henry of Huntingdon. *Historia Anglorum.* Edited by Diana Greenway. Oxford: Clarendon Press, 1996.

Herbert de Losinga. *The Life, Letters, and Sermons of Bishop Herbert de Losinga.* Edited by Edward Myrick Goulburn and Henry Symonds. 2 vols. Oxford: Parker and Co., 1878.

Hermannus. "De miraculis Sancti Eadmundi." In *Memorials of St. Edmund's Abbey,* edited by Thomas Arnold, vol. I. London: Rolls Series, 1890.

Jacobs, Joseph, ed. and trans. *The Jews of Angevin England: Documents and Records from Latin and Hebrew Sources.* London: D. Nutt, 1893; repr. Westmead, Farnborough, Hampshire: Gregg, 1969.

Jessopp, Augustus, and M. R. James. *See* Thomas of Monmouth below.

Jocelin of Brakelond. *The Chronicle of Jocelin of Brakelond Concerning the Acts of Samson, Abbot of the Monastery of St. Edmund.* Edited and translated by H. E. Butler. London: Thomas Nelson and Sons, 1949.

———. *Chronicle of the Abbey of Bury St. Edmunds.* Edited and translated by Diana Greenway and Jane Sayers. Oxford: Oxford University Press, 1989.

John of Ford. *De vita beati Wulrici anachoretae Haselbergiae.* Edited by Maurice Bell. Somerset Records Society Publications 47. London: Frome, 1933.

Loyd, Lewis C., and Doris Mary Stenton, eds. *Sir Christopher Hatton's Book of Seals, to Which Is Appended a Select List of the Works of Frank Merry Stenton.* Publications of the Northamtonshire Record Society 15. Oxford: Clarendon Press, 1950.

Mabillon, Jean. *Annales Ordinis S. Benedicti Occidentalium Monachorum Patriarchae.* 6 vols. Paris: C. Robustel, 1739–1745.

Marcus, Jacob Rader, and Marc Saperstein, eds. *The Jew in the Medieval World: A Source Book, 319–1791.* Cincinnati: Hebrew Union College Press, 1999.

Merlet, L., and L. Jarry, ed. *Cartulaire de l'abbaye de la Madeleine de Châteaudun.* Châteaudun: Pouillier, 1896.

Mortimer, Richard, ed. *Leiston Abbey Cartulary and Butley Priory Charters.* Ipswich, Suffolk: Boydell Press for the Suffolk Records Society, 1979.

———. *Charters of St. Bartholomew's Priory, Sudbury.* Woodbridge, Suffolk: Boydell Press for the Suffolk Records Society, 1996.

Neubauer, Adolf, and Morris Stern. *Hebräische Berichte über die Judenverfolgung während der Kreuzzüge.* Berlin: Simion, 1892, repr. New York: Olms, 1997.

Orderic Vitalis. *The Ecclesiastical History of Orderic Vitalis.* Edited and translated by Marjorie Chibnall. 6 vols. Oxford Medieval Texts. Oxford: Clarendon Press, 1969–1980.

Patterson, Robert B., ed. *The Original Acta of St. Peter's Abbey, Gloucester, c. 1122 to 1263.* Gloucestershire Record Series 11. Gloucester: Bristol and Gloucestershire Archaeological Society, 1998.

Pipe Rolls

Second, Third, and Fourth Years of the Reign of King Henry II, 1155–1158. London: G. E. Eyre and A. Spottiswoode, 1844; facsimile edition, HMSO, 1930.

Sixteenth Year of the Reign of King Henry II, 1169–1170. Pipe Roll Society Publications 15. London, 1892.

Thirty-First Year of Henry I, Michaelmas, 1130. London: G. E. Eyre and A. Spottiswoode, 1833; facsimile edition, HMSO, 1929.

Quodvultdeus *Sermo contra judaeos, paganos et arianos de symbolo.* In Patrologia Latina, ed. J. P. Migne, 42:1115–1130.

Reginald of Durham. *Libellus de vita et miraculis S. Godrici, Heremitae de Finchale.* Edited by Joseph Stevenson. Surtees Society Publications 20. London: J. B. Nichols and Son, 1847.

Resnick, Irven, Ed. *Peter the Venerable, Against the Inveterate Obduracy of the Jews.* Washington, DC: Catholic University of America Press, 2013.

Resnick, Irven M. *Petrus Alfonsi's Dialogue against the Jews.* Translated by Irven M. Resnick. Fathers of the Church, Medieval Continuation. Vol. 8, Washington DC: Catholic University of America Press, 2006.

Richard of Devizes. *The Chronicle of Richard of Devizes of the Time of Richard the First.* Edited by John T. Appleby. Oxford Medieval Texts. Oxford: Oxford University Press, 1963.

Rigord. *Histoire de Philippe Auguste* [Gesta Philippi Augusti, Francorum Regis] in H.-Francois Delaborde, ed., *Oeuvres de Rigord et de Guillaume le Breton,* 1:1–167. Paris: Librairie Renouard, 1885.

Robertson, James Craigie, and J. Brigstocke Sheppard, eds. *Materials for the History of Thomas Becket, Archbishop of Canterbury.* 7 vols. Rerum Britannicarum medii aevi scriptores 67. London: Longman, 1875–1885.

Roger of Hoveden. *Chronica magistri Rogeri de Houedene.* Edited by William Stubbs. 4 vols. London: Longman, 1964 (repr. of 1868 edition).

Roger of Wendover, *Matthæi Parisiensis: Monachi Santi Albani, Chronica Majora.* Edited by H. L. Luard. Rolls Series. 2 vols. London: Longman, 1874.

Salfeld, Siegmund, ed. *Das Martyrologium des Nürnberger Memorbuches.* Quellen zur Geschichte der Juden in Deutschland 3. Berlin: Simion, 1898.

Saunders, H. W., ed. *The First Register of Norwich Cathedral Priory.* Norfolk Record Society 11. Norwich: Norfolk Record Society, 1939.

Simonsohn, Simon. *The Apostolic See and the Jews.* 8 vols. Toronto: Pontifical Institute of Medieval Studies, 1988–1993.

Slack, Corliss Konwiser. *Crusade Charters, 1138–1270.* Medieval and Renaissance Texts and Studies 197. Tempe: Arizona Center for Medieval and Renaissance Studies, 2001.

Southern, R. W., and F. S. Schmitt, eds. *Memorials of St. Anselm.* London: Oxford University Press for the British Academy, 1969.

Stone, E. N. *A Translation of Chapters XI–XVI of the Pseudo-Augustinian Sermon Against Jews, Pagans, and Arians, Concerning the Creed.* Seattle: University of Washington Press, 1928.

Swanton, Michael J., ed. and trans. *The Anglo-Saxon Chronicle.* London: Dent, 1996.

Sweetman, H. S., ed. *Calendar of Documents Relating to Ireland Preserved in Her Majesty's Public Record Office.* 5 vols. London: Longman, 1875–1886.

Thillier, Joseph, and Eugène Jarry, eds. *Cartulaire de Sainte-Croix d'Orléans (814–1300), contenant le "Chartularium ecclesiae Aurelianensis vetus," suivi d'un appendice et d'un supplément.* Paris: Picard, 1906.

Thomas of Monmouth. *Liber de vita et passione Sancti Willelmi Martyris Norwicensis* (Cambridge University Library, Add. ms 3037).

———. *The Life and Miracles of St. William of Norwich by Thomas of Monmouth.* Ed. and trans. Augustus Jessopp and M. R. James. Cambridge: Cambridge University Press, 1896.

———. *The Life and Passion of William of Norwich.* Edited and translated by Miri Rubin. London: Penguin Books, 2014.

———. Ed. Miri Rubin. http://yvc history.qmul.ac.uk/WN-joined 17 08-09.pdf.

West, J. R., ed. *St. Benet of Holme, 1102–1210: The Eleventh and Twelfth Century Sections of Cott. Ms. Galba E. ii. The Register of the Abbey of St. Benet of Holme.* 3 vols. Norfolk Record Society, 1932.

Whitelock, Dorothy, ed. and trans. *The Anglo-Saxon Chronicle: A Revised Translation.* London: Eyre and Spottiswoode, 1961; repr. Westport, CT: Greenwood Press, 1986.

William of Malmesbury. *Historia Novella.* Edited by William Stubbs. London, 1887–1889.

———. *Historia Novella.* Edited and translated by K. R. Potter. London: Thomas Nelson and Sons, 1955.

———. *Historia Novella.* In Joseph Stephenson, ed. *Contemporary Chronicles of the Middle Ages.* Felinfach, Dyfed: Llanerch Enterprises, 1988.

———. *Wilhelmi Malmesbiriensis Monachi de gestis pontificum Anglorum: Libri quinque.* Edited by N.E.S.A. Hamilton. Roll Series 52. London: Longman, 1870; repr. Wiesbaden: Kraus, 1965.

William of Newburgh. *Historia Rerum Anglicarum.* Edited by Richard Howlett. Rolls Series 82. London: Longman, 1885.

Williamson, E. W., ed. *The Letters of Osbert of Clare, Prior of Westminster.* Oxford: Oxford University Press, 1929.

Young, Karl, ed. and trans. *Ordo Rachelis.* Madison: University of Wisconsin, 1919.

B. Secondary Sources

Abou-El-Haj, Barbara. "Bury St. Edmunds Abbey between 1070 and 1124: A History of Property, Privilege, and Monastic Art Production." *Art History* 6 (1983): 1–29.

Abulafia, Anna Sapir. *Christians and Jews in the Twelfth-Century Renaissance.* London: Routledge, 1995.

———, ed. *Religious Violence Between Christians and Jews: Medieval Roots, Modern Perspectives.* New York: Palgrave, 2002.

———. *Christian Jewish Relations 1000–1300: Jews in the Service of Medieval Christendom.* London: Routledge, 2011.

Adler, Michael. "The Medieval Jews of Exeter." *Transactions of the Devonshire Association for the Advancement of Science, Literature, and Art* 63 (1931): 221–240.

———. "The Jews of Medieval Bristol." In Michael Adler, *Jews of Medieval England,* 175–254. London: Jewish Historical Society of England, 1939.

———. *Jews of Medieval England.* London: Jewish Historical Society of England, 1939.

Albrecht, Otto. *Four Latin Plays of St. Nicholas from the Twelfth-Century Fleury Play-book: Text and Commentary.* Philadelphia: University of Pennsylvania Press, 1935.

Alexander, James W. "Herbert of Norwich, 1091–1119: Studies in the History of Norman England." *Studies in Medieval and Renaissance History* 6 (1969): 115–232.

Alexandre-Bidon, D., and D. Lett. *Children in the Middle Ages: Fifth-Fifteenth Centuries.* Notre Dame, IN: University of Notre Dame Press, 1999.

Allen, Derek F. *A Catalogue of English Coins in the British Museum: The Cross-and-Crosslets ('Tealby') Type of Henry II.* London: Trustees of the British Museum, 1951.

Allen, Martin. "Documentary Evidence for the Output, Profits and Expenditure of the Bury St Edmunds Mint." *British Numismatic Journal* 69 (1999): 210–213.

———. "Ecclesiastical Mints in Fifteenth-Century England." *Numismatic Chronicle* 160 (2000): 249–259.

———. "Henry II and the English Coinage." In *Henry II: New Interpretations,* edited by Christopher Harper-Bill and Nicholas Vincent, 257–277. Woodbridge, Suffolk: Boydell Press, 2007.

———. "Mints and Money in Norman England." *Anglo-Norman Studies* 34 (2012): 1–21.

———. *Mints and Money in Medieval England.* Cambridge: Cambridge University Press, 2012.

Anchel, Robert. "The Early History of the Jewish Quarters in Paris." *Jewish Social Studies* 2:1 (1940): 45–60.

Anderson, Freda. "St. Pancras Priory, Lewes: Its Architectural Development to 1200." *Anglo-Norman Studies* 11 (1989): 1–35.

Anderson, George. *The Legend of the Wandering Jew.* Providence, RI: Brown University Press, 1965; repr. 1991.

Anderson, Mary-Désirée. *A Saint at Stake: The Strange Death of William of Norwich, 1144*. London: Faber & Faber, 1964.

Appleby, John T. *Henry II: The Vanquished King*. London: G. Bell & Sons, 1962.

Areford, David S. *The Viewer and the Printed Image in Late Medieval Europe*. Aldershot, Hampshire: Ashgate, 2010.

Aries, Philippe. *Centuries of Childhood: A Social History of Family Life*. Translated by Robert Baldick. New York: Knopf, 1962.

Arnold, John H. *Belief and Unbelief in Medieval Europe*. London: Hodder Arnold, 2005.

Arnold-Foster, Frances. *Studies in Church Dedications*. London: Skeffington and Son, 1899.

Atherton, Ian, ed. *Norwich Cathedral: Church, City and Diocese, 1096–1996*. London: Hambledon Press, 1996.

Auslander, Diane Peters. "Victims or Martyrs: Children, Antisemitism, and the Stress of Change in Medieval England." In *Childhood in the Middle Ages and the Renaissance: The Results of a Paradigm Shift in the History of Mentality*, edited by Albrecht Classen, 105–135. Berlin: Walter de Gruyter, 2005.

Backhouse, Janet, ed. *The Sherborne Missal*. London: British Library, 1999.

Baldwin, John. *The Government of Philip Augustus*. Berkeley: University of California Press, 1986.

Bale, Anthony P. "House Devil, Town Saint": Anti-Semitism and Hagiography in Medieval Suffolk." In *Chaucer and the Jews*, edited by Sheila Delany, 185-209. New York: Routledge, 2002.

———. *The Jew in the Medieval Book: English Antisemitisms, 1350–1500*. Cambridge Studies in Medieval Literature. Cambridge: Cambridge University Press, 2006.

———. ed. *St Edmund, King and Martyr: Changing Images of a Medieval Saint*. York: York Medieval Press, 2009.

———. *Feeling Persecuted: Christians, Jews and Images of Violence in the Middle Ages*. London: Reaktion Books, 2010.

———. "Some Blood, and a Lot More Ink." *Journal for the Study of Antisemitism* 3, no. 2 (2011): 781–3.

Barbezat, Michael D. "The Fires of Hell and the Burning of Heretics in the Accounts of the Executions at Orleans in 1022." *Journal of Medieval History* 40, no. 4 (2014): 399–420.

Barlow, Frank. *The Feudal Kingdom of England, 1042–1216*. 3rd ed. Longman's History of England. London: Longman, 1972.

———. *Thomas Becket*. London: Weidenfeld & Nicolson, 1987.

Barnes, Patricia M. "The Anstey Case." In *A Medieval Miscellany for Doris Mary Stenton*, edited by Patricia Barnes and C. F. Slade, 1–24. London: J. W. Ruddock and Sons, 1962.

Bartlett, Robert. *Trial by Fire and Water: The Medieval Judicial Ordeal*. Oxford: Oxford University Press, 1986.

————. *England under the Norman and Angevin Kings, 1075–1225.* Oxford: Oxford University Press, 2000.

————. *Why Can the Dead Do Such Great Things?: Saints and Worshippers from the Martyrs to the Reformation.* Princeton, NJ: Princeton University Press, 2013.

Bates, David. "The Building of a Great Church: The Abbey of St Peter's, Gloucester and Its Early Norman Benefactors." *Transactions of the Bristol and Gloucestershire Archeological Society* 102 (1984): 129–132.

Bautier, Robert-Henri. "Paris au temps d'Abélard." In *Abélard en son temps: Actes du colloque international organisé à l'occasion du 9. centenaire de la naissance de Pierre Abélard (14–19 mai 1979),* edited by J. Jolivet, 21–78. Paris: Belles Lettres, 1981.

Bearman, Robert. "Baldwin De Redvers, Some Aspects of a Baronial Career in the Reign of King Stephen." *Anglo-Norman Studies* 18 (1985): 19–46.

Beit-Arié, Malachi. *The Makings of the Medieval Hebrew Book: Studies in Paleography and Codicology.* Jerusalem: Magnes Press, 1993.

Benjamin, Sandra. *The World of Benjamin of Tudela: A Medieval Mediterranean Travelogue.* Teaneck, NJ: Fairleigh Dickinson University Press, 1995.

Bennett, Gillian. "Towards a Revaluation of the Legend of 'Saint' William of Norwich and Its Place in the Blood Libel Legend." *Folklore* 116, no. 2 (August 2005): 119–139.

————. "William of Norwich and the Expulsion of the Jews." *Folklore* 116, no. 3 (December 2005): 311–314.

Bennett, Matthew. "Military Aspects of the Conquest of Lisbon, 1147." In *The Second Crusade: Scope and Consequences,* edited by Jonathan Phillips and Martin Hoch, 71–89. Manchester: Manchester University Press, 2001.

Bensly, W. T. "St. Leonard's Priory, Norwich." *Norfolk Archeology* 12 (1895): 190–227.

Benson, Robert L., Giles Constable, and Carol D. Lanham, eds. *Renaissance and Renewal in the Twelfth Century.* Cambridge, MA: Harvard University Press, 1982.

Benton, John F. "The Court of Champagne as a Literary Center." *Speculum* 36 (1961): 551–591.

Benveniste, François. *Balade autour de la muraille de Philippe Auguste.* Saint-Cyr-sur-Loire: A. Sutton, 2004.

Berg, Roger. *Histoire des juifs à Paris: de Chilpéric à Jacques Chirac.* Paris: Éditions du Cerf, 1997.

Berger, David. "The Attitude of St. Bernard of Clairvaux towards the Jews." *Proceedings of the American Academy for Jewish Research* 40 (1972): 89–108.

————. "Mission to the Jews and Jewish-Christian Contacts in the Polemical Literature of the High Middle Ages." *American Historical Review* 91 (1986): 576–591.

————. *From Crusades to Blood Libels to Expulsions: Some New Approaches to Medieval Antisemitism.* New York: Touro College Graduate School of Jewish Studies, 1997.

Berier, F. "L'humaniste, le prêtre et l'enfant mort: Le sermon 'De Sanctis Innocentibus' de Nicolas de Clamanges." In *L'Enfant au Moyen Âge: littérature et civilisation: Communications du quatrième colloque du CUERMA*. Sénéfiance 9. Aix-en-Provence: CUERMA, 1980.

Bernier, Jean. *Histoire de Blois, contenant les antiquitez et singularitez du comté de Blois, les éloges de ses comtes et les vies des hommes illustres qui sont nez au païs blésois, avec les noms et les armoiries des familles nobles du mesme païs.* Paris: Chez François Muguet, 1682.

Berry, Virginia G. "The Second Crusade." In *A History of the Crusades*, 6 vols., edited by Kenneth M. Setton, 2nd ed., Vol. 1: *The First Hundred Years*, edited by M. W. Baldwin, 463–512. Madison: University of Wisconsin Press, 1969.

Bethell, D. "The Making of a Twelfth Century Relic Collection." In *Popular Belief and Practice*, edited by G. J. Cuming and D. Baker. Studies in Ecclesiastical History, 61–72. Cambridge: Ecclestiastical History Society, 1972.

Biale, David. "Blood Libels and Blood Vengeance." *Tikkun* 9, no. 4 (1994): 39–40, 75.

———. *Blood and Belief: The Circulation of a Symbol Between Jews and Christians.* Berkeley: University of California Press, 2007.

Bisson, Thomas N. *Conservation of Coinage, Monetary Exploitation and Its Restraint in France, Catalonia, and Aragon (c. A.D. 1000–c. 1225).* Oxford: Clarendon Press, 1979.

———. *The Crisis of the Twelfth Century: Power, Lordship, and the Origins of European Government.* Princeton, NJ: Princeton University Press, 2009.

Blumenkranz, Bernard. "Les juifs à Blois au Moyen Âge: À propos de la démographie historique des juifs." In *Études de civilisation médiévale (IXe—XIIe siècles): Mélanges offerts à E. R. Labande*, 33–38. Poitiers: Centre d'études supérieurs de civilization médiévale, 1974. Repr. in Bernhard Blumenkranz, *Juifs en France: Écrits dispersés.* Paris: Commission française des archives juives, 1989.

Blurton, Heather. "Narratives of Ritual Crucifixion in Twelfth-Century England." Paper presented at the conference *Antisemitism and English Culture*, July 9–11, 2007, Birkbeck College, University of London.

———. "Egyptian Days: From Passion to Exodus in the Representation of Twelfth-Century Jewish-Christian Relations." In *Christians and Jews in Angevin England: The York Massacre of 1190, Narratives and Contexts*, edited by Sarah Rees Jones and Sethina C. Watson, 222–237. York: York Medieval Press, 2013.

———. "William of Norwich Between History and Liturgy." Paper presented at the conference *Putting England in Its Place: Cultural Production and Cultural Relations in the High Middle Ages*, Fordham University, March 9–10, 2013.

Bolton, John. *Money in the Medieval English Economy 973–1489.* Manchester: Manchester University Press, 2012.

Boon, George C. *Coins of the Anarchy, 1135–54.* Cardiff: National Museum of Wales, 1988.

Boswell, John. *The Kindness of Strangers: The Abandonment of Children in Western Europe from Late Antiquity to the Renaissance*. New York: Pantheon Books, 1988.

Boulton, Maureen. "Anti-Jewish Attitudes in Anglo-Norman Religious Texts: Twelfth and Thirteenth Centuries." In *Christian Attitudes Towards the Jews in the Middle Ages: A Casebook*, edited by Michael Frassetto, 151–166. New York: Routledge, 2007.

Boussard, Jacques. *Nouvelle histoire de Paris: De la fin du siège de 885–886 à la mort de Philippe Auguste*, 2nd ed. Paris: Association pour la publication d'une histoire de Paris, Hachette, 1997.

Boyarin, Adrienne Williams. *Miracles of the Virgin in Medieval England: Law and Jewishness in Marian Legends*. Woodbridge, Suffolk: Boydell and Brewer, 2010.

Boynton, Susan. "Performative Exegesis in the Fleury Interfectio Puerorum." *Viator* 29 (1998): 39–64.

———. "Boy Singers in Medieval Monasteries and Cathedrals." In *Young Choristers, 650–1700*, edited by Susan Boynton and Eric N. Rice 37–48. Woodbridge, Suffolk: Boydell and Brewer, 2008.

Bradbury, C. A. "A Norfolk Saint for a Norfolk Man: William of Norwich and Sir James Hobart at Holy Trinity Church in London." *Norfolk Archaeology* 46,no. 4 (2013), 452–461.

Bradbury, Jim. *Stephen and Matilda: The Civil War of 1139–53*. Stroud, Gloucestershire: Sutton, 1996.

———. "The Civil War of Stephen's Reign: Winners and Losers." In *Armies, Chivalry, and Warfare in Medieval Britain and France*, edited by Matthew Strickland, 115–132. Stamford, Lincolnshire: Paul Watkins, 1998.

———. *Philip Augustus, King of France, 1180–1223*. London: Longman, 1998.

Brand, John D. *The English Coinage, 1180–1247: Money, Mints and Exchanges*. British Numismatic Society, Special Publication 1. Glasgow: British Numsimatic Society, 1994.

Broadhurst, Karen M. "Henry II of England and Eleanor of Aquitaine: Patrons of Literature in French?" *Viator* 27 (1996): 53–84.

Brockett, Clyde W. "*Persona in Cantilena*: St. Nicholas in Music in Medieval Drama." In *The Saint Play in Medieval Europe*, edited by Clifford Davidson, 11–30. Kalamazoo, MI: Medieval Institute Publications EDAM, 1986.

Brooke, Christopher. *The Monastic World 1000–1300*. London: Paul Elek, 1974.

———. Review of *Religious and Laity in Western Europe, 1000–1400: Interaction, Negotiation, and Power*, edited by E. Jamroziak and J. Burton. *Reviews in History*, no. 608, www.history.ac.uk/reviews/review/608.

Brown, Carleton. "The Prioress's Tale." In *Sources and Analogues of Chaucer's Canterbury Tales*, edited by William Frank Brown et al., 447–485. New York: Humanities Press, 1958.

Brown, R. Allen. "Early Charters of Sibton Abbey, Suffolk." In *A Medieval Miscellany in Honour of Doris Mary Stenton*, edited by Patricia Barnes and C. F. Slade, 65–76. London: Pipe Roll Society, 1962.

———. "The Status of the Norman Knight." In *Anglo-Norman Warfare*, edited by Matthew Strickland, 128–142. Woodbridge, Suffolk: Boydell Press, 1992.

Brown, Reva Berman, and Sean McCartney. "The Business Activities of Jewish Women Entrepreneurs in Medieval England." *Management Decision* 39, no. 9 (2001): 699–709.

Brown, S. D. B. "The Servant and His Master: Military Service and Monetary Reward in the Eleventh and Twelfth Centuries." *History* 74 (1989): 20–38.

Brundage, James A. "Intermarriage Between Christians and Jews in Medieval Canon Law." *Jewish History* 3 (1988): 25–40.

Buc, Philippe. "David's Adultery with Bathsheba and the Healing Power of Capetian Kings." *Viator* 24 (1993): 101–120.

Bull, Marcus. *Knightly Piety and the Lay Response to the First Crusade, the Limousin and Gascony, c. 970–1130*. Oxford: Clarendon Press, 1993.

———. "The Capetian Monarchy and the Early Crusade Movement: Hugh of Vermandois and Louis Vii." *Nottingham Mediaeval Studies* 40 (1996): 25–46.

Bull, Marcus, and Norman Housley, eds. *The Experience of Crusading*. Cambridge: Cambridge University Press, 2003.

Bur, Michel. *La formation du comté de Champagne v. 950–v. 1150*. Mémoires des Annales de l'Est 54. Nancy: l'Université de Nancy, 1977.

Buston, William. "The Monastic Infirmary, Norwich." *Norfolk Archeology* 28 (1944): 124–132.

Bynum, Caroline Walker. "The Presence of Objects: Medieval Anti-Judaism in Modern Germany." *Common Knowledge* 10, no. 1 (Winter 2004): 1–32.

Bysted, Ane L. *The Crusade Indulgence. Spiritual Rewards and the Theology of the Crusades, c. 1095–1216*. Leiden: Brill, 2014.

Callahan, Daniel F. "Ademar of Chabannes, Millennial Fears and the Development of Western Anti-Judaism." *Journal of Ecclesiastical History* 46 (1995): 19–35.

Callahan, Thomas, Jr. "A Reevaluation of the Anarchy of Stephen's Reign, 1135–1154: The Case of the Black Monks." *Revue Benedictine* (1974): 338–351.

———. The Impact of the Anarchy on English Monasticism, 1135–54." *Albion* 6 (1974): 219–232.

———. "Sinners and Saintly Retribution: The Timely Death of King Stephen's Son Eustace, 1153." *Studia Monastica* 18 (1976): 109–117.

———. "Ecclesiastical Reparations and the Soldiers of 'The Anarchy.'" *Albion* 10 (1978): 300–318.

Cam, Helen. "An East Anglian Shire-Moot of Stephen's Reign, 1148–1153." *English Historical Review* 39 (1924): 568–571.

Campbell, James. "The East Anglian Sees before the Conquest." In *Norwich Cathedral, Church, City and Diocese, 1096–1996*, edited by Iam Atherton, Eric Fernie, Christopher Harper-Bill, and Hassell Smith, 3–21. London: The Hambledon Press, 1996.

Carter, Peter. "The Historical Content of William of Malmesbury's Miracles of the Virgin Mary." In *The Writing of History in the Middle Ages: Essays Presented to*

Richard William Southern, edited by R. H. Davis and J. M. Wallace-Hadrill, 127–164. Oxford: Clarendon Press, 1981.

Chadych, Danielle, and Dominique Leborgne. *Atlas de Paris: Évolution d'un paysage urbain*. Paris: Parigramme, 1999.

Challis, C. E., ed. *A New History of the Royal Mint*. Cambridge: Cambridge University Press, 1992.

Chazan, Robert. "The Blois Incident of 1171: A Study in Jewish Intercommunal Organization." *Proceedings of the American Academy for Jewish Research* 36 (1968): 13–31.

———. "Emperor Frederick I, the Third Crusade, and the Jews." *Viator* 8 (1977): 83–93.

———. *Church, State and Jew in the Middle Ages*. New York: Behrman House, 1980.

———. "The Timebound and the Timeless: Medieval Jewish Narration of Events." *History and Memory* 6 (1994): 5–34.

———. *The Jews of Western Christendom, 1000–1500*. Cambridge: Cambridge University Press, 2006.

Cheney, C. R. "Church-Building in the Middle Ages." *Bulletin of the John Rylands Library* 34 (1951): 20–36. Repr. in C. R. Cheney, *Medieval Texts and Studies*. Oxford: Clarendon Press, 1973.

Chibnall, Marjorie M. "Mercenaries and the *Familia Regis* under Henry I." *History* 62 (1977): 15–23.

Clark, Cecily. "Women's Names in Post Conquest England: Observations and Speculations." *Speculum* (1978): 223–251.

Classen, Albrecht, ed. *Childhood in the Middle Ages and the Renaissance: The Results of a Paradigm Shift in the History of Mentality*. Berlin: Walter de Gruyter, 2005.

Cluse, Christoph. "*Fabula Ineptissima*: Die Ritualmordlegende um Adam von Bristol nach der Handschrift London, British Library, Harley 957." *Aschkenas* 5 (1995): 293–330.

———, ed. *Europas Juden im Mittelalter: Beiträge des internationalen Symposiums in Speyer vom 20.–25. Oktober 2002*. Trier: Kliomedia, 2004. English edition: *The Jews of Europe in the Middle Ages (Tenth to Fifteenth Centuries). Proceedings of the International Symposium held at Speyer, 20–25 October 2002*. Cultural Encounters in Late Antiquity and the Middle Ages 4. Turnhout: Brepols, 2004.

Codreanu-Windauer, Silvia. "Regensburg: The Archaeology of the Medieval Jewish Quarter." In *Europas Juden im Mittelalter: Beiträge des internationalen Symposiums in Speyer vom 20.–25. Oktober 2002*, edited by Christoph Cluse, 391–403. Trier: Kliomedia, 2004.

Cohen, Jeffrey J. "The Flow of Blood in Medieval Norwich." *Speculum* 79 (2004): 26–65.

———. *Hybridity, Identity and Monstrosity in Medieval Britain*. London: Palgrave MacMillan, 2006.

Cohen, Jeremy, ed. *From Witness to Witchcraft: Jews and Judaism in Medieval Christian Thought*. Wiesbaden: Harrassowitz, 1996.

————, ed. *Essential Papers on Judaism and Christianity in Conflict, from Late Antiquity to the Reformation*. Essential Papers on Jewish Studies. New York: New York University Press, 1999.

————. *Christkillers: The Jews and the Passion from the Bible to the Big Screen*. Oxford: Oxford University Press, 2007.

Cole, Penny J. *The Preaching of the Crusades to the Holy Land, 1095–1270*. Cambridge, MA: Medieval Academy of America, 1991.

Collins, Fletcher, Jr. "The Home of the Fleury Playbook." In *The Fleury Playbook: Essays and Studies*, edited by C. Clifford Flanigan, Thomas P. Campbell, and Clifford Davidson, 26–34. Kalamazoo, MI: Medieval Institute Publications, 1985.

Constable, Giles. "A Note on the Route of the Anglo-Flemish Crusaders of 1147." *Speculum* 28 (1953): 525–526.

————. "The Second Crusade as Seen by Contemporaries." *Traditio* 9 (1953): 213–279.

————. "A Report of a Lost Sermon by St Bernard on the Failure of the Second Crusade." In *Studies in Medieval Cistercian History Presented to Jeremiah F. O'Sullivan*, edited by Joseph F. O'Callaghan, 49–54. Spencer, MA: Cistercian Publications, 1971.

————. "The Financing of Crusades in the Twelfth Century." In *Outremer: Studies in the History of the Crusading Kingdom of Jerusalem Presented to Joshua Prawer*, edited by B. Z. Kedar, H. E. Mayer, and R. C. Smail, 64–88. Jerusalem: Yad Izhak Ben-Zvi Institute, 1982.

————. "Medieval Charters as a Source for the History of the Crusades." In *Crusade and Settlement: Papers Read at the First Conference for the Society for the Study of the Crusades and the Latin East and Presented to R. C. Smail*, edited by Peter W. Edbury, 73–89. Cardiff: University College Cardiff Press, 1985.

————. "The Language of Preaching in the Twelfth Century." *Viator* 25 (1994): 131–152.

————. "A Further Note on the Conquest of Lisbon in 1147." In *The Experience of Crusading*, ed. Marcus Bull and Norman Housley, 39–44. Cambridge: Cambridge University, 2003.

Copinger Hill, H. "S. Robert of Bury St. Edmunds." *Proceedings of the Suffolk Institute of Archaeology* 21, part 2 (1932): 98–107.

Coquelle, P. "Les clochers romans du Vexin français et du Pincerais." *Memoires de la Societé historique et archéologique de Pontoise et du Vexin* 25 (1903): 47–65.

Corbin, Solange "Le Manuscrit 201 d'Orléans: Drames liturgiques dits de Fleury." *Romania* 74 (1953): 1–43.

Coulton, G. G. *Life in the Middle Ages*. Cambridge: Cambridge University Press, 1928.

Couzy, Hélène. "L'Église des Saints Innocents à Paris." *Bulletin monumental* (1972): 279–302.

Cowdrey, H. E. J. "An Early Record at Dijon of the Export of Becket's Relics." In *Popes, Monks and Crusaders*, edited by H. E. J. Cowdrey, 251–253. London: Hambledon Press, 1985.

Cownie, Emma. *Religious Patronage in Anglo-Norman England, 1066–1135.* Woodbridge, Suffolk, UK; Boydell and Brewer, 1998.

Cowper, Frederick A. G. "The New Manuscript of 'Ille et Galeron.'" *Modern Philology* 18 (1921): 601–608.

Cranage, D. H. S, ed. *Thirteenth-Hundredth Anniversary of the Diocese of East Anglia.* Norwich: Jarrold & Sons, 1930.

Cronne, H. A. *The Reign of Stephen, 1135–54: Anarchy in England.* London: Weidenfeld & Nicolson, 1970.

Crosby, Everett U. *Bishop and Chapter in Twelfth-Century England, a Study of the Mensa Episcopalis.* Cambridge Studies in Medieval Life and Thought. Cambridge: Cambridge University Press, 1994.

Crouch, David. "King Stephen and Northern France." In *King Stephen's Reign (1135–1154),* edited by Paul Dalton and Graeme J. White, 44–57. Woodbridge, UK: Boydell Press, 2008.

Cuffel, Alexandra. *Gendering Disgust in Medieval Religious Polemic.* Notre Dame, IN: University of Notre Dame Press, 2007.

Cuming Geoffrey John, and Derek Baker, eds. *Popular Belief and Practice.* Cambridge: Ecclesiastical History Society, 1972.

Curtis, Edmund. *A History of Medieval Ireland from 1086 to 1513.* New York: Barnes and Noble, 1968.

Dalton, Paul, and Graeme J. White, eds. *King Stephen's Reign (1135–1154).* Woodbridge, UK ; Rochester, NY: Boydell, 2008.

Davis, H. W. C. "The Anarchy of Stephen's Reign." *English Historical Review* 18 (1903): 630–641.

Davis, R. H. C. "The Monks of St. Edmund, 1021–1148." *History* 40 (1955): 227–239.

———. "What Happened in Stephen's Reign." *History* 64 (1964): 35–54.

———. *King Stephen, 1135–1154.* London: Longman, 1980.

Delany, Sheila, ed. *Chaucer and the Jews: Sources, Contexts, Meanings.* New York: Routledge, 2002.

Despres, Denise L. "Immaculate Flesh and the Social Body: Mary and the Jews." *Jewish History* 12, no. 1 (1998): 47-69.

Despres, Denise L. "Adolescence and Sanctity: *The Life and Passion of Saint William of Norwich.*" *Journal of Religion* 90 (2010): 33–62.

Dinn, Robert. "'Monuments Answerable to Mens Worth': Burial Patterns, Social Status and Gender in Late Medieval Bury St. Edmunds." *Journal of Ecclesiastical History* 46 (1995): 237–255.

Dobson, Richard B. *The Jews of Medieval York and the Massacre of March 1190.* Borthwick Papers 45. York: St. Anthony's Press, 1974.

———. "The Jews of Medieval Cambridge." *Jewish Historical Studies* 32 (1990–1992): 1–24.

———. *Clifford's Tower and the Jews of Medieval York.* London: English Heritage, 1995.

Dodwell, Barbara. "The Foundation of Norwich Cathedral." *Transactions of the Royal Historical Society* 7, 5th ser. (1957): 1–18.

———. "The Honour of the Bishop of Thetford/Norwich in the Late Eleventh and Early Twelfth Centuries." *Norfolk Archeology* 33 (1962–1965): 185–199.

———. "Herbert de Losinga and the Foundation." In *Norwich Cathedral: Church, City and Diocese, 1096–1996,* edited by Ian Atherton, 231–254. London: Hambledon Press, 1996.

Dolley, Michael. *Anglo-Norman Ireland, c. 1100–1318.* Dublin: Gill and MacMillan, 1972.

Druery, John Henry. "On the Retirement of Bishop Eborard from the See of Norwich." *Norfolk Archeology* 5 (1859): 41–48.

Dudley, Martin R. "*Natalis Innocentum*: The Holy Innocents in Liturgy and Drama." In *The Church and Childhood: Papers Read at the 1993 Summer Meeting and the 1994 Winter Meeting of the Ecclesiastical History Society,* edited by Diana Wood, 233–242. Studies in Church History 31. Oxford: Blackwell, 1994.

Dulaure, Jacques-Antoine. *Histoire physique, civile et morale de Paris: Depuis les premiers temps historiques jusqu'à nos jours.* 10 vols. Paris: Guillaume, 1823.

Dunbabin, Jean. *France in the Making, 843–1180.* Oxford: Oxford University Press, 2000.

Dundes, Alan. "The Ritual Murder or Blood Libel Legend: A Study of Anti-Semitic Victimization through Projective Inversion." *Temenos* 25 (1989): 7–32. Repr. in Alan Dundes, ed., *The Blood Libel Legend: A Casebook in Anti-Semitic Folklore,* 336–376. Madison: University of Wisconsin Press, 1991.

———, ed. *The Blood Libel Legend: A Casebook in Anti-Semitic Folklore.* Madison: University of Wisconsin Press, 1991.

Dutton, Kathryn "'Ad crudiendum tradidit': The Upbringing of Angevin Comital Children." *Anglo-Norman Studies* 32 (2010): 24–39.

Eaglen, Robin J. "The Mint at Bury St Edmunds." In *Bury St. Edmunds: Medieval Art, Architecture, Archaeology and Economy,* British Archaeological Association Conference Transactions 20, edited by Antonia Grandsen, 111–121. Leeds: British Archeological Association, 1998.

Robin J. Eaglen. *The Abbey and Mint of Bury St. Edmunds to 1279.* London: Spink, for the British Numismatic Society, 2006.

Eales, Richard. "The Political Setting of the Becket Translation of 1220." In *Martyrs and Martyrologies,* Studies in Church History 30, edited by Diana Wood, 127–139. Oxford and Cambridge, MA: Blackwell Publishers for the Ecclesiatical History Society, 1993.

Edgington, Susan B. "The Lisbon Letter of the Second Crusade." *Historical Research* 69 (1996): 328–339.

———. "Albert of Aachen, St Bernard and the Second Crusade." In *The Second Crusade: Scope and Consequences,* edited by Jonathan Philips and Martin Hoch, 54–70. Manchester: Manchester University Press, 2001.

————. "The Capture of Lisbon: Premeditated or Opportunistic?" *The Second Crusade. Holy War on the Periphery of Latin Christendom*, edited by Jason T. Roche and Janus Møller Jensen. Turnhout: Brepols, 2015 forthcoming.

Eidelberg, Shlomo. "Trial by Ordeal in Medieval Jewish History: Laws, Customs and Attitudes." *Proceedings of the American Academy for Jewish Research* 46 [Jubilee volume] (1979–1980): 105–120.

Einbinder, Susan. "Pulcellina of Blois: Romantic Myths and Narrative Conventions." *Jewish History* 12, no. 1 (1998): 29–46.

————. "The Jewish Martyrs of Blois." In *Medieval Hagiography* edited by Thomas Head, 537-561. New York: Garland, 2000.

————. *Beautiful Death: Jewish Poetry and Martyrdom in Medieval France.* Princeton, NJ: Princeton University Press, 2002.

Elbogen, Ismar. *Jewish Liturgy: A Comprehensive History.* Philadelphia: Jewish Publication Society, 1993.

Eley, Penney. *Partonopeus de Blois: Romance in the Making.* Woodbridge, Suffolk: Boydell and Brewer, 2011.

Elukin, Jonathan. *Living Together, Living Apart: Rethinking Jewish-Christian Relations in the Middle Ages.* Princeton, NJ: Princeton University Press, 2007.

Emanuel, R. R., and M. W. Ponsford. "Jacob's Well, Bristol: Britain's Only Known Medieval Jewish Ritual Bath (Mikveh)." *Transactions of the Bristol and Gloucestershire Archeological Society* 112 (1994): 73–86.

Encyclopaedia Judaica. 16 vols. Jerusalem and New York: Keter and Macmillan, 1971–1985, 2nd ed. 2007.

Enders, Jody. "Theatre Makes History: Ritual Murder by Proxy in the *Mistere de la Sainte Hostie.*" *Speculum* 79 (2004): 991–1016.

————. *Death by Drama and Other Medieval Urban Legends.* Chicago: University of Chicago Press, 2005.

England, Robert. *The Central European Immigrant in Canada.* Toronto: Macmillan, 1929.

English, Richard. *History of Ireland.* Dublin: Gill & Macmillan, 1991.

Evergates, Theodore. "Blois." In *Medieval France: An Encyclopedia.* New York: Garland, 1998.

Evitt, Regula Meyer. "Undoing the Dramatic History of the Riga *Ludus Prophetarum.*" *Comparative Drama* 25 (1990/1991): 242–256.

Fassler, Margot. "The Feast of Fools and *Danielis Ludus*: Popular Tradition in a Medieval Cathedral Play." In *Plainsong in the Age of Polyphony,* edited by Thomas Forrest Kelly, 65–99. Cambridge: Cambridge University Press, 1992.

Fernie, Eric. *An Architectural History of Norwich Cathedral.* Oxford: Clarendon Press, 1993.

Finkelstein, Louis. *Jewish Self-Government in the Middle Ages.* 2nd ed. New York: Philip Feldheim, 1964.

Finucane, Ronald C. "The Use and Abuse of Medieval Miracles." *History* 60 (1975): 1–10.

————. *Miracles and Pilgrims: Popular Beliefs in Medieval England.* London: Dent, 1977.

————. *The Rescue of the Innocents: Endangered Children in Medieval Miracles.* New York: St. Martin's Press, 1997.

Flanagan, Marie-Thérèse. "Strongbow, Henry II and Anglo-Norman Intervention in Ireland." In *War and Government in the Middle Ages: Essays in Honour of J. O. Prestwich*, edited by John Gillingham and James C. Holt, 62–77. Cambridge: D. S. Brewer, 1984.

Flanigan, C. Clifford, Thomas P. Campbell, and Clifford Davidson, eds. *The Fleury Playbook: Essays and Studies.* Kalamazoo, MI: Medieval Institute Publications, 1985.

Flannery, Edward H. *The Anguish of the Jews : Twenty-Three Centuries of Anti-Semitism.* New York: Paulist Press, 2004.

Fletcher, R. A. "Reconquest and Crusade in Spain, C. 1050–1150." *Transactions of the Royal Historical Society*, 5th series 37 (1987): 31–47.

Fleury, Michel. "Les fouilles récentes du Square des Innocents." *Les Dossiers de l'archéologie* 7 (1974): 65–76.

Flint, Valerie. "The Career of Honorius Augustodunensis: Some Fresh Evidence." *Revue Bénédictine* 82 (1972): 63–86.

————. "Anti-Jewish Literature and Attitudes in the Twelfth Century." *Journal of Jewish Studies* 37 (1986), no. 1, 39–57; no. 2, 183–205.

Florence, Ronald. *Blood Libel: The Damascus Affair of 1840.* Madison: University of Wisconsin Press, 2004.

Foreville, Raymonde. *L'église et la royauté en Angleterre sous Henri II Plantagenet (1154–1189).* Paris: Bloud et Gay, 1943.

Forey, Alan. "The Siege of Lisbon and the Second Crusade." *Portuguese Studies* 20, no. 1 (2004): 1–13.

Fox, Paul A. "A Study of Kinship and Patronage: The Rise of the House of Bek." *Medieval Prosopography* 24 (2003): 171–193.

Frame, Robin. *Ireland and Britain, 1170–1450.* London: Hambledon Press, 1998.

France, John. *The Crusades and the Expansion of Catholic Christendom, 1000–1714.* London: Routledge, 2005.

————. "Logistics and the Second Crusade." In *Logistics of Warfare in the Age of the Crusades*, edited by John H. Pryor, 77–93. Aldershot, Hampshire: Ashgate, 2006.

Frank, Grace. *The Medieval French Drama.* Oxford: Clarendon Press, 1954.

Franke, Daniel P. "The Crusades and Medieval Anti-Judaism: Cause or Consequence?" In *Seven Myths of the Crusades*, edited by Alfred J. Andrea and Andrew Holt. Indianapolis: Hackett Publishing, 2015 forthcoming.

Frankel, Jonathan. *The Damascus Affair: Ritual Murder, Politics, and the Jews in 1840.* Cambridge: Cambridge University Press, 1996.

Franklin, M. J. "Bodies in Medieval Northampton: Legatine Intervention in the Twelfth Century." In *Medieval Ecclesiastical Studies in Honour of Dorothy*

M. Owen, edited by M. J. Franklin and Christopher Harper-Bill, 57–82. Woodbridge, Suffolk: Boydell Press, 1995.

Frassetto, Michael, ed. *Christian Attitudes Towards the Jews in the Middle Ages: A Casebook*. New York: Routledge, 2007.

Fredriksen, Paula. "*Excaecati occulta iustitia Dei*: Augustine on Jews and Judaism." *Journal of Early Christian Studies* 3 (1995): 299–324.

———. *Augustine and the Jews: A Christian Defense of Jews and Judaism*. New York: Doubleday, 2008.

Freedman, Jacob. *Polychrome Historical Haggadah for Passover*. Springfield, MA: Jacob Freedman Liturgy Research Foundation, 1974.

Friedenberg, Daniel M. *Jewish Minters and Medalists*. Philadelphia: Jewish Publication Society of America, 1976.

Fudeman, Kirsten Anne. *Vernacular Voices: Language and Identity in Medieval French Jewish Communities*. Philadelphia: University of Pennsylvania Press, 2010.

Galignani, A. and W. Galignani. *The History of Paris, from the Earliest Period to the Present Day: Containing a Description of Its Antiquities, Public Buildings, Civil, Religious, Scientific, and Commercial Institutions*. 3 vols. Paris: A. and W. Galignani, 1825.

Geary, Patrick. "Saint Helen of Athyra and the Cathedral of Troyes in the Thirteenth Century." *Journal of Medieval and Renaissance Studies* 7 (1977): 149–168.

———. *Furta Sacra: Thefts of Relics in the Central Middle Ages*. 2nd ed. Princeton, NJ: Princeton University Press, 1990.

Gerrard, Daniel. "Jocelin of Brakelond and the Power of Abbot Samson." *Journal of Medieval History* 40, no. 1 (2014): 1–23.

Gervers, Michael, ed. *The Second Crusade and the Cistercians*. New York: St. Martin's Press, 1992.

Gilchrist, Roberta. *Norwich Cathedral Close: The Evolution of the English Cathedral Landscape*. Woodbridge, Suffolk: Boydell Press, 2005.

Gillingham, John. *Richard the Lionheart*. London: Weidenfeld & Nicolson, 1989.

Golb, Norman. "New Light on the Persecution of French Jews at the Time of the First Crusade." *Proceedings of the American Academy for Jewish Research* 34 (1966): 1–45.

———. *The Jews in Medieval Normandy: A Social and Intellectual History*. Cambridge: Cambridge University Press, 1998.

———. "The Rabbinic Master Jacob Tam and Events of the Second Crusade at Reims," *Crusades* 9 (2010): 57–67.

Goldin, Simha. "The Socialization for Kiddush Ha-Shem among Medieval Jews." *Journal of Medieval History* 23 (1997): 117–138.

Golding, Brian. "The Coming of the Cluniacs." In *Proceedings of the Third Battle Conference on Anglo-Norman Studies*, edited by R. Allen Brown, 65–77. Woodbridge, Suffolk: Boydell Press, 1981.

Goodich, Michael. *Violence and Miracle in the Fourteenth Century: Private Grief and Public Salvation*. Chicago: University of Chicago Press, 1995.

Gransden, Antonia. "Propaganda in English Medieval Historiography." *Journal of Medieval Studies* 1 (1975): 363–382.

———. "The Growth of the Glastonbury Traditions and Legends in the Twelfth Century." *Journal of Ecclesiastical History* 27 (1976): 337–358.

———. "Legends and Traditions Concerning the Abbey of Bury St. Edmunds." *English Historical Review* 100 (1985): 1–24.

———. "John de Northwold, Abbot of Bury St. Edmunds (1279–1301) and His Defence of Its Liberties." *Thirteenth-Century England* 4, edited by Peter R. Coss and S. D. Lloyd, 91–112. Woodbridge, Suffolk: Boydell Press, 1991.

———. "The Alleged Incorruption of the Body of St. Edmund, King and Martyr." *Antiquaries Journal* 74 (1994): 135–168.

———. "The Composition and Authorship of the *De miraculis Sancti Eadmundi* Attributed to 'Hermann the Archdeacon.'" *Journal of Medieval Latin* 5 (1995): 1–52.

———, ed. *Bury St. Edmunds: Medieval Art, Architecture, Archaeology and Economy*. British Archaeological Association Conference Transactions 20. Leeds: British Archeological Association, 1998.

Grant, Judith. "A New *Passio beati Edmundi: Regis [et] martyris.*" *Medieval Studies* 40 (1978): 81–95.

Greatrex, Joan. *Biographical Register of the English Cathedral Priories of the Province of Canterbury, c. 1066 to 1540*. Oxford: Clarendon Press, 1997.

Green, Barbara, and Rachel M. R. Young. *Norwich. The Growth of a City*. Norwich: Norwich Museums Committee, 1963.

Green, Judith. "Financing Stephen's War." *Anglo-Norman Studies* 14 (1991): 91–114.

———. *The Aristocracy of Norman England*. Cambridge: Cambridge University Press, 1997.

Gregg, Joan Young. *Devils, Women, and Jews: Reflections of the Other in Medieval Sermon Stories*. Albany: State University of New York Press, 1997.

Gross, Abraham. "The Blood Libel and the Blood of Circumcision: An Ashkenazic Custom That Disappeared in the Middle Ages." *Jewish Quarterly Review* n.s. 86, no. 1–2 (1995): 171–174.

Gross, Henri. *Gallia Judaica*. Paris: Librairie Léopold Cerf, 1897.

Halbrook, Stephen P. "Nazi Firearms Law and the Disarming of the German Jews." *Arizona Journal of International and Comparative Law* 17, no. 3 (2000): 483–535.

ha-Levi, Eleazar. "Jewish Naming Convention in Angevin England." 2005. http://heraldry.sca.org/laurel/names/jewish.html.

Hallam, Elizabeth M. *Capetian France, 987–1328*. London: Longman, 1980.

Hames, Harvey J. "The Limits of Conversion: Ritual Murder and the Virgin Mary in the Account of Adam of Bristol." *Journal of Medieval History* 33 (2007): 43–59.

Hamilton, Marie Padgett. "Echoes of Childermas in the Tale of the Prioress." *Modern Language Review* 34, no. 1 (1939): 1–8.

Harper-Bill, Christopher. "Church and Society in Twelfth-Century Suffolk." *Proceedings of the Suffolk Institute of Archeology* 35 (1983): 203–211.

―――. "Bishop William Turbe and the Diocese of Norwich, 1146–1174." In *Proceedings of the Seventh Battle Conference on Anglo-Norman Studies*, edited by R. Allen Brown, 142–160. Woodbridge, Suffolk: Boydell Press, 1985.

―――. "The Struggle for Benefices in Twelfth Century East Anglia." *Anglo-Norman Studies* 11 (1989): 113–132.

―――. "The Medieval Church and the Wider World." In *Norwich Cathedral: Church, City and Diocese, 1096–1996*, edited by Ian Atherton, 281–313. London: Hambledon Press, 1996.

Harper-Bill, Christopher, and Nicholas Vincent, eds. *Henry II: New Interpretations*. Woodbridge, Suffolk, and Rochester, NY: Boydell & Brewer, 2007.

Harris, Max. *Sacred Folly: A New History of the Feast of Fools*. Ithaca NY: Cornell University Press, 2011.

Hasan-Rokem, Galit, and Alan Dundes, eds. *The Wandering Jew: Essays in the Interpretation of a Christian Legend*. Bloomington: Indiana University Press, 1986.

Haskins, Charles Homer. *The Renaissance of the Twelfth Century*. Cambridge, MA: Harvard University Press, 1955.

Haverkamp, A., ed. *Juden und Christen zur Zeit der Kreuzzüge*. Sigmaringen: Jan Thorbecke Verlag, 1999.

Hayward, Paul. "The Idea of Innocent Martyrdom in Late Tenth- and Eleventh-Century English Hagiology." In *Martyrs and Martyrologies* [Studies in Church History 30], edited by Diana Wood, 81–92. Oxford and Cambridge, MA: Blackwell Publishers for the Ecclesiastical History Society, 1993.

―――. "The Idea of Innocent Martyrdom in Medieval England, c. 700 to 1150 A.D." Ph.D. thesis, University of Cambridge, 1994.

―――. "Geoffrey of Wells' *Liber de infantia sancti Edmundi* and the 'Anarchy' of King Stephen's Reign." *St Edmund, King and Martyr: Changing Images of a Medieval Saint*, edited by Anthony Bale, 63–86. York: York Medieval Press, 2009.

Head, Thomas. "Saints, Heretics, and Fire: Finding Meaning Through the Ordeal." In *Monks and Nuns, Saints and Outcasts: Religious Expression and Social Meaning in the Middle Ages*, edited by Barbara Rosenwein and Sharon Farmer, 220–238. Ithaca, NY: Cornell University Press, 2000.

Heliot, Pierre, and Marie-Laure Chastang. "Quêtes et voyages de reliques au profit des églises françaises du Moyen Age." *Revue d'Histoire Écclesiastique* 59 (1964): 789–822, and 60 (1965): 5–32.

Heslin, Anne. "The Coronation of the Young King." *Studies in Church History* 2 (1965): 165–178.

Heslop, T. A. *Norwich Castle Keep: Romanesque Architecture and Social Context*. Norwich: University of East Anglia: Center of East Anglian Studies, 1994.

————. "The Medieval Conventual Seals." In *Norwich Cathedral, Church, City and Diocese, 1096–1996*, edited by Ian Atherton et al., 443–450. London: Hambledon Press, 1996.

————, ed. *Art, Faith and Place in East Anglia from Prehistory to the Present.* Woodbridge, Suffolk: Boydell and Brewer, 2012.

Heywood, Stephen. "The Romanesque Building." In *Norwich Cathedral, Church, City and Diocese, 1096–1996*, edited by Ian Atherton et al., 73–115. London: Hambledon Press, 1996.

Hillaby, Joe. "The Ritual-Child-Murder Accusation: Its Dissemination and Harold of Gloucester." *Jewish Historical Studies* 34 (1997): 69–110.

Hillaby, Joe, and Richard Sermon. "Jacob's Well, Bristol: Mikveh or Bet Tohorah?" *Transactions of the Bristol and Gloucestershire Archaeological Society* 122 (2005): 127–511.

Hillairet, Jacques. *Evocation du Vieux Paris.* Paris: Éditions de Minuit, 1952.

Hoch, Martin. "The Price of Failure: The Second Crusade as a Turning-Point in the History of the Latin East?" In *The Second Crusade, Scope and Consequences*, edited by Jonathan Phillips and Martin Hoch, 180–200. Manchester: Manchester University Press, 2001.

Hollister, C. Warren. "Stephen's Anarchy." *Albion* 6 (1974): 233–239.

————. "Royal Acts of Mutilation: The Case Against Henry I." In C. Warren Hollister, *Monarchy, Magnates and Institutions in the Anglo-Norman World*, 291–301. London: Hambledon Press, 1986.

James Hooper, "Curious Church Dedications in Norfolk; and Some Rood Screen Figures." In *Memorials of Old Norfolk*, ed. Hugh J. D. Astley, 253–273. Norwich: Bemrose and Sons, 1909.

Horowitz, Elliot. "The Rite to Be Reckless: On the Perpetuation and Interpretation of Purim Violence." *Poetics Today* 15, no. 1 (1994): 9–54.

————. *Reckless Rites: Purim and the Legacy of Jewish Violence, Jews, Christians, and Muslims from the Ancient to the Modern World.* Princeton, NJ: Princeton University Press, 2006.

————. "Dangerous Liaisons: Twentieth-Century Scholars and Medieval Relations between Jews and Christians." *Jewish Review of Books* Spring, (2014): 44-47.

Hsia, R. Po-Chia. The *Myth of Ritual Murder: Jews and Magic in Reformation Germany.* New Haven, CT, and London: Yale University Press, 1988.

Hudson, W. "The Parish Churches and Religious Houses of Norwich." In *Memorials of Old Norfolk*, edited by H. J. D. Astley, 48–59. London: Bemrose, 1908.

Hunnisett, R. F. *The Medieval Coroner.* Cambridge Studies in English Legal History. Cambridge: Cambridge University Press, 1961.

Hurnard, Naomi. *The King's Pardon of Homicide before 1300.* Oxford: Oxford University Press, 1968.

Hyams, Paul. "The Jewish Minority in Medieval England, 1066–1290." *Journal of Jewish Studies* 25:2 (1974): 270–293.

————. "Trial by Ordeal: The Key to Proof in the Early Common Law." In *On the Laws and Customs of England: Essays in Honor of Samuel E. Thorne*, edited by M. S. Arnold, 90–126. Chapel Hill: University of North Carolina Press, 1981.

————. "The Jews in Medieval England, 1066–1290." In *England and Germany in the High Middle Ages: In Honour of Karl J. Leyser*, edited by Alfred von Haverkamp and Hanna Volrath, 173–92. London: German Historical Institute, Oxford University Press, 1996.

Hyamson, A. M. *A History of the Jews in England*. London: Chatto & Windus for the Jewish Historical Society, 1908.

Iogna-Prat, Dominique. *Order and Exclusion: Cluny and Christendom Face Heresy, Judaism, and Islam (1000–1150)*. Ithaca, NY: Cornell University Press, 2002.

Israeli, Raphael. *Poison: Modern Manifestations of a Blood Libel*. Lanham, MD; Oxford: Lexington Books, 2002.

Jacobs, Joseph. *The Jews of Angevin England*. London: David Nutt, 1893.

————. "St. William of Norwich." *Jewish Quarterly Review* 9 (1897): 748–755.

Jaeglé, Marianne. *Histoire de Paris et des parisiens*. Paris: Cie 12, 2005.

James, John. "Evidence for Flying Buttresses before 1180." *Journal of the Society of Architectural Historians* 51 (1992): 261–287.

James, M. R. *On the Abbey of St. Edmund at Bury*. Cambridge Antiquarian Society, Octavo Publications 28. Cambridge, 1895.

Jaspert, Nikolas. "*Capta est Dertosa, Clavis Christianorum*: Tortosa and the Crusades." In *The Second Crusade: Scope and Consequences*, edited by Jonathan Philips and Martin Hoch, 90–110. Manchester and New York: Manchester University Press, 2001.

————. The *Crusades*. New York: Routledge, 2006.

Jeauneau, Édouard. *Rethinking the School of Chartres*. Toronto: University of Toronto Press, 2009.

Jennings, J. C. "The Origins of the 'Elements Series' of the Miracles of the Virgin." *Medieval and Renaissance Studies* 6 (1968): 84–93.

Jensen, Janus Møller, and Jason T. Roche, eds. *The Second Crusade: Holy War on the Periphery of Latin Christendom*, Outremer: Studies in the Crusades and the Latin East, 2. Turnhout: Brepols, 2015 forthcoming.

Jessopp, Augustus. "On Married Clergy in Norfolk in the Thirteenth Century." *Norfolk Archeology* 9 (1884): 187–200.

Jewish Encyclopedia: A Descriptive Record of the History, Religion, Literature, and Customs of the Jewish People from the Earliest Times to the Present Day, edited by Cyrus Adler and Isidore Singer. 12 vols. New York and London: Funk and Wagnalls, 1901–1906. Digitized at http://www.jewishencyclopedia.com/.

Johnson, Hannah. *Blood Libel: The Ritual Murder Accusation at the Limit of Jewish History*. Ann Arbor: The University of Michigan Press, 2012.

Johnson, Willis. "The Myth of Jewish Male Menses." *Journal of Medieval History* 24, no. 3 (1998): 273–295.

Jones, Charles W. *The Saint Nicholas Liturgy and Its Literary Relationships (Ninth to Twelfth Centuries)*. Berkeley: University of California Press, 1963.

Jones, Sarah Rees, and Sethina Watson, eds. *Christians and Jews in Angevin England: The York Massacre of 1190, Narratives and Contexts*. York: York Medieval Press, 2013.

Jong, Mayke de. *In Samuel's Image: Child Oblation in the Early Medieval West*. Leiden and Boston: E. J. Brill, 1996.

Jordan, Karl. *Henry the Lion: A Biography*, translated by P. S. Falla. Oxford: Clarendon Press, 1986.

Jordan, William Chester. *The French Monarchy and the Jews, from Philip Augustus to the Last Capetians (1179–1328)*. Philadelphia: University of Pennsylvania Press, 1989.

———. "Princely Identity and the Jews in Medieval France." In *From Witness to Witchcraft: Jews and Judaism in Medieval Christian Thought*, Wolfenbütteler Mittelalter-Studien 11, edited by Jeremy Cohen, 257–273. Wiesbaden: Harrassowitz, 1996. Repr. in William Chester Jordan, *Ideology and Royal Power in Medieval France*. Aldershot, Hampshire: Ashgate, 2001.

Judd, Robin. "The Politics of Beef: Animal Advocacy and the Kosher Butchering Debates in Germany." *Jewish Social Studies* 10, no. 1 (2003): 117–150.

———. *Contested Rituals: Circumcision, Kosher Butchering, and Jewish Political Life in Germany, 1843–1933*. Ithaca, NY: Cornell University Press, 2007.

Julius, Anthony. *Trials of the Diaspora: A History of Anti-Semitism in England*. Oxford: Oxford University Press, 2010.

Kahl, Hans-Dieter. "Crusade Eschatology as Seen by St. Bernard in the Years 1146–48." In *The Second Crusade and the Cistercians*, edited by Michael Gervers, 35–47. New York: St. Martin's Press, 1992.

Kalman, Julie. "Sensuality, Depravity, and Ritual Murder: The Damascus Blood Libel and Jews in France." *Jewish Social Studies* 13, no. 3 (2007): 35–58.

Kanarfogel, Ephraim. "R. Judah he-Hasid and the Rabbinic Scholars of Regensburg: Interactions, Influences, and Implications." *Jewish Quarterly Review* 96, no. 1 (2006): 17–37.

Kangas, Sini. "Slaughter of the Innocents and Depiction of Children in the Twelfth-Century Sources of the Crusades." In *The Uses of the Bible in Crusading Sources*, edited by Elizabeth Lapina and Nicholas Morton: Leiden: Brill, 2015 forthcoming.

Katz, Jacob. *Exclusiveness and Tolerance, Studies in Jewish-Gentile Relations in Medieval and Modern Times*. New York: Behrman House/ Oxford University Press, 1961.

Keats-Rohan, K. S. B. *Domesday Descendants: A Prosopography of Persons Occurring in English Documents 1066–1166*. Woodbridge: Boydell Press, 2002.

Kedar, Benjamin Z. "Crusade Historians and the Massacres of 1096." *Jewish History* 12, no. 2 (1998): 11–32.

Keefe, Thomas K. *Feudal Assessments and the Political Community under Henry II and His Sons*. Berkeley: University of California Press, 1983.

Kelly, Amy. *Eleanor of Aquitaine and the Four Kings*. Cambridge, MA: Harvard University Press, 1974.

Kent, Ernest A. "Isaac's Hall, or the Music House, Norwich." *Norfolk Archeology* 28 (1945): 31–36.

King, E. J. "The Anarchy of King Stephen's Reign." *Transactions of the Royal Historical Society*, 5th ser. 34 (1984): 133–153.

Knowles, David. "The Growth of Monastic Exemption." *Downside Review* 50 (1932): 201–231, 396–436.

———. *The Episcopal Colleagues of Archbishop Thomas Becket*. Cambridge: Cambridge University Press, 1951.

Knowles, David, and R. Neville Hadcock. *Medieval Religious Houses: England and Wales*. 2nd ed. London: Longman, 1971.

Knowles, David, C. N. L. Brooke, and Vera London, eds. *The Heads of Religious Houses: England and Wales, 940–1216*. Cambridge: Cambridge University Press, 1972.

Kolve, V. A. "Ganymede/Son of Getron: Medieval Monasticism and the Drama of Same-Sex Desire." *Speculum* 73, no. 4 (1998): 1014–1067.

Koopmans, Rachel. *Wonderful to Relate: Miracle Stories and Miracle Collecting in High Medieval England*. Philadelphia: University of Pennsylvania Press, 2011.

Kowaleski, Maryanne. "Town and Country in Late Medieval England: The Hide and Leather Trade." In *Work in Towns, 850–1850*, edited by Penelope J. Corfield and Derek Keene, 57–73. Leicester: Leicester University Press, 1990.

Kruger, Steven. *The Spectral Jew: Conversion and Embodiment in Medieval Europe*. Minneapolis: University of Minnesota Press, 2006.

Krummel, Miriamne Ara. *Crafting Jewishness in Medieval England: Legally Absent, Virtually Present*. New York: Palgrave Macmillan, 2011.

Labande, Edmond-René. "Les filles d'Alienor d'Aquitaine: Étude comparative." *Cahiers de civilization médiévale* 29 (1986): 101–112.

Landon, L. "Everard Bishop of Norwich." *Suffolk Institute of Archeology Proceedings* 20, no. 2 (1929): 186–198.

Langham, Raphael. "William of Norwich," paper presented to *The Jewish Historical Society of England* (2005) and posted online in 2008 at http://www.jhse.org/node/44.

Langmuir, Gavin. "Thomas of Monmouth: Detector of Ritual Murder." *Speculum* 59, no. 4 (1984): 820–846. Repr. in Langmuir, *Toward a Definition of Antisemitism*, 209–236. Berkeley: University of California Press, 1990.

———. *Toward a Definition of Antisemitism*. Berkeley: University of California Press, 1990.

———. *History, Religion and Antisemitism*. Berkeley: University of California Press, 1990.

Lavezzo, Kathy. "Shifting Geographies of Anti-Semitism: Mapping Jew and Christian in Thomas of Monmouth's Life and Miracles of St William of Norwich." *Mapping Medieval Geographies: Geographical Encounters in the Latin*

West and Beyond, 300–1600, edited by Keith D. Lilley, 250–270. Cambridge: Cambridge University Press, 2014.

Lay, Stephen. "Miracles, Martyrs and the Cult of Henry the Crusader in Lisbon." *Portuguese Studies* 24, no. 1 (2008): 7–31.

Lazar, Moshe. "The Lamb and the Scapegoat: The Dehumanization of the Jews in Medieval Propaganda Imagery." In *Anti-Semitism in Times of Crisis*, edited by Sander L. Gilman and Steven T. Katz, 38–101. New York: New York University Press, 1991.

Lebeuf, Jean. *Histoire de la ville et de tout le diocèse de Paris*. 6 vols. Paris: Féchoz et Letouzey, 1883–1890.

Lesueur, Frédéric. "L'église et l'abbaye bénédictine de St.-Lomer de Blois." *Mémoires de la Société des sciences et lettres de Loir-et-Cher* 25 (1924): 59–155.

———. *Les églises de Loir-et-Cher*. Paris: A. et J. Picard, 1969.

Levin, Chaviva. "Constructing Memories of Martyrdom: Contrasting Portrayals of Martyrdom in the Hebrew Narratives of the First and Second Crusade." In *Remembering the Crusades: Myth, Image, and Identity*, edited by Nicholas Paul and Suzanne Yeager, 50–69. Baltimore, MD: Johns Hopkins University Press, 2012.

Levin, Edmund. *A Child of Christian Blood: Murder and Conspiracy in Tsarist Russia: The Beilis Blood Libel*. New York: Schocken Books, 2014.

Lewis, C. P. "The King and Eye: A Study in Anglo-Norman Politics." *English Historical Review* 412 (1989): 569–587.

Licence, Tom. "History and Hagiography in the Late Eleventh Century: The Life and Work of Herman the Archdeacon, Monk of Bury St Edmund." *English Historical Review* 508 (2009): 516–544.

———. "Herbert Losinga's Trip to Rome and the Bishopric of Bury St Edmunds." *Anglo-Norman Studies* 34 (2010): 151–168.

Liebeschutz, H. "The Crusading Movement and Its Bearing on the Christian Attitude Towards Jewry." *Journal of Jewish Studies* 10 (1959): 97–111, reprinted in Jeremy, Cohen, ed. *Essential Papers on Judaism and Christianity in Conflict, from Late Antiquity to the Reformation*. New York: New York University Press, 1999.

Lipman, V. D. *The Jews of Medieval Norwich*. London: Jewish Historical Society of England, 1967.

Lipton, Sara. *Dark Mirror: The Medieval Origins of Anti-Jewish Iconography*. New York: Metropolitan Books, 2014.

Little, Lester. "The Jews in Christian Europe." In *Essential Papers on Judaism and Christianity in Conflict*, edited by J. Cohen, 276–297. New York: New York University Press, 1991.

Lobel, Mary D. "The Gaol of Bury St Edmund's." *Suffolk Institute of Archeology and Natural History* 21, no. 3 (1933): 203–207.

Lombard-Jourdan, Anne. *Paris, genèse de la ville: La rive droite de la Seine des origines à 1223*. Paris: Éditions du CNRS, 1976.

———. *Aux Origines de Paris: la genèse de la rive droite jusqu'en 1223.* Paris: Editions du CNRS, 1985.

LoPrete, Kimberly. "Adela of Blois and Ivo of Chartres: Piety, Politics and the Peace in the Diocese of Chartres." *Anglo-Norman Studies* XIV (1991): 131–152.

———. *Adela of Blois: Countess and Lord (c. 1067–1137).* Dublin: Four Courts Press, 2007.

Lotter, Friedrich. "Innocens virgo et martyr: Thomas von Monmouth und die Verbreitung der Ritualmordlegende im Hochmittelalter." In *Die Legende vom Ritualmord: Zur Geschichte der Blutbeschuldigung gegen Juden,* edited by R. Erb, 25–72. Berlin: Metropol, 1993.

Loud, Graham A. "Some Reflections on the Failure of the Second Crusade." *Crusades* 4 (2005): 1–14.

Lower, Michael. "The Burning at Mont-Aimé: Thibaut of Champagne's Preparations for the Barons' Crusade of 1239." *Journal of Medieval History* 29 (2003): 95–108.

Luchaire, Achille. *Social France at the Time of Philip Augustus.* Translated by Edward B. Krehbiel. New York: H. Holt, 1912.

Luxford, Julian M. "St William of Norwich in Late Medieval Art," paper given at *Youth, Violence and Cult* conference, based at Queen Mary College, University of London, January 29, 2010.

———. "The Iconography of St William of Norwich and the Nuremberg Chronicle." *Norfolk Archeology* 47 (2015) forthcoming.

Mack, R. P. "Stephen and the Anarchy, 1135–1154." *British Numismatic Journal* 35 (1967): 38–112.

MacLehose, William F. *"A Tender Age": Cultural Anxieties over the Child in the Twelfth and Thirteenth Centuries.* New York: Columbia University Press, 2007.

Malkiel, David J. "Infanticide in Passover Iconography." *Journal of the Warburg and Courtauld Institutes* 56 (1993): 85–99.

Marcus, Ivan G. *Rituals of Childhood: Jewish Acculturation in Medieval Europe.* New Haven, CT: Yale University Press, 1996.

———. "The Dynamics of Jewish Renaissance and Renewal in the Twelfth Century." In *Jews and Christians in Twelfth-Century Europe,* edited by Michael A. Signer and John Van Engen, 27–45. Notre Dame, IN: University of Notre Dame Press, 2001.

Mason, E. "A Truth Universally Acknowledged." *Studies in Church History* 16 (1979): 171–186.

Mayhew, N. J. "From Regional to Central Minting, 1158–1464." In *A New History of the Royal Mint,* edited by C. E. Challis, 83–178. Cambridge: Cambridge University Press, 1992.

Mayr-Harting, H. "Functions of a Twelfth-Century Recluse." *History* 60 (1975): 337–352.

McCulloh, John A. "Jewish Ritual Murder: William of Norwich, Thomas of Monmouth, and the Early Dissemination of the Myth." *Speculum* 72, no. 3 (1997): 698–740.

McGuire, Desmond. *History of Ireland*. Twickenham: Hamlyn, 1987.

McLaughlin, Mary Martin. "Survivors and Surrogates: Children and Parents from the Ninth through Thirteenth Centuries." In *The History of Childhood*, edited by Lloyd de Mause, 101–181. New York: Psychohistory Press, 1974.

Medieval France: An Encyclopedia. Edited by William Westcott Kibler et al. New York: Garland Publishing, 1995.

Medieval Jewish Civilization: An Encyclopedia. Edited by Norman Roth. New York: Routledge, 2003.

Mellinkoff, Ruth. *The Mark of Cain*. Berkeley: University of California Press, 1981.

Mentgen, Gerd. "Über den Ursprung der Ritual Mordfabel." *Aschenaz* 4 (1994): 405–416. Revision of "The Origins of the Blood Libel" (in Hebrew). *Zion* 59 (1994): 343–349.

Miller, Naomi. "The Form and Meaning of the Fontaine des Innocents." *Art Bulletin* 50, no. 3 (1968): 270–277.

Milway, Michael. "Boy Bishops in Early Modern Europe: Ritual, Myth, and Reality." In *The Dramatic Tradition of the Middle Ages*, edited by Clifford Davidson, 87–97. New York: AMS Press, 2005.

Minois, Georges. *History of Suicide: Voluntary Death in Western Culture*. Translated into English by Lydia G. Cochrane. Baltimore, MD: Johns Hopkins University Press, 1999.

Minty, Mary. "Kiddush Ha-Shem in German Christian Eyes in the Middle Ages" (in Hebrew). *Zion* 59 (1994): 209–266.

Mollat, Michel, ed. *Histoire de l'Île-de-France et de Paris*. Toulouse: Privat, 1991.

Moore, R. I. *The Formation of a Persecuting Society: Authority and Deviance in Western Europe, 950–1250*. 2nd ed. Malden. Blackwell, 2007.

Morris, Colin. "From Synod to Consistory: The Bishops' Courts in England, 1150–1250." *Journal of Ecclesiastical History* 22 (1971): 115–123.

———. "A Critique of Popular Religion: Guibert of Nogent on the Relics of the Saints." In *Popular Belief and Practice*, edited by Geoffrey John Cuming and Derek Baker, 55–60. Cambridge: Ecclesiastical History Society, 1972.

Morrison, Susan S. *Women Pilgrims in Late Medieval England: Private Piety as Public Performance*. London; New York: Routledge, 2000.

Müller, Karlheinz. "Würzburg—The World's Largest Find from a Medieval Jewish Cemetery." In *The Jews of Europe in the Middle Ages (Tenth to Fifteenth Centuries): Proceedings of the International Symposium held at Speyer, 20–25 October 2002*, edited by Christoph Cluse, 379–389. Turnhout: Brepols, 2004.

Mundill, Robin. *England's Jewish Solution: Experiment and Expulsion, 1262–1290*. New York: Cambridge University Press, 1998.

Murray, Alexander. *Suicide in the Middle Ages*. 2 vols. Oxford: Oxford University Press, 1998.

Nahon, Gérard. "La communauté juive de Paris au XIIIe siècle: Problèmes topographiques, démographiques et institutionnels." In Comité des travaux historiques et scientifiques, *Études sur l'histoire de Paris et de l'Île-de-France*, 143–156. Paris: Bibliothèque nationale, 1978.

———. "From the *Rue aux Juifs* to the *Chemin du Roy*: The Classical Age of French Jewry, 1108–1223." In *Jews and Christians in Twelfth-Century Europe*, edited by Michael A. Signer and John Van Engen, 311–339. Notre Dame, IN: University of Notre Dame Press, 2001.

Narin van Court, Elisa. "Invisible in Oxford: The 'Public Face' of Medieval Jewish History in Modern England." *Engage* 3 (2006). http://www.engageonline.org.uk/.

Neale, F. *Report on Planned Archaeological Excavations of St. Peter's/Bristol Jewry*. Bristol: Bristol Record Office, 1975.

Nelson, Lynn H. *The Normans in South Wales, 1070–1171*. Austin: University of Texas Press, 1966.

Nichols, Ann Eljenholm. *The Early Art of Norfolk: A Subject List of Extant and Lost Art, Including Items Relevant to Early Drama*. Early Drama, Art, and Music Reference Series 7. Kalamazoo, MI: Medieval Institute Publications, 2002.

Nicholson, Helen, ed. *Palgrave Advances in the Crusades*. Basingstoke and New York: Palgrave Macmillan, 2005.

Nightingale, Pamela. "Some London Moneyers and Reflections on the Organization of English Mints in the Eleventh and Twelfth Centuries." *Numismatic Chronicle* 142 (1982): 34–50.

Nilson, Ben. *Cathedral Shrines of Medieval England*. Woodbridge, Suffolk: Boydell & Brewer, 1998.

Nirenberg, David. *Communities of Violence: Persecution of Minorities in the Middle Ages*. Princeton, NJ: Princeton University Press, 1996.

———. *Anti-Judaism: The Western Tradition*. New York: W. W. Norton, 2013.

Noble, Peter S. "*Partonopeu de Blois* and Chrétien de Troyes." In *Studies in Honor of Hans-Erich Keller: Medieval French and Occitan Literature and Romance Linguistics*, edited by Rupert T. Pickens, 195–211. Kalamazoo, MI: Medieval Institute Publications, 1993.

Nolan, Kathleen. "'Ploratus et Ululatus': The Mothers in the Massacre of the Innocents at Chartres Cathedral." *Studies in Iconography* 17 (1996): 95–141.

Novikoff, Alex. *The Medieval Culture of Disputation: Pedagogy, Practice, and Performance*. Philadelphia: University of Pennsylvania Press, 2013.

O'Brien, Bruce R. "From Mordor to Murdrum: The Preconquest Origin and Norman Revival of the Murder Fine." *Speculum* 71, no. 2 (1996): 321–357.

O'Brien, Darren. *The Pinnacle of Hatred: The Blood Libel and the Jews*. Jerusalem: Magnes Press, 2011.

Ocker, Christopher. "Ritual Murder and the Subjectivity of Christ: A Choice in Medieval Christianity." *Harvard Theological Review* 91 (1998): 153–192.

Ogden, Dunbar H. *The Staging of Drama in the Medieval Church*. Newark: University of Delaware Press, 2003.

Oosterwijk, Sophie. "'Long Lullynge Haue I Lorn!': The Massacre of the Innocents in Word and Image." *Medieval English Theatre* 25 (2003): 3–53.

Orpen, Goddard Henry. *Ireland under the Normans.* 4 vols. Oxford: Clarendon Press, 1911–1920.

Otway-Ruthven, A. J. *A History of Medieval Ireland.* 2nd ed. London: Ernest Benn Ltd., 1980.

Parkes, James. *Antisemitism.* London: Valentine, Mitchell, 1963.

Partner, Nancy F. *Serious Entertainments: The Writing of History in Twelfth-Century England.* Chicago: University of Chicago Press, 1977.

Patterson, Robert B. "Anarchy in England, 1135–54: The Theory of the Constitution." *Albion* 6 (1974): 189–200.

———. "Robert Fitz Harding of Bristol: Profile of an Early Angevin Burgess-born Patrician and His Family's Urban Involvement." *Haskins Society Journal* 1 (1989): 109–122.

Patterson, Lee. "'The Living Witnesses of Our Redemption': Martyrdom and Imitation in Chaucer's *Prioress's Tale.*" *Journal of Medieval and Early Modern Studies* 31, no. 3 (2001): 507–560.

Paul, Nicholas. *To Follow in Their Footsteps: the Crusades and Family Memory in the High Middle Ages.* Ithaca, NY: Cornell University Press, 2013.

——— and Suzanne Yeager, eds. *Remembering the Crusades: Myth, Image, and Identity.* Baltimore, MD: Johns Hopkins University Press, 2012.

Pernoud, Régine. *Eleanor of Aquitaine.* Translated by Peter Wiles. London: Collins, 1967.

Phillips, Jonathan. "Saint Bernard of Clairvaux, the Low Countries and the Lisbon Letter of the Second Crusade." *Journal of Ecclesiastical History* 48 (1997): 485–497.

———. "The Murder of Charles the Good and the Second Crusade: Household Nobility, and Traditions of Crusading in Medieval Flanders." *Medieval Prosopography* 19 (1998): 55–75.

———. *The Second Crusade: Extending the Frontiers of Christendom.* New Haven, CT: Yale University Press, 2007.

Phillips, Jonathan, and Martin Hoch, eds. *The Second Crusade: Scope and Consequences.* Manchester: Manchester University Press, 2001.

Pitte, Jean-Robert. *Paris, histoire d'une ville.* Paris: Hachette, 1993.

Poliakov, Leon. *The History of Anti-Semitism* 2 vols. London: Elek, 1974.

Poole, Austin Lane. *From Domesday Book to Magna Carta, 1087–1216.* Oxford: Clarendon Press, 1955.

Potter, Robert. "The *Auto da Fé* as Medieval Drama." In *Festive Drama*, edited by Meg Twycross, 110–118. Cambridge: D. S. Brewer, 1996.

Power, Daniel. *The Norman Frontier in the Twelfth and Early Thirteenth Centuries.* Cambridge: Cambridge University Press, 2004.

Redstone, Lilian J. "The Liberty of St. Edmund." *Proceedings of the Suffolk Institute of Archeology and History* 15 (1913): 200–211.

Rees Jones, Sarah, and Sethina Watson, eds. *Christians and Jews in Angevin England: The York Massacre of 1190, Narratives and Contexts.* York: York Medieval Press, 2013.

Reif, Stefan C. *Judaism and Hebrew Prayer: New Perspectives on Jewish Liturgical History*. Cambridge: Cambridge University Press, 1995.

Resnick, Irven M. "Race, Anti-Jewish Polemic, Arnulf of Séez and the Contested Papal Election of Anaclet II AD 1130." In *Jews in Medieval Christendom: "Slay Them Not,"* edited by Kristine T. Utterback and Merrall LLewelyn Price, 45–70. Leiden: Brill, 2013.

Richardson, H. G. *The English Jewry under Angevin Kings*. London: Methuen & Co., 1960.

Richmond, Colin. "Englishness and Medieval Anglo-Jewry." In *The Jewish Heritage in British History: Englishness and Jewishness*, edited by Tony Kushner, 42–59. London: Frank Cass, 1992. Repr. in *Chaucer and the Jews: Sources, Contexts, Meanings*, edited by Sheila Delany, 213–227. New York and London: Routledge, 2002.

Richter, Michael. "*Urbanitas-Rusticitas*: Linguistic Aspects of a Medieval Dichotomy." In *The Church in Town and Countryside*, edited by Derek Baker, 149–157. Oxford: Ecclesiastical History Society, 1979.

Ridyard, Susan J. "Condigna Veneratio: Post-Conquest Attitudes to the Saints of the Anglo-Saxons." *Anglo-Norman Studies* 9 (1987): 179–206.

Riley-Smith, Jonathan. "Crusading as an Act of Love." *History* 65 (1980): 177–192.

———. "Family Traditions and Participation in the Second Crusade." In *The Second Crusade and the Cistercians*, edited by Michael Gervers, 101–108. New York: St. Martin's Press, 1992.

———. "Early Crusaders to the East and the Cost of Crusading, 1095–1130." In *Cross Cultural Convergence in the Crusader Period: Essays Presented to Aryeh Grabois on His Sixty-Fifth Birthday*, edited by Michael Goodich, Sophia Menache, and Sylvia Schein, 237–258. New York: Peter Lang, 1995.

———. *The First Crusaders, 1095–1113*. Cambridge: Cambridge University Press, 1997.

Rimbault, Edward. "Two Sermons Preached by the Boy Bishop," *Camden Miscellany* 14 n.s. (1875): 1–34.

Robert, Ulysse. *Signes d'infamie au Moyen Âge: Juifs, sarrasins, hérétiques, lépreux, cagots et filles publiques*. Paris: H. Champion, 1889.

Roblin, Michel. *Les juifs de Paris: Démographie, économie, culture*. Paris: A. et J. Picard, 1952.

Roche, Jason T. "The Second Crusade: Main Debates and New Horizons." In *The Second Crusade: Holy War on the Periphery of Latin Christendom*, edited by Jason T. Roche and Janus Møller Jensen. Turnhout: Brepols, 2015 (forthcoming).

Roche, Richard. *The Norman Invasion of Ireland*. Dublin: Anvil Books, 1995.

Rose, E. M. "Gregory of Tours and the Conversion of the Jews of Clermont." In *The World of Gregory of Tours*, edited by Ian Wood and Kathleen Mitchell, 307–320. Leiden and Boston: E. J. Brill for the Medieval Academy of America, 2002.

———. "Distinctions without Much Difference? Ritual Murder, Blood Libel and the Need to Classify." Paper delivered at the *Association for Jewish Studies* annual meeting, Washington D. C. December 21, 2008.

————. "Hugh of Lincoln, Ritual Murder, Henry III and the Crown of Sicily." Paper delivered at the *Harvard Medieval Seminar,* Harvard University, October 3, 2011.

————. "Royal Power and Ritual Murder: Notes on the Expulsion of the Jews from the Royal Domain of France, 1182." In *Center and Periphery: Studies on Power in the Medieval World in Honor of William Chester Jordan,* edited by Katherine L. Jansen, G. Geltner, and Anne E. Lester, 51–63. Leiden: Brill, 2013.

Roth, Cecil. "The Feast of Purim and the Origins of the Blood Accusation." *Speculum* 8 (1933): 520–526. Repr. in *The Blood Libel Legend: A Casebook in Anti-Semitic Folklore,* edited by Alan Dundes, 261–272. Madison: University of Wisconsin Press, 1991.

————. *The Ritual Murder Libel and the Jew: The Report by Cardinal Lorenzo Ganganelli (Pope Clement XIV).* London: Woburn Press, 1935.

————. *A History of the Jews in England.* Oxford: Clarendon Press, 1949, 1964.

————. *The Jews of Medieval Oxford.* Oxford: Clarendon Press for the Oxford Historical Society, 1951.

Roth, Norman. *Medieval Jewish Civilization: An Encyclopedia.* London: Routledge, 2003.

Round, J. H. *Geoffrey De Mandeville: A Study of the Anarchy.* London: Longman, Green and Co., 1892.

————. "The Origin of the Stewarts and Their Chesney Connection." *The Genealogist* 18 (1901): 1–16.

————. "The Early Sheriffs of Norfolk." *English Historical Review* 35, no. 140 (1920): 481–496.

Roy, Neil J. "The Feast of the Holy Innocents and Its Orations in the Missale Romanum of 1970." *Antiphon* 8, no. 1 (2003): 28–33.

Rubenstein, Jay. *Guibert of Nogent: Portrait of a Medieval Mind.* New York: Routledge, 2002.

Rubin, Miri. *Gentile Tales: The Narrative Assault on Late Medieval Jews.* New Haven, CT: Yale University Press, 1999.

Rudich, Vasily A. *Religious Dissent in the Roman Empire: Violence in Judaea at the Time of Nero.* London: Routledge, 2015.

Rutledge, Elizabeth. "The Medieval Jews of Norwich and Their Legacy." In *Art, Faith and Place in East Anglia From Prehistory to the Present,* edited by T. A. Heslop, 117–129. Woodbridge, Suffolk: Boydell and Brewer, 2012.

Ruud, Marylou. "'Unworthy Servants': The Rhetoric of Resignation at Canterbury, 1070–1170." *Journal of Religious History* 22, no. 1 (1998): 1–13.

Rye, Walter. *Some Historical Essays Chiefly Relating to Norfolk,* Part 2. Norwich: R. W. Hunt, 1926.

Saltman, Avrom. *Theobald, Archbishop of Canterbury.* London: University of London, Athlone Press, 1956.

Salzman, L. F. "Sussex Domesday Tenants IV. The Family of Chesney or Cheyney." *Sussex Archeology* 65 (1924): 20–53.

Samaran, C. "Fragments de manuscrits latins et français du Moyen Age." *Romania* 51 (1925): 161–202.

Samuel, Judith. *Jews in Bristol: The History of the Jewish Community in Bristol from the Middle Ages to the Present Day*. Bristol: Redcliffe, 1997.

Sassier, Yves. *Louis VII*. Paris: Fayard, 1991.

Sauvage, Jean-Paul. "Le massacre des juifs à Blois en 1171." *Mémoires de la Société des Sciences et Lettres du Loire-et-Cher* 49 (1994): 5–22.

Scarfe, Norman. "The Bury St. Edmunds Cross: The Work of Master Hugo?" *Proceedings of the Suffolk Institute of Archeology* 33 (1973–1975): 75–85.

Schacter, Jacob J. "Remembering the Temple: Commemoration and Catastrophe in Ashkenazi Culture." In *The Temple of Jerusalem : From Moses to the Messiah : In Honor of Professor Louis H. Feldman*, edited by Steven Fine and Louis H. Feldman, 275-301. Leiden, Boston: Brill, 2011.

Schäfer, Peter. *Judeophobia: Attitudes toward the Jews in the Ancient World*. Cambridge, MA; London: Harvard University Press, 1997.

———. *Mirror of His Beauty: Feminine Images of God from the Bible to the Early Kabbalah*. Princeton, NJ: Princeton University Press, 2002.

Schama, Simon. *The Story of the Jews. Finding the Words, 1000 BCE–1492 CE*. London: Bodley Head, 2013.

Schenk, Jochen. *Templar Families: Landowning Families and the Order of the Temple in France, C. 1120–1307*. Cambridge: Cambridge University Press, 2012.

Schreckenberg, Heinz. *The Jews in Christian Art: An Illustrated History*. New York: Continuum, 1996.

Schultz, Magdalene. "The Blood Libel: A Motif in the History of Childhood." *Journal of Psychohistory/History of Childhood Quarterly* 14 (1986): 1–24. Repr. in Alan Dundes, ed., *The Blood Libel Legend: A Casebook in Anti-Semitic Folklore*, 273–303. Madison: University of Wisconsin Press, 1991.

Shahar, Shulamith. *Childhood in the Middle Ages*. London: Routledge, 1990.

———. "The Boy Bishop's Feast: A Case-Study in Church Attitudes Towards Children in the High and Late Middle Ages." In *The Church and Childhood*, edited by Diana Wood, 243–260. Oxford: Published for the Ecclesiastical History Society by Blackwell Publishers, 1994.

Shachar, Uri Z. "Inspecting the Pious Body: Christological Morphology and the Ritual-Crucifixion Allegation." *Journal of Medieval History* 41, no. 1 (2015): 21–40.

Shatzmiller, Joseph. "Jewish Converts in Medieval Europe 1200–1500." In *Cross Cultural Convergences in the Crusader Period*, edited by Sophia Menache, Michael Goodich, Sylvia Schein, 297–318. New York: Peter Lang, 1995.

Shea, Jennifer. "Adgar's *Gracial* and Christian Images of Jews in Twelfth-Century Vernacular Literature." *Journal of Medieval History* 33, no. 2 (2007): 181–196.

Shepkaru, Shmuel. *Jewish Martyrs in the Pagan and Christian World*. Cambridge: Cambridge University Press, 2005.

Shinners, John R. "The Veneration of Saints at Norwich Cathedral in the Fourteenth Century." *Norfolk Archaeology* 40 (1988): 133–144.

Shoham-Steiner, Ephraim. "'Vitam Finivit Infelicem': Madness Conversion and Adolescent Suicide among Jews in Late Twelfth Century England." In *Jews in Medieval Christendom: "Slay Them Not,"* edited by K. T. Utterback and M. L. Price, 71–90. Leiden: Brill, 2013.

Siberry, Elizabeth. *Criticism of Crusading, 1095–1274.* Oxford: Clarendon Press, 1985.

———. "The Crusader's Departure and Return: A Much Later Perspective." In *Gendering the Crusades*, edited by Susan Edgington and Sarah Lambert, 177–190. Cardiff: University of Wales Press, 2001.

Signer, Michael A., and John Van Engen, eds. *Jews and Christians in Twelfth-Century Europe.* Notre Dame, IN: University of Notre Dame Press, 2001.

Skinner, Patricia, ed. *The Jews in Medieval Britain: Historical, Literary and Archaeological Perspectives.* Woodbridge: Boydell & Brewer, 2003.

Southern, R. W. "The English Origins of the Miracles of the Virgin." *Medieval and Renaissance Studies* 4 (1958): 176–216.

———. "The School of Paris and the School of Chartres." In *Renaissance and Renewal*, edited by Robert L. Benson and Giles Constable, 113–137. Oxford: Clarendon Press, 1982.

Spector, Stanley. "Anti-Semitism and the English Mystery Plays." In *The Drama of the Middle Ages: Comparative and Critical Essays*, edited by G. J. Gianakaris, Clifford Davidson, and John H. Stroupe, 328–341. New York: AMS Press, 1982.

Spiegel, Gabrielle M., and Paul Freedman. "Medievalisms Old and New: The Rediscovery of Alterity in North American Medieval Studies." *American Historical Review* 103, no. 3 (1998): 677–704.

Spiegel, Shalom. "In *Monte Dominus Videbitur*: The Martyrs of Blois and the Early Accusations of Ritual Murder" (in Hebrew). In *The Mordecai M. Kaplan Jubilee Volume*, Hebrew section, 267–287. New York: Jewish Theological Seminary of America, 1953.

Stacey, Robert C. "History, Religion and Antisemitism: A Response to Gavin Langmuir." *Religious Studies Review* 20, no. 2 (1994): 95–101.

———. "Jewish Lending and the Medieval English Economy." In *A Commercializing Economy: England 1086 to c. 1300*, edited by Richard H. Britnell and Bruce M. S. Campbell, 78–101. Manchester: Manchester University Press, 1995.

———. "From Ritual Crucifixion to Host Desecration: Jews and the Body of Christ." *Jewish History* 12 (1998): 11–28.

———. "Crusades, Martyrdoms and the Jews of Norman England, 1096–1190." In *Juden und Christen zur Zeit der Kreuzzüge*, edited by A. Haverkamp, 233–251. Sigmaringen: Jan Thorbecke Verlag, 1999.

———. "Jews and Christians in Twelfth-Century England: Some Dynamics of a Changing Relationship." In *Jews and Christians in Twelfth-Century Europe*, edited by Michael Signer and John Van Engen, 340–354. Notre Dame, Ind.: University of Notre Dame Press, 2001.

———. "'Adam of Bristol' and the Development of Ritual Crucifixion Tales in Medieval England." In *Thirteenth Century England* 11, edited by Björn K. U. Weiler et al., 1–15. Woodbridge, Suffolk: Boydell & Brewer, 2007.

Stewart, Ian. "Moneyers in the 1130 Pipe Roll." *British Numismatic Journal* 61 (1991): 1–8.

———. "The English and Norman Mints, c. 600–1158." In *A New History of the Norman Mint*, edited by C. E. Challis, 1–82. Cambridge: Cambridge University Press, 1992.

Stocker, David. "The Shrine of Little Saint Hugh." In *Medieval Art and Architecture at Lincoln Cathedral*, edited by T. A. Heslop and V. A. Sekules, 109–117. Oxford: British Archeological Association, 1986.

Stokes, H. P. *Studies in Anglo-Jewish History*. Edinburgh: Jewish Historical Society of England, 1913.

Stone, Eric. "The Estates of Norwich Cathedral Priory 1100-1300." Unpublished Ph.D. thesis, Oxford University, 1956.

Stow, Kenneth R. *Alienated Minority: The Jews of Medieval Latin Europe*. Cambridge, MA: Harvard University Press, 1992.

———. *Jewish Dogs: An Image and Its Interpreters; Continuity in the Catholic-Jewish Encounter*. Stanford, CA: Stanford University Press, 2006.

Streit, Kevin T. "The Expansion of the English Jewish Community in the Reign of King Stephen." *Albion* 25 (1993): 1177–1192.

Strickland, Matthew. *War and Chivalry: The Conduct and Perception of War in England and Normandy, 1066–1217*. New York: Cambridge University Press, 1996.

Stroll, Mary. *The Jewish Pope: Ideology and Politics in the Papal Schism of 1130*. Leiden: E. J. Brill, 1987.

Taitz, Emily. *The Jews of Medieval France: The County of Champagne*. Westport, CT: Greenwood Press, 1994.

Ta-Shma, Yisrael. "The Source and Place of the Prayer *Alenu le-shabeah*" (in Hebrew). In *The Frank Talmage Memorial Volume*, 2 vols., edited by Barry Walfish, 1:85–98. Haifa: Haifa University Press, 1993.

Tatlock, J. S. P. "The English Journey of the Laon Canons." *Speculum* 8 (1933): 454–465.

Thomas, Hugh M. "Violent Disorder in King Stephen's England: A Maximum View." In *King Stephen's Reign (1135–1154)*, edited by Paul Dalton and Graeme J. White, 139–170. Woodbridge, Suffolk: Boydell, 2008.

Thomas, I. G. "The Cult of Saints' Relics in Medieval England," unpublished Ph.D. thesis, University of London, 1974.

Thomas, Wyndham. "The Cultural Context of the Fleury Playbook: Liturgy and Drama in a Corner of Twelfth Century France." *Proceedings of the Bath Royal Literary and Scientific Institution* 9 (2005) unpaginated.

Thomson, Rodney M. "Early Romanesque Book-Illustration in England: The Dates of the Pierpont Morgan *Vitae Sancti Edmundi* and the Bury Bible." *Viator* 2 (1971): 211–225.

———. "The Library of Bury St Edmunds Abbey in the Eleventh and Twelfth Centuries." *Speculum* 47 (1972): 617–645.

Thornton, T. C. G. "The Crucifixion of Haman and the Scandal of the Cross." *Journal of Theological Studies* 37 (1986): 419–426.

Throop, Susanna A. *Crusading as an Act of Vengeance, 1095–1216.* Farnham, Surrey: Ashgate, 2011.

Tinkle, Theresa. "Exegesis Reconsidered: The Fleury Slaughter of Innocents and the Myth of Ritual Murder." *Journal of English and Germanic Philology* 102, no. 2 (2003): 211–243.

———. "Jews in the Fleury Playbook." *Comparative Drama* 38 (2004): 1–38.

Trachtenberg, Joshua. *The Devil and the Jews: The Medieval Conception of the Jew and Its Relation to Modern Antisemitism.* 2nd paperback ed. Philadelphia: Jewish Publication Society, 1983 .

Tudor, Virginia. "Reginald of Durham and St. Godric of Finchale: Learning and Religion on a Personal Level." In *Studies in Church History: Religion and Humanism,* edited by Keith Robbins, 37–48. Oxford: Ecclesiastical History Society, 1981.

Turner, Ralph V. *Men Raised from the Dust: Administrative Service and Upward Mobility in Angevin England.* Philadelphia: University of Pennsylvania Press, 1988.

Tyerman, Christopher *England and the Crusades, 1095–1588.* Chicago: University of Chicago Press, 1988.

———. *God's War: A New History of the Crusades.* London: Allen Lane/ Penguin, 2006.

———. "Paid Crusaders. 'Pro Honoris Vel Pecunie'; 'Stipendiarii Contra Paganos'; Money and Incentives on Crusades." In *The Practices of Crusading: Image and Action from the Eleventh to the Sixteenth Centuries,* edited by Christopher Tyerman, 1–40. Farnham: Ashgate, 2013.

———. *The Practices of Crusading, Images and Action from the Eleventh to the Sixteenth Centuries.* Farnham: Ashgate, 2013.

Utterback, Kristine T., and Merrall Llewelyn Price, eds. *Jews in Medieval Christendom: "Slay Them Not."* Leiden: Brill, 2013.

Utz, Richard. "The Medieval Myth of Jewish Ritual Murder: Toward a History of Literary Reception." *The Year's Work in Medievalism,* 14, 1999, 23–37.

Valdez del Alamo, Elizabeth. "Lament for a Lost Queen: The Sarcophagus of Dona Blanca in Najera." *Art Bulletin* 78, no. 2 (1996): 311–333.

Vauchez, André. *The Laity in the Middle Ages: Religious Beliefs and Devotional Practices.* Notre Dame, IN: University of Notre Dame Press, 1993.

———. *Sainthood in the Later Middle Ages.* Cambridge: Cambridge University Press, 1997.

Vincent, Nicholas. "Warin and Henry Fitz Gerald, the King's Chamberlains: The Origins of the Fitzgeralds Revisited." *Anglo-Norman Studies* 21 (1998): 233–260.

———. "The Pilgrimages of the Angevin Kings of England, 1154–1272." In *Pilgrimage: The English Experience from Becket to Bunyan*, edited by Colin Morris, 12–45. Cambridge and New York: Cambridge University Press, 2002.

Wagenarr-Nolthenius, Hélène. "Der *Planctus Iudei* und der Gesang jüdischer Märtyrer in Blois anno 1171." In *Mélanges offerts à René Crozet*, edited by Pierre Gallait, part 2: 881–885. Poitiers: [n.p.], 1966.

Walcott, Mackenzie Edward Charles. *Sacred Archæology: A Popular Dictionary of Ecclesiastical Art and Institutions, from Primitive to Modern Times*. London: L. Reeve, 1868.

Ward, Benedicta. *Miracles and the Medieval Mind: Theory, Record, Event, 1000–1215*. Philadelphia: University of Pennsylvania Press, 1982.

Ward, Jennifer C. "Fashions in Monastic Endowment: The Foundations of the Clare Family, 1066–1314." *Journal of Ecclesiastical History* 32, no. 4 (1981): 427–451.

Wareham, Andrew. "The Motives and Politics of the Bigod Family, c. 1066–1177." *Anglo-Norman Studies* 17 (1994): 223–242.

Warren, W. L. *Henry II*. London: Eye Methuen, 1973.

Wasyliw, Patricia Healy. *Martyrdom, Murder and Magic. Child Saints and Their Cults in Medieval Europe*. Studies in Church History 2. New York: Peter Lang, 2005.

Watt, J. A. "The English Episcopate, the State and the Jews: The Evidence of the Thirteenth Century Conciliar Decrees." In *Thirteenth Century England* 2, edited by Peter Coss and Simon Lloyd, 137–147. Woodbridge, Suffolk: Boydell & Brewer, 1988.

Weil, Louis. "The Debate about Anti-Semitism in the Good Friday Liturgy with Special Reference to the Reproaches," 2005 <http://www.stmvirgin.org/archives/article19433c2290727.htm>.

Weinberg, Robert. *Blood Libel in Late Imperial Russia: The Ritual Murder Trial of Mendel Beilis*. Bloomington: Indiana University Press, 2013.

Weinstein, Donald, and Rudolph Bell. *Saints and Society: The Two Worlds of Western Christendom, 1000–1700*. Chicago: University of Chicago Press, 1982.

Welander, David. *The History, Art, and Architecture of Gloucester Cathedral*. Wolfeboro Falls, NH: A. Sutton, 1991.

West, Jeffrey. "A Taste for the Antique? Henry of Blois and the Arts." *Anglo-Norman Studies* 30 (2008): 213–230.

White, Graeme J. "Were the Midlands 'Wasted' during Stephen's Reign?" *Midland History* 10 (1985): 26–46.

———. "Royal Income and Regional Trends." In *King Stephen's Reign (1135–1154)*, edited by Paul Dalton and Graeme J. White, 27–43. Woodbridge, UK: Boydell, 2008.

Williams, John Robert. "William of the White Hands and Men of Letters." In *Anniversary Essays in Medieval History by Students of Charles Homer Haskins,* edited by Charles Holt Taylor, 365–387. Boston: Houghton Mifflin, 1929.

Wilson, Dolores. "Multi-Use Management of the Medieval Anglo-Norman Forest." *Journal of the Oxford University History Society* 1 (2004): 1–16.

Wood, Anthony. *The History and Antiquities of the University of Oxford: Annals.* 2 vols. Oxford: 1792.

Wood, Diana, ed. *The Church and Childhood.* Oxford: Published for the Ecclesiastical History Society by Blackwell Publishers, 1994.

Yarrow, Simon. *Saints and Their Communities: Miracle Stories in Twelfth-Century England.* Oxford: Clarendon Press, 2007.

Yaxley, Susan. *Herbert de Losinga, First Bishop of Norwich.* Dereham, Norfolk: Larks Press, 1995.

Yerushalmi, Josef Hayim. *Zakhor: Jewish History and Jewish Memory.* Seattle: University of Washington Press, 1982.

Youth, Violence, and Cult: Interdisciplinary Workshops for the Investigation of the First Known Ritual Murder Charge Against Jews: The Case of William of Norwich, c. 1144. Arts and Humanities Research Council (AHRC) workshops, 2009–2010. http://yvc.history.qmul.ac.uk/index.html.

Yuval, Israel J. "Vengeance and Damnation, Blood and Defamation: From Jewish Martyrdom to Blood Libel Accusation" (in Hebrew). *Zion* 58 (1993): 33–96.

———. "Blood Libels and Blood Vengeance." *Tikkun* 9, no. 4 (1994): 39–40.

———. "Jews and Christians in the Middle Ages: Shared Myths, Common Language." In *Demonizing the Other: Antisemitism, Racism and Xenophobia,* edited by Robert S. Wistrich, 88–107. Jerusalem: Vidal Sassoon International Center for the Study of Antisemitism, 1999.

———. "'They Tell Lies: You Ate the Man': Jewish Reactions to Ritual Murder Accusations." In *Religious Violence Between Christians and Jews: Medieval Roots, Modern Perspectives,* edited by Anna Sapir Abulafia, 86–106. New York: Palgrave, 2002.

———. *Two Nations in Your Womb: Perceptions of Jews and Christians in Late Antiquity and the Middle Ages.* Berkeley: University of California Press, 2006.

Zafran, Eric. "The Iconography of Antisemitism: A Study of the Representation of the Jews in the Visual Arts of Europe, 1400–1600." Ph.D. diss., Institute of Fine Arts, New York University, 1973.

Photo Credits

Map of Europe from *The European World, 400–1450* (Oxford University Press, 2005).
Map of Norwich Augustus Jessopp and M. R. James, *The Life and Miracles of St. William of Norwich* (Cambridge University Press, 1896).

Figure 1.1: Photograph courtesy of Tim Caynes.
Figure 2.1a: © The Fitzwilliam Museum, Cambridge.
Figure 2.1b: IX.1082 Sword. European, 12th century. © Royal Armouries.
Figure 3.1a: Wikimedia Creative Commons, photograph by Fae.
Figure 3.1b: Wikimedia Creative Commons, courtesy of Pipin81.
Figure 4.1: Wikimedia Creative Commons.
Figure II.1 Courtesy of Norfolk Medieval Graffiti Survey.
Figure 5.1: Gospels of Henry the Lion, Codex Guelf. Noviss. 2°, Herzog August Bibliothek (1188). Wikimedia Creative Commons.
Figure 6.1: Bibliothèque nationale de France.
Figure 7.1: Los Angeles, The J. Paul Getty Museum, MS 101 fol. 44.
Figure 8.1a: Wikimedia Creative Commons, photograph by C. J. Dub, 2007.
Figure 8.1b: Wikimedia Creative Commons, Th. Hoffbauer 1550.
Figure 8.1c: Courtesy of François Benveniste, "Paris à l'époque de Philippe Auguste," www.philippe-auguste.com.
Figure C.1: Photograph courtesy of Katherine J. Lewis.

Index